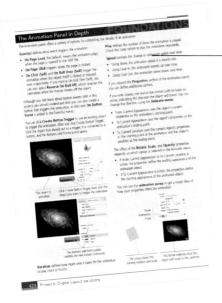

InDesign Foundations

Additional functionality, related tools, and underlying graphic design concepts are included throughout the book.

Advice and Warnings

Where appropriate, sidebars provide shortcuts, warnings, or helpful tips.

Project Review

After completing each project, students can complete these fill-in-the-blank and short-answer questions to test their understanding of the concepts in the project.

Portfolio Builder Projects

Each step-by-step project is accompanied by a freeform project, allowing students to practice skills and creativity, resulting in an extensive and diverse portfolio of work.

Visual Summary

Using an annotated version of the finished project, students can quickly identify the skills used to complete different aspects of the job.

PROJECTS AT A GLANCE

The Against The Clock *Portfolio Series* teaches graphic design software tools and techniques entirely within the framework of real-world projects; we introduce and explain skills where they would naturally fall into a professional workflow. For example, rather than an entire chapter about printing, which most students find boring, we teach printing in conjunction with a print-based project.

The project-based approach in *The Professional Portfolio Series* allows you to get in depth with the software beginning in Project 1. You don't have to read several chapters of introductory material before you can start creating artwork.

Our approach also prevents "topic tedium." That means, for example, we don't require you to read pages and pages of information about text. Instead, we explain text tools and options as part of larger projects, such as placing text on a letterhead layout.

Clear, easy-to-read, step-by-step instructions walk you through every phase of each job, from creating a new file to saving the finished piece. Wherever logical, we also offer practical advice and tips about underlying concepts and graphic design practices that will benefit students as they enter the job market.

The projects in this book reflect a range of different types of InDesign jobs, from creating a corporate identity package and implementing a newsletter template to compiling a multi-chapter book. When you finish this book's eight projects and accompanying Portfolio Builder exercises, you will have a substantial body of work that should impress any potential employer.

The eight InDesign projects are described briefly here; more detail is provided in the full table of contents (beginning on Page viii).

project 1 — Letterhead Design

- ❑ Setting up the Workspace
- ❑ Creating Basic Page Elements
- ❑ Placing External Images
- ❑ Creating and Formatting Basic Text
- ❑ Printing InDesign Files

project 2 — Festival Poster

- ❑ Building Graphic Interest
- ❑ Importing and Formatting Text
- ❑ Working with Text as Graphics
- ❑ Adjusting Layout Size
- ❑ Outputting PDF Files

project 3 — Aerospace Newsletter

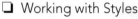

- ❑ Working with Templates
- ❑ Working with Styles
- ❑ Working with Tables
- ❑ Preflighting and Packaging the Job

project 4
Museum Exhibits Booklet

- ❏ Working with Master Pages
- ❏ Controlling the Flow of Text
- ❏ Outputting Variations of Files

project 7
Repurposed Content Layouts

- ❏ Working with XML
- ❏ Creating Alternate Layouts

project 5
Folding Travel Brochure

- ❏ Building a Folding Template
- ❏ Advanced Frame Options
- ❏ Advanced Text Formatting

project 8
Multi-Chapter Booklet

- ❏ Combining Documents into Books
- ❏ Building a Table of Contents
- ❏ Building an Index
- ❏ Exporting Book Files
- ❏ Merging Data into a Page Layout

project 6
Digital Layout Variations

- ❏ Controlling Color for Output
- ❏ Creating Interactive PDF Elements
- ❏ Exporting an HTML File
- ❏ Exporting an EPUB File

Our goal throughout the projects in this book is to familiarize you with the tool set so you can be more productive and more marketable in your career as a graphic designer.

It is important to keep in mind that InDesign is an extremely versatile and powerful application. The sheer volume of available tools, panels, and features can seem intimidating when you first look at the software interface. With a bit of background information and a little practice however, most of these tools are fairly simple to use.

Wherever necessary, we explain the underlying concepts and terms required for understanding the software. We're confident these projects provide the practice necessary for you to create sophisticated artwork by the end of the first project.

CONTENTS

Project 3
Aerospace Newsletter

Project 4
Museum Exhibits Booklet

CONTENTS

GETTING STARTED

Prerequisites

To use *The Professional Portfolio Series,* you should know how to use your mouse to point and click, as well as how to drag items around the screen. You should be able to resize and arrange windows on your desktop to maximize your available space. You should know how to access drop-down menus and understand how check boxes and radio buttons work. It also doesn't hurt to have a good understanding of how your operating system organizes files and folders and how to navigate your way around them. If you're familiar with these fundamental skills, then you know all that's necessary to use *The Professional Portfolio Series.*

Resource Files

All files you need to complete the projects in this book — except, of course, the application files — are on the Student Files web page at againsttheclock.com. See the inside back cover of this book for access information.

Each archive (ZIP) file is named according to the related project (e.g., **CACouncil_ID20_RF.zip**). At the beginning of each project, you must download the archive file for that project and expand it to access the resource files that you need to complete the exercises. Detailed instructions for this process are included in the Interface chapter.

Files required for the related Portfolio Builder exercises at the end of each project are also available on the Student Files page; these archives are also named by project (e.g., **Market_ID20_PB.zip**).

ATC Fonts

You must download and install the ATC fonts from the Student Files web page to ensure your exercises and projects will work as described in the book. You should replace older (pre-2013) ATC fonts with the ones on the Student Files web page.

Software Versions

This book was written and tested using the original 2020 release of Adobe InDesign CC (v 15.0) software. You can find the specific version number in the Splash Screen that appears while your application is launching or by choosing About InDesign in the InDesign CC menu (Macintosh) or Help menu (Windows).

Because Adobe releases periodic upgrades throughout the year, some features and functionality might have changed since publication. Please check the Errata section of the Against The Clock website for any significant issues that might have arisen from these periodic upgrades.

System Requirements

The Professional Portfolio Series was designed to work on both Macintosh or Windows computers. We include specific instructions relative to each platform where differences exist from one platform to another. One issue that remains different from Macintosh to Windows is the use of different modifier keys (Control, Shift, etc.) to accomplish the same task. When we present key commands, we always follow the same Macintosh/Windows format: Macintosh keys are listed first, then a slash, followed by the Windows key commands.

THE INDESIGN USER INTERFACE

Adobe InDesign is a robust publishing application that allows you to integrate text and graphics, either prepared in the program or imported from other sources, to produce files that can be printed to a local or networked printer, taken to a commercial printer, or published digitally. This book is designed to teach you how InDesign can be used to complete virtually any type of project, from a one-page flyer to a 500-page book.

The sheer volume of available options in InDesign means there are numerous tools and utilities you need to learn to make the most of the application. The simple exercises in this introduction are designed to let you explore the InDesign user interface. Whether you are new to the application or upgrading from a previous version, we strongly encourage you to follow these steps to click around and become familiar with the basic workspace.

 ## Explore the InDesign Interface

The user interface (UI) is what you see when you launch the application. The specific elements you see — including which panels are open and where they appear on the screen — depend on what was done the last time the application was open. The first time you launch InDesign, you see the default workspace settings defined by Adobe. When you relaunch the application after you or another user has quit, the workspace defaults to the last-used settings.

1. **Create a new empty folder named WIP (Work In Progress) on any writable disk (where you plan to save your work in progress).**

2. **Download the InterfaceID_ID20_RF.zip archive from the Student Files web page.**

3. **Macintosh users: Place the ZIP archive in your WIP folder, then double-click the file icon to expand it.**

   Windows users: Double-click the ZIP archive file to open it. Click the folder inside the archive, and drag it into your primary WIP folder.

   This **InterfaceID** folder contains all the files you need to complete this introduction.

Macintosh: Double-click the archive file icon to expand it.

Windows: Open the archive file, then drag the InterfaceID folder from the archive to your WIP folder.

4. **Macintosh users: While pressing Command-Control-Option-Shift, launch InDesign. Click Yes when asked if you want to delete Preference files.**

   Windows users: Launch InDesign, and then immediately press Control-Alt-Shift. Click Yes when asked if you want to delete the Preference files.

5. Macintosh users: Open the Window menu and make sure the Application Frame option is toggled on.

Many menu commands and options in InDesign are **toggles**, which means they are either on or off; when an option is already checked, that option is toggled on (visible or active). You can toggle an active option off by choosing the checked menu command or toggle an inactive option on by choosing the unchecked menu command.

Note:

On Windows, the Application Frame menu command is not available; you can't turn off the Application Frame on the Windows OS.

This option should be checked.

Understanding the Application Frame

On Windows, each running application is contained within its own frame; all elements of the application — including the Menu bar, panels, tools, and open documents — are contained within the Application frame.

Adobe also offers the Application frame to Macintosh users as an option for controlling the workspace. When the Application frame is active, the entire workspace exists in a self-contained area that can be moved around the screen. All elements of the workspace (excluding the Menu bar) move when you move the Application frame.

The Application frame is active by default, but you can toggle it off by choosing Window>Application Frame. If the menu option is checked, the Application frame is active; if the menu option is not checked, it is inactive. (On Windows, the Application Frame menu command is not available; you can't turn off the Application Frame on the Windows OS.)

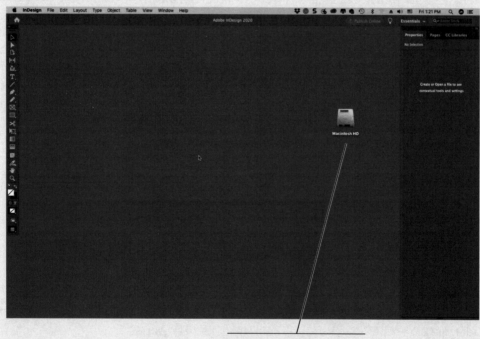

When the Application frame is not active, the desktop is visible behind the workspace elements.

6. Review the options in the Home screen.

The default user interface shows a Home screen when no file is open. No panels are visible in this workspace. Instead, you have one-click access to a list of recently opened files (if any), buttons to create a new file or open an existing one, and links to additional functionality provided by the Adobe Creative Cloud suite.

This workspace appears whenever InDesign is running, but no actual file is open. As soon as you open or create a file, the interface reverts to show the last-used workspace arrangement.

Macintosh

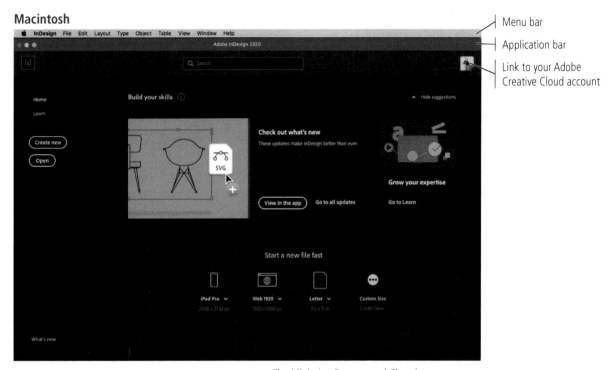

Menu bar

Application bar

Link to your Adobe Creative Cloud account

The Minimize, Restore, and Close buttons appear on the right end of the Menu bar.

Windows

Menu bar

The Macintosh and Windows workspaces are virtually identical, with a few primary exceptions:

- On Macintosh, the application's title bar appears below the Menu bar; the Close, Minimize, and Restore buttons appear on the left side of the title bar, and the Menu bar is not part of the Application frame.

- On Windows, the Close, Minimize, and Restore buttons appear at the right end of the Menu bar, which is part of the overall Application frame.

- Macintosh users have two extra menus, consistent with the Macintosh operating system (OS) structure. The Apple menu provides access to system-specific commands. The InDesign menu follows the Macintosh system-standard format for all applications; this menu controls basic application operations such as About, Hide, Preferences, and Quit.

7. In InDesign with no file open, click the InDesign icon in the top-left corner of the Home screen.

Clicking this icon enters into the InDesign workspace so you can access the various panels, even when no file is open.

Click this icon to enter the InDesign workspace.

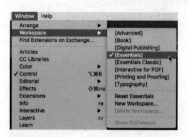

8. Choose Window>Workspace>Essentials.

The software includes a number of built-in saved workspaces, which provide one-click access to a defined group of panels, designed to meet common workflow needs.

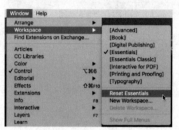

9. Choose Window>Workspace>Reset Essentials.

This step might or might not do anything, depending on what was done in InDesign before you started this project. If you or someone else changed anything, and then quit the application, those changes are remembered when InDesign is relaunched. You are resetting the user interface in this step so what you see will match our screen captures.

10. Macintosh users: Choose InDesign>Preferences>Interface. Windows users: Choose Edit>Preferences>Interface.

Remember that on Macintosh systems, the Preferences dialog box is accessed in the InDesign menu; Windows users access the Preferences dialog box in the Edit menu.

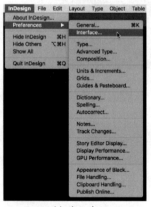
Macintosh

Windows

Note:

As you work your way through the projects in this book, you'll learn not only what you can do with these different collections of preferences, but also why and when you might want to use them.

Preferences customize the way many of the program's tools and options function. When you open the Preferences dialog box, the active pane is the one you chose in the Preferences submenu. Once open, however, you can access any of the Preference categories by clicking a different option in the left pane; the right side of the dialog box displays options related to the active category.

Note:

If a menu item has a keyboard shortcut, that shortcut is listed on the right side of the menu.

11. In the Appearance section, choose any Color Theme option you prefer.

You might have already noticed the rather dark appearance of the panels and interface background. InDesign uses the medium-dark "theme" as the default. (We used the Light option throughout this book because text in the interface elements is easier to read in printed screen captures.)

12. In the Panels section, check the option to Auto-Collapse Icon Panels.

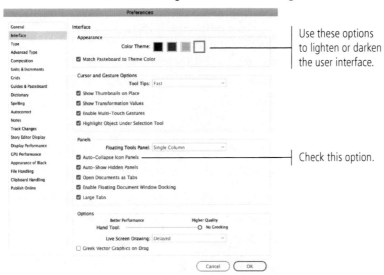

Use these options to lighten or darken the user interface.

Check this option.

Note:

You can also activate the Auto-Collapse Icon Panels option in the panel dock title bar's contextual menu.

13. Click OK to close the Preferences dialog box.

14. Continue to the next exercise.

Customizing Keyboard Shortcuts and Menus

At the bottom of the Edit menu, you can open the Keyboard Shortcuts and Menus dialog boxes to define custom sets.

In the Keyboard Shortcuts dialog box, **Product Area** lists categories of options that can be modified (primarily menu commands, but also some task-specific commands such as manipulating tables and frames).

The **Commands** window lists all options (in the selected product area) for which you can assign a keyboard shortcut.

Current Shortcuts for the selected command are listed immediately below the commands. You can use the **New Shortcut** field to assign an alternative shortcut.

If you edit the default keyboard shortcuts, you see a message asking you to save changes as a new set. You cannot override the application's default options in the Default set.

In the Menu Customization dialog box, clicking the visibility (eye) icon for any menu command hides it in the application menu. You can also use the Color option to define a colored background for a specific item in a menu.

If you hide certain menu commands, you can temporarily show them again by choosing Show All Menu Items at the bottom of the primary application menus.

Explore the Arrangement of InDesign Panels

InDesign includes a number of options for managing the numerous panels, so you can customize and personalize the workspace to suit your specific needs. We designed the following exercise to give you an opportunity to explore different ways of controlling InDesign panels. Because workspace preferences are largely a matter of personal taste, the projects in this book instruct you to use certain tools and panels, but where you place those elements within the interface is up to you.

1. With InDesign open, review the options available in the user interface.

The default Essentials workspace includes the Tools panel on the left side of the screen, the Control panel at the top of the screen, and a set of panels attached to the right side of the screen. (The area where the panels are stored is called the **panel dock**.)

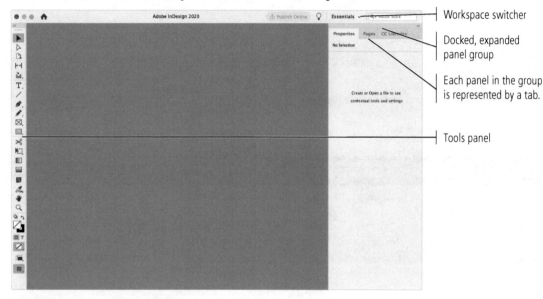

Workspace switcher

Docked, expanded panel group

Each panel in the group is represented by a tab.

Tools panel

2. Choose Window>Stroke.

All InDesign panels can be toggled on and off from the Window menu.

- If you choose a panel that is already open but iconized, the panel expands to the left of its icon.
- If you choose a panel that is already open in an expanded group but is not the active panel, that panel comes to the front of the group.
- If you choose a panel that isn't currently open, it opens in the same place as it was when it was last closed.

When you expand a panel that is part of a panel group, the entire group expands.

The panel you selected is the active panel in the expanded group.

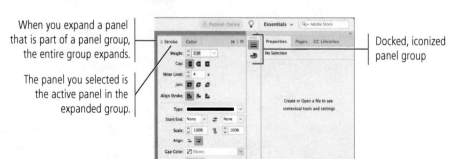

Docked, iconized panel group

3. Control/right-click the Color panel tab and choose Close from the contextual menu.

Control/right-clicking opens a contextual menu, which provides options specific to the item you click. In this case, you access commands related to the Color panel because you clicked on that panel tab. You can choose to close the individual panel or close all tabs in the active panel group. The lower three options in the menu relate to the behavior of all panels, not only to the specific panel where you opened the contextual menu.

Control/Right-click to access contextual menus.

The Stroke panel remains open after closing the Color panel.

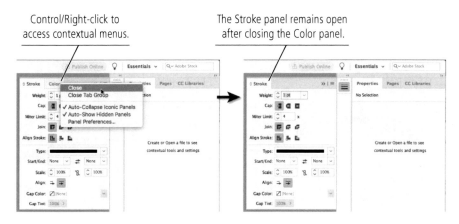

Note:

Macintosh users who do not have right-click mouse capability can press the Control key and click to access the contextual menu.

You do not have to press Control and right-click to access the menus.

Note:

A panel group is still considered a group even if it has only one panel.

4. Click away from the expanded panel group to collapse it.

By default, expanded panels remain open until you manually close them or expand another panel in the same dock column. Because you activated the Auto-Collapse Iconic Panels option in the previous exercise, the expanded panel collapses as soon as you click away from it.

5. Choose Window>Layers.

6. Click the drop zone behind the Layers/Links panel tabs and drag left away from the dock.

Panels and panel groups can be **floated** by clicking a panel tab and dragging away from the dock. By clicking the panel group's drop zone, you can move the entire group at once.

Note:

If a panel group is floating, you can also click the group's close button to close all panels in that groups.

Macintosh

Windows

Click the panel group drop zone and drag to move the panel group out of the dock.

When you release the mouse button, the panel group floats freely in the workspace.

Floating panel Close button

Nested Tools and Keyboard Shortcuts

Any tool with an arrow in the bottom-right corner includes related tools below it. When you click a tool and hold down the mouse button (or Control/right-click a tool), the **nested tools** appear in a pop-up menu. When you choose one of the nested tools, that variation becomes the default choice in the Tools panel.

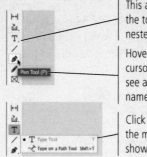

This arrow means the tool has other nested tools.

Hover the mouse cursor over the tool to see a tool tip with the name of the tool.

Click and hold down the mouse button to show the nested tools.

Most of the default InDesign tools can be accessed with a keyboard shortcut. When you hover the mouse cursor over a tool, the pop-up **tool tip** shows the name of the tool and a letter in parentheses. Pressing that letter on the keyboard activates the associated tool (unless you're working with type). If you don't see tool tips, check the Interface pane of the Preferences dialog box, and set the Tool Tips menu to Fast or Normal.

Finally, if you press and hold a tool's keyboard shortcut, you can temporarily call the appropriate tool (called **spring-loaded keys**); after releasing the shortcut key, you return to the tool you were using previously.

The image to the right offers a quick reference of nested tools, as well as the keyboard shortcut for each tool (if any). Nested tools are shown indented.

Tools Panel Options

In addition to the basic tool set, the bottom of the Tools panel includes options that control the fill and stroke colors, options for what attribute is being affected by color changes, options to show or hide various non-printing elements, and which screen preview mode to use.

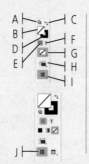

A	Fill color
B	Stroke color
C	Swap Fill and Stroke
D	Default Fill and Stroke
E	Formatting Affects Container
F	Formatting Affects Text
G	Apply Color/Gradient/None menu
H	View Options menu
I	Preview Mode menu
J	Normal view mode

In the two-column Tools panel, the position of some elements is slightly different. In addition to the position of certain elements, the Apply Color/Gradient/None options appear as individual buttons and are not consolidated into a menu, and the Normal viewing mode has a separate button from the Preview Mode menu button.

Tool Hints

The Tool Hints panel (Window>Utilities>Tool Hints) provides useful tips about the active tool, including a brief description of the tool and an explanation of the tool's behavior if you press one or more modifier keys and the tool's keyboard shortcut.

▶ Selection tool (V)

▷ Direct Selection tool (A)

⬚ Page tool (Shift-P)

⊢⊣ Gap tool (U)

🖾. Content Collector tool (B)

   🖾. Content Placer tool

T. Type tool (T)

   ↜. Type on a Path tool (Shift-T)

/ Line tool (\\)

🖊. Pen tool (P)

   ⁺🖊. Add Anchor Point tool (=)

   🖊. Delete Anchor Point tool (-)

   ⌐. Convert Direction Point tool (Shift-C)

✎. Pencil tool (N)

   🖊. Smooth tool

   ✎. Erase tool

⊠. Rectangle Frame tool (F)

   ⊗. Ellipse Frame tool

   ⊗. Polygon Frame tool

▢. Rectangle tool (M)

   ○. Ellipse tool (L)

   ○. Polygon tool

✂ Scissors tool (C)

▷⊏ Free Transform tool (E)

   ↻. Rotate tool (R)

   🔲. Scale tool (S)

   📐. Shear tool (O)

▣ Gradient Swatch tool (G)

▤ Gradient Feather tool (Shift-G)

🗐 Note tool

🔖. Color Theme tool (Shift-I)

   🖊. Eyedropper tool (I)

   🖊. Measure tool (K)

✋ Hand tool (H)

🔍 Zoom tool (Z)

7. **Click the drop zone behind the floating Layers/Links panel tabs and drag right until a blue line appears at the right edge of the user interface.**

   Panels and panel groups can be dragged to different locations (including into different groups) by dragging the panel's tab; the target location — where the panel will reside when you release the mouse button — is identified by the blue highlight.

Note:

Drag a panel tab onto a panel group's drop zone to make the dragged panel part of the target group.

The blue line indicates where the panel group will be placed when you release the mouse button.

The expanded panel group is added as a third column in the dock.

8. **Click the Properties panel tab in the left dock column. Drag the Properties panel tab until a blue line appears above the Layers/Links panel group.**

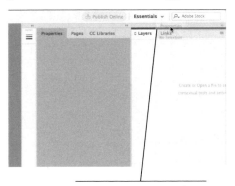
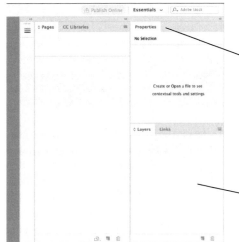

When you release the mouse button, the moved panel becomes a separate panel group in the right dock column.

The blue line indicates where the panel will be placed when you release the mouse button.

Other docked panel groups expand or contract to make room for the new panel.

9. **In the right dock column, click the line separating the two panel groups and drag down until the Properties panel occupies approximately two-thirds of the space in the column.**

   Dragging the bottom edge of a docked panel group changes the height of that panel group. Other panels in the same column expand or shrink as necessary to fit the column.

   Each column of the dock can also be made wider or narrower by dragging the left edge of the column. (Dragging the left edge of a dock column changes the width of all panels in that column.)

When the cursor is a double-headed arrow, click and drag to resize panel groups vertically.

10. Double-click the title bar above the right dock column to collapse it to icons.

Double-clicking the dock title bar expands a collapsed column or collapses an expanded column.

Collapsed panels are referred to as **iconized** or **iconic**. When panels are iconized, they default to show only the panel icon. You can move your mouse cursor over an icon to see the panel name in a pop-up tool tip.

Each dock column, technically considered a separate dock, can be expanded or collapsed independently of other columns. You can also independently iconize or expand each floating panel (group).

Double-click the title bar at the top of the dock column to collapse or expand it independently of other dock columns.

Note:

You can click the left edge of an iconized dock column and drag left to show the panel name as well as the icon.

11. Choose Window>Control.

The Control panel, which appears at the top of the workspace below the Application/Menu bar, is context-sensitive, which means it shows different options depending on what is selected in the layout. You will use the Control panel extensively throughout this book.

The Control panel appears immediately below the Application/Menu bar, above all other interface elements.

12. On the left side of the workspace, review the Tools panel. If you don't see all of the panel options, double-click the Tools panel title bar.

The Tools panel can be displayed as either one or two columns; double-clicking the Tools panel title bar toggles between these two modes.

Some monitors — especially laptops — might be too small to display the number of tools available in InDesign's Tools panel. If this is the case, you should use the two-column mode.

The Tools panel can also be floated (moved out of the dock) by clicking its title bar and dragging away from the edge of the screen. To re-dock the floating Tools panel, simply click the panel's title bar and drag back to the left edge of the screen; when a blue line highlights the edge of the workspace, releasing the mouse button places the Tools panel back in the dock. If the Tools panel is floating, you can toggle through three different modes — one-column vertical, two-column vertical, and one-row horizontal.

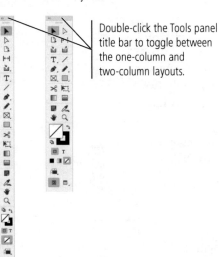

Double-click the Tools panel title bar to toggle between the one-column and two-column layouts.

Note:

Double-clicking the drop zone behind an expanded panel group minimizes that group, collapsing it to show only the panel tabs.

You can click any tab in a minimized panel group to expand the group and make the selected panel active.

Double-click the drop zone to minimize a panel group.

Create a Saved Workspace

Over time you will develop personal preferences — for example, the Colors panel always appearing at the top — based on your work habits and project needs. Rather than re-establishing every workspace element each time you return to InDesign, you can save your custom workspace settings so you can recall them with a single click.

1. **Click the Workspace switcher in the Application/Menu bar and choose New Workspace.**

   Again, keep in mind that we list differing commands in the Macintosh/Windows format. On Macintosh, the Workspace switcher is in the Application bar; on Windows, it's in the Menu bar.

The Workspace switcher shows the name of the last-called workspace.

Note:

The Delete Workspace option opens a dialog box where you can choose a specific user-defined workspace to delete. You can't delete the default workspaces that come with the application.

2. **In the New Workspace dialog box, type Portfolio. Make sure the Panel Locations option is checked and click OK.**

   You didn't define custom menus, so that option is not relevant in this exercise.

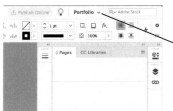

After saving the current workspace, the Workspace switcher shows the name of the newly saved workspace.

3. **Open the Workspace switcher again and review the options.**

   User-defined workspaces always appear at the top of the menu.

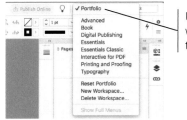

User-defined workspaces appear at the top of the menu.

Note:

If you are using a shared computer, you might want to also include your own name in the workspace name.

Keep in mind that calling a saved workspace restores the panels exactly as they were the last time you used that workspace. For example, if you close a panel that is part of a saved workspace, the closed panel will not be reopened the next time you call the same workspace. To restore the saved state of the workspace, including opening closed panels or repositioning moved ones, you have to use the Reset option.

Note:

If a menu option is grayed out, it is not available for the active selection.

4. **Continue to the next exercise.**

Explore InDesign Document Views

There is far more to using InDesign than arranging panels around the workspace. What you do with those panels — and even which panels you need — depends on the type of work you are doing in a particular file. In this exercise, you open an InDesign file and explore the interface elements you'll use to create documents.

1. **In InDesign, choose File>Open. Navigate to your WIP>Interface folder and select sfaa1.indd in the list of available files.**

   The Open dialog box is a system-standard navigation dialog box. You can also press Command/Control-O to access the Open dialog box.

2. **Press Shift, and then click sfaa5.indd in the list of files.**

   Pressing Shift allows you to select multiple contiguous (consecutive) files in the list. You can also press Command/Control to select and open non-contiguous files.

Note:

On Windows, file extensions might not be visible in the Open dialog box.

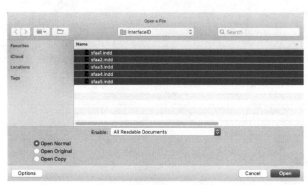

Macintosh   Windows

One final reminder: we list differing commands in the Macintosh/Windows format. On Macintosh, you need to press the Command key; on Windows, press the Control key. (We will not repeat this explanation every time different commands are required for each OS.)

3. **Click Open to open all five selected files.**

4. **If you see a Profile or Policy Mismatch warning, click OK.**

   InDesign files open in the document window. Across the top of the document window, each open document is represented by a separate tab; the document tabs show the file name and current view percentage.

Note:

If the file name includes the word "(Converted)" in the document tab, it was created in a previous version of InDesign.

The active file tab is lighter than the other document tabs.

5. **Click the sfaa2.indd tab to make that document active.**

6. **Highlight the current value in the View Percentage field (in the bottom-left corner of the document window). Type 200, then press Return/Enter.**

   Different people prefer larger or smaller view percentages, depending on a number of factors (eyesight, monitor size, and so on). As you complete the projects in this book, you'll see our screen shots zoom in or out as necessary to show you the most relevant part of a particular file. In most cases we do not tell you what specific view percentage to use for a particular exercise unless it is specifically required for the work being done.

Note:

All open files can be accessed at the bottom of the Window menu.

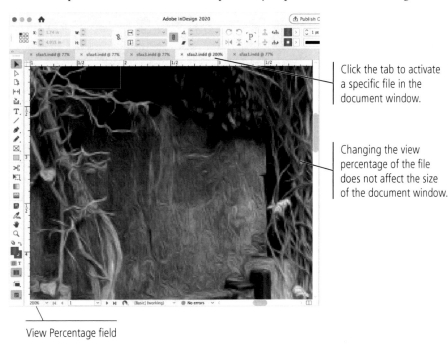

Click the tab to activate a specific file in the document window.

Changing the view percentage of the file does not affect the size of the document window.

View Percentage field

7. **Choose View>Fit Page in Window.**

   Fit Page in Window automatically calculates the view percentage based on the size of the document window.

These six options affect the view percentage of a file.

Note:

Fit Spread in Window relates to documents that have left- and right-facing pages, such as a book.

8. **Click the Zoom tool in the Tools panel. Click in the document window and drag a marquee around the logo in the top-left corner.**

   Dragging a marquee with the Zoom tool enlarges the selected area to fill the document window.

Zoom tool cursor

The marquee area enlarges to fill the document window.

9. **With the Zoom tool selected, Option/Alt-click in the document window.**

   One final reminder: When commands are different for the Macintosh and Windows OS, we include the different commands in the Macintosh/Windows format. In this case, Macintosh users should press the Option key while clicking; Windows users should press the Alt key.

   Clicking with the Zoom tool enlarges the view percentage in specific, predefined steps. Pressing Option/Alt while clicking with the Zoom tool reduces the view percentage in the reverse sequence of the same percentages.

Note:

You can set the viewing percentage of an InDesign document to any value from 5% to 4000%.

With the Zoom tool active, press Option/Alt and click to zoom out.

10. Click the Hand tool near the bottom of the Tools panel.

11. Click in the document, hold down the mouse button, and drag around.

The Hand tool is a very easy and convenient option for changing the visible area of an image in the document window.

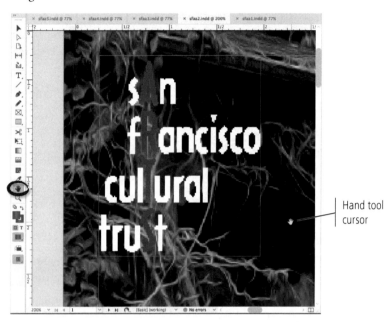

Hand tool
cursor

Note:

Press the Z key to access the Zoom tool.

Press the H key to access the Hand tool.

Note:

If you click and hold down the mouse button when the Hand tool is active, the page zooms out and a red "view box" appears. You can drag the view box and release the mouse button to recenter the view on the area inside the view box.

Understanding InDesign View Options

Most InDesign projects require some amount of zooming in and out to various view percentages, as well as navigating around the document within its window. As we show you how to complete various stages of the workflow, we usually won't tell you when to change your view percentage because that's largely a matter of personal preference. But you should understand the different options for navigating an InDesign file so you can easily and efficiently get to the place you want.

View Menu

The View menu provides options for changing the view percentage. You should also become familiar with the keyboard shortcuts for these commands:

Zoom In	Command/Control-equals (=)
Zoom Out	Command/Control-minus (-)
Fit Page in Window	Command/Control-0 (zero)
Fit Spread in Window	Command-Option-0/Control-Alt-0
Actual Size (100%)	Command/Control-1
Entire Pasteboard	Command-Option-Shift-0/Control-Alt-Shift-0

Zoom Level Field/Menu

You can use the Zoom Level field in the Application/Menu bar to type a specific view percentage, or you can use the attached menu to choose from the predefined view percentage steps.

Zoom Tool

You can click with the **Zoom tool** to increase the view percentage in specific, predefined intervals (the same intervals you see in the View Percentage menu in the bottom-left corner of the document window). Pressing Option/Alt with the Zoom tool allows you to zoom out in the same predefined percentages. If you drag a marquee with the Zoom tool, you can zoom into a specific location; the area surrounded by the marquee fills the available space in the document window.

Hand Tool

Whatever your view percentage, you can use the **Hand tool** to drag the file around in the document window and scroll from one page to another. The Hand tool changes only what is visible in the window; it has no effect on the actual content of the file.

12. Choose View>Display Performance>High Quality Display.

When Typical Display mode is active, InDesign displays a low-resolution preview of placed images to save time when the screen redraws (i.e., every time you change something). The images appear bitmapped and don't look very good, which is even more evident when you zoom in to a high view percentage. Fortunately, however, you have the option to preview the full-resolution images placed in a file.

Note:

Depending on your computer's graphics capabilities, InDesign might default to either Typical Display or High Quality Display.

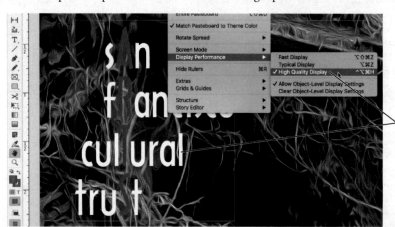

Using the High Quality Display, images do not show the bitmapping of the default low-resolution previews.

Controlling Display Performance

By default, files display in the document window using the Typical display performance settings. In the Display Performance pane of the Preferences dialog box, you can change the Default View settings (Fast, Typical, or High Quality). In the Adjust View Settings section, individual sliders control the display of raster images, vector graphics, and objects with transparency.

In the layout, you can change the document display performance using the View>Display Performance menu.

If **Allow Object-Level Display Settings** is checked in the View>Display Performance submenu, you can also change the preview for a specific image in the Object>Display Performance submenu or using the object contextual menu.

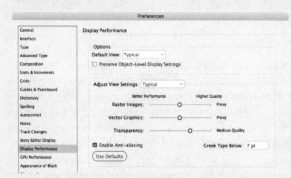

To remove object-level settings, choose **Clear Object-Level Display Settings**. (Object-level display settings are maintained only while the file remains open; if you want to save the file with specific object-level display settings, check the **Preserve Object-Level Display Settings** option in the Preferences dialog box.)

Fast displays gray boxes in place of graphics.

Typical shows the low-resolution proxy images.

High-quality shows the full resolution of placed files.

13. Using the Selection tool, click the background image to select it. Control/right-click the selected image and choose Display Performance> Typical Display from the contextual menu.

Control/right-clicking an object on the page opens a contextual menu, which makes it easy to access item-specific options.

In the View menu, the Allow Object-Level Display Settings option is active by default (see the image in the previous step); this means you can change the display of individual objects on the page.

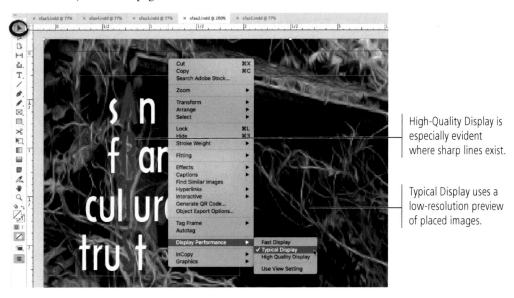

High-Quality Display is especially evident where sharp lines exist.

Typical Display uses a low-resolution preview of placed images.

14. Choose View>Fit Page in Window to see the entire page.

15. In the Pages panel, double-click the Page 2 icon to show that page in the document window.

The Pages panel is the easiest way to move from one page to another in a multi-page document. You will use this panel extensively as you complete the projects in this book.

Double-click a page icon to display that page in the document window.

16. **Control/right-click the Page 2 icon in the Pages panel and choose Page Attributes>Rotate Spread View>90° CW from the contextual menu.**

Rotating the view only changes the display of the page; the actual page remains unchanged in the file. This option makes it easier to work on objects or pages oriented differently than the overall document. In this example, the front side of the postcard has portrait orientation, but the mailer side has landscape orientation.

Note:

You can also rotate page views using the options in the View>Rotate Spread menu.

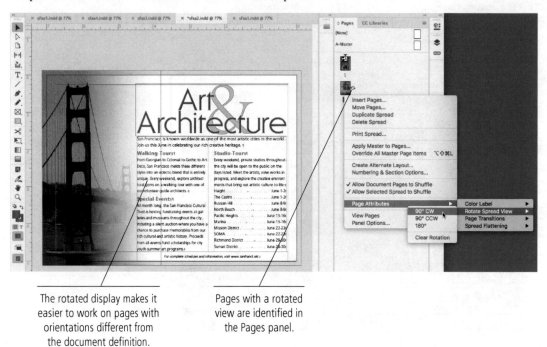

The rotated display makes it easier to work on pages with orientations different from the document definition.

Pages with a rotated view are identified in the Pages panel.

17. **Continue to the next exercise.**

Explore the Arrangement of Multiple Documents

In many cases, you will need to work with more than one layout at the same time. InDesign incorporates a number of options for arranging multiple documents. We designed the following simple exercise so you can explore these options.

1. **With sfaa2.indd active, choose Window>Arrange>Float in Window.**

You can also separate all open files by choosing Window>Arrange>Float All In Windows.

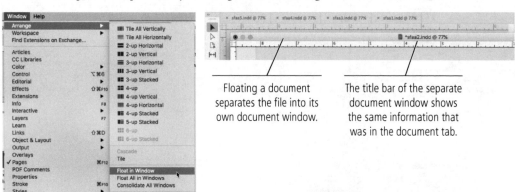

Floating a document separates the file into its own document window.

The title bar of the separate document window shows the same information that was in the document tab.

2. **Choose Window>Arrange>2-up Vertical.**

The defined arrangements provide a number of options for tiling multiple open files within the available workspace. These arrangements manage all open files, including those in floating windows.

Each option's icon suggests the result of that command. The active file remains active; this is indicated by the brighter text in the active document's tab.

Extra documents remain as tabs in the left document window.

The 2-Up Horizontal arrangement divides the document window in half.

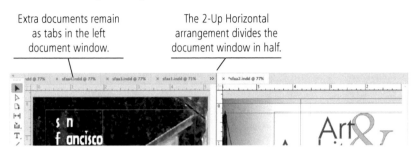

Note:

The Consolidate All option restores all floating documents into a single, tabbed document window.

3. **Click the sfaa2.indd document tab and drag left until a blue highlight appears around the document tabs in the other panel.**

When you release the mouse button, all open files are again part of the same document window.

4. **At the bottom of the Tools panel, click the Screen Mode button and hold down the mouse button.**

InDesign has five different **screen modes**. The files you explored in this project were saved in Normal screen mode. In Normal mode, you can see all non-printing elements including guides and frame edges (if those are toggled on). You can now also see the pasteboard surrounding the defined page area; your development work is not limited by the defined page size.

If your Tools panel is displayed two-column mode, the Normal Mode button appears to the left of the Screen Mode button, where the other views are available.

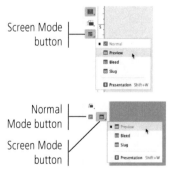

Screen Mode button

Normal Mode button

Screen Mode button

5. Choose Preview from the Screen Mode menu.

Preview screen mode surrounds the page with a neutral gray background. Page guides, frame edges, and other non-printing areas are not visible in the Preview mode.

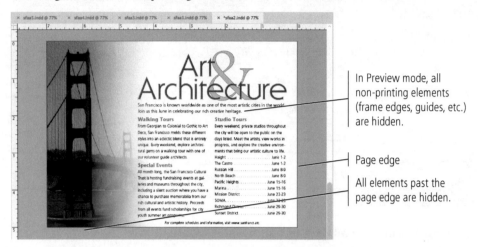

In Preview mode, all non-printing elements (frame edges, guides, etc.) are hidden.

Page edge

All elements past the page edge are hidden.

6. Open the Screen Mode menu again and choose Bleed.

The Bleed screen mode is an extension of the Preview mode; it shows an extra area (which was defined when the document was originally set up) around the page edge. This bleed area is a required part of print document design — objects that are supposed to print right up to the edge of the page must extend past the page edge, usually 1/8″ or more. (Bleed requirements and setup are explained in Project 1: Letterhead Design.)

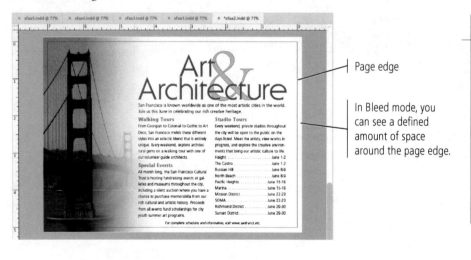

Page edge

In Bleed mode, you can see a defined amount of space around the page edge.

Note:

By default, the pasteboard matches the color defined for the user interface in the Interface pane of the Preferences dialog box. If you uncheck the Match Pasteboard to Theme Color option, the pasteboard is white.

7. **Using either Screen Mode button, choose the Presentation mode.**

Presentation mode fills the entire screen with the active spread. By default, the area around the page is solid black; you can press W to change the surround to white, press G to change it to neutral gray, or press B to change it back to black. In Presentation mode, clicking anywhere on the screen shows the next spread; Shift-clicking shows the previous spread.

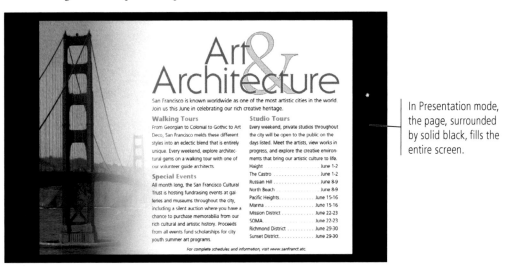

In Presentation mode, the page, surrounded by solid black, fills the entire screen.

8. **Press ESC to exit Presentation mode.**

9. **Click the Close button on the active document tab.**

Clicking the Close button on a document tab closes only that file.

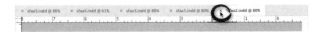

10. **Click Don't Save/No when asked if you want to save changes to sfaa2.indd.**

In the document tab, an asterisk before the file name indicates the file has been changed but not yet saved. By rotating the spread view on Page 2, the file has technically been changed.

InDesign automatically asks if you want to save any file that has been changed before closing it.

11. **Macintosh users: Click the Close button in the top-left corner of the Application frame.**

Closing the Macintosh Application frame closes all open files but does not quit the application.

Macintosh Close button

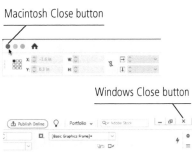

Windows Close button

Windows users: Click the Close button on each open document tab to close the remaining files.

Clicking the Close button on the Windows Application frame (Menu bar) closes all open files *and* quits the application. To close open files *without* quitting, you have to manually close each open file, or Control/right-click any of the document tabs and choose Close All.

Letterhead Design

Your client has hired you to create a letterhead design that incorporates the corporate logo and a set of images representing the kind of products that are available at the client's retail location. They are going to have the letterhead printed commercially so they can use it to print letters, invoices, and other business correspondence.

This project incorporates the following skills:

❏ Creating a new file to meet defined project requirements

❏ Using the basic InDesign drawing tools to develop visual interest

❏ Selecting objects and object contents

❏ Creating and formatting basic text attributes

❏ Placing and manipulating external graphics files

❏ Printing a desktop proof sample

client comments

Until now, we've just added the logo and address at the top of a Word document whenever we sent out correspondence. The business has been growing lately, and we want something more professional.

I sent you our logo, which was created in Adobe Illustrator. I also selected a bunch of images that represent the different stores at the market; I want to include at least a few of those on the letterhead.

Can you get our address information from our website, or do we need to send that to you as a separate document?

art director comments

I've looked over the client's images, and I think we should use all of them. InDesign has everything you need to create the necessary graphics directly on the page layout.

I already reviewed the size of the photos. They should be fine to place into the layout as they are; you won't need to manipulate the actual image files.

I also copied the client's contact info into a file for you. I noticed they have a tagline — Grand Cuisine. Grand Culture. Grand Central. — fairly prominent throughout the site, so I think we should include that in the print design work, as well.

It might feel like there's a lot involved in creating this piece, but it's not too complicated. The client liked the initial sketch, so putting in the effort at this point will be worth it.

project objectives

To complete this project, you will:

- ❑ Create a new document based on the requirements of a commercial printer.
- ❑ Place ruler guides to define "safe" areas on the page.
- ❑ Draw basic shapes using native InDesign tools.
- ❑ Use a variety of methods to arrange multiple objects.
- ❑ Work with anchor points and handles to create a complex shape.
- ❑ Apply color to fills and strokes.
- ❑ Create and format basic text elements.
- ❑ Import external text and graphics files.
- ❑ Print a desktop proof.

Setting up the Workspace

As you learned in the Interface chapter, InDesign gives you extensive control over your workspace — you can choose where to place panels, whether to collapse or expand open panels, and even to save workspaces with sets of panels in specific locations. Because workspace issues are largely a matter of personal preference, we tell you what tools to use, but we don't tell you where to keep the various panels. Many of our screen captures show floating panels so we can clearly focus on a specific issue. Likewise, we typically don't tell you what view percentage to use; you should use whatever you are comfortable with to accomplish the specific goal of an exercise.

 Define a New Layout File

Some production-related concerns will dictate how you design a letterhead. If a letterhead is being printed commercially, it's probably being printed with multiple copies on a large press sheet from which the individual letterhead sheets will be cut. Most commercial printing happens this way. This type of printing typically means design elements can run right off the edge of the sheet, called **bleeding**.

If you're designing for a printer that can run only letter-size paper, you have to allow enough of a margin area for your printer to hold the paper as it moves through the device (called the **gripper margin**); in this case, you can't design with bleeds.

The most basic process in designing a layout is creating a new InDesign file. The New Document dialog box has a large number of options, and the following exercise explains them. Don't be overwhelmed by the length of this process; in later projects, we simply tell you what settings to define without re-explaining every field.

> **Note:**
>
> *Some desktop printers have a minimum margin at the page edges; you're usually safe with 3/8".*
>
> *Many newer inkjet printers have the capability to print 8.5 × 11" with full bleed. Consult your printer documentation to be sure.*

1. **Download GCMarket_ID20_RF.zip from the Student Files web page.**

2. **Expand the ZIP archive in your WIP folder (Macintosh), or copy the archive contents into your WIP folder (Windows).**

   This results in a folder named **GCMarket**, which contains all the files you need for this project. You should also use this folder to save the files you create in this project.

   If necessary, refer to Page 1 of the Interface chapter for specific information on expanding or accessing the required resource files.

3. **In InDesign, choose File>New>Document.**

   You have several options for creating a new file:

   - Choose File>New> Document
   - Use the associated keyboard shortcut Command/Control-N
   - Click the Create New button in the Home screen

If the Home screen is visible, click the Create New button to open the New Document dialog box.

4. **Click the Print option at the top of the resulting New Document dialog box.**

Click a category name to show related presets.

5. **Choose the Letter preset on the left side of the dialog box.**

The New Document dialog box presents a number of preset sizes and prebuilt starter templates, broken into categories based on the intended output.

When you choose the Print category, you see common page sizes such as Letter and Legal. The Print presets automatically default to the CMYK color mode, which is required for commercial printing applications. For all the Web and Mobile categories of presets, the new document defaults to the RGB color mode.

Click to select an existing preset or template.

6. **On the right side of the dialog box, choose Inches in the Units menu.**

By default, InDesign uses picas as the unit of measurement for print documents; measurements in this dialog box are shown in picas and points, using the "ApB" notation (for A picas and B points).

After you choose a different option in this menu, the dialog box fields change to reflect the new default unit of measurement. Because you selected the Letter preset in Step 5, the Width and Height fields default to 8.5 inches and 11 inches respectively.

If you choose Web or Digital Publishing, InDesign changes the default unit of measurement to pixels, which is more appropriate for web design.

Regardless of which unit of measurement you choose when you create a new file, you can change the setting for a specific file in the Units and Increments pane of the Preferences dialog box. InDesign supports all modern units of measurement, including points, picas, inches, millimeters, centimeters, and pixels (as well as a few others from historic typography).

You can also type different measurement units, such as "2cm", in a dialog box or panel field. As long as you include the unit in your entry, the software accurately translates the value you type into the default unit for the active file.

> *Note:*
>
> *Picas are the measuring units traditionally used in typography; they are still used by many people in the graphic communications industry.*
>
> *1 point = 1/72 inch*
>
> *12 points = 1 pica*
>
> *1 pica = 1/6 inch*
>
> *6 picas = 1 inch*

7. **Type gcm-letterhead in the Name field (below the words "Preset Details").**

8. **Make sure the Portrait Orientation option is selected.**

Portrait documents are higher than they are wide; **landscape** documents are wider than they are high. If you click the Orientation option that is not currently selected, the Width and Height values are automatically reversed.

Click here to highlight the field, then type to define a new file name.

Landscape

Portrait

9. **Leave the Number of Pages field set to 1.**

A letterhead is a single page, usually printed on only one side. This project needs only a single layout page in the InDesign file.

10. **Leave the Start Page # field set to 1.**

    This option is useful when you work with multi-page files. Odd-numbered pages always appear on the right, as you see in any book or magazine; you can define an even-numbered starting page to force the first page of a layout to the left.

11. **Uncheck the Facing Pages check box.**

    Facing pages are used when a printed job will be read left to right like a book, with Page 1 starting on the right, then Page 2 facing Page 3, and so on. Facing-page layouts are based on **spreads**, which are pairs of left-right pages as you flip through a book (e.g., Page 6 facing Page 7). (You work extensively with facing pages starting in Project 4: Museum Exhibits Booklet.)

12. **Leave the Primary Text Frame option unchecked.**

    When this option is checked, InDesign creates a text frame that automatically fills the area created by the defined page margins. A letterhead design primarily focuses on the area outside the margins, so you don't need to add a primary text frame to this file.

13. **Expand the Margins section of the preset details.**

14. **If the chain icon to the right of the Margin fields shows two connected links, click the icon to break the link between the fields.**

    When the chain icon is active (connected links), all four margin fields will be the same; changing one field changes all margin values to the same value. For this project, the top and bottom values need to be different from the left and right values, so you need to unlink (unconstrain) the fields.

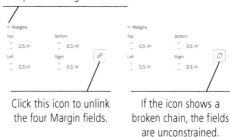

Click the arrow to expand or collapse the Margins section.

Click this icon to unlink the four Margin fields.

If the icon shows a broken chain, the fields are unconstrained.

15. **Highlight the first Margins field (Top) and type 2.**

    When you define values using the default unit of measurement, it is not necessary to type the unit; you can simply type the numbers.

16. **Press Tab to move to the Bottom field.**

    You can tab through the fields of most dialog boxes and panels in InDesign. Press Shift-Tab to move the highlight to the previous field in the tab order.

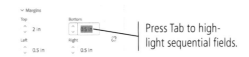

Press Tab to high-light sequential fields.

17. **Change the Bottom field to 1.75, then press Tab to highlight the Left field.**

18. **Change the Left field to 0.75, press Tab, and then change the Right field to 0.75.**

    It is not necessary to type the preceding zero when you define a value. We include it here for clarity.

Note:

When you work with non-facing pages, the Inside and Outside margin fields change to Left and Right respectively. Technically, non-facing pages do not have an inside (spine edge) or outside (face or trim edge), so there are only left and right sides.

19. **Click the arrow button to the left of the Bleed and Slug heading.**

20. **Make sure the chain icon to the right of the Bleed fields is active (unbroken links), then change the first Bleed field to 0.125 (the decimal equivalent of 1/8). Press Tab to apply the new Bleed value to all four sides.**

Bleed is the amount an object needs to extend past the edge of the artboard or page to meet the mechanical requirements of commercial printing.

The letterhead for this project will be printed commercially; the printer said the design can safely bleed on all four sides, and its equipment requires a 1/8″ bleed allowance.

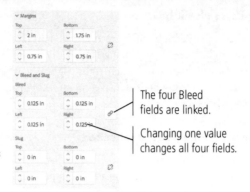

The four Bleed fields are linked.

Changing one value changes all four fields.

Note:

You should become familiar with the common fraction-to-decimal equivalents:

1/8 = 0.125

1/4 = 0.25

3/8 = 0.375

1/2 = 0.5

5/8 = 0.625

3/4 = 0.75

7/8 = 0.875

21. **Make sure all four Slug fields are set to 0.**

A **slug** is an area outside the bleed, where designers typically add job information that will not appear in the final printed piece. The slug area can be used for file/plate information, special registration marks, color bars, and/or other elements that need to be printed on the press sheet but do not appear within the job area.

22. **Check the Preview box at the bottom of the New Document dialog box.**

When this option is active, you can see the result of your choices (behind the dialog box) before you click OK to create the new file.

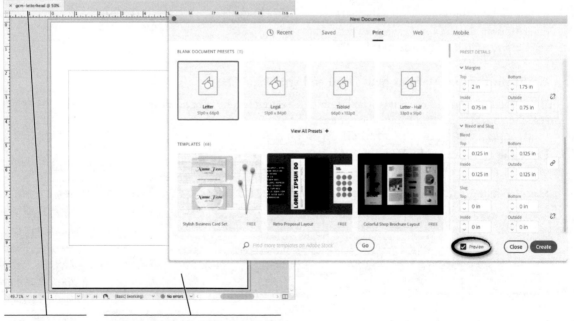

The name you defined appears in the document tab.

When the Preview option is checked, the new document appears behind the dialog box to show the results of your choices.

23. Click Create to create the new document.

The document appears, filling the available space in the document window. (Your view percentage might appear different than what you see in our images.)

The letter-size page edge is represented by a dark black line. Pink/purple lines identify margin guides, and red lines identify bleed guides. The color of the pasteboard (the area around the artboard) defaults to match the brightness of the user interface. You can change this setting to show a white pasteboard by unchecking Match Pasteboard to Theme Color in the Interface pane of the Preferences dialog box.

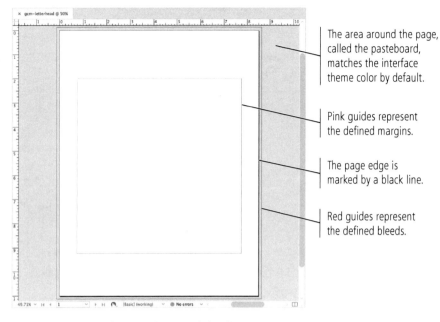

The area around the page, called the pasteboard, matches the interface theme color by default.

Pink guides represent the defined margins.

The page edge is marked by a black line.

Red guides represent the defined bleeds.

As we explained in the Interface chapter, the panels you see depend on what was done the last time you (or someone else) used the application. Because workspace arrangement is such a personal preference, we tell you what panels you need to use, but we don't tell you where to place them. In our screen shots, we typically float panels over the relevant area of the document so we can focus the images on the most important part of the file at any particular point. Feel free to dock the panels, grouped or ungrouped, iconized or expanded, however you prefer.

24. Choose File>Save As and navigate to your WIP>GCMarket folder.

If you assign a name in the New Document dialog box (as you did in Step 7), that name becomes the default file name in the Save As dialog box.

The dialog box defaults to the InDesign 2020 (.indd) format, and the extension is automatically added to the name you defined. If the Hide Extension option is checked at the bottom of the dialog box, the ".indd" will not appear in the file name.

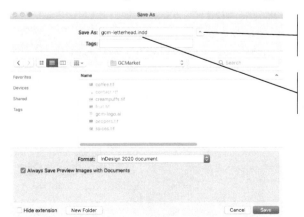

Click here if you don't see the full navigation options on Macintosh.

The extension ".indd" is automatically added to the file name.

Note:

The first time you save a file, the Save command opens the same dialog box as the File>Save As command. After saving the file once, you can use Save to save changes to the file or use Save As to create another file under a new file name.

Note:

The Save As dialog box follows a system-standard format. Macintosh and Windows users see slightly different options, but the basic functionality is the same.

25. Click Save, then continue to the next exercise.

Understanding Document Presets

If you frequently define the same new-document settings, you can click the Save Document Preset button to save those choices as a preset so you can create the same document settings with minimal repetition. You can access your user-defined presets in the Saved pane of the New Document dialog box.

Click the Save Document Preset button...

...then type here to define a name for the custom preset.

Click here to access saved presets.

You can also access and manage your document presets in the File>Document Presets submenu. Choosing one of the existing presets in the menu opens the legacy New Document dialog box, which defaults to the values in the preset that you called.

Choosing Define in the Document Presets submenu opens a dialog box that lists the existing presets.

- Click New to open the New Document Preset dialog box, which is basically the same as the New Document dialog box, except the Preset menu is replaced with a field where you type the preset name instead of clicking the Save Preset button.
- Select a preset and click Edit to change the preset's associated options.
- Select a preset and click Delete to remove the preset from the application.
- Click Load to import presets from another computer.
- Click Save to save a preset (with the extension ".dcst") so it can be sent to and used on another computer.

Create Ruler Guides

In addition to the margin and bleed guides you defined when you created the document, you can also place ruler guides to mark whatever other positions you need to identify in your layout.

The **live area** is the "safe" area inside the page edge where important design elements should reside. Because printing and trimming are mechanical processes, there will always be some variation, however slight. Elements placed too close to the page edge run the risk of being accidentally trimmed off. The printer for this job recommended a 1/4″ live-area margin. You defined the margins for this file to describe the area that would typically occupy the content of a letter; in this exercise you will create ruler guides to mark the live area.

1. **With gcm-letterhead.indd open, choose View>Show Rulers if you don't see rulers at the top and left edges of the document window.**

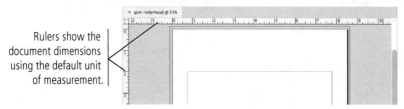

Rulers show the document dimensions using the default unit of measurement.

Note:

You can change the default units of measurement for a file in the Units & Increments pane of the Preferences dialog box or by Control/right-clicking a ruler and choosing a new option. Each ruler (horizontal and vertical) can have a different unit of measurement.

2. **Zoom in to 100% so you can clearly see the top of the page.**

3. **Click the horizontal page ruler (at the top of the document window) and drag down until cursor feedback indicates the guide is positioned at Y: 0.25 in. With the cursor inside the page area, release the mouse button.**

   As you drag, the Control panel and cursor feedback show the current position of the guide you are placing; this makes it very easy to precisely position guides.

   If the Control panel is not visible, you can show it by choosing Window>Control. If you don't see the cursor feedback, make sure Show Transformation Values is checked in the Interface pane of the Preferences dialog box.

The Control panel, ruler, and cursor feedback all show the location of the guide.

4. **Click the horizontal page ruler again and drag a guide to Y: 10.75 in.**

5. **Click the vertical ruler and drag a guide to X: 0.25 in.**

   Watch the marker on the horizontal ruler to judge the guide's position.

Drag from the vertical ruler to add a vertical guide.

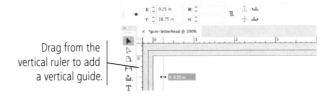

6. **Click the vertical ruler again and drag a second vertical guide to X: 8.25 in.**

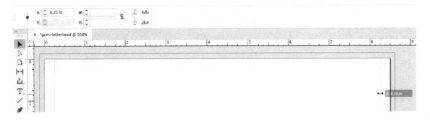

7. **Using the Selection tool, click anywhere in the document space to deselect the guide you just created.**

8. **Save the file and continue to the next stage of the project.**

Raster image quality depends directly on the file's resolution; when you work with raster image files, you need to understand the resolution requirements from the very beginning of the process:

- **Pixels per inch (ppi)** is the number of pixels in one horizontal or vertical inch of a digital raster file.

- **Lines per inch (lpi)** is the number of halftone dots produced in a linear inch by an output device to simulate the appearance of continuous-tone color.

- **Dots per inch (dpi)** or **spots per inch (spi)** is the number of dots produced by an output device in a single line of output. Dpi is sometimes used interchangeably (although incorrectly) with pixels per inch.

When reproducing a photograph on a printing press, the image must be converted into a set of different-size dots that fool the eye into seeing continuous tones. The result of this conversion process is a halftone image; the dots used to simulate continuous tone are called **halftone dots**. Light tones in a photograph are represented as small halftone dots; dark tones are represented as large halftone dots. (In pre-digital design processes, images were converted to halftones by photographing the image through a screen to create halftone dots; different screens produced different numbers of dots in an inch — hence the term "dots per inch".)

Screen Ruling

The screens used with old graphic-arts cameras had a finite number of available dots in a horizontal or vertical inch. That number was the **screen ruling**, or lines per inch. A screen ruling of 133 lpi means that in a square inch there are 133 × 133 (17,689) possible locations for a halftone dot. If the screen ruling is decreased, there are fewer total halftone dots, producing a grainier image; if the screen ruling is increased, there are more halftone dots, producing a clearer image.

Line screen is a finite number based on a combination of the intended output device and paper. You can't randomly select a line screen. Ask your printer what line screen will be used before you begin creating your images. If you can't find out ahead of time or are unsure, follow these general guidelines:

- Newspaper or newsprint: 85–100 lpi

- Magazine or general commercial printing: 133–150 lpi

- Premium-quality-paper jobs (such as art books): 150–175 lpi (some specialty jobs use 200 lpi or more)

If you find this information a bit confusing, don't worry. As a general rule for preparing commercial print layouts, most raster images should have twice the pixel resolution at 100% size as the line screen that will be used.

Image Resolution

When an output device creates halftone dots, it calculates the average value of a group of pixels and generates a spot of appropriate size. An image's resolution controls the quantity of pixel data that the printer can read. Regardless of the source — camera, scanner, or files created from scratch in a program such as Photoshop — images need to have sufficient resolution for the output device to generate enough halftone dots to create the appearance of continuous tone.

The relationship between pixels and halftone dots defines the rule of resolution for raster-based images — the resolution of a raster image (ppi) should be two times the screen ruling (lpi) that will be used for printing.

In the image below, each white square represents a pixel. The highlighted area shows the pixel information used to generate a halftone dot. Ideally, the printer has four pixels for each halftone dot created.

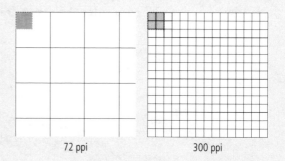

72 ppi   300 ppi

If an image only has 72 pixels per inch, the output device has to generate four halftone dots per pixel, resulting in poor printed quality.

In the images below, the same raster image is reproduced at 300 ppi (left) and 72 ppi (right); notice the obvious degradation in quality in the 72-ppi version.

For line art, the general rule is to scan the image at the same resolution as the output device. Many laser printers and digital presses image at 600–1,200 dots per inch (dpi); imagesetters used to make printing plates for a commercial press typically output at much higher resolution, possibly 2,400 dpi or more.

To complete this project, you need to create a graphic near the bottom of the page, which will serve as a container for the client's images. Fortunately, InDesign includes sophisticated drawing tools that can create what you need. Before you begin, however, you should understand the different types of elements you will encounter when you design files in InDesign.

Vector graphics are composed of mathematical descriptions of lines and shapes. Vector graphics are resolution-independent; they can be freely scaled and are automatically output at the resolution of the output device. The shapes you create in Adobe InDesign, or in drawing applications such as Adobe Illustrator, are vector graphics.

Raster images, such as photographs or files created in Adobe Photoshop, are made up of a grid of pixels (rasters or bits) in rows and columns (called a bitmap). Raster files are resolution-dependent; their resolution is determined when you scan, photograph, or create the file. You can typically reduce raster images, but you cannot significantly enlarge them without losing image quality.

Line art is a type of raster image made up entirely of 100% solid areas; the pixels in a line-art image have only two options: they can be all black or all white. Examples of line art are UPC bar codes or pen-and-ink drawings.

 Create a Simple Line

Although much drawing work is done in a dedicated illustration program such as Adobe Illustrator, you can use drawing tools in InDesign to create vector artwork.

InDesign includes two tools for creating lines: the Line tool for creating straight lines and the Pen tool for creating curved lines called **Bézier curves** (although you can also create straight lines with the Pen tool). In this exercise, you create the most basic element possible: a straight line. You then add anchor points to the line to create a multi-segment path.

1. **With gcm-letterhead.indd open, make sure nothing is selected in the file. Review the Properties panel (Window>Properties).**

    The Properties panel is context-sensitive, which means it provides access to different options depending on which tool is active and what is selected in the document.

    When nothing is selected in the file, you can use the Properties panel to change document-related settings such as page size and margins. Clicking the Adjust Layout button opens a dialog box where you can change the document settings and at the same time adjust layout elements to match the new page size and/or margin.

    You can use the Page Number field to navigate to a specific page in the layout. Clicking the Page button activates the Page tool, which you can use to dynamically change the page size in the document window.

    The three buttons in the Rulers & Grids section toggle the visibility of rulers (▛), the baseline grid(▤), and the document grid(▦).

    The three buttons in the Guides section toggle the visibility of page guides(▦), lock and unlock page guides(▦), and toggle the visibility of smart guides(▦).

The Control panel combines many common formatting options into a single, compact format. It is context-sensitive, which means different options are available depending on what is selected in the layout. It is also customizable, which means you can change the options available in the panel. (It is also important to note that the options available in the Control panel might be limited by the active workspace and by the width of your monitor or Application frame.)

Default Control panel when a graphics frame is selected on a 21-inch monitor:

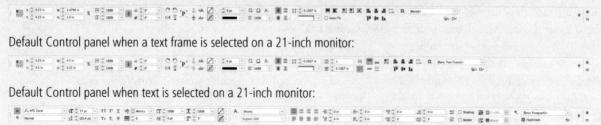

Default Control panel when a text frame is selected on a 21-inch monitor:

Default Control panel when text is selected on a 21-inch monitor:

When anything other than text is selected, the panel Options menu includes options for controlling the position of the panel (top, bottom, or floating), as well as how transformations affect selected objects:

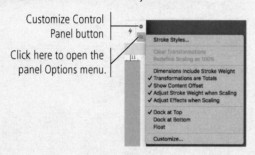

Customize Control Panel button

Click here to open the panel Options menu.

- **Stroke Styles.** This opens a dialog box where you can edit or define custom styles for lines and object strokes.
- **Clear Transformations.** Choosing this option resets an object to its original position (also clearing rotation).
- **Dimensions Include Stroke Weight.** When checked, width and height values include the object width, as well as the defined stroke width. For example, a square that is 72 points wide with a 1-point stroke would be 73 points wide overall (when using the default stroke position that aligns the stroke on the center of object edge).
- **Transformations are Totals.** When checked, transformations are cumulative for the frame and its contents. For example, say an image frame is rotated 10°.
  - When checked, the frame content also shows a 10° rotation; you can change the content rotation to 0° to return the image (but not the frame) to horizontal.
  - When not checked, the frame content shows 0° because the content is not rotated relative to its container. You have to rotate the content −10° to return it to horizontal without affecting the frame's rotation.

- **Show Content Offset.** When checked, the Control panel shows X+ and Y+ values for a frame's content when the actual content (not the frame) is selected.
- **Adjust Stroke Weight when Scaling.** When checked, resizing an object changes the stroke weight proportionally. For example, resizing an object with a 1-pt stroke to 50% results in a 0.5-pt stroke.

Clicking the Customize Control Panel button, or choosing Customize in the panel Options menu, opens a dialog box where you can define the available options in the panel; anything with a checkmark will be available when it's relevant to the selection in the document.

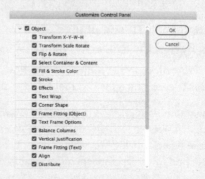

Clicking the Quick Apply button (⚡) opens a special navigation dialog box. This feature enables you to easily find and apply what you want (menu commands, user-defined styles, and so on) by typing a few characters in the text entry field and then clicking the related item in the list.

2. **Choose View>Grids & Guides>Smart Guides to make sure this option is toggled on. If the option is already checked, move the cursor away from the menu and click to dismiss it.**

Smart guides are a useful function of the application, making it easy to create and precisely align objects. Smart guides show the dimensions of an object when you create it, the position of an object when you drag it, the edge and center position of nearby objects and the distance between nearby similar objects.

This option should be checked (active).

3. **Choose the Line tool in the Tools panel, then click the Default Fill and Stroke button at the bottom of the Tools panel.**

The default option for the Line tool is a black stroke with no fill.

4. **Near the bottom of the page, click at the left bleed guide and drag to the right bleed guide. Press Shift, and then release the mouse button.**

As you drag, cursor feedback shows the length of the line you are drawing. The blue line previews what will appear when you release the mouse button. Pressing Shift as you draw forces (constrains) the line to exact 45° angles, including exactly horizontal.

Note:

You can turn off specific Smart Guide functions in the Guides & Pasteboard pane of the Preferences dialog box.

Note:

When drawing lines, cursor feedback shows the length of the segment you are drawing.

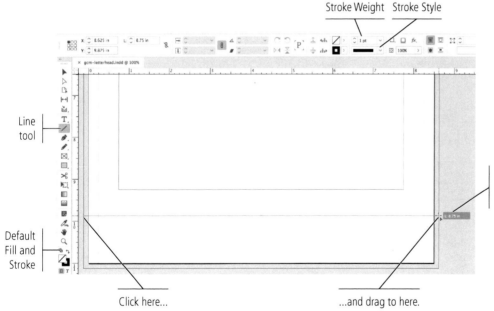

Stroke Weight   Stroke Style

Line tool

Cursor feedback shows the length of the line.

Default Fill and Stroke

Click here...   ...and drag to here.

5. **In either the Control or Properties panel, open the Stroke Weight menu and choose 2 pt.**

Because a line is selected in the layout, both the Control panel and Properties panel present options related to the selected line: stroke weight, style, color, etc. You can choose one of the stroke weight presets from the menu or simply type any value in the field.

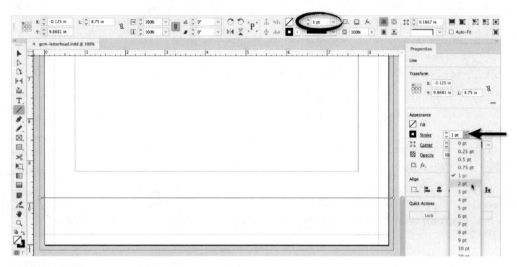

Like the Properties panel, the Control panel is context-sensitive; both present options that specifically relate to whatever is selected in the layout.

We primarily use the Properties panel throughout this book, unless a required option is only available in the Control panel. You should realize, however, that the Properties panel options are typically duplicated in the Control panel.

6. **In either the Control or Properties panel, change the Y field to 9.75 in and press Return/Enter to apply the change.**

X defines the horizontal (left-to-right) position, and Y defines the vertical (top-to-bottom) position. Because you constrained this line to horizontal, changing the Y field moves the entire line.

Remember, you do not need to type the units if you are entering a measurement in the default unit of measurement. We include the units in our steps for the sake of clarity.

7. **Choose the Pen tool in the Tools panel, then move the cursor over the line you just created.**

When the Pen tool is over an existing, selected line, it automatically switches to the Add Anchor Point tool cursor; clicking adds a new point to the selected line.

If the Pen tool is over a specific point on a selected line, it automatically switches to the Delete Anchor Point tool cursor; clicking removes that point from the line.

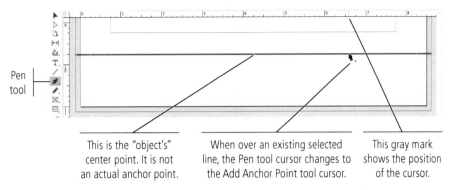

Pen tool

This is the "object's" center point. It is not an actual anchor point.

When over an existing selected line, the Pen tool cursor changes to the Add Anchor Point tool cursor.

This gray mark shows the position of the cursor.

8. **When the cursor is at the 4.5″ mark of the horizontal page ruler, click to add a point to the line.**

The visible center point of the selected line is a bit deceptive. This simply marks the center of the shape (a line, in this case); it is not an actual point on the line.

9. **Move the cursor right to the 6″ mark and click to add another point.**

All vector objects are composed of anchor points and connecting line segments, even if you don't create each point manually. The original line had two regular points (one at each end) and a straight connecting segment. You added two new points for a total of four points and three connecting segments.

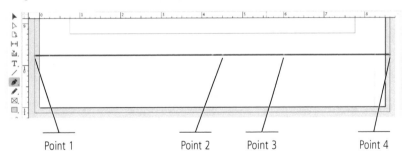

Point 1   Point 2   Point 3   Point 4

Note:

Although the center point might be difficult to see in our screenshots, you should be able to see it more clearly on your screen.

10. **Choose the Direct Selection tool in the Tools panel, and click away from the line to deselect it.**

The Direct Selection tool is used to select individual pieces of objects, such as a specific point on a line or a specific line segment between two points. However, you have to first deselect the entire line before you can select only part of it.

11. Move the cursor over the right part of the line.

When the Direct Selection tool cursor shows a small line in the icon, clicking will select the specific segment under the cursor.

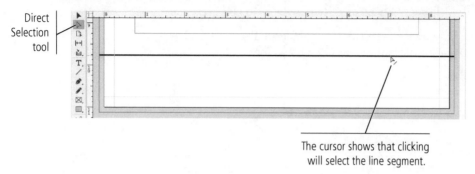

The cursor shows that clicking
will select the line segment.

12. Click anywhere between the third and fourth points on the line. Press Shift, and drag down until the cursor feedback shows the Y position of 10.2 in.

The segment you selected moves, and the segment between points 2 and 3 adjusts as necessary to remain connected. The segment between points 1 and 2 is not affected.

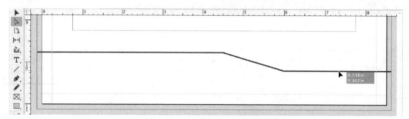

13. Using the Direct Selection tool, click the second point from the left (Point 2).

When the Direct Selection tool cursor shows a small circle in the icon, clicking will select the specific point under the cursor.

14. In the Control or Properties panel, change the X position of the selected point to 4.875 in.

As you can see, you can control the precise position of every point in a shape.

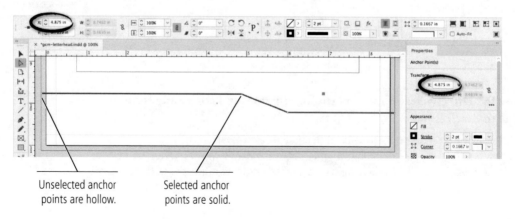

Unselected anchor
points are hollow.

Selected anchor
points are solid.

15. Save the file and continue to the next exercise.

Create Bézier Curves

Every line is composed of anchor points and line segments that connect those points. Even a simple, straight line has two points, one at each end. More sophisticated shapes can be created by adding anchor points and manipulating the direction handles of those points to control the shape of segments that connect the different points.

This concept is the heart of Bézier curves and vector-based drawing and can be one of the most challenging skills for new designers to master. The Pen tool and its variations are extremely powerful but also very confusing for new users. The best way to understand this tool is simply to practice. As you gain experience, you will become more comfortable with manipulating anchor points, handles, and line segments.

In this exercise you will make very simple manipulations to the straight line you just created. We also encourage you to practice as much as possible using the Pen tool until you are more proficient; for example, try copying the outlines of various shapes in photographs.

Note:

Bézier curves can be difficult, at first, to master. The best training is to practice until you can recognize and predict how moving a point or handle will affect the connected segments.

1. **With gcm-letterhead.indd open, make sure the line at the bottom of the page is selected.**

2. **Choose the Convert Direction Point tool nested under the Pen tool.**

   The Convert Direction Point tool changes a corner point to a smooth point (and vice versa). **Smooth points** have handles that control the size and shape of curves connected to that point. You can then use the Direct Selection tool to adjust handles for a selected anchor point.

Note:

Tools with nested options default to show the last-used variation in the main Tools panel.

3. **Click the second point on the line, press Shift, and drag right until the ruler shows the cursor is at 5.625″.**

   When you click a point with the Convert Direction Point tool and immediately drag, you add direction handles to the point. Those direction handles define the shape of the line segments connected to the point. As you drag farther away from the point, the affected segment's curve increases.

   Pressing Shift constrains the new direction handles to 45° angles — in this case, exactly horizontal. If you look closely, you can see the direction handle on the left side of the point is exactly on top of the line.

   By default, clicking and dragging creates a smooth, symmetrical point in which equal-length handles are added to each side of the point directly opposite each other. As long as a point is symmetrical, changing the angle of one handle also affects the handle on the other side of the point.

Note:

Using the Convert Direction Point tool, click a smooth point to convert it to a corner point.

Click the point and drag right to add handles.

The connected line bends in the direction in which you pull the handle.

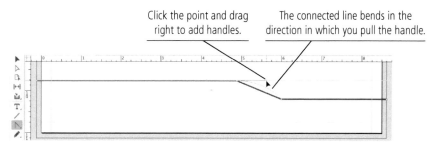

4. **Click the third point, press Shift, and drag right until the ruler shows the cursor is at 6.5".**

As we just explained, the affected curve gets larger as you drag farther away from the point. Because you're dragging exactly horizontally, the horizontal segment on the right is not curving.

On the left side of the point, however, you can see the effect of converting Point 3 to a symmetrical point. Dragging to the right side of the point adds direction handles on *both sides* of the point; the length and position of the left handle defines the shape of the curve on the left side of the point, which is the one you want to affect in this step.

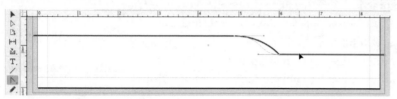

Note:

If you add points to a curved line segment, the new points automatically adopt the necessary direction handles to maintain the original curve shapes.

Note:

The lines that connect anchor points based on the angle and length of the control handles are called Bézier curves.

5. **Choose the Pen tool in the Tools panel. It is now nested under the Convert Direction Point tool.**

When you choose a nested tool variation, the nested tool becomes the default option in that position on the Tools panel.

6. **Move the cursor over the left endpoint of the line. When you see a diagonal line in the cursor icon, click to connect to the existing endpoint.**

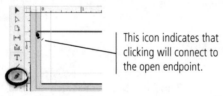

This icon indicates that clicking will connect to the open endpoint.

Note:

When you drag direction handles, the blue lines preview the effects of your changes.

Note:

If you move an anchor point that has direction handles, the handles don't change angle or length. The related curves change shape based on the new position of the point.

7. **Press Shift, then click at the bottom-left bleed guide.**

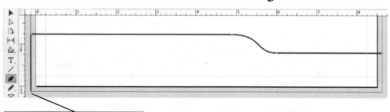

Shift-click to create a vertical line connected to the previous point.

8. **Press Shift, then click the bottom-right bleed guide.**

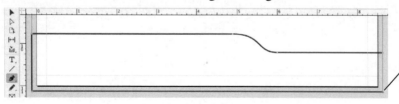

Shift-click to create a horizontal line between the previous point and the point where you click.

9. **Move the cursor over the open endpoint at the right end of the original line. When you see a small circle in the cursor icon, click to close the shape.**

You could have created this shape as a regular rectangle and then modified the top line with the Pen tool. However, our goal was to teach you how to create a basic line and how to perform some basic tasks with the Pen tool and its variations.

This icon indicates that clicking will close the shape.

It's important to realize there is almost always more than one way to accomplish a specific goal in InDesign. As you gain experience, you will develop personal preferences for the most effective and efficient methods of doing what you need to do.

10. **Save the file and continue to the next exercise.**

Understanding Anchor Points and Handles

An **anchor point** marks the end of a line **segment**, and the point **handles** determine the shape of that segment. Each segment in a path has two anchor points and can have two associated handles.

You can create corner points by simply clicking with the Pen tool instead of clicking and dragging. Corner points do not have their own handles; the connected segments are controlled by the handles of the other associated points.

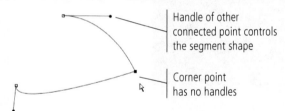

Handle of other connected point controls the segment shape

Corner point has no handles

In the image shown here, we first clicked to create Point A and dragged (without releasing the mouse button) to create Handle A1. We then clicked and dragged to create Point B and Handle B1; Handle B2 was automatically created as a reflection of B1 (Point B is a **symmetrical point**).

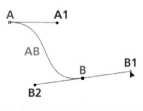

This image shows the result of dragging Handle B1 to the left instead of to the right when we created the initial curve. Notice the difference in the curve here compared to the curve above. When you drag a handle, the connecting segment arcs away from the direction in which you drag.

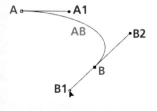

It's important to understand that every line segment is connected to two handles. In this example, Handle A1 and Handle B2 determine the shape of Segment AB. Dragging either handle affects the shape of the connected segment.

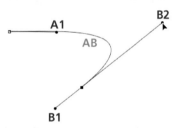

When you use the Pen tool, clicking and dragging a point creates a symmetrical (smooth) point; both handles start out at equal length, directly opposite one another. Changing the angle of one handle of a symmetrical point also changes the opposing handle of that point.

In the example here, repositioning Handle B1 also moves Handle B2, which affects the shape of Segment AB. (You can, however, change the length of one handle without affecting the length of the other handle.)

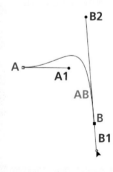

Change Color Values

Although there are several default color choices built into the Swatches panel of every InDesign file, you are not limited to these few options. You can define virtually any color based on specific values of component colors.

When you are building a page to be printed, you should use CMYK colors. The CMYK color model, also called **process color**, uses subtractive color theory to reproduce the range of printable colors by overlapping semitransparent layers of cyan, magenta, yellow, and black inks in varying percentages from 0–100.

In process-color printing, these four colors of ink are imaged (or separated) onto individual printing plates. Each color separation is printed with a separate unit of a printing press. When printed on top of each other in varying percentages, the semitransparent inks produce the CMYK **gamut**, or the range of possible colors. Special (spot) colors can also be included in a job by using specifically formulated inks as additional color separations.

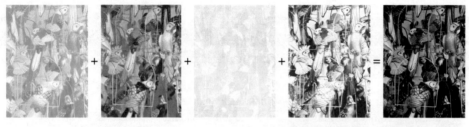

Using theoretically pure pigments, a mixture of equal parts of cyan, magenta, and yellow should produce black. Real pigments, however, are not pure; the actual result of mixing these three colors usually appears as a muddy brown. In the image to the right, the left block is printed with 100% black ink. The right block is a combination of 100% cyan, 100% magenta, and 100% yellow inks.

The fourth color, black (K), is added to the three subtractive primaries to extend the range of printable colors and to allow much purer blacks to be printed than is possible with only the three primaries. Black is abbreviated as "K" because it is the "key" color to which others are aligned on the printing press. Using K for black also avoids confusion with blue in the RGB color model, which is used for jobs that will be distributed digitally (websites, some PDF files, etc.).

1. **With gcm-letterhead.indd open, use the Selection tool to make sure the shape at the bottom of the page is selected.**

   Every shape you create in an InDesign document has a **bounding box**, which is a non-printing rectangle marking the outer dimensions of the shape. (Even a circle has a square bounding box, marking the largest height and width of the object.) The bounding box has eight handles, which you can drag to change the size of the rectangle. If you can see an object's bounding box handles, that object is selected.

2. **Click the button at the right end of the Control panel to open the panel Options menu.**

3. **If the Dimensions Include Stroke Weight option is checked, click that item to toggle the option off.**

When this option is active, the size of an object's stroke is factored as part of the overall object size. Consider, for example, a frame that is 72 points wide with a 1-point stroke. If you remove the stroke from the frame, the frame would then be only 71 points wide.

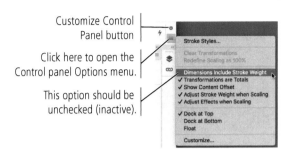

Customize Control Panel button

Click here to open the Control panel Options menu.

This option should be unchecked (inactive).

Note:

These options remember the last-used settings.

4. **At the bottom of the Tools panel, click the Swap Fill and Stroke button.**

The object now has a black fill and a stroke of none. Because you turned off the Dimensions Include Stroke Weight option, removing the stroke has no effect on the object's size.

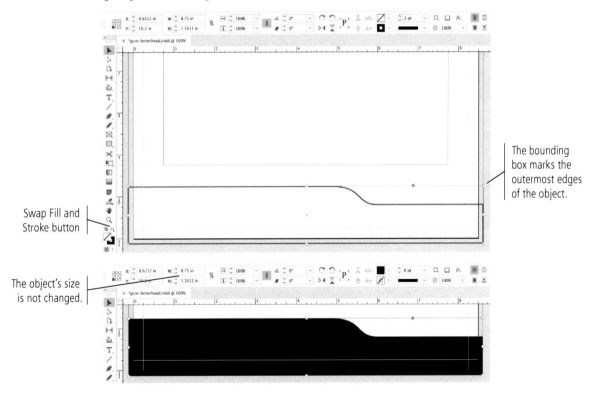

The bounding box marks the outermost edges of the object.

Swap Fill and Stroke button

The object's size is not changed.

5. **Open the Color panel (Window>Color>Color).**

Remember, all panels can be accessed in the Window menu. Because workspace arrangement is a matter of personal preference, we won't tell you where to place panels.

6. **Click the Fill swatch to bring it to the front (if it isn't already).**

When you apply color from any of the Swatches panels (including the ones in the Control panel), the Color panel shows a swatch of that color as a single slider. You can use this slider to easily apply a percentage of the selected swatch.

7. **Click the Options button in the top-right corner of the Color panel and choose CMYK from the Options menu.**

   This option converts the single swatch slider to the four process-color sliders. You can change any ink percentage to change the object's fill color.

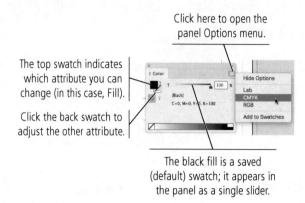

Click here to open the panel Options menu.

The top swatch indicates which attribute you can change (in this case, Fill).

Click the back swatch to adjust the other attribute.

The black fill is a saved (default) swatch; it appears in the panel as a single slider.

8. **Highlight the C (cyan) field and type 85%.**

   You do not need to type the "%" character; we include it here for clarity.

9. **Press Tab to highlight the M (magenta) field, then type 50%.**

10. **Repeat the process from Step 9 to define the Y (yellow) value as 85% and the K (black) value as 40%.**

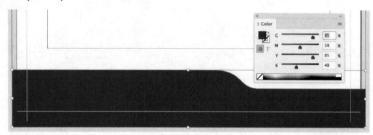

11. **With the object selected and the Fill swatch on the top of the stack, open the Color panel options menu and choose Add to Swatches.**

    This command creates a saved swatch from the active values; the new swatch will appear in the standalone Swatches panel as well as in the pop-up panels attached to the Control panel. After saving the swatch, the Color panel shows the fill color as a single slider of that swatch.

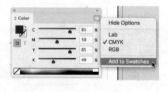

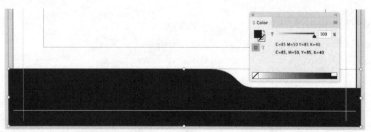

12. **Save the file and continue to the next exercise.**

Note:

You can change the color by typing a specific value or by dragging the slider below the color gradient.

Note:

If you change the fill or stroke color value with no object selected, you define the values for the next object you create.

Note:

You are going to use this color again later when you format text. By creating a saved custom color swatch, you will be able to apply the same color values in a single click.

Create a Basic Graphics Frame

When you place an external image file into an InDesign layout, it is contained in a frame. If you simply place the file into a layout, a containing frame is automatically created for you based on the dimensions of the placed image. You can also create graphic frames *before* placing images, which can be useful if you want to define the available space without using the actual external files.

InDesign includes two groups of tools for creating basic shapes in a layout: the frame tools and the shape tools. There is no practical difference between the shapes created with the two sets of tools (for example, a rectangle created with the Rectangle Frame tool or with the Rectangle tool). The frame tools create empty graphic frames, which are identified by crossed diagonal lines when Frame Edges are visible in the layout (View>Extras>Show Frame Edges). Basic shapes do not have these lines; however, if you place content into a shape created with one of the basic shape tools, it is automatically converted to a graphic frame.

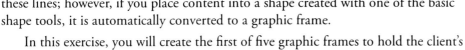

In this exercise, you will create the first of five graphic frames to hold the client's thumbnail images.

1. **With gcm-letterhead.indd open, choose the Rectangle Frame tool in the Tools panel.**

   If you don't see the Rectangle Frame tool, click and hold the default shape tool until the nested tools appear; slide over and down to select the Rectangle Frame tool.

2. **Press Command/Control, then click away from the existing shape to make sure it is deselected.**

   If you don't deselect the existing shape, the changes you make in the next step would affect the selected object.

   Pressing Command/Control temporarily switches to the last-used Selection tool (Selection or Direct Selection). This allows you to easily make selections — or, in this case, deselect an object — without changing the active tool.

Note:

To deselect objects, you can also choose Edit>Deselect All.

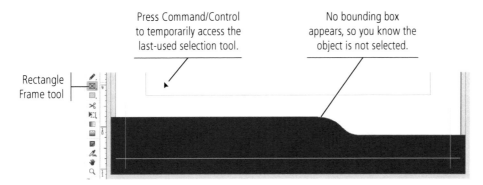

Press Command/Control to temporarily access the last-used selection tool.

No bounding box appears, so you know the object is not selected.

Rectangle Frame tool

3. **Click the Default Fill and Stroke button at the bottom of the Tools panel.**

   In InDesign, the default fill is None, and the default stroke is 1-pt black.

4. **Click anywhere on the page, press and hold the Shift key, then drag down and right to draw a rectangle 1.25″ high and 1.25″ wide.**

   As you draw, cursor feedback shows the size of the shape you are creating.

   Pressing Shift while drawing a shape constrains the horizontal and vertical dimensions of the shape to have equal height and width — in other words, this creates a perfect square or circle.

   Default Fill and Stroke button

   The blue line previews the shape you are drawing.

   Cursor feedback shows the size of the shape you're drawing.

   Note:

   If you simply click a basic shape or frame tool on the page, a dialog box opens so you can define a specific size for the new shape.

5. **Release the mouse button to create the rectangle.**

   The new shape appears in the position where you drew it. Notice the new frame has both a Fill and Stroke color of None even though you reset the Black stroke color in Step 3.

   New graphics frames always default to a Fill and Stroke color of None with a 0-pt stroke weight regardless of the settings you define before creating the frame. Fortunately, you can always change these settings after creating the frame.

   Note:

   If you use the regular shape tools instead of the frame tools, the Fill and Stroke settings you define before drawing are reflected in the new shape.

   Position and dimensions of the selected object

   Bounding box handles

   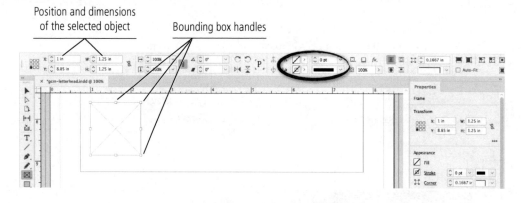

6. **In either the Control panel or Properties panel, select the bottom-left reference point.**

As we already explained, the Control and Properties panels are context-sensitive, which means different options are available depending on what is selected. The Transform section of the Properties panel defaults to show only the position and size of the selected object; clicking the More Options button reveals the other transformations that can be applied.

The **reference point** determines how transformations will occur (in other words, which point of the object will remain in place if you change one of the position or dimension values). These points correspond to the object's bounding box handles as well as to the object's exact center point.

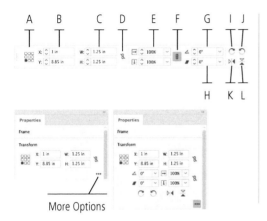

More Options

A	Transformation reference point
B	Object position
C	Object dimensions
D	Constrain proportions for width & height
E	Scale the object by a specific percentage
F	Constrain proportions for scaling
G	Rotation Angle
H	Shear X Angle
I	Rotate 90° Clockwise
J	Rotate 90° Counterclockwise
K	Flip Horizontal
L	Flip Vertical

Note:

You can use math operators to add (+), subtract (-), divide (/), or multiply (*) existing values in the Control panel. This is useful when you want to move or change a value by a specific amount.

Type **+.5** after the value to move the object down half an inch.

7. **Highlight the X field in either panel and type 1, then press Tab to move the highlight to the Y field.**

As in dialog boxes, you can use the Tab key to move through the fields in a panel. The X and Y fields determine the position of the selected object. X defines the horizontal (left-to-right) position, and Y defines the vertical (top-to-bottom) position.

8. **With the Y field highlighted, type 9 and then press Return/Enter.**

Pressing Return/Enter applies your changes. (You can also simply click away from the object to apply the change.)

The bottom-left reference point is selected.

The bottom-left corner of the object is positioned at X: 1 in, Y: 9 in.

9. **Save the file and continue to the next exercise.**

Clone, Align, and Distribute Multiple Objects

As you should have already noticed, there is often more than one way to accomplish the same task in InDesign. Aligning multiple objects on a page is no exception. In this exercise you will explore a number of alignment options as you create the remaining graphics frames for the client's thumbnail images.

1. **With gcm-letterhead.indd open, choose the Selection tool in the Tools panel.**

   The Selection tool is used to select entire objects; the Direct Selection tool is used to select parts of objects or the contents of a frame.

   Using the Selection tool, you can

   - Click and drag a handle to resize selected objects.
   - Shift-click and drag to resize objects proportionally.
   - Command/Control-click and drag to scale selected objects.
   - Command/Control-Shift-click and drag to scale selected objects proportionally.
   - Press Option/Alt with any of these to apply the transformation around the selection's center point.

2. **Click inside the area of the empty graphics frame to select the shape.**

3. **Press and hold Option/Alt, then click the frame and drag right. Release the mouse button when green lines connect the top, center, and bottom edges of the two shapes and when the horizontal ruler shows 1/8″ space between the two objects.**

   Pressing Option/Alt as you drag moves a copy of the selected object (called **cloning**).

   As you drag, a series of green lines marks the top, center, and bottom of the original object. These green lines are a function of InDesign's Smart Guides, which make it easy to align objects to each other by simply dragging.

Note:

You might need to zoom in to the object you are dragging to see the Smart Guides.

Note:

You can also press Shift to constrain the drag/cloning movement to 45° angles from the original object.

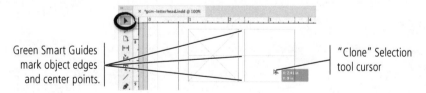

Green Smart Guides mark object edges and center points.

"Clone" Selection tool cursor

4. **Click the second shape, press Option/Alt, and drag right. Release the mouse button when the horizontal edges align and when you see opposing arrows below/between the three frames.**

   In addition to aligning edges, Smart Guides also make it easy to identify and match the distances between multiple objects. Smart Guides also identify equal dimensions when you create a new object near an existing one.

Note:

Smart guides do not function when moving objects on the paste-board (outside the page boundaries).

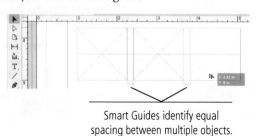

Smart Guides identify equal spacing between multiple objects.

5. **With the third object still selected, choose Object>Transform Again>Transform Again.**

This command applies the last-used transformation to the selected object. Because you used the cloning movement in the previous step, the result is a fourth copy spaced at the same distance used in Step 4. (The Transform Again command can be used to reapply rotation, scaling, sizing, and other transformations.)

Note:

You can choose Object>Step and Repeat to make more than one copy of an object using specific horizontal and vertical distances for each copy.

6. **With the fourth frame selected, choose Edit>Duplicate.**

This command makes a copy of the selected object using the last-applied distance.

Note:

If you start by clicking inside an existing shape, you will drag that shape instead of drawing a selection marquee.

7. **Zoom out so you can see the entire bottom of the document.**

8. **Using the Selection tool, click outside the existing shapes and then drag a marquee touching any part of all five frames.**

As we stated previously, the Selection tool is used to access and manipulate entire objects; any object partially selected by the marquee will be included in the selection.

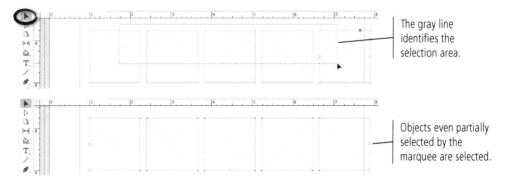

The gray line identifies the selection area.

Objects even partially selected by the marquee are selected.

9. **Click the right-center bounding box handle of the active selection. Press and hold the Spacebar, then drag left. When you see no space between the five frames, release the mouse button.**

As you drag, the space between the selected objects changes; the size of the actual objects is not affected (called **live distribution**).

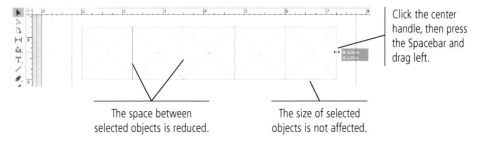

Click the center handle, then press the Spacebar and drag left.

The space between selected objects is reduced.

The size of selected objects is not affected.

10. Click the right-center handle again. Without pressing the Spacebar, drag left until the cursor feedback shows the width of the selection is 5.5″.

Simply dragging the handle resizes the entire selection; the spacing and position of various selected objects relative to one another is not affected.

Note:

Dragging a center handle changes the object size in only one direction.

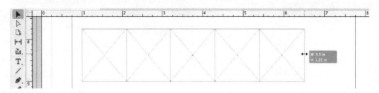

11. With the five frames selected, choose Object>Group.

Grouping multiple objects means you can treat them as a single unit.

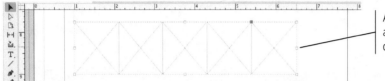

After grouping, a single bounding box outlines the entire group.

12. Open the Align panel (Window>Object & Layout>Align).

You can use the Align panel to align multiple objects relative to one another, to the page, or to the spread. The Align Objects options are fairly self-explanatory; when multiple objects are selected, they align based on the edge(s) or center(s) you click.

Note:

Group objects by pressing Command/Control-G.

Ungroup objects by pressing Command/Control-Shift-G.

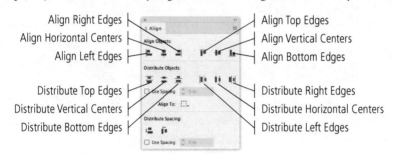

Align Right Edges
Align Horizontal Centers
Align Left Edges
Align Top Edges
Align Vertical Centers
Align Bottom Edges
Distribute Top Edges
Distribute Vertical Centers
Distribute Bottom Edges
Distribute Right Edges
Distribute Horizontal Centers
Distribute Left Edges

Note:

When the insertion point is not flashing in text, choosing Edit>Select All selects all objects on the active spread.

13. With the grouped graphics frames selected, press Shift and then click to add the green-filled shape to the active selection.

You can Shift-click an object to select it in addition to the previously selected object(s) or Shift-click an already selected object to deselect it without deselecting other objects.

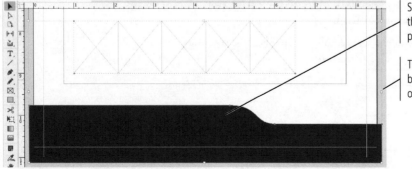

Shift-click to add this shape to the previous selection.

The selection bounding box now surrounds all objects on the page.

14. In the Align panel, open the Align To menu and make sure Align To Selection is the active option.

Using the (default) Align To Selection option, selected objects align to one another based on the outermost edges of the entire selection. In other words, aligning the top edges moves all objects to the same Y position as the highest selected object.

If you use the Key Object option, you can click any object in the selection to designate it as the key. (The key object shows a heavier border than other objects in the selection.)

Because you can align objects relative to the document, the align buttons are also available when only one object is selected, allowing you to align any single object to a precise location on the page or spread.

Note:

Align options are also available in the Properties panel and, depending on the width of your monitor and the workspace you are using, in the Control panel.

15. With all objects selected, click the Align Left Edges and Align Bottom edges buttons in the Align panel.

Because you grouped the five graphics frames, they are treated as one object during alignment; their positions relative to each other do not change.

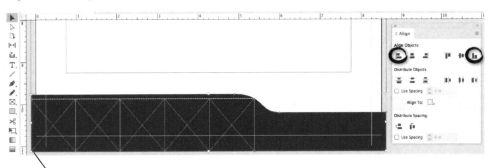

Selected objects are aligned to the bottom-most and left-most edges of the selection.

Understanding Object Distribution

The Distribute Objects options in the Align panel control the positions of multiple objects relative to each other.

Original position   Distribute Horizontal Centers position

By default, objects are equally distributed within the dimensions of the overall selection. You can check the Use Spacing option to space edges or centers by a specific amount.

Distribute Horizontal Centers with 1″ spacing value

Distribute Spacing options place equal space between selected objects, using the value defined in the Use Spacing field. You can also check Use Spacing to add a specific amount of space between the selected objects.

Distributed Spacing with 0.25″ spacing value

16. **Using the Selection tool, click away from the selected shapes to deselect all objects.**

17. **Using the Selection tool, click the right empty graphics frame to select it.**

    Because the frames are grouped, clicking once selects the entire group containing the frame you clicked.

18. **In the Control panel, change the Stroke Weight field to 3 pt.**

19. **Click the arrow button to the right of the Stroke swatch to open the attached Swatches panel. Choose Paper from the pop-up panel.**

    Because the active selection is a group, the new stroke weight and color apply to every object in the group.

    There is a difference between no fill and 0% of a color. The "None" color option essentially removes color from that attribute; underlying objects will be visible in areas where None is applied.

    Using 0% of a color — or using the Paper color — effectively creates a solid "white" fill. (In printing, solid white areas **knock out** or hide underlying shapes.)

Note:

Paper is basically white but more accurately named because the paper for a specific job might not be white.

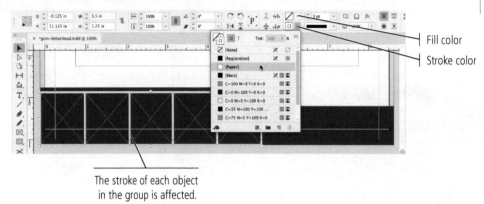

Fill color

Stroke color

The stroke of each object in the group is affected.

You can also use the Properties panel to change an object's stroke and fill attributes. Clicking the fill or stroke swatch opens a pop-up panel where you can define the color of the related attribute. The pop-up panel defaults to show saved swatches; you can click the Color button at the top to show the same options as you see in the stand-alone Color panel or click the Gradient button to show options from the Gradient panel.

Swatches   Color   Gradient

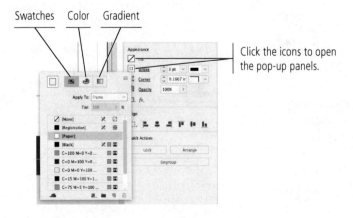

Click the icons to open the pop-up panels.

20. **Save the file and continue to the next exercise.**

Create a Rounded Rectangle

In addition to basic rectangles, you can create frames with a number of special corner treatments. In this exercise, you modify one corner of the right-most graphics frame to smoothly blend with the curve of the underlying background shape.

1. **With gcm-letterhead.indd open, make sure nothing is selected in the layout.**

2. **Using the Selection tool, double-click the right-most graphics frame in the group.**

   Double-clicking a group allows you to select only one object in a group without ungrouping the various objects. This is called "entering into the group."

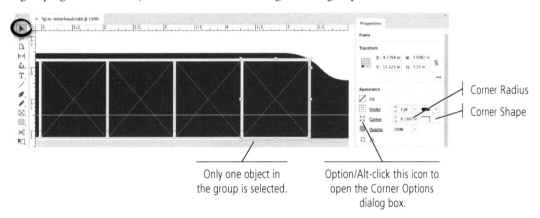

Corner Radius

Corner Shape

Only one object in the group is selected.

Option/Alt-click this icon to open the Corner Options dialog box.

3. **With the single frame selected, Option/Alt-click the Corner Shape icon in the Properties panel.**

   You can also choose Object>Corner Options to access the same dialog box.

   You can use the fields in the Properties panel to change the corner shape and radius of all corners on a selected shape. In this case, however, you want to change the shape of only one corner. Option/Alt-clicking the icon in the panel opens the related dialog box — in this case, the Corner Options dialog box — where you can exercise greater control over various settings.

4. **Check the Preview option in the bottom-left corner of the dialog box.**

   Many dialog boxes in InDesign have a Preview checkbox. When checked, you can see the effects of your selections before finalizing them.

5. **Click the Constrain icon in the dialog box to unlink the four corners.**

6. **Open the Corner Shape menu for the top-right corner and choose Rounded.**

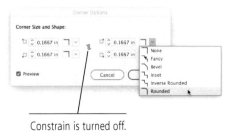

Constrain is turned off.

7. **Type 0.45 in the top-right Corner Size field, then press the Tab key.**

   For the dialog box Preview option to work properly, you have to move the highlight away from the field you changed. Pressing Tab while the dialog box is open allows you to see the results of your changes.

   Remember, you don't need to type the unit of measurement as long as the new value is the same unit as the default; we use units in our directions for clarity. We will not continue to repeat this explanation.

   A rounded-corner rectangle is simply a rectangle with the corners cut at a specific distance from the end (the corner radius). The two sides are connected with one-fourth of a circle, which has a radius equal to the amount of the rounding.

Radius

   Even though the adjusted frame now has one rounded corner, the **bounding box** still marks the outermost corners of the shape.

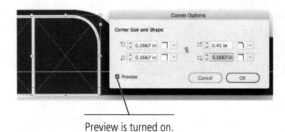

Preview is turned on.

8. **Click OK to return to the document.**

9. **Save the file and continue to the next stage of the project.**

Note:

The Polygon Frame and Polygon tools can be used to create odd shapes with a defined number of straight edges (including triangles).

Polygon Frame tool
Polygon tool

Clicking once with either Polygon tool opens the Polygon dialog box, where you can define the size of the new object as well as the number of points on the new shape. Star Inset determines how much closer those inside points will be to the center. (An inset of 0% creates all points at the same distance from the object's center.)

Editing Live Corners

FOUNDATIONS

When a rectangular frame is selected in the layout, a small yellow square appears on the right edge of the shape's bounding box. You can click this button to enter Live Corner Effects edit mode, where you can dynamically adjust the appearance of corner effects for all corners or for one corner at a time. Simply clicking away from the object exits the edit mode.

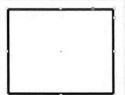

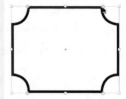

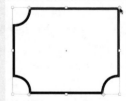

Click the yellow square to enter Live Corner Effects edit mode.

Drag a yellow corner diamond left or right to change the radius of all four corners.

Option/Alt-click a yellow diamond to change the shape of corner effects.

Shift-click a yellow diamond to change the radius of only one corner. Option/Alt-Shift-click to change the shape of one corner.

Transforming Objects Manually

You have a number of options for transforming objects in an InDesign layout. Using the Selection tool, you can

- Click a center bounding-box handle and drag to resize an object in one direction.
- Click a corner handle and drag to resize an object in both directions at once.
- Click outside a corner handle and drag to rotate an object.

When you drag a handle, you can press Shift to maintain the object's original height-to-width proportions during the transformation. Press Option/Alt while dragging to transform the object around its center point.

You can also use one of the Transformation tools to rotate, scale, or shear an object (or use the fields in the Control, Transform, or Properties panels to apply transformations).

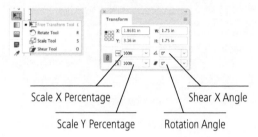

Scale X Percentage   Shear X Angle

Scale Y Percentage   Rotation Angle

Using the Pathfinder

You can apply a number of transformations to objects using the Pathfinder panel (Window>Object & Layout>Pathfinder).

Paths	Pathfinder	Convert Shape	Convert Point
Join Path	Add	Rectangle	Plain Point
Open Path	Subtract	Rounded Rectangle	Corner Point
Close Path	Intersect	Beveled Rectangle	Smooth Point
Reverse Path	Exclude Overlap	Inverse Rounded Rectangle	Symmetrical Point
	Minus Back	Ellipse	
		Triangle	
		Polygon	
		Line	
		Horizontal/Vertical Line	

Path options break (open) a closed path, connect (close) the endpoints of an open path, or reverse a path's direction (start becomes end and vice versa).

Pathfinder options create objects by combining multiple existing objects. When you use the Pathfinder (other than Subtract), attributes of the front object are applied to the resulting shape; Subtract maintains attributes of the back object.

- **Add** results in a single combined shape from selected objects.
- **Subtract** results in the shape of the back object minus any overlapping area of the front object.
- **Intersect** results in the shape of only the overlapping areas of selected objects.
- **Exclude Overlap** results in the shape of all selected objects minus any overlapping areas.
- **Minus Back** results in the shape of the front object minus any area where it overlaps other selected objects.

Convert Shape options change the overall appearance of an object using one of the six defined basic shapes or using the default polygon settings; you can also convert any shape to a basic line or an orthogonal (horizontal or vertical) line.

Convert Point options affect the position of direction handles when a specific anchor point is selected.

- **Plain** creates a point with no direction handles.
- **Corner** creates a point that produces a sharp corner; changing the direction handle on one side of the point does not affect the handle on the other side of the point.
- **Smooth** creates a point with opposing direction handles that are exactly 180° from one another; the two handles can have different lengths.
- **Symmetrical** creates a smooth point with equal-length opposing direction handles; changing the length or position of one handle applies the same change to the opposing handle.

Tips and Tricks for Working with Layout Objects

Copying and Pasting

The standard Cut, Copy, and Paste options are available in InDesign, just as they are in most applications. Whatever you have selected will be copied or cut to the Clipboard, and whatever is in the Clipboard will be pasted. InDesign has a number of special pasting options in the Edit menu:

Paste. If you are pasting an object (frame, etc.), the object will be pasted in the center of the document window. If you are pasting text, it will be pasted at the location of the current insertion point; if the insertion point is not currently placed, the text is placed in a new basic text frame in the middle of the document window.

Paste without Formatting. This command is available when text is in the Clipboard; the text is pasted using the default type formatting options (12-pt black Minion Pro, if it hasn't been changed on your system).

Paste Into. This command is available when an object is in the Clipboard and another object is selected. The pasted object becomes the contents of the object that is selected when you choose this command.

Paste in Place. This command pastes an object at the exact position as the original. If you paste on the same page as the original, you create a second object exactly on top of the first. You can also use this command to place a copy in the exact position as the original but on a different page in the layout.

Managing Stacking Order

The top-to-bottom order of objects is called **stacking order**. When you have multiple stacked objects, it can be difficult to select exactly what you want. Fortunately, the application provides a number of options to make it easier.

When you move the Selection tool cursor over an object, the edges of the object are highlighted. This lets you know what will be selected if you click.

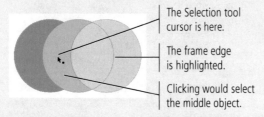

The Selection tool cursor is here.

The frame edge is highlighted.

Clicking would select the middle object.

When an object is already selected, InDesign favors the already selected object. This prevents you from accidentally selecting an object higher in the stacking order (for example, if you want to drag only the middle object).

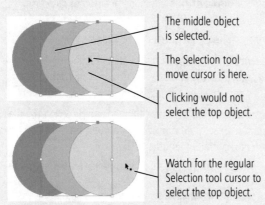

The middle object is selected.

The Selection tool move cursor is here.

Clicking would not select the top object.

Watch for the regular Selection tool cursor to select the top object.

You can select the next object down in the stacking order by pressing Command/Control while clicking within the area of the object stack.

You can use the Object>Select submenu commands (or their related keyboard shortcuts) to access objects relative to their order in the stack.

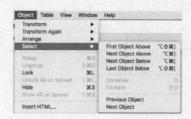

You can use the Object>Arrange submenu commands (or their related keyboard shortcuts) to change the stacking-order position of objects.

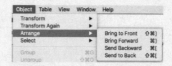

Finally, you can use the individual item listings in the Layers panel to select exactly the object you want or to rearrange objects in the layer stack.

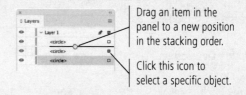

Drag an item in the panel to a new position in the stacking order.

Click this icon to select a specific object.

STAGE 3 / **Placing External Images**

As you saw in the first stage of this project, InDesign incorporates a number of tools for building graphics directly in a layout. Of course, most page-layout projects will include files from other sources. Logos created in Adobe Illustrator, raster-based images created in Adobe Photoshop, digital photographs, stock images, and many other types of files can be incorporated into a larger project.

 Place an Adobe Illustrator File

Every image in a layout exists in a frame. You can either create the frame first and place a file into it, or you can simply place an image and create the containing frame at the same time. In this exercise, you are going to place the client's logo, and transform it to fit into the margin space at the top of the layout.

Note:

Artwork in an Illustrator file must be entirely within the bounds of the artboard (page) edge. Anything outside the artboard edge will not be included when you place the file into InDesign.

1. **With gcm-letterhead.indd open, make sure nothing is selected.**

2. **Choose File>Place. Navigate to the WIP>GCMarket folder and select gcm-logo.ai. At the bottom of the dialog box, check Show Import Options.**

   Macintosh users: if you don't see three checkboxes at the bottom of the dialog box, click the Options button to reveal those checkboxes.

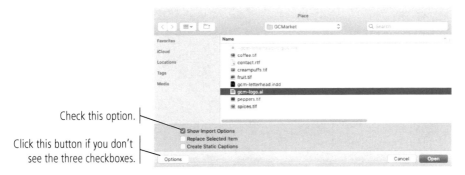

Check this option.

Click this button if you don't see the three checkboxes.

3. **Click Open.**

   When Show Import Options is checked, the Place [Format] dialog box opens with the options for the relevant file format. Every file format has different available options.

   If you press Shift when clicking Open in the Place dialog box, the Place [Format] dialog box for the selected file appears even if Show Import Options is not checked.

   When you place a native Illustrator file, the dialog box shows Place PDF options because the PDF format is the basis of Illustrator files that can be placed into InDesign.

4. **In the General tab, choose Art in the Crop To menu.**

You can use the Preview area on the left to determine which page/artboard you want to place.

The Crop To menu determines what part of the file will be placed:

- **Bounding Box** places the file based on the minimum area enclosing the objects on the page. You can also choose to include all layers or only visible layers in the calculation.

- **Art** uses the outermost dimensions of artwork in the file.

- **Crop** uses a crop area defined in the file.

- **Trim** uses trim marks defined in the file.

- **Bleed** uses the defined bleed area in the file.

- **Media** uses the physical size at which a PDF file was created.

Note:

If Crop, Trim, or Bleed is not defined in a file, the file will be placed based on the defined artboard size.

When Transparent Background is checked, background objects in the InDesign layout show through empty areas of the placed file. If this option is not checked, empty areas of the placed file knock out underlying objects.

5. **Click the Layers tab to display those options.**

PDF and native Illustrator files can include multiple layers. You can determine which layers to display in the placed file by toggling the eye icons on or off in the Show Layers list. In the Update Link Options menu, you can determine what happens when/if you update the link to the placed file.

- **Keep Layer Visibility Overrides** maintains your choices regarding which layers are visible in the InDesign layout.

- **Use PDF's Layer Visibility** restores the layer status as saved in the placed file.

6. **Click OK to load the cursor with the placed file.**

By default, the loaded Place cursor shows a small thumbnail of the file you're placing. You can turn off the thumbnail preview feature by unchecking the Show Thumbnails on Place option in the Interface pane of the Preferences dialog box.

7. **Click near the top-left corner of the page to place the image.**

   Every image in an InDesign layout exists in a frame. When you click an empty area of the page to place an image, the containing frame is automatically created for you.

   In the layout, blue handles and frame edges indicate the frame, and not its contents, is selected on the page; values in the Properties panel relate to the actual containing frame.

8. **Using the Properties panel, choose the top-left reference point and then change the frame's position to X: 0.25 in, Y: 0.25 in.**

Position the object's top-left corner at X: 0.25 in, Y: 0.25".

The blue handles show the edge of the graphics frame that contains the logo.

9. **Open the Interface pane of the Preferences dialog box. Choose Immediate in the Live Screen Drawing menu, then click OK.**

   Remember, preferences are accessed in the InDesign menu on Macintosh and in the Edit menu on Windows.

   Live Screen Drawing controls the appearance of an image when you move or resize it. The default behavior, Delayed, means the image does not appear inside the frame while you change the frame parameters (position, etc.).

   Using the Immediate Live Screen Drawing option, the image inside the frame always appears inside the frame when you move or resize the frame. If Delayed is selected, you can click and hold down the mouse button for a couple seconds to temporarily access the Immediate preview behavior.

10. **With the placed image selected, check the Auto-Fit option in the Frame Fitting section of the Properties panel.**

11. Click the bottom-right corner of the frame, then drag up to make the frame smaller. When cursor feedback shows the frame is 1.6 in high, release the mouse button.

When the Auto-Fit option is checked, resizing the frame automatically resizes the contained image to fit the new frame size; the image remains centered inside the frame. Areas of the image outside the resized frame remain visible, but slightly ghosted, while you hold down the mouse button.

When Auto-Fit is not selected, you can press Command/Control while resizing a frame to also scale the frame's content.

12. Uncheck the Auto-Fit option in the Properties panel.

If you don't turn off this option, you will not be able to manually apply other frame fitting commands in the next steps.

13. With the graphics frame still selected, click the Fit Content Proportionally button in the Properties panel.

The fitting options can resize the image relative to its frame or resize the frame relative to its content.

- **Fill Frame Proportionally** resizes content to fill the entire frame while preserving the content's proportions. Some of the image area might be cropped.

- **Fit Content Proportionally** resizes content to fit entirely within its containing frame, maintaining the current aspect ratio of the image. Some empty space might result along one dimension of the frame.

- **Fit Content to Frame** resizes content to fit the dimensions of the container, even if that means scaling the content out of proportion (stretched in one direction or another).

- **Fit Frame to Content** resizes the frame to the dimensions of the placed content.

- **Center Content** centers content within its containing frame, but neither the frame nor the content is resized.

- **Content-Aware Fit** allows the software to evaluate the placed image, then scale the image inside the frame to show what it determines to be the most important part of the image.

In this case, you defined the available frame height; you are using the fitting options to force the content proportionally into that available space.

Auto-Fit is turned off.

Note:

Frame fitting options can also be accessed in an object's contextual menu or in the Control panel.

14. With the Selection tool active, move the cursor inside the resized frame.

This reveals the Content Grabber, which you can use to access and manipulate the frame's content without the need to switch tools.

Content Grabber

15. Click the Content Grabber in the logo frame.

When the frame's content is selected, the X+ and Y+ fields define the position of the image *within the frame* and not to the frame itself. The Scale X and Scale Y fields show the file's current size as a percentage of the original.

These fields now show the parameters of the content in the frame.

The red frame and handles indicate you are now editing the content instead of the containing frame.

Note:

You can also use the Direct Selection tool to access and edit the content inside a graphics frame.

16. With the frame content selected, select the top-left reference point in the Properties panel and change the X+ field to 0.

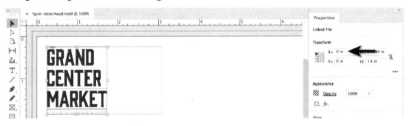

17. Press Esc to return to the frame of the selected object.

The graphics frame is again selected, and the Selection tool is still active.

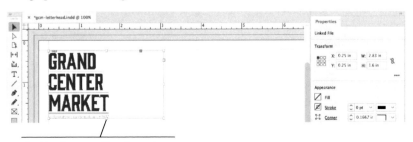

The blue frame and handles indicate you are again editing the frame and not the frame's content.

18. With the graphics frame still selected, click the Fit Frame to Content button in the Properties panel.

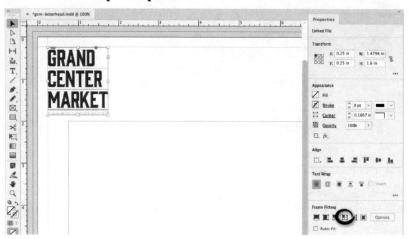

19. Save the file and continue to the next exercise.

Place Images into Existing Frames

In many cases, you will need to place an image or graphic into an existing frame and then manipulate the placed file to suit the available space. In the previous stage of this project, you created five empty graphics frames at the bottom of the layout; in this exercise, you will place the client's photos into those frames.

1. With gcm-letterhead.indd open, make the bottom of the page visible in your document window.

2. Using the Selection tool, click one of the empty graphics frames.

Remember, when objects are grouped, the Selection tool selects the entire group.

The Selection tool is active.

Clicking part of a group selects the entire group.

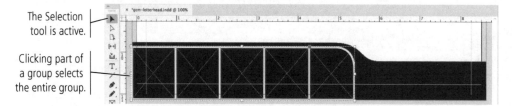

3. Open the Layers panel (Window>Layers), then click the arrow to the left of Layer 1 to expand the layer.

Every file has a default layer named "Layer 1" where objects you create exist automatically. Every object on a layer is listed in the Layers panel, nested under the appropriate layer name. Groups, which you created in an earlier exercise, can be expanded so you can access and manage the individual components of the group.

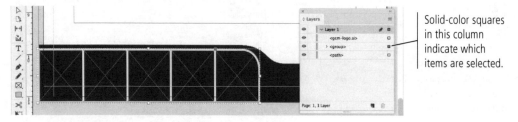

Solid-color squares in this column indicate which items are selected.

4. **Click the arrow to the left of the <group> item to expand the group.**

5. **Click the Select Item button for the first <rectangle> item in the group.**

   This method makes it easy to work with individual items in a group without first breaking apart the group.

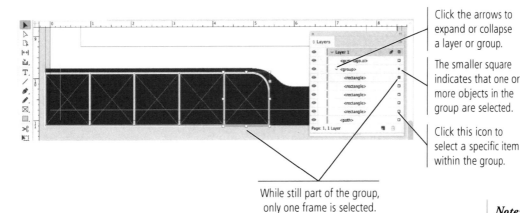

Click the arrows to expand or collapse a layer or group.

The smaller square indicates that one or more objects in the group are selected.

Click this icon to select a specific item within the group.

While still part of the group, only one frame is selected.

Note:

You can also use the Direct Selection tool to select individual objects within a group.

6. **In the Properties panel, check the Auto-Fit box, then click the Options button.**

   In this case, you know how much space is available, but you don't yet know the size of the images intended to fill the space. You can use the Frame Fitting options to determine what will happen when you place any image into the existing frames.

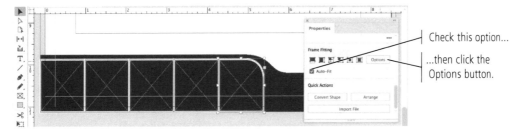

Check this option...

...then click the Options button.

7. **In the Frame Fitting Options dialog box, choose Fill Frame Proportionally in the Fitting menu, choose the top-left point in the Align From proxy, and click OK.**

   When an image is placed into this frame, it will fill the entire frame, and the aspect ratio of the image will be maintained.

   The Align From reference points determine the position of the placed content relative to the frame. In this case, the top-left corner of the content will be anchored to the top-left corner of the frame.

Check this option...

...then choose the top-left registration point.

8. **With the Selection tool still active, click the fourth frame to select it.**

   When you are already "inside" a group, you can use the Selection tool to select another individual object within the same group.

   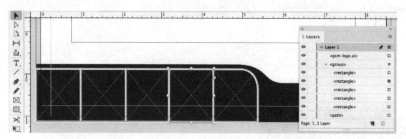

   When you use the Auto-Fit checkbox in the Control panel, the center registration point is the default Content Fitting option. To change the registration point for each frame, you need to use the Frame Fitting Options dialog box.

9. **Repeat Steps 6–8 for the remaining placeholder frames, selecting each frame and changing the frame fitting options for the selected frame.**

10. **Choose File>Place. If necessary, navigate to the WIP>GCMarket folder.**

11. **Uncheck all options at the bottom of the dialog box.**

    Macintosh users: Remember, you might have to click the Options button to show the Options checkboxes. We will not continue to repeat this instruction.

    If you leave Show Import Options checked, you would see the TIFF Options dialog box for each of the selected images. In this case you simply want to place the images so you don't need to review the file options.

12. **Press Command/Control, then click the following files to select them:**

    coffee.tif
    creampuffs.tif
    fruit.tif
    peppers.tif
    spices.tif

    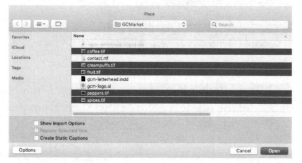

    In many cases, you will need to place more than one image from the same location into an InDesign layout. You can streamline the process by loading multiple images into the cursor at once, and then clicking to place each image in the correct location.

Note:

Press Shift to select multiple contiguous files in a dialog box.

Press Command/Control to select multiple non-contiguous files.

Note:

You can press Command/Control to select non-consecutive files in the list, or press Shift to select consecutive files.

13. Click Open to load the selected files into the Place cursor.

When you select multiple files in the Place dialog box, the cursor is loaded with all selected pictures; a number in the cursor shows the number of files loaded.

Five images are currently loaded in the Place cursor.

Note:

When more than one file is loaded in the Place cursor, the Links panel shows "LP" for the item that is active in the Place cursor.

The thumbnail in the cursor shows the active file, which will be placed when you click. You can use the Left Arrow and Right Arrow keys to navigate through the loaded images, watching the cursor thumbnails to find the one you want to place.

14. Click inside the left placeholder frame to place the first image.

As soon as you place the first file, the next loaded image appears as the cursor thumbnail.

In the Layers panel, the <rectangle> object is replaced with the name of the file you placed into the frame.

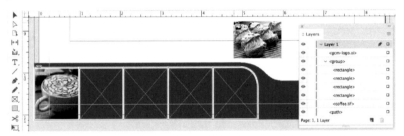

15. Click inside each empty frame to place the remaining loaded images.

16. Save the file and continue to the next stage of the project.

STAGE 4 / Creating and Formatting Basic Text

InDesign is ultimately a page-layout application; **page layout** means combining text and graphic elements in a meaningful way to convey a message. Text can be a single word (as in the logo used in this project) or thousands of pages of consecutive copy (as in a dictionary). Virtually every project you build in InDesign will involve text in one way or another; this letterhead is no exception.

Create a Simple Text Frame

Adding text to a page is a relatively simple process: draw a frame, and then type. In this exercise, you'll create a new text frame and add the client's tag line, then apply some basic formatting options to style the text.

Keep in mind this project is an introduction to creating elements on a layout page; there is far more to professional typesetting than the few options you use here. InDesign provides extremely precise control over virtually every aspect of every letter and word on the page. In the following projects, you will learn about the vast number of options available for setting and controlling type, from formatting a single paragraph to an entire multi-page booklet.

Note:

Remember from the Getting Started section at the beginning of this book: to complete the projects in this book, you should install and activate the ATC fonts provided with the book's resource files.

1. **With gcm-letterhead.indd open, select the Type tool in the Tools panel.**

2. **Click in the empty space above the green-filled shape and drag to create a frame.**

   To type text into a layout, you must first create a frame with the Type tool; when you release the mouse button, you see a flashing bar (called the **insertion point**) where you first clicked to create the text frame.

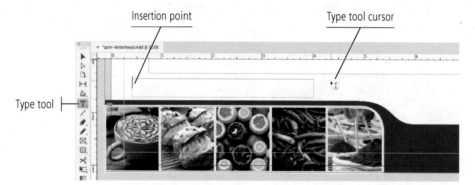

3. **Type Grand Cuisine. Grand Culture. Grand Central.**

The text appears beginning at the flashing insertion point. Depending on the size of your frame, the text might automatically wrap to a second line within the frame or might not fit into the frame (indicated by a red X, called an **overset text icon**).

New text in InDesign is automatically set in black 12-pt Minion Pro. This font is installed along with the application, so it should be available on your computer unless someone has modified your system fonts. Don't worry if your type appears in some other font; you will change it shortly.

When the insertion point is flashing, the Properties panel includes a fairly large number of text formatting options, consolidated from a variety of other panels and dialog boxes. Depending on the height of your monitor or application frame, you might need to scroll through the panel to find specific formatting options that appear at the bottom of the panel.

Note:

Type defaults to a 100% black fill with no stroke. (You can apply a stroke to type, but you should be very careful when you do to avoid destroying the letter shapes.)

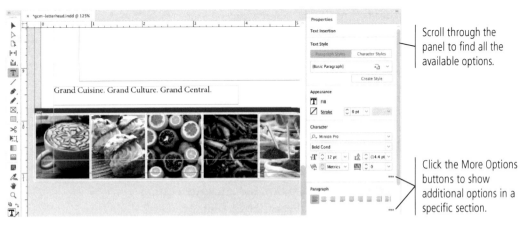

Scroll through the panel to find all the available options.

Click the More Options buttons to show additional options in a specific section.

4. **Choose the Selection tool in the Tools panel.**

You must use the Selection tool to change the position and size of a text frame. You can either drag the handles to manually change the frame or use the Control panel options to define specific parameters.

5. **In the Properties panel, make sure the constrain option is not active for the W and H fields. Choose the top-left reference point, and then change the frame's dimensions to:**

X: 0.25 in	W: 4.5 in
Y: 9.5 in	H: 0.25 in

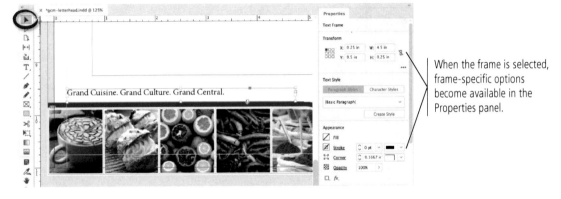

When the frame is selected, frame-specific options become available in the Properties panel.

6. **Choose the Type tool, and click inside the repositioned text frame to place the insertion point.**

7. **Choose Edit>Select All to select all text in the frame.**

   Character formatting such as the font, style, size, and fill color apply only to selected characters.

   In addition to using the Select All command to select all text in a story, you have a number of options for selecting type characters in a frame:

   - Select specific characters by clicking with the Type tool and dragging.
   - Double-click a word to select the entire word.
   - Triple-click a word to select the entire line containing the word.
   - Quadruple-click a word to select the entire paragraph containing the word.
   - Press Shift-Right Arrow or Shift-Left Arrow to select the character to the immediate right or left of the insertion point, respectively.
   - Press Shift-Up Arrow or Shift-Down Arrow to select all characters up to the same position as the insertion point in the previous or next line, respectively.
   - Press Command/Control-Shift-Right Arrow or Command/Control-Shift-Left Arrow to select the word immediately to the right or left of the insertion point, respectively.
   - Press Command/Control-Shift-Up Arrow or Command/Control-Shift-Down Arrow to select the rest of paragraph immediately before or after the insertion point, respectively.

Note:

When a type frame is selected with the Selection tool, you can double-click inside the frame to place the insertion point inside that frame. The Type tool automatically becomes active.

8. **In the Properties panel, open the Fill swatch panel and click the custom green swatch at the bottom of the list color. Press Return/Enter to close the pop-up Swatches panel.**

   This is the swatch you defined and saved earlier when you changed the fill color of the green-filled shape. By clicking the swatch, you change the color of all selected text.

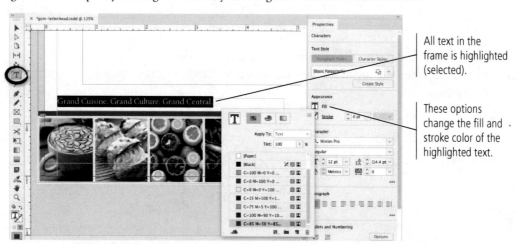

All text in the frame is highlighted (selected).

These options change the fill and stroke color of the highlighted text.

9. **With the text still selected, click in the Font Family field to highlight the current font name.**

10. With the font name highlighted, type ATC.

When you type in the Font Family field, the application automatically presents a menu of all fonts that include the letters you type.

By default, the application presents any font that includes the search characters *anywhere in the font name*; a search for "gar" would find both Garamond and Devangari. This kind of search returns all matching fonts in the pop-up menu.

If you click the magnifying glass icon, you can also choose to Search First Word Only. In this case, typing "gar" would automatically change the Font Family field to the first font that begins with those characters; no menu is presented.

11. Move your mouse cursor over various fonts in the menu.

You can use this method in the font menu to show a live preview of various fonts before actually applying them to the selected text.

Individual characters do not need to be selected to change text formatting. Changes made while a type *object* is selected apply to all text in that type object.

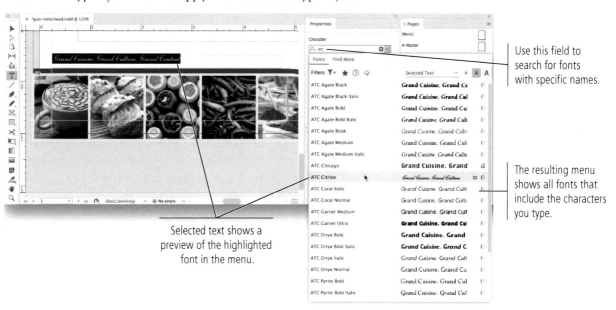

Selected text shows a preview of the highlighted font in the menu.

Use this field to search for fonts with specific names.

The resulting menu shows all fonts that include the characters you type.

12. Click ATC Coral Normal in the Font menu to select that font.

After you select the font, you should notice the Font Family menu shows "ATC Coral" and the secondary Font Style menu shows "Normal." When you use the Font Search option (as in Step 10), the resulting menu shows all font variations that include the letters you type — including different styles within the same family.

The applied font appears in the Font Family menu.

The specific style appears in the Font Style menu.

More about Working with Fonts

You can click the arrow to the right of the Font Family menu to open the Font panel, which provides a number of options for finding fonts you want to use in your design. (The same options are available wherever you see a Font Family menu — the Character panel, the Control panel, and the Properties panel.)

The top section of the menu lists up to ten most recently used fonts. These appear in the order they were used, with the most recent at the top of the menu. (You can change the number of displayed fonts in the Type pane of the Preferences dialog box.)

The second section lists SVG fonts. The third section lists all other fonts that are available to InDesign.

The font family names in each section appear in alphabetical order. An arrow to the left of a font name indicates that a specific font family includes more than one style. You can click the arrow to show all possible styles in the panel.

If you apply a font that includes more than one style, the style you choose appears in the Font Style menu. You can open the Font Style menu to change the style without changing the font family.

Each font in the panel includes a sample of the font, which defaults to show the currently selected text. If no text is selected, the sample text simply shows the word "Sample." You can choose a different sample text from the menu at the top of the panel. You can also change the size of the sample text using the three icons to the right of the menu.

Change the
sample text size

Click to change
the sample text.

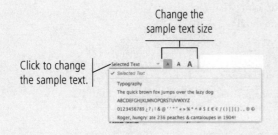

Click here to change the search behavior when you type in the Font Family field.

Clear the Font Family field   Open the Font menu

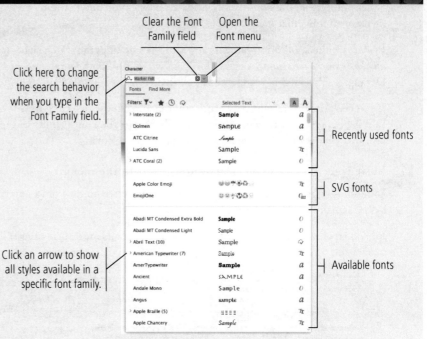

Click an arrow to show all styles available in a specific font family.

Recently used fonts

SVG fonts

Available fonts

The right column in the Font menu shows an icon to identify the type of font:

a **PostScript (Type 1) fonts** have two file components (outline and printer) that are required for output.

T **TrueType fonts** have a single file but (until recently) were primarily used on the Windows platform.

O **OpenType fonts** are contained in a single file that can include more than 60,000 glyphs (characters) in a single font. OpenType fonts are cross-platform; the same font can be used on both Macintosh and Windows systems.

SVG **OpenType SVG fonts** allow font glyphs to be created as SVG (scalable vector graphics) artwork, which means glyphs can include multiple colors and gradients. These fonts, which are relatively new, are most commonly used for emojis.

VAR **OpenType Variable fonts**, introduced in 2016, were developed jointly by Adobe, Apple, Google, and Microsoft to allow a single font file to store a continuous range of variants. If you apply a variable font, you can adjust the width and weight of the applied font without the need for different font files for variations such as Bold, Black, Condensed, or Extended.

↻ **Adobe fonts** are those that have been activated in your Creative Cloud account.

Above the list of fonts in the Font panel, you can use the Filters options to show only certain fonts in the panel. Clicking the Filter Fonts by Classification button opens a menu where you can find fonts of a certain style (serif, sans serif, etc.), as well as fonts with specific properties:

▼⌄ Filter Fonts by Classification

★ Show Favorite Fonts

🕓 Show Recently Added Fonts

♻ Show Activated (Adobe) Fonts

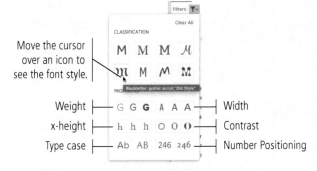

Move the cursor over an icon to see the font style.

Weight — Width
x-height — Contrast
Type case — Number Positioning

- Weight, or the thickness of strokes in the letterforms
- Width of the individual letterforms
- x-height, or the ratio of lowercase letter height compared to uppercase
- Contrast, or the ratio of thin strokes compared to thick strokes in individual letterforms
- Typecase, or whether a font includes both uppercase and lowercase or all capitals/small caps
- Number positioning, which refers to whether numbers all align to the baseline or extend above or below the baseline

When you use any of the filtering options, the Font panel shows only fonts that match the selected filter. You can click the Clear All link in the top-right corner of the panel to restore the default font list.

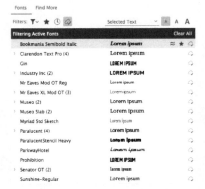

When the mouse cursor hovers over a font in the list, two additional icons appear on the right side of the panel for the highlighted font.

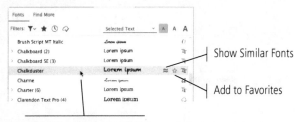

Show Similar Fonts

Add to Favorites

Move the cursor over a font to reveal additional options.

You can click the Show Similar Fonts ≈ button to show only fonts similar to one you selected; clicking the Back hot-text link returns to the full Font panel.

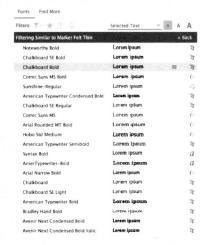

Clicking the Add to Favorites ☆ button designates a font as a Favorite; Favorite fonts are identified by a solid star icon even when the cursor is not hovering over that particular font. You can also use the Filtering option at the top of the panel to show only Favorite fonts.

Working with Adobe Fonts

Adobe Fonts (formerly called Typekit) is an online library of high-quality fonts that are available to anyone with a Creative Cloud subscription.

The Find More option at the top of the Font panel provides a link to Adobe Fonts directly from the InDesign interface.

When you find a font you want to use, move your mouse over that font to show the Activate icon ⊕; click that icon to activate it in your Creative Cloud account. (A separate icon shows that a particular font is currently being activated ☁.) Synced fonts will be available for use in any application on your device.

If only certain fonts in a family are active, you can click the Active Remaining icon ☁ to activate all fonts in that family.

If a font is already active, move your mouse over the Active icon ☁ to access the Deactivate icon ☁; click that icon to unsync that font.

Verifying your Adobe ID

To use Adobe Fonts in an Adobe application, you must first verify you are signed in using the username and password associated with your individual user subscription. (Adobe Font functionality is not available if you are working on a computer that has an Adobe software Device license instead of an individual user subscription.)

If you open the Help menu, you will see an option to either Sign In or Sign Out. If you see the words "Sign Out," the menu option also shows the email address (username) that is currently signed in.

If you see your own username, you are already signed in and can use the Adobe Font functionality. If you see a different username, you should choose the Sign Out option, and then sign in with your own username. If you see the words "Sign In," you should choose that menu option and follow the on-screen directions to sign in with your own username.

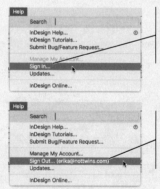

If this option shows "Sign In," you are not yet signed in to your Creative Cloud account.

If this option shows "Sign Out," this is the email (Adobe ID) that is currently signed in to the Adobe Creative Cloud.

13. Click the Up-Arrow button for the Font Size field until you see a red icon on the right edge of the frame.

Each time you click, you increase the type size by one point. The red X is the **overset text icon**; it indicates more text exists than will fit into the frame.

You can also choose from the common preset type sizes in the menu or type a specific size in the field.

If you type in the Font Size field, you don't need to type the unit "pt" for the type size; InDesign automatically applies the measurement for you.

Note:

Press Command/Control-Shift-> to increase the type size by 2 pt, or Command/Control-Shift-< to decrease the type size by 2 pt.

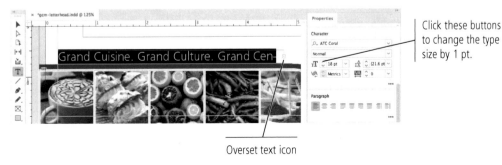

Click these buttons to change the type size by 1 pt.

Overset text icon

14. Click the Down-Arrow button once to reduce the type size by 1 pt.

This allows all the type to fit in the frame.

15. Click anywhere in the selected text to place the insertion point.

This removes the highlight, indicating the characters are now deselected.

16. Save the file and continue to the next exercise.

Place an External Text File

You just learned how to create a text frame and create new text. You can also import text created in an external word-processing application, which is a common situation when creating page-layout jobs (more common, perhaps, than manually typing text in a frame). In this exercise, you import text saved in a rich-text format (RTF) file, which can store type-formatting options as well as the actual text.

1. **With `gcm-letterhead.indd` open, make sure nothing is selected in the layout and then choose File>Place.**

   Remember, you can choose Edit>Deselect All, or simply click in an empty area of the workspace to deselect any selected objects.

2. **Navigate to `contact.rtf` in the WIP>GCMarket folder. Make sure none of the options are checked at the bottom of the dialog box and click Open.**

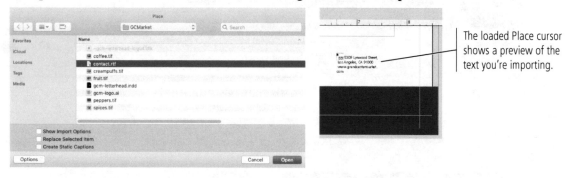

The loaded Place cursor shows a preview of the text you're importing.

3. **Click the loaded Place cursor within the pink margin guides, approximately 0.5″ up from the bottom margin guide.**

   The address is supposed to appear in the green area to the right of four small images. However, if you click inside that area with the Type tool, it will convert the existing shape to a type area. In this case you want a simple rectangular text frame, so you are creating it in an empty area and then moving it into place.

   The resulting text frame is automatically created as wide as the defined margin guides and extending down to the bottom margin guide on the page.

Placing text from a file automatically creates a text frame to contain the text.

4. **Choose the Selection tool. Click the bottom-right corner of the frame and drag until the frame is just large enough to contain the text.**

5. **Click and drag the frame until its bottom-right corner snaps to the page guides in the bottom-right corner of the page.**

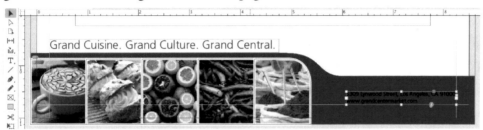

6. **Press Command/Control-Shift, then click the top-left bounding box handle of the frame. While holding down the mouse button, drag to the left. When the Scale X and Scale Y fields in the Control panel show approximately 120%, release the mouse button.**

As you drag the frame handle, pressing Command/Control allows you to resize the type along with the frame. Pressing Shift constrains the scaling to maintain the original height-to-width ratio.

Note:

The same fields are available in the Properties panel if you click the More Options button in the Transform section.

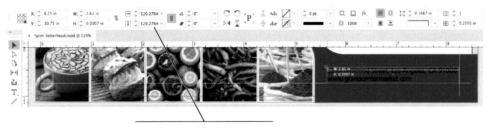

These fields show the percentage to which the frame and its content are being scaled.

7. **With the Selection tool still active, open the Fill color pop-up panel in the Properties panel.**

8. **Choose Text in the Apply To menu at the top of the pop-up panel, then click the Paper color.**

   Keep in mind this changes the color of all text in the selected frame; if you want to change only some characters, you must use the Type tool to highlight the characters you want to affect.

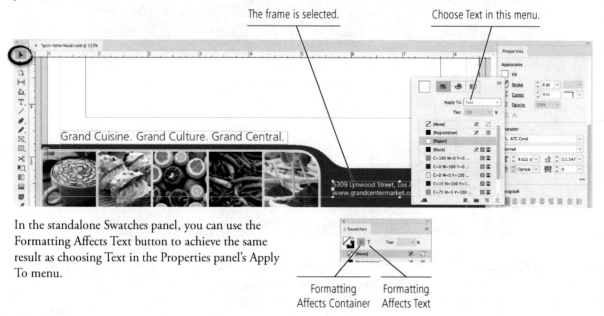

The frame is selected.

Choose Text in this menu.

In the standalone Swatches panel, you can use the Formatting Affects Text button to achieve the same result as choosing Text in the Properties panel's Apply To menu.

Formatting Affects Container

Formatting Affects Text

9. **In the Properties panel, click the [Paragraph] Align Right option.**

   Paragraph formatting (including alignment) applies to all selected paragraphs. If no text is highlighted, it applies only to the paragraph where the insertion point is placed.

   In this case, the containing text frame is selected; all paragraphs in the selected frame are also considered selected and will be affected by formatting changes.

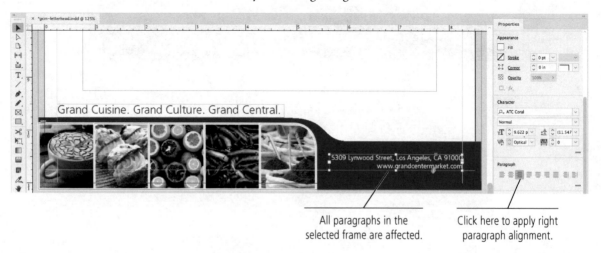

All paragraphs in the selected frame are affected.

Click here to apply right paragraph alignment.

10. **Zoom out so you can see the entire page.**

11. **Use the Screen Mode button at the bottom of the Tools panel to turn on the Preview mode.**

This mode turns off nonprinting indicators, including guides and the blue borders surrounding every frame. These tools can be very valuable when you're working on a layout, but they can be distracting in other cases.

Note:

You can also toggle off just frame edges in the View>Extras submenu.

When frame edges are hidden, moving the Selection tool cursor over a frame reveals its edges. This highlighting can make it easier to find exactly the object you want, especially when working in an area with a number of overlapping or nearby objects.

12. **Save the file and continue to the final stage of the project.**

STAGE 5 / **Printing InDesign Files**

Although the PDF format is the *de facto* standard for submitting files to a commercial printer, you will still need to output printed proofs at some point in your career, whether to show a hard copy to a client or to simply review a document's content away from a monitor. Creating those proofs requires a basic understanding of how software and hardware translate what you see on screen to ink on paper.

For a printer to output high-quality pages from Adobe InDesign, some method of defining the page and its elements is required. These definitions are provided by Page Description Languages (PDLs), the most widely used of which is Adobe PostScript 3.

When a file is output to a PostScript-enabled device, the raster image processor (RIP) creates a file that includes mathematical descriptions detailing the construction and placement of the various page elements; the print file precisely maps the location of each pixel on the page. In the printer, the RIP then interprets the description of each element into a matrix of ones (black) and zeros (white). The output device uses this matrix to reconstruct the element as a series of individual dots or spots that form a high-resolution bitmap image on film or paper.

Not every printer on the market is capable of interpreting PostScript information. Low-cost, consumer-level inkjet printers, common in the modern graphic design market, are generally not PostScript compatible. (Some desktop printers can handle PostScript, at least with an additional purchase; consult the technical documentation that came with your printer to make certain it can print PostScript information.) If your printer is non-PostScript compatible, some features in the InDesign Print dialog box will be unavailable, and some page elements (particularly EPS files) might not output as expected.

If you do not have a PostScript output device, you can work around the problem by first exporting your InDesign files to PDF (see Project 2: Festival Poster) and then opening the PDFs in Acrobat to print a proof. This is a common workflow solution in the current graphic design industry.

Print a Sample Proof

In general, every job you create will be printed at some point in the workflow — whether for your own review, as a client comp, or as a final proof to accompany a file to the commercial printer. So, whether you need a basic proof or a final job proof, you should still understand what is possible in the InDesign Print dialog box.

Composite proofs print all colors on the same sheet, which allows you to judge page geometry and the overall positioning of elements. Final composite proofs provided to the printer should include **registration marks** (special printer's marks used to check the alignment of individual inks when the job is printed), and they should always be output at 100% size.

Note:

It is also important to realize that desktop inkjet and laser printers typically do not accurately represent color.

1. **With gcm-letterhead.indd open, choose File>Print.**

   The Print dialog box includes dozens of options in eight different categories.

   The most important options you'll select are the Printer and PPD (PostScript printer description) at the top of the dialog box. InDesign reads the information in the PPD to determine which of the specific print options are available for the current output.

2. **Choose the printer you want to use in the Printer menu, and choose the PPD for that printer in the PPD menu (if possible).**

3. Review the options in the General pane.

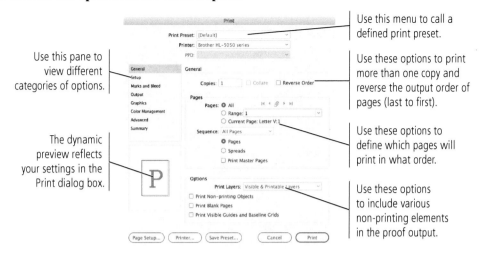

Use this pane to view different categories of options.

Use this menu to call a defined print preset.

Use these options to print more than one copy and reverse the output order of pages (last to first).

The dynamic preview reflects your settings in the Print dialog box.

Use these options to define which pages will print in what order.

Use these options to include various non-printing elements in the proof output.

If you frequently use the same options for printing proofs, simply click the Save Preset button at the bottom of the dialog box after defining those settings. You can then call those same settings by choosing the saved preset in the Print Preset menu.

4. Click the Setup option in the list of categories.

These options determine the paper size that will be used for the output (not to be confused with the page size), paper orientation, and page scaling and positioning options relative to the paper size.

5. If your printer can print to tabloid-size paper, choose Tabloid in the Paper Size menu.

If you can only print to letter-size paper, choose the landscape paper orientation option, and then activate the Tile check box.

To output a letter-size page at 100% on letter-size paper, you have to tile to multiple sheets of paper; using the landscape paper orientation allows you to tile to two sheets instead of four (as shown in the preview area).

The Offset and Gap fields should only be used when a job is output to an imagesetter or high-end proofing device. They define page placement on a piece of oversized film or on a printing plate.

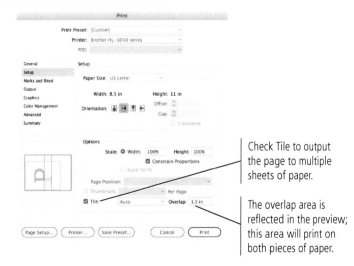

Check Tile to output the page to multiple sheets of paper.

The overlap area is reflected in the preview; this area will print on both pieces of paper.

6. **Click the Marks and Bleed option in the list of categories.**
   Activate the All Printer's Marks option and change the Offset field to 0.125 in.
   Make sure the Use Document Bleed Settings option is checked.

   You can specify individual printer's marks or simply print them all. For proofing purposes, the crop and bleed marks are the most important options to include.

   The Offset value determines how far from the page edge printer's marks will be placed; some printers require printer's marks to stay outside the bleed area, which means the offset should be at least the same as the defined bleed area.

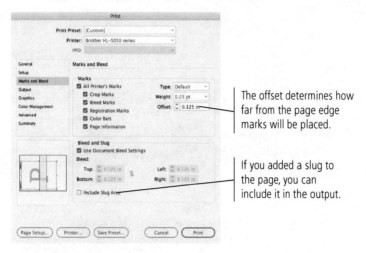

The offset determines how far from the page edge marks will be placed.

If you added a slug to the page, you can include it in the output.

7. **Click the Output option in the list of categories.**
   If you can print color, choose Composite CMYK or Composite RGB in the Color menu; otherwise, choose Composite Gray.

   In the Color menu, you can choose the color model you want to use. (If you only have a black-and-white printer, this menu will default to Composite Gray.) The composite options output all colors to a single page, which is appropriate for a desktop proof. If you choose either Separations option in the menu, the Inks list shows which inks (separations) will be included in the output.

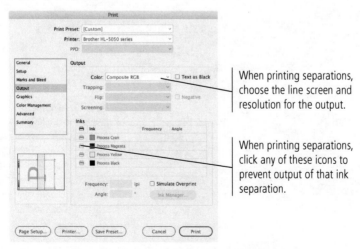

When printing separations, choose the line screen and resolution for the output.

When printing separations, click any of these icons to prevent output of that ink separation.

The Trapping, Flip, Negative, Screening, Frequency, and Angle options should only be used by the output service provider; these options relate to the way separations are imaged on a printing plate for commercial print output.

8. **Click Graphics in the list of categories.**

9. **Choose Optimized Subsampling in the Images Send Data menu.**

This menu determines how much data is sent to the output device for placed images.

- **All**, the default option, sends full-resolution image data.

- **Optimized Subsampling** sends only the necessary data to output the best possible resolution on the printer you are using.

- **Proxy** outputs low-resolution screen previews, which reduces the time required for output.

- **None** outputs all placed images as gray frames with crossed diagonal lines. This is useful for reviewing overall placement when developing an initial layout comp.

If you are using a compatible output device, the Fonts Download menu determines how much font data is downloaded to the printer. (Font data is required by the output device to print the job correctly.)

- **None** sends no font information to the printer. (This can cause output problems, especially if you use TrueType fonts.)

- **Complete** sends the entire font file for every font used in the document.

- **Subset** sends font information only for the characters used in the document.

Professional-quality output devices include a number of resident fonts, from just a few to the entire Adobe type library. If the Download PPD Fonts option is checked, InDesign sends data for all fonts in the document, even if those fonts are installed on the output device. (This can be important because different fonts of the same name might have different font metrics, which can cause text to reflow and appear different in the print than in the file you created.)

The PostScript menu defines which level of PostScript to use. Some older devices cannot process PostScript 3. You should generally leave this menu at the default value.

The Data Format menu defines how image data is transferred. ASCII is compatible with older devices and is useful for cross-platform applications. Binary is smaller than ASCII but might not work on all platforms.

10. **Click Print to output the page.**

11. **When the document comes back into focus, save and close it.**

Note:

We're intentionally skipping the Color Management and Advanced panes in the Print dialog box. We explain them in later projects when they are relevant to the project content.

PROJECT REVIEW

1. _____ is the area of an object that extends past the edge of a page to compensate for variations in the output process.

2. _____ is a special kind of raster image that has only two possible color values, black or white.

3. The _____ defines the outermost dimensions of an object; it is always a rectangle, regardless of the object's specific shape.

4. _____ are based on the concept of anchor points and their defining control handles.

5. _____ are the four primary colors used in process-color printing.

6. The _____ tool is used to select entire frames or other objects.

7. The _____ tool can be used to select specific segments or individual points on a path.

8. The _____ panel can be used to select and rearrange specific objects in a group.

9. The _____ can be used to access a frame's content when the Selection tool is active.

10. The _____ is context sensitive, reflecting different options depending on what is selected in the document.

1. Briefly explain the difference between a vector graphic and a raster image.

2. Briefly explain how resolution affects a page laid out in InDesign.

3. Briefly explain the concept of process color.

PORTFOLIO BUILDER PROJECT

Use what you learned in this project to complete the following freeform exercise.
Carefully read the art director and client comments, then create your own design to meet the needs of the project.
Use the space below to sketch ideas; when finished, write a brief explanation of your reasoning behind your final design.

The owner of your agency is pleased with your work on behalf of your client. She has decided to create more formal branding for the agency and wants you to create a new logo and accompanying collateral pieces.

To complete this project, you should:

❑ Develop a compelling logo that suggests the agency's purpose (graphic design). Incorporate the agency's name — Creative Concepts — in the logo.

❑ Build a letterhead using the same specifications you used to design the market's letterhead.

❑ Build a business card 3.5″ wide by 2″ high, with 1/8″ bleeds.

❑ Build an envelope layout for #10 business-size envelopes (9.5″ × 4.125″).

For the logo, I want something that really says "graphic design" because how can we convince clients that we can design their logos if we don't have a good design for our own? Find or create some kind of imagery people will immediately recognize as graphics- or art-related.

The letterhead should have the company's mailing address, phone number, and website. The business card needs to include a name, title, mailing address, email, and phone number. The envelope should only have the mailing address and the website. Use your own contact information as placeholder text for everything.

For the envelope, we're going to print pre-folded envelopes, so you can't use bleeds. You need to keep objects at least 0.25″ from the edges.

All pieces should have a consistent look. Whatever you do on the letterhead, you should use similar visual elements on all three pieces.

We designed this project to introduce you to the basics of page layout with InDesign; you will expand on these skills throughout this book. Creating a new document to meet specific project needs — including page size, margins, and the printer's stated bleed requirements — is one of the most important tasks you will complete in InDesign.

After the page structure is created, InDesign has many tools for creating objects: basic shapes, lines, and Bézier curves, placeholder frames, and text frames. The built-in drawing tools can create sophisticated artwork directly on the page (although InDesign should not be considered an alternative to Adobe Illustrator for creating all vector artwork). You can also place external image and text files, and then transform those files to meet the specific needs of a given project.

There are many different methods for managing objects and their content. The Selection and Direct Selection tools, the Content Indicator icon, frame edge highlighting, and the Layers panel all provide ways to access only — and exactly — what you want to edit.

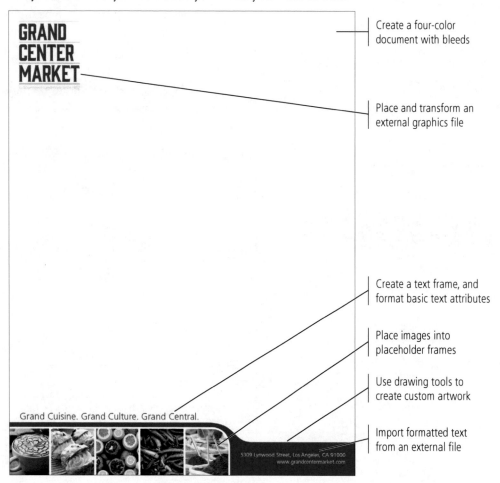

Create a four-color document with bleeds

Place and transform an external graphics file

Create a text frame, and format basic text attributes

Place images into placeholder frames

Use drawing tools to create custom artwork

Import formatted text from an external file

Festival Poster

Your client, the marketing director for the city department of parks and recreation, wants a poster and postcard to advertise the opening festival that kicks off the annual Summer Concert Series. She wants to use very little text and large, vivid graphics.

This project incorporates the following skills:

❑ Creating a file with the appropriate settings for a five-color, commercially printed poster

❑ Using gradients, graphics, and effects to attract the viewer's attention

❑ Adding text elements and applying formatting as appropriate

❑ Threading a single text story across multiple text frames

❑ Understanding the options for formatting characters and paragraphs

❑ Adjusting layouts to different page sizes

❑ Creating PDF files that meets the printer's requirements

PROJECT MEETING

The poster to promote this festival is basically the "play bill," and we will plaster it all over the city. We want the artwork to be very colorful and vivid, so the main focus — and most of the poster real estate — should be on the graphics. But the text also has to be readable; this morning I emailed the text I want to include.

Our posters for past years' festivals have always been 11″ × 17″, but we've been told that 11″ × 8.5″ will fit in the half-page ad space of the local newspaper. We're going to switch to that size for this year's event.

For the postcard, we typically go oversized and use 7″ × 5″ because it stands out a bit more than a typical 6″ × 4.25″ postcard.

The client has provided all the pieces you need, so you can get started composing the layout. Most of this job is going to involve compositing multiple images and formatting text, but I want you to go beyond basic image placement. InDesign includes many tools for manipulating images; use some of those to make sure this poster consists of more than just plain pictures.

Finally, I want you to use a special metallic ink for the date and location. That should give the poster just a bit more visual impact than regular flat colors. I think the gold 8005 in Pantone's metallic collection will work well with the other visual elements.

You already know the page sizes. According to the printer the postcard only needs the standard 1/8″ bleed allowance, but the poster needs a 1/4″ bleed just to be safe.

The final files should be saved as PDFs using the printer's specs, which I'll email to you.

To complete this project, you will:

- ❑ Convert the content type of frames.
- ❑ Create a custom gradient to add visual impact.
- ❑ Create a frame using an image clipping path.
- ❑ Apply effects to unify various graphic elements.
- ❑ Create a QR code.
- ❑ Thread the flow of text through multiple text frames.
- ❑ Format text characters and paragraphs to effectively convey a message.
- ❑ Place inline graphics to highlight important textual elements.
- ❑ Place text on a path.
- ❑ Apply a spot color.
- ❑ Adjust the layout to more than one page size.
- ❑ Create PDF files for commercial output.

SUMMER INDIE ROCK FESTIVAL

www.summerconcertseries.com

STAGE 1 / Building Graphic Interest

Graphics and text are contained in frames, and those objects (including graphics frames) can have stroke and fill attributes. You can use those foundational skills to build virtually any InDesign layout.

InDesign also includes a number of options for extending your artistic options beyond simply compositing text and graphics that were finalized in other applications. The first stage of this project incorporates a number of these creative tools to accomplish your client's stated goal of grabbing the viewer's attention with vivid, attractive graphics.

 Set up the Workspace

1. **Download `Concert_ID20_RF.zip` from the Student Files web page.**

2. **Expand the ZIP archive in your WIP folder (Macintosh), or copy the archive contents into your WIP folder (Windows).**

   This results in a folder named **Concert**, which contains the files you need for this project. You should also use this folder to save the files you create in this project.

3. **In InDesign, choose File>New>Document. Choose the Print option at the top of the dialog box, and choose the Letter document preset.**

   Remember, using the Print category of presets automatically applies inches as the unit of measurement and CMYK as the default color model.

4. **In the Preset Details section, make the following changes to the default values:**

Name:	poster
Units:	Inches
Orientation:	Landscape
Facing Pages:	Unchecked
Margins:	0.25 in on all four sides
Bleed:	0.25 in on all four sides

Note:

If a setting isn't mentioned, leave it at the default setting.

5. **Click Create to create the new file.**

6. **Save the new file as `poster.indd` in your WIP>Concert folder, and then continue to the next exercise.**

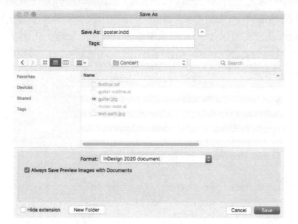

 Define Color Swatches

Before you begin creating colors to use in a layout, you should understand a few basics about the mechanics of designing with color.

Color By Numbers. If you base color choices solely on what you see on your monitor, many colors will probably not look quite right when printed with process-color inks. Even if you have calibrated your monitor, there will always be some discrepancies since monitors display color in RGB and printing uses CMYK.

Every print designer should have some sort of printed process-color chart, which contains small squares of process ink builds so you can see, for example, what a process build of C=10 M=70 Y=30 K=20 will really look like when printed. When you define process colors in InDesign, you should enter specific numbers in the CMYK fields to designate your color choices rather than relying on your screen preview. As you gain experience defining colors, you will become better able to predict the outcome for a given process-ink build.

The same concept also applies when using special ink libraries. You should have, and use, swatch books showing printed samples of the special inks. You cannot rely on the monitor preview to choose a special ink color.

Total Area Coverage. When defining the ink values of a process-color build, you must usually limit your total area coverage (TAC, also called total ink coverage or total ink density), or the amount of ink used in a given color. If you exceed the TAC limits for a given paper-ink-press combination, your printed job might end up with excess ink bleed, smearing, smudging, show-through, or a number of other printing errors because the paper cannot absorb all the ink.

Maximum TAC limits are between 240% and 320% for offset lithography, depending on the paper being used; TAC can be easily calculated by adding the percentages of each ink used to create the color. If a color is defined as C=45 M=60 Y=90 K=0, the total area coverage is 195% (45 + 60 + 90 + 0).

Swatches in InDesign. The Swatches panel (Window>Color>Swatches) is used to apply predefined colors to any element in a layout.

A **Fill** and **Stroke** swatches determine the active attribute; whichever appears at the top of the stack is the one that will be changed by clicking a swatch.

B The **Swap Fill and Stroke** button reverses the current fill and stroke colors.

C The **Formatting Affects Container** option is active by default when an object is selected with the Selection tool; when selected, clicking a color changes the fill or stroke of the selected object.

D If a text frame is selected, you can click the **Formatting Affects Text** button to change the color of text inside that frame. This option is active by default when the insertion point is placed in a text frame.

E Use the **Tint** field to change the tint of the applied color, from 0% to 100%.

F Clicking the **Add Selected Swatch to my Current CC Library** button adds the selected swatch to the active CC Library (see Page 327 for more information).

G Use the **Swatch Views** menu to show all swatches, show only color swatches, show only gradient swatches; or show only color groups.

H Click the **New Color Group** button to create a new color group (folder) for organizing swatches. Selected swatches move into the new color group.

I Click the **New Swatch** button to create a new color swatch based on the active color. If the active color is an existing swatch, the new swatch is a duplicate of the existing swatch with "2" appended to the swatch name.

J Click the **Delete Selected Swatch/Group** button to remove selected color swatches/groups; objects where those colors had been applied are not affected.

A number of options are included in the default swatches panel for new print files:

- **None.** This swatch removes any applied color from the active attribute.

- **Registration.** This swatch appears on every separation in a job. This "color" should only be used for special marks and information placed outside the design's trim area.

- **Paper.** In four-color printing, there is no white ink; instead, you have to remove or "knock out" underlying colors so the paper shows through, regardless of whether it is white or some other color. This is why InDesign refers to this swatch as "Paper" instead of "White."

- **Black.** This is a 100% tint of only black ink.

- **Colors.** Six default color swatches represent the subtractive (CMY) and additive (RGB) color models.

The right side of the panel has two columns of icons for each color swatch:

- The left icon identifies whether a swatch is a process (▣) or a spot color (◉).

- The right icon identifies the color model used to define the color: CMYK (▣), RGB (▪), or LAB (▣).

Note:

Using the Fill and Stroke swatches at the top of the Swatches panel, you can apply different colors to the fill and stroke of selected text.

Note:

You cannot edit or delete the None, Registration, or Black color swatches.

You can edit the Paper swatch to more accurately represent the color of paper being used for a specific job. Editing the appearance of the Paper swatch only affects the on-screen preview; it does not appear in the print output.

1. With **poster.indd** open, open the Swatches panel (Window>Color>Swatches).

2. In the Swatches panel, double-click the default blue color swatch (C=100 M=90 Y=10 K=0).

Double-clicking a swatch opens the Swatch Options dialog box, where you can change the settings of that swatch. The top of the dialog box shows this swatch is a Process CMYK color named according to the color values.

Note:

Remember, all panels (whether docked or not) can be accessed from the Window menu. If you don't see a specific menu command, choose Edit>Show All Menu Items.

3. Change the ink percentages to the following:

Cyan:	70%
Magenta:	80%
Yellow:	0%
Black:	0%

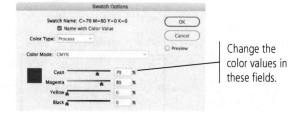

Change the color values in these fields.

4. Click OK to apply the change.

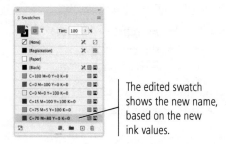

The edited swatch shows the new name, based on the new ink values.

5. Repeat Steps 2–4 to change the definition of the default red color swatch (C=15 M=100 Y=100 K=0) to:

Cyan:	20%
Magenta:	100%
Yellow:	100%
Black:	10%

6. With nothing selected in the layout, click the default green color swatch and drag it to the panel's Delete button.

Although it isn't necessary to delete the swatch, you should know how the process works. If you delete a swatch used in the layout, you will be asked what color to use in place of the one you are deleting.

Drag the swatch to the panel's Delete button.

7. Open the Swatches panel Options menu.

This menu has options for creating four types of color swatches: Color, Tint, Gradient, and Mixed Ink.

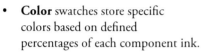

Click here to open the panel Options menu.

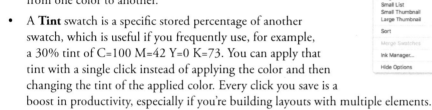

- **Color** swatches store specific colors based on defined percentages of each component ink.

- **Gradient** swatches store specific transitions from one color to another.

- A **Tint** swatch is a specific stored percentage of another swatch, which is useful if you frequently use, for example, a 30% tint of C=100 M=42 Y=0 K=73. You can apply that tint with a single click instead of applying the color and then changing the tint of the applied color. Every click you save is a boost in productivity, especially if you're building layouts with multiple elements.

- **Mixed Ink** swatches allow you to combine percentages of spot and process colors, or of multiple spot colors; this option is only available when at least one spot color exists in the file. The **Mixed Ink Group** option allows you to build multiple swatches at once. Be very careful if you use mixed ink swatches; they can be a source of unpredictable color reproduction and potential output problems.

8. Choose New Color Swatch in the panel Options menu.

9. Leave the Name with Color Value option checked. Make sure the Color Type is set to Process and the Color Mode is set to CMYK.

There is no industry standard for naming colors, but InDesign comes close with the Name with Color Value option when you define a new swatch. This type of naming convention serves several purposes:

- You know exactly what components the color contains, so you can easily see if you are duplicating colors.

- You can immediately tell the color should be a process build rather than a special ink or spot color.

- You avoid mismatched color names and duplicated spot colors, which are potential disasters in the commercial printing production process.

Mismatched color names occur when a defined color name has two different values — one defined in the page layout and one defined in a file you placed into your layout. When the files are output, the output device might be confused by different definitions for the same color name; the imported value might replace the project's value for that particular color name (or vice versa). The change could be subtle, or it could be drastic.

A similar problem occurs when the same spot color is assigned different names in different applications. For example, you define a spot color in InDesign as "Border Color"; another designer might define the same spot color in Illustrator as "Spec Blue." When the illustration is placed into the InDesign layout, two different spot-color separations exist even though the different color names have the same values.

Note:

Use the Load Swatches option to import color swatches from another InDesign file.

Use the Add Unnamed Colors option to find and add colors that are applied in the layout without using a defined swatch (e.g., using the Color panel).

Use the Sort submenu options to sort swatches by name or color value.

10. Define the swatch color percentages as

Cyan:	**0%**
Magenta:	**40%**
Yellow:	**0%**
Black:	**100%**

Leave this option checked.

Choose Process color type.

Choose CMYK color mode.

Define ink percentages here.

Uncheck this option.

100% black and some percent of another color is called **rich black** or **super black**. Remember, when the inks are printed, adding another ink to solid black enhances the richness of the solid black. Adding cyan typically creates a cooler black, while adding magenta typically creates a warmer black.

11. At the bottom of the dialog box, uncheck the option to add the swatch to a CC Library.

CC Libraries are useful for sharing assets such as color swatches across multiple Adobe CC applications if you have an individual Creative Cloud user account.

12. Click the Add button to create the new color swatch.

By clicking the Add button, you can add more color swatches without having to reopen the New Color Swatch dialog box. If you click OK, the swatch is created and the dialog box closes.

13. In the New Color Swatch dialog box, choose Spot in the Color Type menu.

14. Choose Pantone+ Metallic Coated in the Color Mode menu.

Spot colors are created with special premixed inks to produce a certain color with one ink layer; they are not built from the process inks used in CMYK printing. When you output a job with spot colors, each spot color appears on its own separation.

Spot-color inks are commonly used when an exact color, such as a corporate color, is required. InDesign includes a number of built-in color libraries, including spot-color systems such as the Pantone Matching System (PMS), the most popular collections of spot colors in the United States.

Even though you can choose a color directly from the library on your screen, you should look at a swatch book to verify you are using the color you intend. Special inks exist because many of the colors cannot be reproduced with process inks, nor can they be accurately represented on a computer monitor. If you specify special colors and then convert them to process colors later, your job probably won't look exactly as you expect.

Note:

Spot colors are safely chosen from a swatch book — a book of colors printed with different inks, similar to the paint chip cards used in home decorating.

When choosing spot colors, ask your printer which ink system it supports. If you designate TruMatch but they use Pantone inks, you won't get the colors you expect.

15. **Place the insertion point in the Pantone field and type 8005.**

You can also scroll through the list and simply click a color to select it.

Type a specific color number in this field.

16. **Click Add, then click Done to return to the document window.**

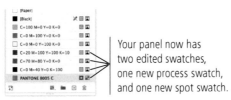

Your panel now has two edited swatches, one new process swatch, and one new spot swatch.

17. **Save the file and continue to the next exercise.**

Working with Color Groups

Color groups are a convenient way to manage swatches, much as you might organize files in folders on your desktop.

When you click the New Color Group button at the bottom of the Swatches panel, a new group is added to the panel with the default name "Color Group X," where X is simply a sequential number.

Clicking the New Color Group button adds a color group with the default naming convention.

You can double-click the color group name to open the Edit Color Group dialog box, where you can define a specific name for the group.

Choosing New Color Group in the panel Options menu automatically opens the Edit Color Group dialog box, where you can name the new group at the time it is created.

If one or more swatches are selected in the panel when you create a new color group, the selected swatches are automatically moved to the new group.

After a group is created, you can drag existing swatches in the group using the following steps:

1a. Click to select a single swatch;
  b. Shift-click to select multiple consecutive swatches; or
  c. Command/Control-click to select multiple nonconsecutive swatches.

2. Release the mouse button.

3. Click one of the selected swatches away from the swatch name.

4. While holding down the mouse button, drag the selected swatches until a heavy line appears immediately below the color group name.

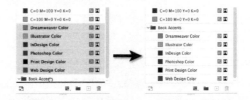

If an existing group, or a swatch inside an existing group, is selected when you create a new swatch, the new swatch is automatically added to the selected group.

Create the Poster Background

The background of this poster is going to be a solid fill of the rich black swatch you defined in the previous exercise. However, an object filling the entire page can cause certain problems. For example, if you try to create a text frame inside the area, you end up converting the frame to a text frame. In this exercise, you use the Layers panel to prevent problems that could be caused by the background shape.

1. **With poster.indd open, choose the Rectangle tool in the Tools panel.**

2. **In the Swatches panel, make sure the Fill swatch is on top and click the C=0 M=40 Y=0 K=100 swatch.**

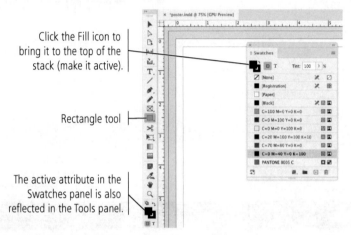

Click the Fill icon to bring it to the top of the stack (make it active).

Rectangle tool

The active attribute in the Swatches panel is also reflected in the Tools panel.

3. **Click the Stroke icon at the top of the panel to activate that attribute, then click the None swatch.**

By changing the fill and stroke attributes when no object is selected, you define those attributes for the next object you create.

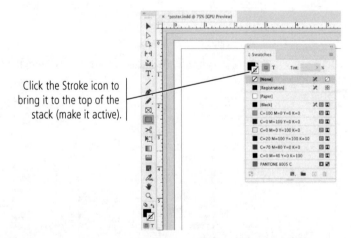

Click the Stroke icon to bring it to the top of the stack (make it active).

4. **Using the Rectangle tool, create a rectangle covering the entire page and extends to the defined bleed guides.**

You can single-click to define the rectangle size, and then drag it into position with the Selection tool. Alternatively, you can simply click and drag with the Rectangle tool, using the Bleed guides to snap the edges of the shape.

5. **In the Layers panel (Window>Layers), click the arrow to expand Layer 1.**

6. **Click the empty space to the right of the eye icon for the <rectangle> item.**

   The second column in the Layers panel can be used to lock individual items or entire layers. (If you lock a whole layer, all items on that layer are automatically locked.) You can click an existing lock icon in the Layers panel to unlock an object or layer.

Note:

You can also click a lock icon on the page to unlock a specific object.

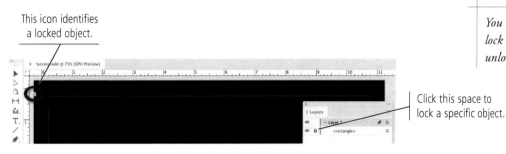

This icon identifies a locked object.

Click this space to lock a specific object.

7. **With the Rectangle tool still selected, change the stroke color to the custom blue swatch. Using the Control panel, change the stroke weight to 6 pt.**

   When you locked the rectangle in Step 6, it was automatically deselected. This means changing the stroke and fill attributes does not affect the rectangle.

Note:

You cannot use the Properties panel to define settings for the next object you create; in this case you must use the Control panel.

8. **Click and drag to draw a rectangle anywhere on the page.**

9. **Using the Control panel, choose the top-left reference point and then change the frame's dimensions to**

X: -0.25 in	W: 11.5 in
Y: 1 in	H: 6.5 in

   These dimensions create a frame extending the entire width of the layout (including bleeds), with 1″ of space above and below the frame.

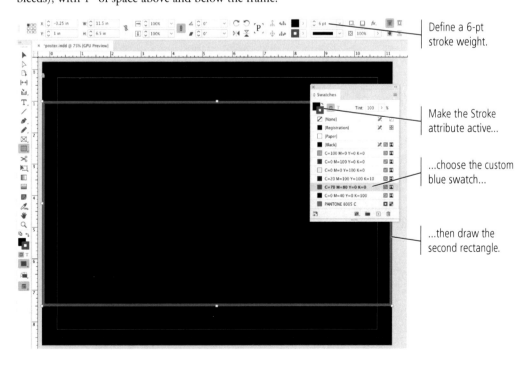

Define a 6-pt stroke weight.

Make the Stroke attribute active...

...choose the custom blue swatch...

...then draw the second rectangle.

10. In the Layers panel, click the Eye icon to the left of the locked <rectangle>.

The visible rectangle has the same fill color as the background shape (which is now hidden). To make it easier to see and work with only specific objects, you can use the Layers panel to toggle the visibility of individual objects or entire layers.

Note:

If you hide an entire layer, all objects on that layer are hidden.

Click an Eye icon to hide a specific object or layer.

11. Save the file and continue to the next exercise.

 Define and Apply a Gradient

A **gradient**, also called a **blend**, can be used to create a smooth transition from one color to another. You can apply a gradient to any object using the Gradient panel (Window>Color>Gradient), or you can save a gradient swatch if you plan to use it again. The Gradient panel controls the type and position of applied gradients.

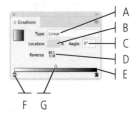

A **Type.** Choose either linear or radial gradient.

B **Location.** This field defines the position (from 0 on the left to 100 on the right) of the selected stop along the gradient ramp.

C. **Angle.** This field defines the angle of the gradient around a circle:

- 0° is horizontal, left to right
- 90° is vertical, bottom to top
- 180° is horizontal, right to left
- −90° (270°) is vertical, top to bottom

D. **Reverse.** This button changes the colors in the gradient left to right, as if flipping it horizontally.

E. **Gradient Ramp.** This shows a sample of the defined gradient. You can click below the ramp to add a new stop.

F. **Gradient Stops.** These show positions where specific colors are defined along the gradient. You can click and drag stops to new positions along the ramp or drag them off the ramp to remove stops from the gradient.

G. **Center Point.** The center point between two stops is the point where the two adjacent stops blend equally. You can drag the center points to change the percentage of the gradient occupied by a specific color.

Note:

You can drag a swatch from the Swatches panel to the gradient ramp in the Gradient panel to add a new color stop or to change the color of an existing stop.

1. With **poster.indd** open, choose the Selection tool. Click outside the area of the visible rectangle to deselect it.

2. Choose New Gradient Swatch from the Swatches panel Options menu.

3. Click the gradient stop on the left end of the gradient ramp to select it.

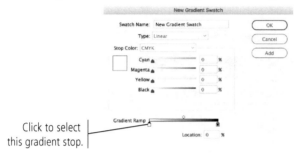

Click to select this gradient stop.

4. Make sure Linear is selected in the Type menu, and then choose Swatches in the Stop Color menu.

   You can define gradients using LAB values, CMYK percentages, RGB values, or existing color swatches.

5. With the first stop selected, click the blue CMYK swatch.

6. Select the second gradient stop (on the right end of the ramp), and then click the custom red swatch.

7. **Type Blue to Red in the Swatch Name field and then click OK.**

The new gradient swatch
is selected by default.

8. **Using the Selection tool, click the visible rectangle on the page to select it.**

9. **Make the Fill icon active in the Swatches panel, and then click the Blue to Red gradient swatch.**

   It is important to remember but easy to forget: make sure the correct attribute (fill or stroke) is active when you change a color.

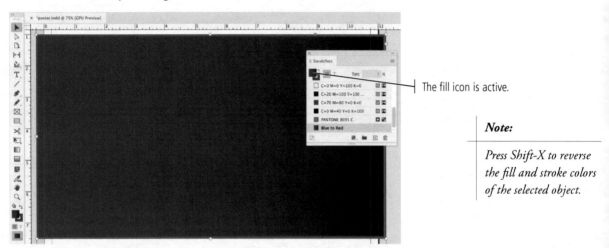

The fill icon is active.

Note:

Press Shift-X to reverse the fill and stroke colors of the selected object.

10. **Make the Stroke icon active in the Swatches panel, and then click the Blue to Red gradient swatch.**

Note:

Remember, all panels can be accessed in the Window menu.

11. **Using the Gradient panel (Window>Color>Gradient), change the Angle field to 180° so the stroke goes from red on the left to blue on the right (the reverse of the fill).**

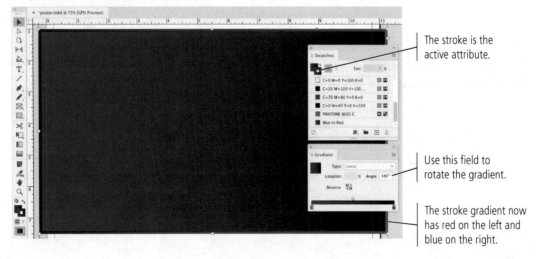

The stroke is the
active attribute.

Use this field to
rotate the gradient.

The stroke gradient now
has red on the left and
blue on the right.

12. **Click away from the rectangle to deselect it.**

13. Use the Screen Mode button at the bottom of the Tools panel to display the layout in Preview mode.

This option hides all guides and frame edges, which makes it easier to see the subtle effect created by the opposing gradients.

Screen Mode button

14. Restore the document view to the Normal mode in the Screen Mode menu.

15. Save the file and continue to the next exercise.

Using the Gradient Tools

Clicking a gradient swatch adds a gradient to the selected object, beginning at the left edge and ending at the right edge for linear gradients, or beginning at the object's center and ending at the object's outermost edge for radial gradients. When you drag with the **Gradient tool**, you define the length of the gradient without regard to the object you're filling.

This frame is filled with the Green to Blue gradient.

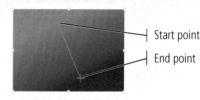

The Gradient tool defines a new angle, start point, and end point for the gradient.

Start point

End point

The **Gradient Feather tool** has a similar function but produces different results. Rather than creating a specific-colored gradient, the Gradient Feather tool applies a transparency gradient, blending the object from solid to transparent.

The image frame is placed over a cyan-filled frame.

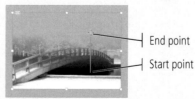

The Gradient Feather tool defines transparency, from 0 at the start point to 100 at the end point.

End point

Start point

Create an Irregular Graphics Frame

You can create basic graphics frames using the Rectangle, Ellipse, and Polygon Frame tools. You can also create a Bézier shape with the Pen tool, and then convert the shape to a graphics frame, which means you can create a frame in virtually any shape. However, it requires a lot of work to trace complex graphics with the Pen tool; fortunately, you can use other options to create complex frames from placed graphics.

1. **In the open `poster.indd` file, select the gradient-filled rectangle in the layout.**

2. **Choose File>Place. Navigate to `guitar-outline.ai` in the WIP>Concert folder. Check Show Import Options and Replace Selected Item, then click Open.**

    Macintosh users: Remember, you might have to click the Options button to reveal the three options checkboxes. We will not continue to repeat this instruction.

This frame should be selected.

Make sure both options are checked.

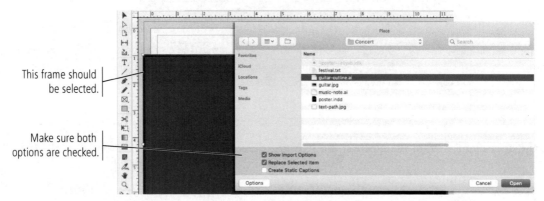

3. **In the resulting dialog box, choose Art in the Crop To menu, then click OK.**

    If Replace Selected Item was not checked in the Place dialog box, the image would be loaded into the cursor.

    Because the existing rectangle was selected and the Replace Selected Item option was checked, the new image automatically appears in the selected frame. If another image had already been placed in the frame, the guitar graphic would replace the existing image (hence the name of the command).

Note:

Refer back to Project 1: Letterhead Design for an explanation of the Crop To options.

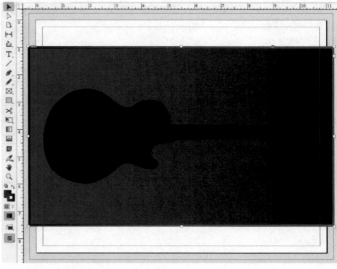

4. Choose Edit>Undo Replace.

If you accidentally replace a selected item, undoing the placement loads the last-placed image into the cursor.

This is an easy fix if you accidentally replace an image. Simply choose Edit>Undo Replace, and then click to place the loaded image in the correct location.

Note:

The Undo command undoes the single last action. In this case, placing the image into the frame — even though it happened automatically — was the last single action.

5. Click in the white area near the top-left corner to place the loaded image.

Do not click inside the gradient-filled rectangle; if you do, the loaded image will be placed back into that frame instead of in a new frame.

6. Using the Properties panel, select the top-left reference point and then change the new image frame's position to X: 0.25 in, Y: 4.75 in.

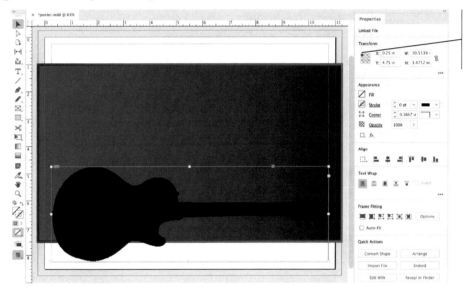

Use the top-left reference point to position the graphics frame.

7. With the same frame selected, choose Object>Clipping Path>Options.

A **clipping path** is a hard-edged outline that masks an image. Areas inside the path are visible; areas outside the path are hidden.

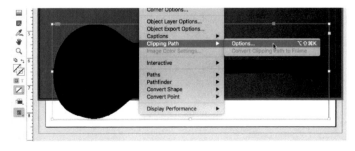

8. **In the resulting dialog box, check the Preview option and then choose Detect Edges in the Type menu.**

   InDesign can access Alpha channels and clipping paths saved in an image, or you can create a clipping path based on the image content. Because this graphic is a vector graphic with well-defined edges filled with a solid color, InDesign can create a very precise clipping path based on the information in the file.

Note:

The Include Inside Edges option generates a compound clipping path that removes holes in the middle of the outside path.

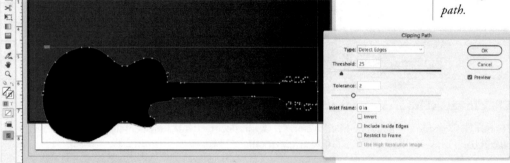

9. **Click OK to close the dialog box and create the clipping path.**

10. **Choose Object>Clipping Path>Convert Clipping Path to Frame.**

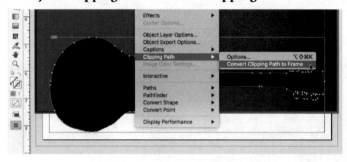

Understanding Clipping Path Options

Threshold specifies the darkest pixel value that will define the resulting clipping path. In this exercise, the placed image is filled with solid black, so you can set a very high Threshold value to define the clipping path. In images with greater tone variation (such as a photograph), increasing the Threshold value removes lighter areas from the clipped area.

Tolerance specifies how similar a pixel must be to the Threshold value before it is hidden by the clipping path. Increasing the Tolerance value results in fewer points along the clipping path, generating a smoother path. Lowering the Tolerance value results in more anchor points and a potentially rougher path.

Inset Frame shrinks the clipping path by a specific number of pixels. You can also enter a negative value to enlarge the clipping path.

Invert reverses the clipping path, making hidden areas visible and vice versa.

Include Inside Edges creates a compound clipping path, removing inner areas of the object if they are within the Threshold and Tolerance ranges.

Restrict to Frame creates a clipping path that stops at the visible edge of the graphic. You can include the entire object, including areas beyond the frame edges, by unchecking this option.

Use High Resolution Image generates the clipping path based on the actual file data instead of the preview image.

11. **Using the Direct Selection tool, select the image inside the irregular frame.**

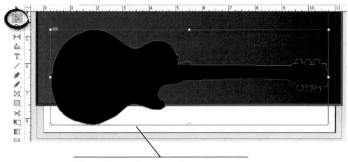

The red bounding box indicates that you have selected the image inside the frame.

12. **With the frame content selected, press Delete/Backspace to delete the placed file but leave the frame you created.**

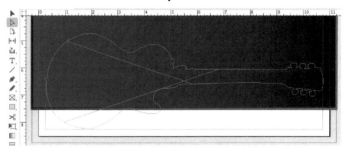

Note:

If you don't see the frame edges, make sure you reset the screen mode to Normal instead of Preview (which you used in the last exercise).

13. **Using the Selection tool, click the irregular graphics frame to select it.**

14. **Choose File>Place and navigate to guitar.jpg in the WIP>Concert folder. Uncheck all options at the bottom of the dialog box and click Open.**

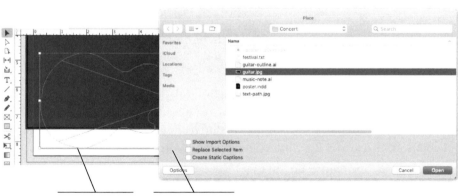

This frame should be selected.   This option should not be checked.

Although the existing frame was selected when you opened the Place dialog box, the new image is loaded into the cursor because you unchecked the Replace Selected Item option.

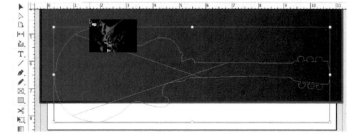

15. Click inside the empty frame with the loaded cursor to place the image inside the frame.

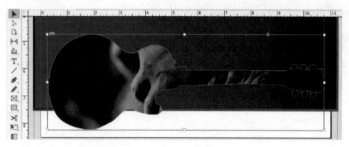

16. Save the file and continue to the next exercise.

 Create Visual Impact with Transparency

The image effects and transparency controls in InDesign provide options for adding dimension and depth directly in the page layout. You can change the transparency of any object (or individual object attributes), apply different blending modes, and apply creative effects such as drop shadows and beveling.

Transparency and effects are controlled in the Effects panel. You can change these options for an entire object (fill and stroke), only the stroke, only the fill, the text (if you're working with a text frame), the graphic (if you're working with a graphics frame), or all objects in a group. The selected item in the panel list is referred to as the **target**.

A   Blending Mode
B   Opacity
C   Clear all effects and make object opaque
D   Add an object effect to the selected target
E   Remove effects from the selected target

Technical Issues of Transparency

Before you use these features and effects, you should understand what transparency is and how it affects your output. **Transparency** is the degree to which light passes through an object so that objects in the background are visible. In terms of page layout, transparency means being able to "see through" objects in the front of the stacking order to objects lower in the stacking order.

Because of the way printing works, applying transparency in print design is a bit of a contradiction. Commercial printing is, by definition, accomplished by overlapping a mixture of (usually) four semitransparent inks in different percentages to reproduce a range of colors. In that sense, all print design requires transparency.

But *design* transparency refers to the objects on the page. The trouble is, when a halftone dot is printed, it's either there or it's not. There is no "50% opaque" setting on a printing press. This means a transformation needs to take place behind the scenes, translating what we create on screen into what a printing press produces.

When transparent objects are output, overlapping areas of transparent elements are actually broken into individual elements where necessary to produce the best possible results. Ink values in the overlap areas are calculated by the application and based on the capabilities of the mechanical printing process; the software converts what we create on screen into the elements necessary to print.

When you get to the final stage of this project, you'll learn how to preview and control the output process for transparent objects.

Note:

The Graphic option is only available when a placed graphic within a frame is selected. Group replaces Object in the list only when a group is selected.

Note:

Effects applied to text apply to all text in the frame; you can't apply effects to individual characters.

Note:

Transparency is essentially the inverse of opacity. If an object is 20% transparent, it is also 80% opaque.

1. In the open **poster.indd** file, use the Selection tool to select the gradient-filled rectangle.

2. Choose Object>Content>Graphic.

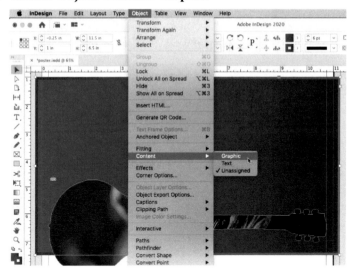

Note:

You can also Control/ right-click an object and change its content type in the contextual menu.

When you create a frame with one of the basic shape tools, it is considered "unassigned" because it is neither a text frame nor a graphics frame. You can convert any type of frame (graphics, text, or unassigned) to another type using this menu.

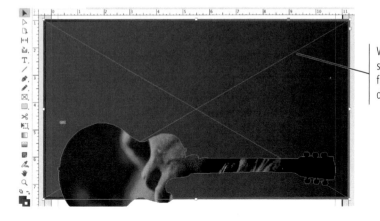

When frame edges are showing, an empty graphics frame shows crossed diagonal lines.

3. With the gradient-filled rectangle still selected on the page, choose File>Place. Navigate to the WIP>Concert folder and choose **guitar.jpg**. At the bottom of the dialog box, check the Replace Selected Item option.

This option should be checked.

4. **Click Open to place the selected file.**

   Because Replace Selected Item was active in the dialog box, the image is placed directly into the selected frame.

5. **Using the Selection tool, click the guitar-shaped graphics frame to select it.**

6. **Move the Selection tool cursor over the image frame to reveal the Content Grabber.**

The Selection tool is active.

The frame is selected.

Content Grabber

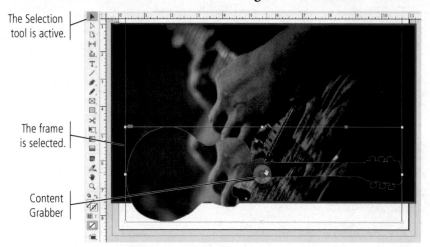

Note:

You can turn off the Content Grabber by choosing View>Extras> Hide Content Grabber.

7. **Click the Content Grabber to access the image in the frame.**

   Remember, when you select an image within a frame using either the Content Grabber or the Direct Selection tool, the Control panel fields define the position of the graphic *relative to* its containing frame. Negative numbers move the graphic up and to the left from the frame edge; positive numbers move the graphic down and to the right.

8. **Using the Properties panel, change the image's position inside the frame to X: -0.75 in, Y: -4.5 in (based on the top-left reference point).**

   This position aligns the image in the guitar-shaped frame with the image in the rectangle frame, giving the impression of a single image in both frames. In the next few steps, you will use transparency effects to differentiate the two versions of the image.

The Selection tool is still active.

The image in this frame is now aligned with the image in the other frame.

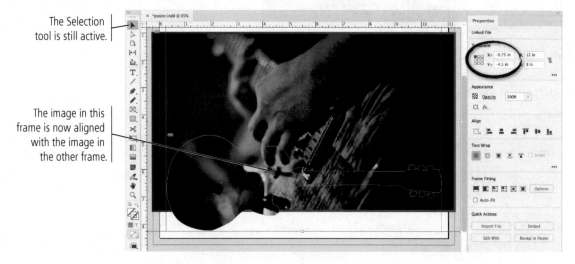

9. **Press ESC to restore the frame (not the frame content) as the active selection.**

10. **In the Properties panel, click the *fx* button and choose Drop Shadow from the menu.**

When a frame is selected, you can use this menu to apply effects to the entire object. The Effects dialog box opens to show options for the effect you selected in the menu.

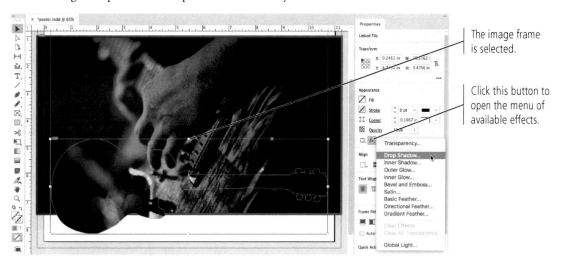

The image frame is selected.

Click this button to open the menu of available effects.

11. **In the resulting dialog box, check the Preview option so you can preview your results before accepting/applying them.**

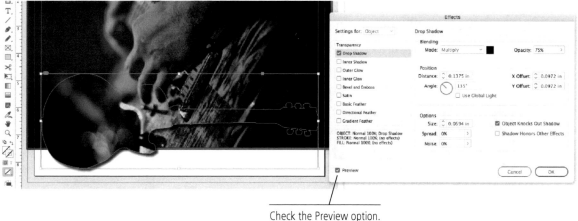

Check the Preview option.

12. **With the Drop Shadow options showing in the dialog box, click the color swatch in the Blending section to open the Effect Color dialog box.**

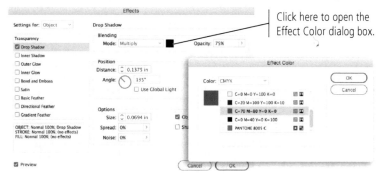

Click here to open the Effect Color dialog box.

13. **Select the custom blue swatch in the list, then click OK.**

   If the Preview option is checked in the Effects dialog box, you should see the result of changing the drop shadow color.

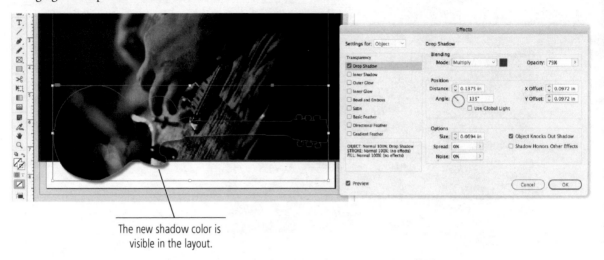

The new shadow color is visible in the layout.

14. **Click OK to apply your changes and return to the layout.**

15. **Using the Direct Selection tool, click to select the image inside the rectangular graphics frame.**

16. **Open the Effects panel (Window>Effects).**

   When the content inside a graphics frame is selected, you can apply effects to the image itself, independent of the frame.

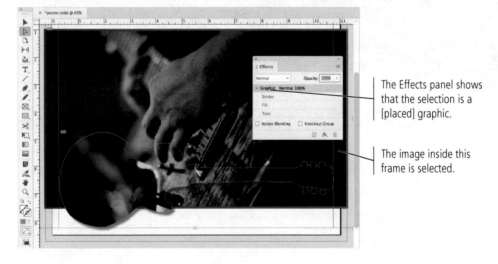

The Effects panel shows that the selection is a [placed] graphic.

The image inside this frame is selected.

17. **With the Graphic option selected in the Effects panel, choose the Multiply option in the Blending Mode menu.**

    The image now blends into the gradient background.

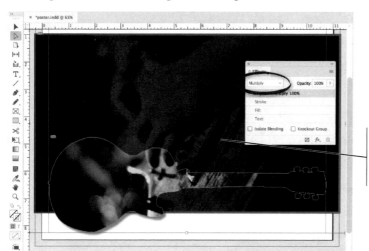

Note:

Effects in InDesign are non-destructive, which means they have no effect on the physical file data.

The Multiply blending mode merges the image colors into the object's gradient fill.

Understanding Blending Modes   FOUNDATIONS

Blending modes control how colors in an object interact with underlying colors.

- **Multiply** multiplies the base color by the blend (top) color, resulting in a darker color. Multiplying with black produces black; multiplying with white has no effect.

- **Screen** is basically the inverse of Multiply, always returning a lighter color. Screening with black has no effect; screening with white produces white.

- **Overlay** multiplies or screens the blend color to preserve the original lightness or darkness of the base.

- **Soft Light** darkens or lightens base colors depending on the blend color. Blend colors lighter than 50% lighten the base; blend colors darker than 50% darken the base.

- **Hard Light** combines the Multiply and Screen modes. Blend colors darker than 50% are multiplied, and blend colors lighter than 50% are screened.

- **Color Dodge** brightens the base color. Blend colors lighter than 50% significantly increase brightness; blending with black has no effect.

- **Color Burn** darkens the base color by increasing the contrast. Blend colors darker than 50% significantly darken the base color by increasing saturation and reducing brightness; blending with white has no effect.

- **Darken** returns the darker of the blend or base color. Base pixels lighter than the blend color are replaced; base pixels darker than the blend color do not change.

- **Lighten** returns whichever is the lighter color. Base pixels darker than the blend color are replaced; base pixels lighter than the blend color do not change.

- **Difference*** inverts base color values according to the brightness value in the blend layer. Lower brightness values in the blend layer have less of an effect on the result; blending with black has no effect.

- **Exclusion*** is similar to Difference, except that midtone values in the base color are completely desaturated.

- **Hue*** results in a color with the luminance and saturation of the base color and the hue of the blend color.

- **Saturation*** results in a color with the luminance and hue of the base and the saturation of the blend color.

- **Color*** results in a color with the luminance of the base color and the hue and saturation of the blend color.

- **Luminosity*** results in a color with the hue and saturation of the base color and the luminance of the blend color (basically the opposite of the Color mode).

*Avoid applying the Difference, Exclusion, Hue, Saturation, Color, and Luminosity modes to objects with spot colors. It could create unpredictable results when the file is separated for commercial print requirements.

18. **Click the *fx* button at the bottom of the Effects panel, and choose Gradient Feather.**

    The Gradient Feather effect creates a transparency gradient so an object blends into underlying objects instead of leaving a hard edge. The effect is created using a gradient that shifts from 100% opacity to 0% opacity. The levels of opacity in the gradient determine the opacity of the object to which the feather effect is applied.

Note:

The Gradient Feather effect is automatically applied if you use the Gradient Feather tool.

19. **In the Effects dialog box, click the button to the right of the gradient ramp sample to reverse the gradient.**

20. **Click in the Angle circle and drag until the field shows 90°. The line should point straight up.**

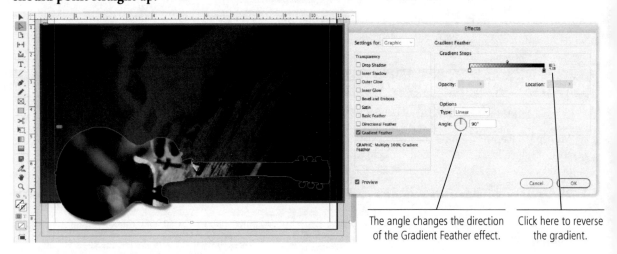

The angle changes the direction of the Gradient Feather effect.

Click here to reverse the gradient.

21. **Drag the right gradient stop until the Location field shows approximately 85%.**

    Extending the solid black part of the gradient extends the entirely visible part of the image.

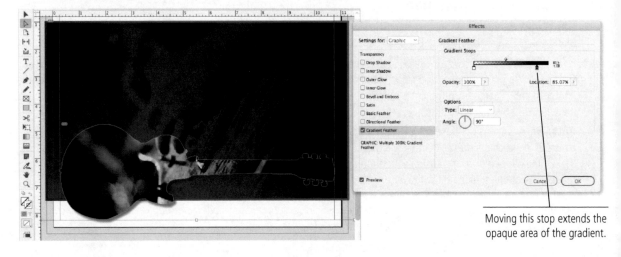

Moving this stop extends the opaque area of the gradient.

Nine different InDesign effects can be applied by clicking the *fx* button at the bottom of the Effects panel, by clicking the *fx* button in the Control panel, or by choosing from the Object>Effects menu.

Drop Shadow and Inner Shadow

Drop Shadow adds a shadow behind the object. **Inner Shadow** adds a shadow inside the edges of the object. For both types, you can define the blending mode, color, opacity, angle, distance, offset, and size of the shadow.

- **Distance** is how far away the shadow will be from the original object. The **Offset** fields allow you to define different horizontal and vertical distances.
- **Size** is the blur amount applied to the shadow.
- **Spread** (for Drop Shadows) is the percentage that the shadow expands beyond the original object.
- **Choke** (for Inner Shadows) is the percentage that the shadow shrinks into the original object.
- **Noise** controls the amount of pixels added to the effect.

When the **Object Knocks Out Shadow** option is checked, areas of the shadow under the object are knocked out or removed. This option is particularly important if the original object is semitransparent above its shadow.

Use Global Light is available for the Drop Shadow, Inner Shadow, and Bevel and Emboss effects. When this option is checked, the style is linked to the "master" light source angle for the entire file. Changing the global light setting affects any linked effect applied to any object in the entire file. (You can also change the Global Light settings by choosing Object>Effects>Global Light.)

Outer Glow and Inner Glow

Outer Glow and **Inner Glow** add glow effects to the outside and inside edges, respectively, of the original object. For either kind of glow, you can define the blending mode, opacity, noise, and size values.

- You can define the **Technique** as **Precise**, which creates a glow at a specific distance, or **Softer**, which creates a blurred glow and does not preserve detail as well.
- For Inner Glows, you can define the **Source** of the glow: **Center** applies a glow from the object center, and **Edge** applies the glow starting from the object's inside edges.
- The **Spread** and **Choke** sliders affect the percentages of the glow effects.

Satin

Satin applies interior shading to create a satiny appearance. You can change the blending mode, color, and opacity of the effect, as well as the angle, distance, and size.

Bevel and Emboss

This effect has four variations or styles:

- **Inner Bevel** creates a bevel on an object's inside edges.
- **Outer Bevel** creates a bevel on an object's outside edges.
- **Emboss** creates the effect of embossing the object against the underlying layers.
- **Pillow Emboss** creates the effect of stamping the edges of the object into the underlying layers.

Any of these styles can be applied as **Smooth** (blurs the edges of the effect), **Chisel Hard** (creates a distinct edge to the effect), or **Chisel Soft** (creates a distinct, slightly blurred edge to the effect).

You can change the **Direction** of the bevel effect. **Up** creates the appearance of the layer coming out of the image; **Down** creates the appearance of something stamped into the image. The **Size** field makes the effect smaller or larger, and the **Soften** option blurs the edges of the effect. **Depth** increases or decreases the three-dimensional effect of the bevel.

In the **Shading** area, you can control the light source's **Angle** and **Altitude** (think of how shadows differ as the sun moves across the sky). Finally, you can change the blending mode, opacity, and color of both highlights and shadows created with the Bevel and Emboss effect.

Basic Feather, Directional Feather, Gradient Feather

Basic Feather equally fades all edges of the selection by a specific width. The **Choke** option determines how much of the softened edge is opaque (higher settings increase opacity). **Corners** can be **Sharp** (following the outer edge of the shape), **Rounded** (according to the Feather Width), or **Diffused** (fading from opaque to transparent). **Noise** adds random pixels to the softened area.

Directional Feather applies different feather widths to individual edges of an object. The **Shape** option defines the object's original shape (First Edge Only, Leading Edges, or All Edges). The **Angle** field allows you to rotate the effect.

Gradient Feather creates a transparency gradient that blends from solid to transparent. This effect underlies the Gradient Feather tool. You can move the start and end stops to different locations along the ramp or add stops to define specific transparencies at specific locations. You can also choose from a Linear or Radial Gradient Feather effect and change the angle of a Linear Gradient Feather effect.

22. Click OK to close the Effects dialog box and apply your choices.

The *fx* icon to the right of the "Graphic" listing indicates effects have been applied to the selected graphic. You can double-click the *fx* icon in the Effects panel to open the Effects dialog box, where you can change the settings of the applied effects.

This icon indicates that effects have been applied to the selected graphic.

23. Click away from the active image to deselect it and its containing frame.

24. Save the file and continue to the next exercise.

Create a QR Code

A **QR code**, short for Quick Response code, is a type of bar code that provides easy access (using a special QR code reader app) to additional information programmed into the code. InDesign includes a built-in option for creating QR codes in a layout, which makes it simple to incorporate this kind of marketing tool.

1. With poster.indd open, create a new rectangle frame in the bottom-left corner of the layout. Define the frame parameters (based on the object's top-left reference point) as

X: 0.25 in	W: 0.8 in
Y: 7.45 in	H: 0.8 in

2. Using the Properties panel, change the frame's stroke weight to 3 pt, change its fill color to Paper, and change its stroke color to the custom blue swatch.

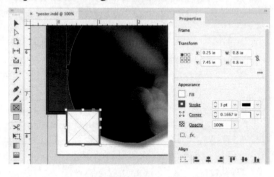

Note:

You can edit the properties of a QR code by choosing Object>Edit QR code (or by choosing Edit QR Code in the object's contextual menu.)

3. With the new frame selected, choose Object>Generate QR Code.

Note:

Keep in mind that distorting the code graphic might prevent it from working.

4. **In the resulting dialog box, choose Web Hyperlink in the Type menu and type www.westonsummerconcertseries.com in the URL field.**

You can use the Type menu to define what the QR code does:

- **Web Hyperlink.** If you choose this option, you can define the specific URL that appears when a user scans the code.

- **Plain Text.** If you choose this option, you can define a plain-text message that appears when a user scans the code.

- **Text Message.** If you choose this option, you can define the phone number and message content sent.

- **Email.** If you choose this option, you can define the email address, subject, and email body included in the resulting email.

- **Business Card.** If you choose this option, you can define the specific fields common in digital contact applications (name, company, address, etc.).

5. **Click the Color tab at the top of the dialog box. Choose C=0 M=40 Y=0 K=100, then click OK.**

The color you define here determines the color of the QR code object. Keep in mind high contrast between the QR code object and the frame background color assures the code will work on all devices and apps.

InDesign automatically generates the QR code inside the frame. The resulting graphic is centered in the frame and scaled to leave a 10-pixel inset from the nearest frame edges. The QR code is actually created as an embedded EPS graphic (although it does not appear in the file's Links panel). If you select the graphic inside the frame, you can scale it as you would any other placed graphic.

6. **Save the file and continue to the next stage of the project.**

STAGE 2 / Importing and Formatting Text

Placing text is one of the most critical functions of page-layout software, whether you create the text directly within InDesign or import it from an external file. InDesign provides all the tools you need to format text, from choosing a font to automatically creating hanging punctuation.

Define Multiple Layers

You are going to create a second layer to hold the text frames for this poster. This allows you to work without distraction from the existing graphics as well as protect the graphics from being accidentally altered while you are working on the text.

1. **With poster.indd open, open the Layers panel.**

2. **Expand Layer 1 in the panel if necessary, then click the empty space to the left of the bottom <rectangle> to show that object.**

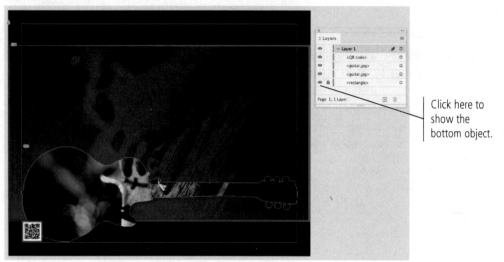

Click here to show the bottom object.

3. **Double-click the Layer 1 name in the panel.**

   The default in every file is named "Layer 1," which is not terribly useful when you use multiple layers. Descriptive names are far better for any asset, including layers.

4. **Change the Name field to Graphics and review the other options.**

   - The **Color** menu determines the color of frame edges and bounding box handles for objects on that layer.

   - If **Show Layer** is checked, the layer contents are visible in the document. You can also change visibility by toggling the eye icon in the Layers panel.

   - If **Lock Layer** is checked, you can't select or change objects on that layer.

   - If **Print Layer** is checked, the layer will output when you print or export to PDF.

   - The **Show Guides** option allows you to create and display different sets of guides for different layers; this is a more versatile option than showing or hiding all guides (which occurs with the View>Grids & Guides>Show/Hide Guides toggle).

   - The **Lock Guides** option allows you to lock and unlock guides on specific layers.

   - If **Suppress Text Wrap When Layer is Hidden** is checked, text on underlying layers reflows when the layer is hidden.

5. **Check the Lock Layer option, then click OK to close the Layer Options dialog box.**

The layer and all objects on it are now locked.

Create New Layer

Delete Selected Layers

Note:

The Layers panel only shows objects on the active page or spread.

6. **In the Layers panel, click the arrow to the left of the Graphics layer to collapse it.**

7. **Click the eye icon for the Graphics layer to hide that layer.**

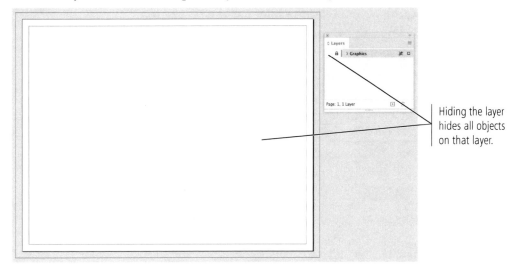

Hiding the layer hides all objects on that layer.

8. **Click the Create New Layer button at the bottom of the Layers panel.**

9. **Double-click Layer 2 in the Layers panel. Change the layer name to Text.**

10. **Click OK to create the new layer.**

The new layer is active, which means objects you create from this point will appear on that layer unless you intentionally create or select another layer in the layout file. Objects on the new layer will have red bounding box handles, matching the layer color as defined in the Layer Options dialog box.

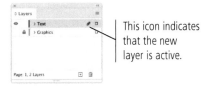

This icon indicates that the new layer is active.

11. **Save the file and continue to the next exercise.**

Control Text Threading

Some layouts require only a few bits of text, while others include numerous pages. Depending on how much text you have to work with, you might place all the layout text in a single frame, or you might cut and paste different pieces of a single story into separate text frames. In other cases, you might thread text across multiple frames, maintaining the text as a single story but allowing flexibility in frame size and position.

1. With **poster.indd** open, zoom into the empty area at the top of the page.

2. **Use the Type tool to create a text frame filling the horizontal space between the margin guides.**

3. **With the text frame active, choose the Selection tool. Use the Properties panel to change the selected frame's parameters (based on the top-left reference point) to**

X: 0.25 in	**W: 10.5 in**
Y: 0.25 in	**H: 0.625 in**

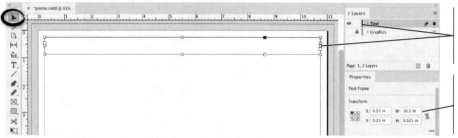

The frame's handles and edges match the color of the layer where it resides.

With Selection tool active, use the Properties panel to change the position and dimensions of a text frame.

4. **Create two more text frames using the following parameters:**

Frame 2	**X: 5.75 in**	**W: 5 in**
	Y: 1.5 in	**H: 4.25 in**
Frame 3	**X: 4.5 in**	**W: 6.25 in**
	Y: 7.9 in	**H: 0.35 in**

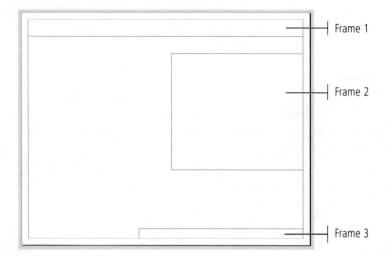

Frame 1

Frame 2

Frame 3

5. **Choose the Type tool, and click inside the first text frame to place the insertion point.**

   When you click in a text frame with the Type tool, you see a flashing insertion point where you click or, if there is no text in the frame, in the top-left corner. This insertion point marks the location where text will appear when you type, paste, or import it.

6. **Choose File>Place. Navigate to the file named festival.txt in the WIP>Concert folder.**

7. **Make sure the Replace Selected Item option is checked and then click Open.**

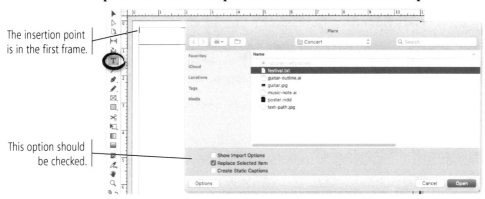

The insertion point is in the first frame.

This option should be checked.

When Replace Selected Item is checked, the text file is automatically imported at the location of the insertion point. If this option is not checked, the text is imported into the cursor.

8. **Choose the Selection tool in the Tools panel.**

   When a text frame is selected, you can see the In and Out ports that allow you to link one text frame to another. In this case, the Out port shows the **overset text icon**, indicating the placed file has more text than can fit within the frame.

   It might help to zoom in to better see the In and Out ports. The overset text icon is visible even when the In and Out ports are not.

   In port   Out port

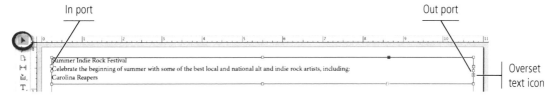

   Summer Indie Rock Festival
   Celebrate the beginning of summer with some of the best local and national alt and indie rock artists, including:
   Carolina Reapers

   Overset text icon

9. **Click the Out port of the first text frame.**

   Clicking the Out port loads the cursor with the rest of the text in the story. When the loaded cursor is over an existing frame, you can click to place the next part of the story in that frame. When the cursor is not over a frame, you can click and drag to create a frame containing the next part of the story. You can do this with the Selection tool (as you just did) or the Direct Selection tool.

This arrow in the out port indicates that the frame is linked to another frame.

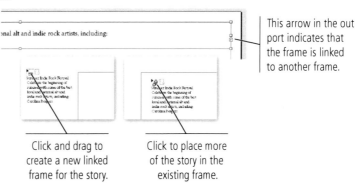

Click and drag to create a new linked frame for the story.

Click to place more of the story in the existing frame.

10. Click inside the second frame to link it to the first frame.

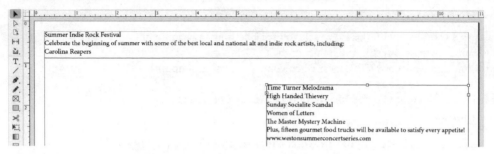

11. Repeat this process to link from the second frame to the third.

You can define the thread of text frames even when there is no text to fill those frames. Simply use the Selection or Direct Selection tool to click the Out port of one frame, and then click anywhere within the next frame to add to the thread.

You can also press Command/Control while the Type tool is active to click a text frame Out port and thread the frames.

12. Choose View>Extras>Show Text Threads.

When this option is toggled on (and you are in Normal viewing mode), you can see all threading arrows whenever any text frame in the thread is selected.

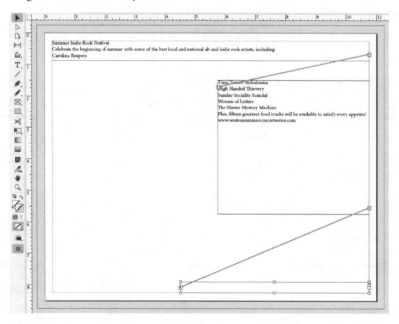

13. Choose View>Extras>Hide Text Threads.

14. Save the file and continue to the next exercise.

Note:

When you load the cursor with overset text, the loaded cursor shows the text from the beginning of the story even though the beginning is already placed. This is a quirk of the software; when you click with the loaded cursor, the text will flow into the new frame at the proper place in the story.

Note:

*Text that appears as a series of gray bars is called **greeked text**. By default, text smaller than 7 pt (at 100%) is greeked to improve screen redraw time. You can change the greeking threshold in the Display Performance pane of the Preferences dialog box.*

View percentage is part of the determination for greeking text; in other words, if your view percentage is 50%, 12-pt text appears as 6-pt text on screen, so it would be greeked using the default preferences.

Define Manual Frame Breaks

When you thread text from one column or frame to another, you often need to control exactly where a story breaks from frame to frame. InDesign includes a number of commands for breaking text in precise locations.

1. **In the open poster.indd file, use the Type tool to click at the end of the first line (after the word "Festival") to place the insertion point.**

    As you complete the following exercises, feel free to zoom in as necessary to work with specific areas of your layout.

2. **Choose Type>Insert Break Character>Frame Break.**

    InDesign provides several special break characters that allow you to control the flow of text from line to line, from column to column, and from frame to frame. The Frame Break character forces all following text into the next frame in the thread.

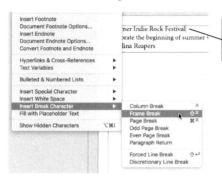

The insertion point is at the end of the first paragraph.

3. **Choose Type>Show Hidden Characters.**

    Each paragraph is separated by a paragraph return character (¶). A paragraph can be one or two words or multiple lines. The important thing is to realize a paragraph is technically any copy between two paragraph returns (or other break characters).

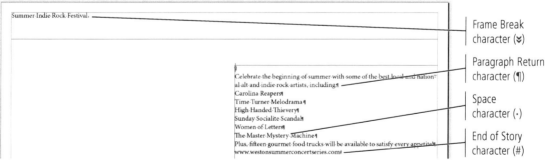

Frame Break character (⬇)

Paragraph Return character (¶)

Space character (·)

End of Story character (#)

When you placed the Frame Break character in Step 2, everything following the insertion point was pushed to the next frame, including the paragraph return character that was at the end of the first line. This created an "empty" paragraph that should be deleted.

4. **With the insertion point flashing at the beginning of the second frame, press Forward Delete to remove the extra paragraph return.**

    The Forward Delete key is the one directly below the Help key on most standard keyboards. If you don't have a Forward Delete key (if, for example, you're working on a laptop), move the insertion point to the beginning of the next line ("Celebrate the beginning...") and press Delete/Backspace.

Note:

You can also toggle the visibility of hidden characters using the View Options button in the Tools panel.

Note:

Press Enter (numeric keypad) to add a Column Break.

Press Shift-Enter (numeric keypad) to add a Frame Break.

Press Command/ Control-Enter (numeric keypad) to add a Page Break, which pushes all text to the first threaded frame on the next page.

5. **With hidden characters visible, highlight the paragraph return character at the end of the next-to-last sentence in the second frame (before the web address).**

6. **Choose Type>Insert Break Character>Frame Break to replace the highlighted paragraph return with a frame break character.**

When text is highlighted — including hidden formatting characters — anything you type, paste, or enter using a menu command replaces the highlighted text.

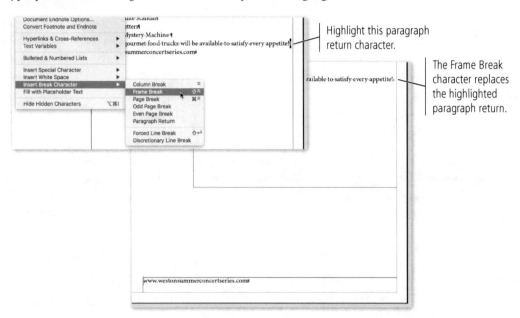

Highlight this paragraph return character.

The Frame Break character replaces the highlighted paragraph return.

7. **Save the file and continue to the next exercise.**

Designing with Placeholder Text

With the insertion point placed in a text frame, choosing Type>Fill with Placeholder Text fills the active frame with **lorem text** (supposedly from a Latin treatise on ethics written by Cicero more than 2,000 years ago) using the default text-format settings. If a text frame is linked to other text frames, the placeholder text fills the entire series of linked text frames.

Lorem placeholder text is valuable for experimenting with the appearance of paragraph text, giving you a better idea of what blocks of copy will look like when real content is placed in the layout.

If you press Command/Control while choosing Fill with Placeholder Text, you can define a different language to use for the placeholder text. These options are useful if you want to experiment with a design for a layout in which the text does not use the Roman alphabet — again, the placeholder more accurately represents what the final copy will look like.

Three threaded text frames are filled with Roman placeholder text.

Three threaded text frames are filled with Japanese placeholder text.

Apply Character Formatting

Once text is in a frame, you can use character formatting attributes to determine the appearance of individual letters, such as the font and type size. These attributes can be controlled in the Character panel (Window>Type & Tables>Character), Control panel, or Properties panel. In the Properties panel, you have to click the More Options button to access some of these options.

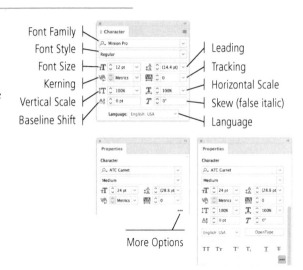

More Options

- A **font** contains all characters (**glyphs**) that make up a typeface, including uppercase and lowercase letters, numbers, special characters, etc. The **font style** is a specific variation of the selected font, such as bold or condensed.

- **Size** is the height of a typeface measured in points.

- **Leading** is the distance from one baseline to the next. By default, InDesign automatically applies leading as 120% of the type size.

  InDesign treats leading as a character attribute, even though leading controls the space between lines of an individual paragraph. (Space between paragraphs is controlled using the Space Before/After options in the Paragraph panel.) This approach means you can change the leading for a single line of a paragraph by selecting any character(s) in that line; however, changing the leading for any character in a line applies the same change to the entire line that contains those characters. You can change this behavior by checking the Apply Leading to Entire Paragraph option in the Type pane of the Preferences dialog box.

- **Vertical Scale** and **Horizontal Scale** artificially stretch or contract the selected characters. This type of scaling is a quick way of achieving condensed or expanded type if those variations of a font don't exist. Type that has been artificially scaled in this fashion tends to look bad because the scaling destroys the type's metrics; if possible, you should always use a condensed or expanded version of a typeface before resorting to horizontal or vertical scaling.

- **Kerning** increases or decreases the space between pairs of letters. Kerning is used in cases where particular letters in specific fonts need to be manually adjusted to eliminate a too-tight or too-spread-out appearance; manual kerning is usually necessary in headlines or other large type. Many commercial fonts have built-in kerning pairs, so you won't need to apply too much hands-on intervention with kerning.

- **Tracking**, also known as "range kerning," refers to the overall space between a range of characters.

- **Baseline Shift** moves the selected type above or below the baseline by a specific number of points. Positive numbers move the characters up; negative values move the text down.

- **Skew** artificially slants the selected text, creating a false italic appearance. This option distorts the look of the type and should be used sparingly (if ever).

Note:

You can use the Up and Down Arrow keys to nudge paragraph and character style values when the insertion point is in a panel field.

Note:

*Tracking and kerning are applied in thousandths of an **em**. An em is technically defined as width that equals the type size.*

In addition to the options in the basic Character panel, several styling options are also available in the panel Options menu.

- **All Caps** changes all the characters to capital letters. This option only changes the appearance of the characters; they are not permanently converted to capital letters. To change the case of selected characters to all capital letters — the same as typing with Caps Lock turned on — use the Type>Change Case menu options.

- **Small Caps** changes lowercase letters to smaller versions of the uppercase letters. If the font is an Open Type font containing true small caps, InDesign uses the true small caps.

- **Superscript** and **Subscript** artificially reduce selected character(s) to a specific percentage of the point size; these options raise (superscript) or lower (subscript) the character from the baseline to a position that is a certain percentage of the leading. (The size and position of Superscript, Subscript, and Small Caps are controlled in the Advanced Type Preferences dialog box.)

- **Underline** places a line below the selected characters.

- **Strikethrough** places a line through the middle of selected characters.

- **Ligatures** are substitutes for certain pairs of letters, most commonly fi, fl, ff, ffi, and ffl. Other pairs such as ct and st are common for historical typesetting, and ae and oe are used in some non-English-language typesetting.

Note:

Most of these character formatting options are also available in the Control panel and in the extended Character options in the Properties panel.

Note:

Choosing Underline Options or Strike-through Options in the Character panel Options menu allows you to change the weight, offset, style, and color of the line for those styles.

1. **With poster.indd open, choose the Type tool in the Tools panel. Triple-click the first line of text in the story to select it.**

   Character formatting options apply only to selected characters.

2. **In the Character panel (Window>Type & Tables>Character), highlight the existing font name and type atc o. Click ATC Onyx Bold in the resulting menu to apply the new font.**

   The characters you type in the Font Family field result in a menu with all fonts that include the letters you type. After you select the font in the menu, ATC Onyx appears in the Font Family menu, and Bold appears in the Font Style menu.

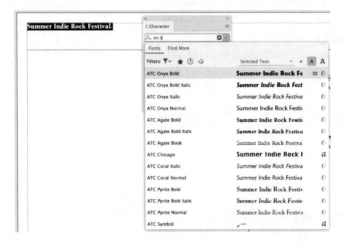

3. **Open the Font Size menu and choose 60 pt.**

You can choose one of the built-in font sizes, type a specific value in the field, or click the arrow buttons to change the font size by 1 pt.

4. **Change the value in the Horizontal Scale field to 80%.**

Horizontal and vertical scaling are useful for artificially stretching or contracting fonts that do not have a condensed or extended version. Be careful using these options, though, because artificial scaling alters the character shapes and can make some fonts very difficult to read (especially at smaller sizes).

5. **Open the Character panel Options menu and choose the All Caps option.**

6. **Click four times to select the first paragraph in the second frame, hold down the mouse button, and then drag down to select the other lines in the same frame.**

Clicking twice selects an entire *word*, clicking three times selects an entire *line*, and clicking four times selects the entire *paragraph*.

7. **Change the selected text to 20-pt ATC Onyx Normal.**

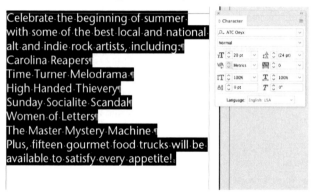

Note:

When you use mouse clicks to highlight text, dragging up or down selects additional text above or below the text you first clicked. If you quadruple-click to select an entire paragraph, for example, dragging down selects entire paragraphs after the first selected.

8. **Highlight the entire last paragraph (in the third frame), and change the text to 24-pt ATC Garnet Medium.**

9. **Save the file and continue to the next exercise.**

 Apply Paragraph Formatting

Paragraph formatting options, available in the Paragraph panel (Window>Type & Tables>Paragraph), affect an entire paragraph, or everything between two paragraph return characters. In the Properties panel, only the paragraph alignment options are available by default; clicking the More Options button shows the hidden paragraph formatting fields.

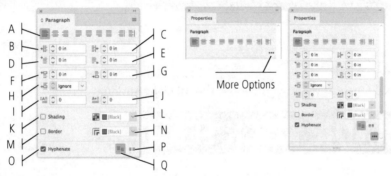

More Options

Paragraph formatting can also be controlled in the Control panel; depending on the width of your monitor, you might have to use the buttons at the left end of the panel to access the paragraph formatting options.

Click this button to show paragraph formatting options.

Click this button to show character formatting options.

A   **Paragraph Alignment** determines how the edges of a paragraph appear in relation to the containing frame. Align Left, Align Right, and Align Center are self-explanatory.

The Justify options force the lines in a paragraph to extend the entire width of the containing frame or column with no ragged edges on either side; if you justify a paragraph, you can also determine the alignment of the last line in the paragraph (left, right, center, or justified).

Align Towards Spine and Align Away from Spine change the paragraph alignment from left to right, depending on the paragraph's position in a facing-page layout.

≡ Align Left
≡ Align Center
≡ Align Right
≡ Justify with Last Line Aligned Left
≡ Justify with Last Line Aligned Center
≡ Justify with Last Line Aligned Right
≡ Justify All Lines
≡ Align Towards Spine
≡ Align Away from Spine

B   **Left Indent** defines the distance a paragraph is moved from the left edge of its containing frame or column.

C   **Right Indent** defines the distance a paragraph is moved from the right edge of its containing frame or column.

D   **First-Line Indent** defines the distance the first line of a paragraph is moved in from the left edge of the overall paragraph.

E   **Last-Line Indent** defines the distance the last line of a paragraph is moved in from the left edge of the overall paragraph.

F   **Space Before** defines space separating a paragraph from the previous one in the same story.

G   **Space After** defines space separating a paragraph from the next one in the same story.

H   **Space Between Paragraphs Using Same Style** can be used to override the Space Before and Space After values for consecutive paragraphs using the same defined paragraph style. For example, you define 10 pts of space after every paragraph of body copy to enhance visual separation and readability. For a list of items, however, you want the 10 pts above and below the overall list but not in between each individual list item. In this case you can use the Space Between... option to define 0 pts of space between the consecutive list item paragraphs without affecting the space above or below the overall list.

I   A drop cap is a stylistic option that enlarges the first one or more characters in a paragraph (usually the first paragraph in a story or section of a story). **Drop Cap Line Count** defines the number of lines drop cap characters extend.

J   **Drop Cap Character Count** defines the number of characters enlarged at the beginning of the paragraph.

K   **Shading** places a color behind the entire paragraph when this box is checked, as if each paragraph was contained in a separate frame.

L   **Shading Color** defines the color of the shading behind the paragraph. Option/Alt-clicking the Shading icon (⊞) opens a dialog box where you can define specific settings for the shading, such as how far the color extends past the edges of the actual paragraph.

M   **Border** places a border around the entire paragraph when this box is checked.

N   **Border Color** defines the color of the border around the paragraph. Option/Alt-clicking the Border icon (⊪) opens a dialog box where you can define specific settings for the borders, such as border thickness and which edges of the paragraph will be bordered.

O   **Hyphenate**, when checked, allows automatic hyphenation at the ends of paragraph lines.

P/Q   **Align to Baseline Grid** and **Do Not Align to Baseline Grid** determine how lines in a paragraph interact with the defined baseline grid, which is explained on Page 129.

1. In the open `poster.indd` file, place the cursor anywhere in the paragraph in the first frame.

2. In the Paragraph panel, click the Justify All Lines button.

   Paragraph formatting applies to the entire paragraph where the insertion point is placed or to any paragraph entirely or partially selected. A paragraph does not have to be entirely selected to change its paragraph formatting attributes.

Insertion point

3. Place the cursor anywhere in the paragraph in the third frame, then apply right paragraph alignment.

Insertion point

4. In the second frame, select any part of the first through seventh paragraphs.

   If you want to apply the same formatting to more than one consecutive paragraph, you can drag to select any part of the target paragraphs. Any paragraph even partially selected will be affected.

5. In the Paragraph panel, change the Space After field to 0.125 in.

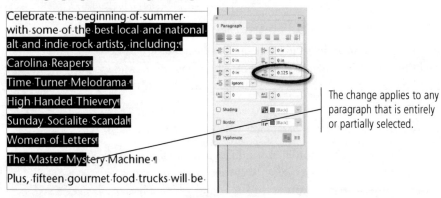

The change applies to any paragraph that is entirely or partially selected.

6. Select any part of the second through sixth paragraphs in the same frame. In the Paragraph panel, click the down-arrow button for the Space After field one time.

   When inches is the unit of measurement, arrows in the Paragraph panel change the values by 1/16″ (0.0625″).

7. **With the same text selected, change the Left Indent field to 0.3 in.**

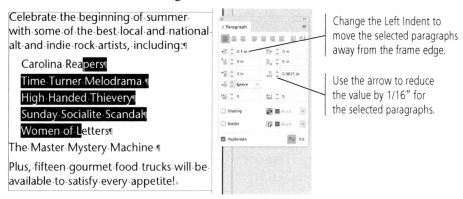

Change the Left Indent to move the selected paragraphs away from the frame edge.

Use the arrow to reduce the value by 1/16" for the selected paragraphs.

8. **Place the insertion point at the beginning of the sixth paragraph (before the words "The Master...") and press Delete/Backspace.**

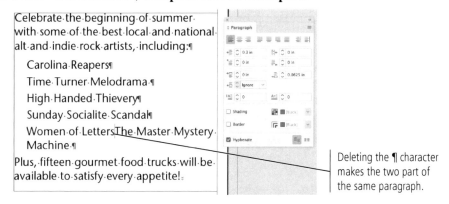

Deleting the ¶ character makes the two part of the same paragraph.

9. **Press Return/Enter to separate the two paragraphs again.**

When you break an existing paragraph into a new paragraph, the attributes of the original paragraph are applied to the new paragraph.

This is an easy way to copy paragraph formatting from one paragraph to the next. When you re-separate the two paragraphs, the "The Master..." paragraph adopts the paragraph formatting attributes of the "Women of..." paragraph.

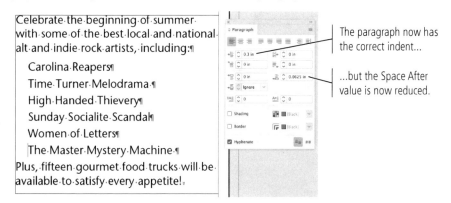

The paragraph now has the correct indent...

...but the Space After value is now reduced.

10. **With the insertion point at the beginning of the seventh paragraph, change the Space After value back to 0.125 in.**

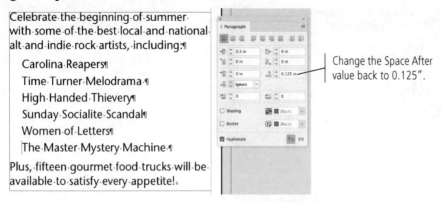

Change the Space After value back to 0.125".

11. **Press Command-Option-I/Control-Alt-I to toggle off the hidden characters.**

Many designers frequently toggle the visibility of hidden characters while working on any given layout. You should become familiar with the keyboard shortcut for this command.

12. **In the Layers panel, click the empty space to the left of the Graphics layer to make that layer — and all its objects — visible again.**

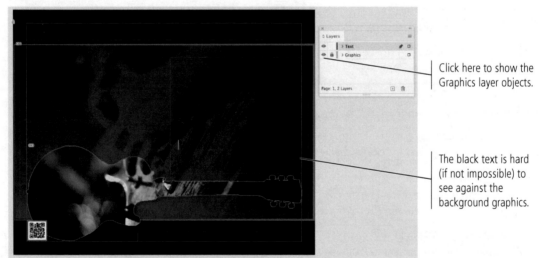

Click here to show the Graphics layer objects.

The black text is hard (if not impossible) to see against the background graphics.

13. **With the insertion point still flashing in the now-obscured text, choose Edit>Select All to select all text in the series of linked frames.**

The Select All command selects all text in the story, whether that story exists in a single frame or threads across multiple frames.

Note:

The Select All command also selects overset text that doesn't fit into the current frame or thread of frames.

14. In the Swatches panel, make sure the Text icon is selected at the top of the panel, and then click the Paper swatch.

This "T" icon means you are changing the text color instead of the object color.

Understanding the Baseline Grid

The **baseline grid**, a series of light blue non-printing guides that extends down the page at specific intervals, is used for controlling and aligning type. You can show the baseline grid by choosing View>Grids & Guides>Show Baseline Grid.

You can force paragraphs to align to the baseline grid, which overrides the defined leading. When **Do Not Align to Baseline Grid** is active, line spacing is defined solely by the applied leading:

When **Align to Baseline Grid** is active, line spacing is defined by the baseline; if the type size or leading is too large to fit lines on sequential baselines, text skips every other baseline:

You can change the baseline grid in the Grids pane of the Preferences dialog box. The Start position can be relative to the top of the page (default) or the top margin, and you can change the increment between lines. View Threshold determines the smallest view percentage at which the grid is visible.

You can also change the baseline grid for a specific frame in the Baseline Options pane of the Text Frame Options dialog box (Object>Text Frame Options).

15. **Select only the first paragraph and change the type fill color to Pantone 8005 C.**

    Remember, type color is a character attribute. Only the highlighted characters are affected by the change.

16. **Repeat Step 15 for the web address in the third frame.**

17. **Click away from the text to deselect it. Use the button at the bottom of the Tools panel to turn on the Preview mode and review the results.**

18. **Return the file to the Normal viewing mode.**

19. **Save the file and continue to the next stage of the project.**

Applying Optical Margin Alignment FOUNDATIONS

At times, specific arrangements of text can cause a paragraph to appear out of alignment even though it's technically aligned properly. Punctuation at the beginning or end of a line, such as commas at the end of a line, often causes this kind of optical problem. InDesign includes a feature called **optical margin alignment** to fix this type of problem.

Optical margin alignment is applied in the Story panel (Window>Type and Tables>Story). When this option is turned on, punctuation marks move outside text margins — either to the left for left-aligned text or right for right-aligned text. (Moving punctuation outside the margins is often referred to as **hanging punctuation**.) The field in the Story panel tells InDesign what size type needs to be adjusted. The best effect is usually created using the same size as the type that needs adjustment.

Optical margin alignment option applies to an entire story (including all text frames in the same thread) and not just the selected paragraph. If necessary, you can toggle on the **Ignore Optical Margin** option (in the Paragraph panel Options menu) for individual paragraphs so that a specific paragraph is not affected by optical margin alignment.

The commas on the right edge of the frame create the impression of misaligned text.

With Optical Margin Alignment active, the commas move outside the frame edge.

STAGE 3 / Working with Text as Graphics

Now that you're familiar with the basic options for formatting characters and paragraphs, you can begin to add style to a layout using two techniques: flowing text along a path and placing graphics inline with text. (You will, of course, learn much more about working with text as you complete the rest of the projects in this book.)

Place Inline Graphics

Any graphics frame you create on a page floats over the other elements in the layout. You can position graphics frames over other objects to hide underlying elements, or you can apply a **runaround** so text will wrap around a picture box.

You can also place images as inline graphics, which means they will be anchored to the text in the position in which they are placed. If text reflows, inline objects reflow with the text and maintain their correct positioning.

There are two methods for creating inline objects. For simple applications, such as a graphic bullet, you can simply place the graphic and format it as a text character. (An inline graphic is treated as a single text character in the story; it is affected by many of the paragraph-formatting commands such as space before and after, tab settings, leading, and baseline position.) For more complex applications, you can use the options in the Object>Anchored Object menu.

1. **With `poster.indd` open, place the insertion point at the beginning of the second line in the third frame (before the word "Carolina").**

2. **Choose File>Place and navigate to `music-note.ai` in the WIP>Concert folder.**

The insertion point is at the beginning of this paragraph.

This option should be checked.

3. **Make sure the Replace Selected Item option is checked, and then click Open.**

   If the insertion point is flashing in a story when you place a graphic using the Replace Selected Item option, the graphic is automatically placed as an inline object.

The line spacing adjusts to fit the placed image.

Note:

You can also select an existing object, cut or copy it, place the insertion point, and then paste the object inline where the insertion point flashes.

4. **Select the inline graphic with the Selection tool.**

5. **In the Transform section of the Properties panel, click the More Options button.**

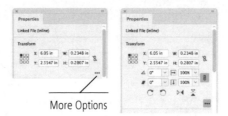

More Options

6. **Using the Properties panel, scale the selected inline graphic and frame to 60% proportionally.**

   Although inline graphics are anchored to the text, they are still graphics contained in graphics frames. You can apply the same transformations to inline graphics you could apply to any other placed graphics.

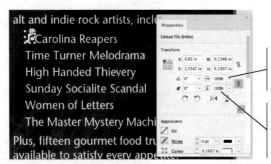

Use these fields to scale the placed graphic and the containing frame.

After you finalize the scaling, the fields show 100% when the frame is selected with the Selection tool.

7. **Choose Object>Anchored Object>Options. Check the Preview option at the bottom of the dialog box.**

8. **With the Inline option selected, change the Y Offset to –0.05 in. Press the Tab key to show the result in the document.**

   A negative number moves the anchored object down; a positive number moves it up.

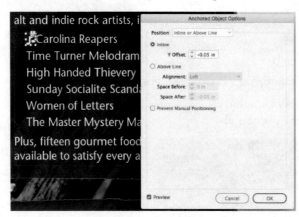

9. **Click OK, and then use the Type tool to place the insertion point between the anchored object and the letter "C." Using the Properties panel, change the Kerning field to 200.**

Because an anchored graphic is treated like a single character, you can use kerning to add space between the anchored graphic and the following character.

Insertion point

10. **Press Shift-Left Arrow to select the anchored object, and then choose Edit>Copy to copy the highlighted object/character.**

You can select an inline graphic just as you would any other text character. Copying text in InDesign is the same as copying text in other applications.

The anchored graphic is selected (highlighted).

Note:

You can also press Command/Control-C to copy selected text.

11. **Place the insertion point at the beginning of the next paragraph and paste the copied object.**

As with copying, pasting text — including inline graphics — in InDesign is the same as in other applications: choose Edit>Paste, or press Command/Control-V.

12. **Paste the anchored graphic again at the beginning of the remaining indented paragraphs.**

13. **Save the file and continue to the next exercise.**

The Anchored Object Options dialog box controls the position of an anchored object relative to text where it is placed.

Using the **Inline** option, the object aligns to text baseline; you can move it up or down relative to the baseline by adjusting the Y Offset value.

Using the **Above Line** option, the object can be anchored to the left, right, or center of the frame. If you're using facing pages, you can also choose Toward Spine or Away from Spine so the object will be placed relative to the spread center. Space Before defines an object's position relative to the bottom of the previous line. Space After defines position relative to the first character in the next line.

By default, you can use the Selection tool to drag an anchored object (in other words, change its position relative to the text to which it is anchored). If **Prevent Manual Positioning** is checked, you can't drag the anchored object in the layout.

When text threads are visible (View>Show Text Threads), a dashed blue line identifies the position of anchored objects relative to the text in which they are anchored.

For complex applications such as moving an anchored object outside a text frame, you can choose Custom in the Anchored Object Options Position menu.

The **Relative to Spine** option, which aligns objects based on the center spread line, is only available if your layout has facing pages. When selected, objects on one side of a spread (such as a sidebar in the outside margin) remain on the outside margin even if the text reflows to a facing page.

The **Anchored Object Reference Point** defines the location on the object that you want to align to the location on the page.

The **Anchored Position Reference Point** defines the page location where you want to anchor an object.

The **X Relative To** field defines what you want to use as the basis for horizontal alignment — Anchor Marker, Column Edge, Text Frame, Page Margin, or Page Edge. The **X Offset** setting moves the object left or right.

The **Y Relative To** field specifies how the object aligns vertically — Line (Baseline), Line (Cap Height), Line (Top of Leading), Column Edge, Text Frame, Page Margin, or Page Edge. The **Y Offset** setting moves the object up or down.

When **Keep Within Top/Bottom Column Boundaries** is checked, the anchored object stays inside the text column if reflowing the text would otherwise cause the object to move outside the boundaries (for example, outside the top edge of the frame if the anchoring text is the first line in a column). This option is only available when you select a line option such as Line (Baseline) in the Y Relative To menu.

Creating Anchored Placeholders

You can use the Object>Anchored Object>Insert option to define an inline placeholder object. You can create a frame (unassigned, graphics, or text) with a specific size and apply object and paragraph styles. The **Position** options are the same as those in the Anchored Object Options dialog box. (You can always resize and reposition the object later.)

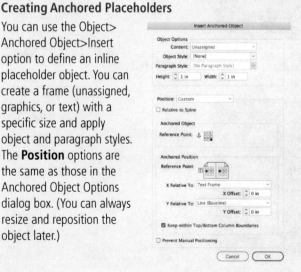

The anchored object is outside the text frame; it is positioned with custom values.

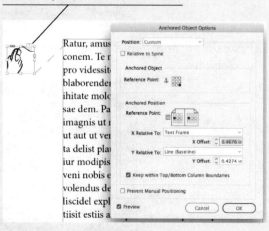

Create Type on a Path

Instead of simply flowing text into a frame, you can also create unique typographic effects by flowing text onto a path. A text path can be any shape you can create in InDesign, whether using one of the basic shape tools, a complex graphic drawn with the Pen tool, or a path created by converting a clipping path to a frame.

1. **With poster.indd open, deselect all objects in the layout.**

   As we explained previously, you can choose Edit>Deselect All or use the Selection tool to click an empty area of the workspace. If you use the click method, make sure you don't click a white-filled object instead of an empty area.

2. **Choose File>Place. Select text_path.jpg in the WIP>Concert folder and click Open. Position the top-left corner of the placed graphic at X: 0 in, Y: 0 in.**

   When this image is loaded into the cursor, click outside the defined bleed area to place the image and not replace the content in one of the existing frames. Then use the Control panel to position the image correctly. (The image you are placing is simply a guide you will use to create the shape of the text path for this exercise.)

3. **Click away from the placed graphic to deselect it.**

4. **Choose the Pen tool. Using the Control panel, change the stroke value to 3-pt Cyan (C=100 M=0 Y=0 K=0), and change the fill value to None.**

   The line in the placed image is magenta, so you're using cyan to help differentiate your line from the one in the image. The white background in the JPEG file makes it easy to focus on the line instead of the elements you have already created.

5. **Using the Pen tool, click once on the left end of the line in the placed image.**

   This first click establishes the first point of the path you're drawing.

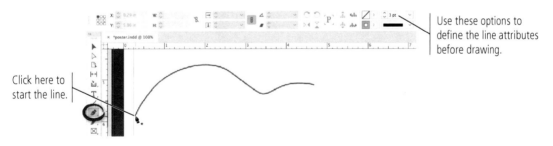

Use these options to define the line attributes before drawing.

Click here to start the line.

6. **Click near the top of the first arc and drag right to create handles for the second anchor point.**

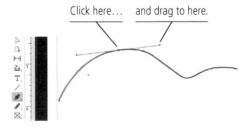

Click here... and drag to here.

7. **Continue clicking and dragging to add the necessary points and handles that create the rest of the line.**

   Use what you learned in Project 1: Letterhead Design to draw the rest of the Bèzier line.

   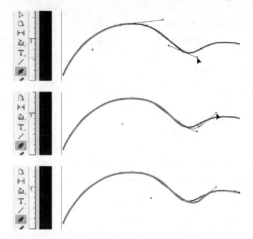

8. **Using the Direct Selection tool, adjust the points and handles until your line closely resembles the one in the placed image.**

   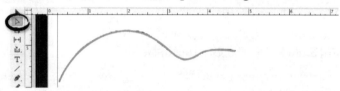

9. **Choose the Type on a Path tool. Move the cursor near the path until the cursor shows a small plus sign in the icon, and then click the path.**

   This action converts the line from a regular path to a type path; the insertion point flashes at the beginning of the text path.

   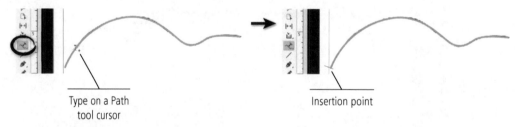

   Type on a Path tool cursor

   Insertion point

10. **Type Weston Summer Concert Series. Choose Edit>Select All to select all text on the path, then format the type as 24-pt ATC Garnet Medium.**

11. **Using the Selection tool, click the text_path.jpg image you used as a guide. Press Delete/Backspace to remove it from the layout.**

12. **Click the text path with the Selection tool to select the actual line.**

13. **Click the bar at the left edge of the text path and drag to the right about 3/8″ (use the following image as a guide).**

When you release the mouse button, the left edge of the text moves to the point where you dragged the line. This marks the orientation point of the text on the path.

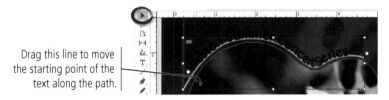

Drag this line to move the starting point of the text along the path.

14. **With the type-path object still selected, use the Swatches panel to change the object's stroke color to None.**

A text path can have a fill and stroke value just like any other path. (When a text path has no stroke color, you can still view the path by choosing View>Extras>Show Frame Edges.)

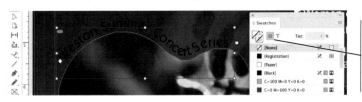

When the actual path is selected, the Swatches panel defaults to show attributes of the path object, not the type.

15. **Click the Text Color button at the top of the Swatches panel, and then click the Pantone 8005 C swatch to change the text color.**

You don't have to select the actual text on a path to change its color. You can use the buttons in the Swatches panel to change the color attributes of either the path or the text.

Click here to change the type fill and stroke colors.

16. **Using the Type tool, place the insertion point immediately before the word "Series" on the path.**

17. **Change the kerning as necessary to separate any letters that run into one another in the type on a path.**

Although your file might be slightly different than ours, depending on the exact path you created and distance you moved the start bar (Step 13), you should probably see some of the lettershapes run or "crash" into each other when the path dips down.

Remember, kerning adjusts the space between two specific characters wherever the insertion point is placed. You should place the insertion point between any crashing letter pairs and adjust the kerning for that pair to separate the lettershapes.

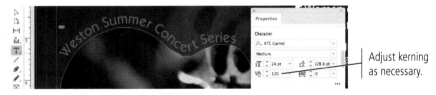

Adjust kerning as necessary.

18. **Save the file and continue to the next stage of the project.**

You can control the appearance of type on a path by choosing Type>Type on a Path>Options. You can apply one of five effects, change the alignment of the text to the path, flip the text to the other side of the path, and adjust the character spacing around curves (higher Spacing values remove more space around sharp curves).

The **Rainbow** (default) effect keeps each character's baseline parallel to the path.

The **Stair Step** effect aligns the left edge of each character's baseline to the path.

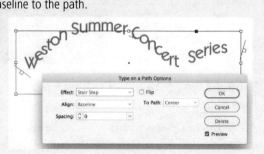

The **Skew** effect maintains the vertical edges of type while skewing horizontal edges around the path.

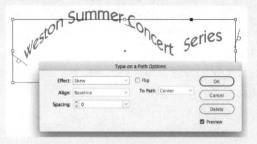

The **Gravity** effect aligns the center of each character's baseline to the path, keeping vertical edges in line with the path's center.

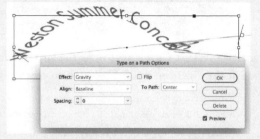

The **3D Ribbon** effect maintains horizontal edges of type while rotating vertical edges to be perpendicular to the path.

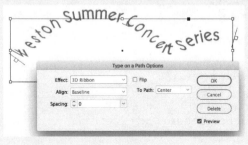

The **Align options** determine which part of the text (Baseline, Ascender, Descender, or Center) aligns to which part of the path (Top, Bottom, or Center).

STAGE 4 / Adjusting Layout Size

Many design projects include more than one required piece. In the case of this project, you also need to create a postcard with the same graphics as the poster you just finished. InDesign's Adjust Layout options makes this process far easier than manually recreating the layout for each required piece.

 ## Adjust the Layout Size

Creating different versions of a layout used to require numerous steps to manually adjusting the page size, bleeds, margins, and layout elements. The new Adjust Layout option consolidates a number of those steps with a single dialog box, allowing the software to calculate adjustments as necessary to create a different page size.

1. **With poster.indd open, choose File>Save As. With WIP>Concert as the destination folder, change the file name to postcard.indd, then click Save.**

   You are going to make substantial changes to the file in this exercise. Saving with a different name before making those changes avoids the potential of overwriting the work you already completed to make the client's poster.

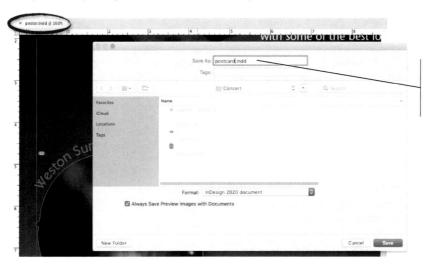

You are re-saving the file with a different name before making significant changes.

2. **With postcard.indd open, choose File>Adjust Layout.**

3. **In the resulting dialog box, change the Width field to 7 in and the Height field to 5 in.**

   You can use this dialog box to define any new Page size, whether larger or smaller than the original. The software will attempt to make the best possible changes based on a comparison of the old and new page aspect ratios (width-to-height comparison).

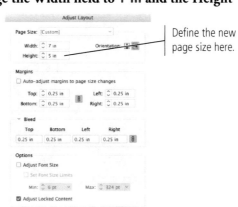

Define the new page size here.

Note:

Click the Adjust Layout button in the Document Setup dialog box (File>Document Setup) to open this dialog box.

4. **Make sure the Constrain icon is active between the Margin fields, then change the Top Margin field to 0.125 in.**

If you check the Auto-Adjust Margins to Page Size Changes option, InDesign will automatically calculate new margins for the adjusted layout. In this case you have been told you need a 1/8″ margin, so you are defining the value rather than letting the software do it for you.

Activate the Constrain icon to change all four fields at once.

5. **Make sure the Constrain icon is active between the Bleed fields, then change the Top Bleed field to 0.125 in.**

Again, the postcard has different output requirements than the poster. This dialog box allows you to automatically adjust the page settings in one step rather than manually adjusting each setting in different places.

Activate the Constrain icon to change all four fields at once.

6. **In the Options settings, check the Adjust Font Size box.**

The rather large font sizes you defined in the poster would not be appropriate for the smaller postcard size. Checking this option allows the software to calculate a font size better suited to the adjusted layout size.

When Adjust Font Size is active, you can also determine minimum and maximum Font Size Limits to keep adjusted type within a defined size range.

7. **Make sure the Adjust Locked Content option is checked.**

Before you started working on the poster text, you locked the Graphics layer to protect it from accidental adjustments. If this option is not checked, all objects on the graphics layer would remain at their original sizes and positions rather than scaling to fit the new layout size.

Check both these options.

8. **Click OK to apply your settings and adjust the layout.**

The adjusted layout is smaller than the original poster, but the page aspect ratio is fairly close to the original. The software's automatic adjustments do a reasonably good job of converting the larger poster elements to fit the smaller postcard size. You will make any necessary fixes in the next exercise.

9. **Save the postcard file, then continue to the next exercise.**

Fine-Tune the Adjusted Layout

As you saw in the previous exercise, changing the layout size is a fairly simple process using the Adjust Layout feature. However, it is important to realize most automatic software functions are not foolproof. Graphic design is a subjective, visual process. Whenever you use automatic adjustments such as Adjust Layout, you should carefully review the results before calling the job finished.

1. **With `postcard.indd` open, review the adjusted layout.**

   You might notice several problems that were created when the software adjusted the various elements to fit the new page size.

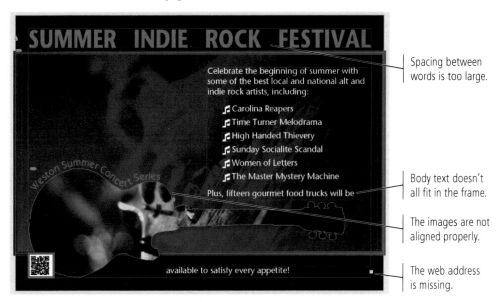

Spacing between words is too large.

Body text doesn't all fit in the frame.

The images are not aligned properly.

The web address is missing.

2. **Using the Selection tool, click the second text frame to select it. Drag the top-center handle up until the Y position is 0.7 in.**

   The body text again fits in the third frame, allowing the web address to move back into place in the third frame.

Drag this handle up.

All body text fits in the frame.

The web address is again visible.

3. **Using the Type tool, click to place the insertion point in the heading (in the first frame) at the top of the layout.**

   This paragraph uses justified alignment. In the adjusted layout and font size, this results in large spaces between words in the heading.

Note:

Make sure you use the regular Type tool, not the Type on a Path tool that you used in the previous exercise.

4. **Open the Paragraph panel Options menu and choose Justification.**

The insertion point is in this paragraph.

Click here to open the panel's Options menu.

5. **In the resulting dialog box, activate the Preview option. Change the Maximum Letter Spacing field to 20%, and change the Maximum Glyph Scaling to 150%. Click OK to finalize the change.**

The Justification dialog box controls the minimum, desired, and maximum spacing allowed for justified paragraph alignment.

- **Word Spacing** defines the space that can be applied between words (where spaces exist in the text). At 100% (the default Desired amount), no additional space is added between words.

- **Letter Spacing** defines the space that can be added between individual letters within a word. All three values default to 0%, which allows no extra space between letters; at 100%, an entire space would be allowed between characters, making the text very difficult to read.

Note:

By changing these two settings, you are basically telling InDesign, "Increase the amount of letter spacing up to 20% of the normal spacing that would be applied by the pressing the spacebar. Also increase the width of individual glyphs up to 150% of their original scale."

- **Glyph Scaling** determines how much individual character glyphs can be scaled (stretched or compressed) to justify the text. At 100%, the default value for all three settings, characters are not scaled.

- In narrow columns, single words sometimes appear on a line by themselves. If the paragraph is set to full justification, a single word on a line might appear to be too stretched out. You can use the **Single Word Justification** menu to center or left-align these single words instead of leaving them fully justified.

- The **Composer** menu defines how InDesign controls the overall flow of text (called composition) within a paragraph: Adobe Paragraph Composer (the default) and Adobe Single-line Composer. Both methods create breaks based on the applied hyphenation and justification for a paragraph.

The settings you defined in this step result in larger spaces throughout the line instead of only stretching the space between whole words. Allowing the software to scale individual glyphs helps reduce the space between individual letters, making the text more readable while still occupying the entire horizontal space.

6. **In the Layers panel, click the Lock icon for the Graphics layer to unlock that layer.**

The original poster layout has a distinct combination of two frames with the same image, carefully aligned to create a specific visual effect. When you reduced the page size, the software automatically adjusted the two frames to fit the new layout size. The software

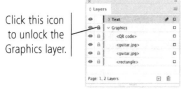

Click this icon to unlock the Graphics layer.

did not, however, consider the visual relationship between the two graphics frames, so they do not properly align in the adjusted layout.

7. **Using the Direct Selection tool, click to select the placed background image in the gradient-filled frame.**

8. **In the Transform section of the Properties panel, click the More Options button to show the scaling percentage of the placed image.**

When the More Options are visible, you can see this image has been reduced to fit into the reduced page size.

The image in the background frame is selected.

More Options button

9. **Change the placed image size to 63% proportionally.**

In the next step you will change the second instance of this graphic to match this one. You are simply rounding the scale percentage to make it easier to exactly match the two images.

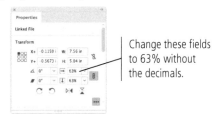

Change these fields to 63% without the decimals.

10. **Still using the Direct Selection tool, click to select the placed image in the guitar-shaped frame.**

The image in the guitar frame is selected.

This image was scaled to a different percentage when the layout was adjusted.

11. **In the Properties panel, change the placed image size to 63% proportionally.**

When the scale percentage matches the background version, the two images align properly.

12. **Save the postcard file, then continue to the final stage of the project.**

STAGE 5 / Outputting PDF Files

If your layout contains transparency or effects, those transparent areas will typically need to be flattened for output. **Flattening** divides transparent artwork into the necessary vector and raster objects. Transparent objects are flattened according to the settings in the selected flattener preset, which you choose in the Advanced options of the Print dialog box (or in the dialog box that appears when you export as PDF, EPS, or another format).

When you work with transparency, InDesign converts affected objects to a common color space (either CMYK or RGB) so transparent objects of different color spaces can blend properly. To avoid color mismatches between different areas of the objects on screen and in print, the blending space is applied for on-screen display and in the flattener. You can define which space to use in the Edit>Transparency Blend Space menu; for print jobs, make sure the CMYK option is selected.

Using the Flattener Panel Preview

You can use the Flattener Preview panel (Window> Output>Flattener Preview) to highlight areas that will be affected by flattening. You can use the Highlight menu to preview different areas and determine which preset to use. Clicking Refresh updates the preview based on your choices (or choose Auto Refresh Highlight).

- **None** displays the normal layout.
- **Rasterized Complex Regions** highlights areas that will be rasterized based on the Raster/Vector Balance of the applied preset.
- **Transparent Objects** highlights objects with opacity of less than 100% as well as objects with blending modes, transparent effects, or feathering.
- **All Affected Objects** highlights all objects affected by transparency, including the transparent objects and objects overlapped by transparent objects.
- **Affected Graphics** highlights all placed image files affected by transparency.

- **Outlined Strokes** highlights all strokes that will be converted to filled objects when flattened.
- **Outlined Text** highlights all text that will be converted to outlines when flattened.
- **Raster-Fill Text and Strokes** highlights text and strokes that result in rasterized fills from flattening.
- **All Rasterized Regions** highlights objects (and parts of objects) that will be rasterized when flattened.

Flattener Presets

InDesign includes three default flattener presets:

- **Low Resolution** works for desktop proofs that will be printed on low-end black-and-white printers and for documents that will be published on the web.
- **Medium Resolution** works for desktop proofs and print-on-demand documents that will be printed on PostScript-compatible color printers.
- **High Resolution** works for commercial output on a printing press and for high-quality color proofs.

You can create your own flattener presets by choosing Edit> Transparency Flattener Presets and clicking New in the dialog box. You can also use the Transparency Flattener Presets dialog box to load presets created on another machine, such as one your service provider created for its specific output device and/or workflow.

Export a PDF File for Print

1. **Open poster.indd from your WIP>Concert folder.**

2. **Choose File>Export. Navigate to your WIP>Concert folder as the target destination and choose Adobe PDF (Print) in the Format/Save As Type menu.**

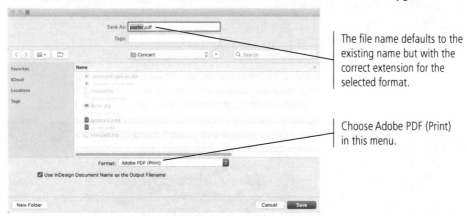

The file name defaults to the existing name but with the correct extension for the selected format.

Choose Adobe PDF (Print) in this menu.

3. **Click Save.**

Before the PDF is saved, you have to define the settings that will be used to generate the PDF file.

4. **Choose [High Quality Print] in the Adobe PDF Preset menu.**

The Adobe PDF Preset menu includes six PDF presets that meet common industry output requirements.

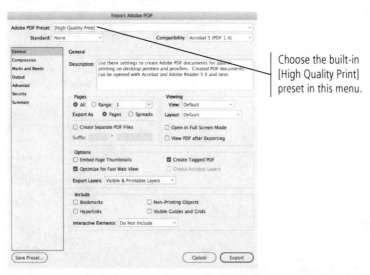

Choose the built-in [High Quality Print] preset in this menu.

Because there are so many ways to create a PDF — and not all of those ways are optimized for the needs of commercial printing — the potential benefits of the file format are often undermined. The PDF/X specification was created to help solve some of the problems associated with bad PDF files entering the prepress workflow. PDF/X is a subset of PDF specifically designed to ensure files have the information necessary for the digital prepress output process. Ask your output provider whether you should apply a PDF/X standard to your files and, if so, which version to use.

5. **Review the options in the General pane, and make sure Visible & Printable Layers is selected in the Export Layers menu.**

- **Pages** options determine which pages to output and whether to output facing pages on a single page. You can also choose to export individual pages or spreads (facing pages) as a single page in the resulting PDF.

- **Create Separate PDF Files** can be used to create individual PDFs of each page included in the Pages section above. When you check this option, you can define the suffix added to the end of the file name to distinguish each exported PDF:

  - **Incremental Numbers** (sequential, beginning with 01 for the first exported page)

  - **Page Number** (the default option, including a preceding "_" character)

  - **Page Size** (useful if you use a single layout to design multiple versions of the same content)

- **View** options determine the default view percentage of the exported PDF file. You can cause the file to open at actual size, fit the page into the Acrobat window based on a number of dimensions, or choose a specific percentage (25, 50, 75, or 100).

- **Layout** determines how spreads appear in the resulting PDF file.

  - The **Single Page** options export each spread separately.

  - The **Continuous** options export files so users can scroll through the document and view parts of successive pages at the same time. Using the non-continuous options, scrolling has the same effect as turning a page; you can't view successive spreads at once.

  - The **Two-Up Facing** options export two spreads side by side.

  - The **Two-Up Cover Page** options export the first spread as a single page and then the remaining spreads two at a time side-by-side. This allows the pages to appear as they would in a book, with even-numbered pages on the left and odd-numbered pages on the right.

- **Open In Full Screen Mode** opens the resulting PDF without showing Acrobat's menus or panels. You can then use the Flip Pages Every field to automatically change pages after a defined interval.

- **View PDF after Exporting** opens the PDF file after it has been created.

- **Embed Page Thumbnails** creates a thumbnail for each page being exported or one thumbnail for each spread if the Spreads option is selected.

- **Optimize for Fast Web View** optimizes the PDF file for faster viewing in a web browser by allowing the file to download one page at a time.

- **Create Tagged PDF** automatically tags elements based on a subset of Acrobat tags, including basic formatting, lists, and so on.

- **Create Acrobat Layers** saves each InDesign layer as an Acrobat layer within the PDF. Printer's marks are exported to a separate "marks and bleeds" layer. Create Acrobat Layers is available only when Compatibility is set to Acrobat 6 (PDF 1.5) or later.

- **Export Layers** determines whether you are outputting All Layers (including hidden and non-printing layers), Visible Layers (including non-printing layers), or Visible & Printable Layers.

- **Include** options can be used to include specific non-printing elements.

6. Review the Compression options.

Compression options determine what and how much data will be included in the PDF file. This set of options is one of the most important when creating PDFs since too-low resolution results in bad-quality printing and too-high resolution results in extremely long download times.

Before you choose compression settings, you need to consider your final goal. In a file for commercial printing, resolution is more important than file size. If your goal is a PDF to be posted on the web, file size is at least equally important as image quality.

You can define a specific compression scheme for color, grayscale, and monochrome images. Different options are available depending on the image type:

- **JPEG compression** options are lossy, which means data is thrown away to create a smaller file. When you use one of the JPEG options, you also define an Image Quality option (from Low to Maximum).

- **ZIP compression** is lossless, which means all file data is maintained in the compressed file.

- **CCITT compression** was initially developed for fax transmission. Group 3 supports two specific resolution settings (203 × 98 dpi and 203 × 196 dpi). Group 4 supports resolution up to 400 dpi.

- **Run Length Encoding** (RLE) is a lossless compression scheme that abbreviates sequences of adjacent pixels. If four pixels in a row are black, RLE saves that segment as "four black" instead of "black-black-black-black."

Note:

Since you chose the High Quality Print preset, these options default to settings that will produce the best results for most commercial printing applications.

Resolution Options for PDF

When you resize an image in the layout, you are changing its effective resolution. The **effective resolution** of an image is the resolution calculated after any scaling has been taken into account. This number is actually more important than the original image resolution. The effective resolution can be calculated with a fairly simple equation:

$$\frac{\text{original resolution}}{1} \div \frac{\%\ \text{magnification}}{100} = \text{effective resolution}$$

If a 300-ppi image is magnified 150%, the effective resolution is

300 ppi / 1.5 = 200 ppi

If you reduce the same 300-ppi image to 50%, the effective resolution is:

300 ppi / 0.5 = 600 ppi

In other words, the more you enlarge a raster image, the lower its effective resolution becomes. Reducing an image results in higher effective resolution, which can result in unnecessarily large PDF files.

When you create a PDF file, you also specify the resolution that will be maintained in the resulting PDF file. The Resolution option is useful if you want to throw away excess resolution for print files or if you want to create low-resolution files for proofing or web distribution.

- **Do Not Downsample** maintains all the image data from the linked files in the PDF file.

- **Average Downsampling To** reduces the number of pixels in an area by averaging areas of adjacent pixels. Apply this method to achieve user-defined resolution (72 or 96 dpi for web-based files or 300 dpi for print).

- **Subsampling To** applies the center pixel value to surrounding pixels. If you think of a 3 × 3-block grid, subsampling enlarges the center pixel — and thus, its value — in place of the surrounding eight blocks.

- **Bicubic Downsampling To** creates the most accurate pixel information for continuous-tone images. This option also takes the longest to process, and it produces a softer image. To understand how this option works, think of a 2 × 2-block grid — bicubic downsampling averages the value of all four of those blocks (pixels) to interpolate the new information.

7. **In the Marks and Bleeds options, check the Crop Marks option and change the Offset field to 0.25 in. Check the Use Document Bleed Settings option.**

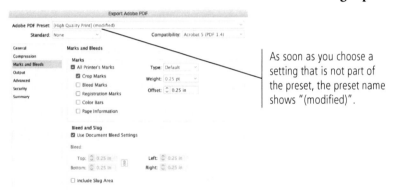

As soon as you choose a setting that is not part of the preset, the preset name shows "(modified)".

Note:

The Output options relate to color management, which you will use in Project 6: Digital Layout Variations. The Security options let you add password protection to a PDF file.

8. **In the Compatibility menu, choose Acrobat 4 (PDF 1.3).**

The Compatibility menu determines which version of the PDF format you will create. This is particularly important if your layout uses transparency. PDF 1.3 does not support transparency, so the file will require flattening. If you save the file to be compatible with PDF 1.4 or later, transparency information will be maintained in the PDF file.

9. **In the Advanced options, choose High Resolution in the Transparency Flattener Preset menu.**

10. **Click Export to create your PDF file. If you see a warning message, click OK.**

Your PDF file will be flattened, so some features (hyperlinks, bookmarks, etc.) will be unavailable. You didn't use those features in this project, so you don't have to worry about this warning.

11. **Choose Window>Utilities>Background Tasks.**

The PDF export process happens in the background, which means you can work on other tasks while the PDF is being created. This panel shows how much of the process has been completed as a percentage and will list any errors that occur. When the PDF file is finished, the export process is no longer listed in the panel.

The export process is listed in the panel.

12. **Save the poster file and close it.**

13. **Open the `postcard.indd` file if necessary, then choose File>Export.**

14. **With your WIP>Concert folder defined as the target destination, choose Adobe PDF (Print) in the Format/Save As Type menu, then click Save.**

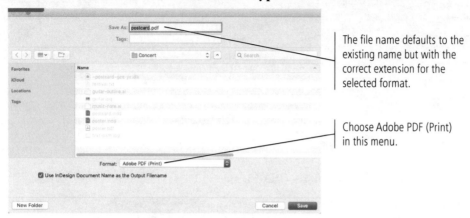

The file name defaults to the existing name but with the correct extension for the selected format.

Choose Adobe PDF (Print) in this menu.

15. **Review the options in the Export Adobe PDF dialog box.**

This dialog box remembers the last-used settings. Because you just defined the required settings for the poster file, those same settings are already selected here.

16. **Click Export, then click OK to dismiss the warning message and create the postcard PDF file.**

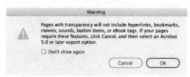

17. **Save the postcard file and close it.**

PROJECT REVIEW

1. The _____ tool can be used to draw the direction and position of a gradient within a frame.

2. The _____ menu command reveals characters such as paragraph returns and tabs.

3. _____ is the space between specific pairs of letters. To change this value, you have to place the insertion point between two characters.

4. The _____ is the theoretical line on which the bottoms of letters rest.

5. The _____ indicates more text exists in the story than will fit into the available frame or series of linked frames.

6. A/an _____ is defined as all text between two ¶ characters.

7. The _____ panel is used to apply optical margin alignment.

8. _____ are objects that are attached to specific areas of text.

9. _____ is the resolution of an image after its scaling in the layout has been taken into account.

10. _____ compression for raster images is lossy, which means data is thrown away to reduce the file size.

1. Briefly explain how transparency is applied to objects in an InDesign page layout.

2. Briefly define a clipping path; provide at least two examples of how they might be useful.

3. Briefly explain the difference between character formatting and paragraph formatting.

PORTFOLIO BUILDER PROJECT

Use what you learned in this project to complete the following freeform exercise.
Carefully read the art director and client comments, then create your own design to meet the needs of the project.
Use the space below to sketch ideas; when finished, write a brief explanation of your reasoning behind your final design.

art director comments

Your local community theater is planning a summer production of "Down the Yellow Brick Rabbit Hole," a satirical mash-up of "The Wizard of Oz" meets "Alice in Wonderland." You have been hired to create several pieces to advertise the play in local media and in the community.

To complete this project, you should:

❏ Design a half-page advertisement for the local newspaper (11.5″ × 10.5″ trim size).

❏ Design a full-page advertisement for the community arts and entertainment magazine (8.5″ × 11″ trim size).

❏ Design a poster that can be placed in local storefronts and other public venues (11″ × 17″ trim size).

❏ Find or create artwork that appropriately illustrates the concept of the play.

client comments

As the director and playwright, I was inspired by Gregory Maguire's interesting rewrites of classic fairy tales. But then I started to think about what would happen if the characters from different books met somehow... and this play is the result.

Some real sparks fly when the Queen of Hearts and the Wizard of Oz get together! And the wicked witch, well, she's got her hands full trying to escape the clutches of an army of talking caterpillars.

This play is one-third mystery, one-third dramedy, and one-third just plain silly! It's got star-crossed lovers, an evil villain, an inept magician, a rather foolish prince, and even a mad flying monkey that wears some very strange hats.

The only text in the ad should be

Down the Yellow Brick Rabbit Hole
by Stacey Wrightwood
at the Preston Theater this August
800-555-PLAY for ticket information

project justification

PROJECT SUMMARY

This project combined form and function, presenting the client's information in a clear, easy-to-read manner while using graphic elements to grab the viewer's attention and reinforce the message of the piece. Completing this poster involved adjusting a number of different text formatting options, including paragraph settings and the flow of text across multiple frames. You should now understand the difference between character and paragraph formatting and know where to find the different options when you need them.

The graphics options in InDesign give you significant creative control over virtually every element of your layouts. Custom colors and gradients add visual interest to any piece while more sophisticated tools like non-destructive transparency and other effects allow you to experiment entirely within your page layout until you find exactly the look you want to communicate your intended message.

Create custom swatches and gradients

Control text flow across multiple text frames

Control various character and paragraph formatting attributes

Place graphics as anchored inline objects

Create and format text on a path

Create a custom graphics frame from an image's clipping path

Use blending modes and effects to blend images in different frames

Generate a QR code to provide additional customer information

Adjust the layout to use a different page size

Make corrections as necessary to clean up automatic adjustments

Aerospace Newsletter

Your client is a non-profit foundation that focuses on preserving the history of American innovation in aerospace. It publishes a monthly newsletter for people on various mailing lists, which are purchased from a list-management vendor. The editor wants to change the existing newsletter template and wants you to take over the layout once the template has been revised.

This project incorporates the following skills:

❏ Opening and modifying an existing layout template

❏ Managing missing font and link requests

❏ Replacing graphics files to meet specific color output needs

❏ Formatting text with template styles

❏ Controlling text-frame inset, alignment, and wrap attributes

❏ Creating a table with data from a Microsoft Excel worksheet

❏ Preflighting the final layout and creating a job package

PROJECT MEETING

client comments

In the past our newsletter was printed using two spot colors in our logo, but the printer just told us that we can save money if we use four-color printing instead.

We also want to go from four columns to three on the front page. Each issue has a highlight image at the top of the front page, which relates to the feature story. The bottom of the front page is a series of photos from one of our affiliates, put together by that organization's staff.

Half of the back is an ad, and the other half features the same affiliate who provides the photos for the bottom of the front page. If there is room, we can include a table with our ArAA contact information.

We sent you the files that will be required to complete July's newsletter — photos, ads, three text files (the main article, a sidebar for the front, and the story for the back), and the Microsoft Excel table with our contact information.

art director comments

Whenever you work with a file that someone else created, there is always the potential for problems. When you open the template, you'll have to check the fonts and images and make any necessary adjustments. Make sure you save the file as a template again before you build the new issue.

The printer said they prefer to work with native application files instead of PDF, so when you're finished implementing the layout, you'll need to check the various elements and then create a final job package.

project objectives

To complete this project, you will:

❏ Handle requests for missing fonts and images.

❏ Edit master page elements to meet new layout requirements.

❏ Save a layout file as a template.

❏ Access master page elements on the layout pages.

❏ Format imported text using template styles.

❏ Build and format a table using data from a Microsoft Excel spreadsheet.

❏ Create a final job package for the output provider.

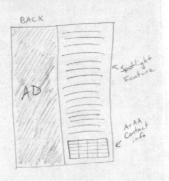

STAGE 1 / Working with Templates

InDesign templates are special types of files that store the basic structure of a project. Well-planned templates can store layout elements such as nonprinting guides to mark various areas of the job; placeholder frames that will contain different stories or images in each revision; elements that remain the same in every revision, such as the nameplate; and even formatting information that will be applied to different elements so the elements can be consistent from one issue to the next.

Manage Missing Fonts

When you work with digital page layouts, whether in a template or in a regular layout file, it's important to understand fonts are external files of data that describe the font for on-screen display and for the output device. The fonts you use in a layout need to be available on any computer that will be used to open the file. InDesign stores a reference to used fonts, but it does not store the actual font data.

1. **Download Aerospace_ID20_RF.zip from the Student Files web page.**

2. **Expand the ZIP archive in your WIP folder (Macintosh) or copy the archive contents into your WIP folder (Windows).**

   This creates a folder named **Aerospace**, which contains the files you need for this project. You should also use this folder to save the files you create in this project.

3. **Choose File>Open. Select araa-newsletter.indt in the WIP>Aerospace folder, and choose the Open [As] Original option.**

   Macintosh users: As with placing images, you might need to click the Options button in the bottom-left corner to reveal the options for opening a template file. We will not repeat this instruction.

   You have several options when you open an existing template file:

   - If you choose **Open [As] Normal** to open a regular InDesign file (INDD), the selected file appears in a new document window or tab. When you use this option to open a template file (INDT), InDesign creates and opens a new untitled file based on the template.

   - When you choose **Open [As] Original**, you open the actual InDesign template file so you can make and save changes to the template.

   - You can use **Open [As] Copy** to open a regular InDesign file as if it were a template; the result is a new, untitled document based on the file you selected.

Note:

Missing fonts are one of the most common problems in the digital graphics output process. This is one of the primary advantages of using PDF files for output — PDF can store actual font data, so you don't need to include the separate font files in your job package. (However, PDF can't solve the problem of missing fonts used in a layout template.)

Macintosh   Windows

4. **Click Open, then review the warning message.**

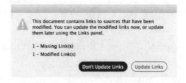

InDesign stores links to images placed in a layout; the actual image data is not stored in the InDesign file. If placed files are not available in the same location as when they were placed or if they have been resaved since you placed them, you'll see a warning message when you open the file. You'll correct these problems shortly.

5. **Click Don't Update Links. If you get a Profile or Policy Mismatch warning, click OK.**

Profile mismatches are explained in Project 6: Digital Layout Variations.

6. **Review the information in the Missing Fonts dialog box.**

When you open a file that calls for fonts not installed on your computer system, you see this warning. You could blindly fix the problem now (without knowing what will be affected), but we prefer to review problem areas before making changes.

Note:

If you have the ATC fonts from previous editions installed, ATC Colada might not appear in the list of missing fonts.

7. **Click Close to dismiss the Missing Fonts dialog box.**

8. **Open the Pages panel (Window>Pages).**

The Pages panel makes it very easy to navigate through the pages in a layout, including master pages. You can navigate to any page by simply double-clicking the page's icon or navigate to a spread by double-clicking the spread page numbers below the page icons.

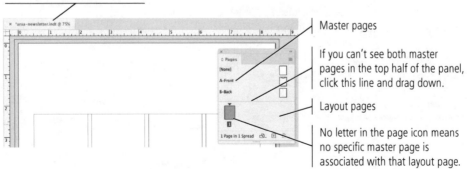

The document tab shows you are editing the actual template file.

Master pages

If you can't see both master pages in the top half of the panel, click this line and drag down.

Layout pages

No letter in the page icon means no specific master page is associated with that layout page.

Think of master pages as templates for different pages in the layout. This file, for example, has two master pages: Front Page and Back Page. The letters preceding each master name are automatically added and used to identify which layout pages are associated with which master page.

9. **Double-click the A-Front icon to display that layout.**

The top area of the newsletter (the **nameplate** area) includes the newsletter logotype as well as the "Published by…" line and the issue date. A pink highlight around the type shows the font used in this area is not available.

The Missing Font highlighting is only a visual indicator on your screen; it is not included when the job is output. If the nameplate information is not highlighted, open the Composition pane of the Preferences dialog box, and make sure the Highlight Substituted Fonts option is checked.

10. **Using the Type tool, click the frame with the missing font to place the insertion point.**

The Control panel shows the missing font name in brackets. Any time you see a font name in brackets, you know you have a potential problem.

Note:

The missing-font highlighting only appears if you are in the Normal viewing mode.

Missing fonts are listed in brackets.

Highlighting indicates an area where the required font is not available.

The name or number of the active page is highlighted.

The icon of the selected page is highlighted.

11. **Choose Type>Find Font.**

The Find Font dialog box lists every font used in the layout, including missing ones (which are identified with a warning icon). You can use this dialog box to replace any font — including missing ones — with another font available on your system.

12. **Highlight ATC Colada Regular in the Fonts in Document list. In the Replace With area, choose ATC Onyx in the Font Family menu and choose Normal in the Font Style menu.**

13. **Check the option to Redefine Style When Changing All.**

When this is checked, the font replacement will be applied in paragraph and character style definitions, even if those styles are not currently applied in the layout.

The warning icon indicates which font is missing.

If you don't check the Redefine Style option, you might later introduce another missing-font problem when you apply a style that calls for a missing font.

Note:

If you select a font that is used in a placed graphic, you can click the Find Graphic button to navigate to the location of the graphic where the font is used.

Note:

If you click the More Info button, you can see specific details about the selected font, such as the type of font and where it is used.

14. **Click Change All to replace all instances of ATC Colada Regular.**

You could also click the Find Next button to review individual instances of a missing font, or click the Change or Change/Find button to replace and review individual instances of the selected font.

When the Redefine Style option is checked and you use the Change All option, InDesign provides a warning when overrides have been applied to existing styles.

15. **Click OK to dismiss the warning message.**

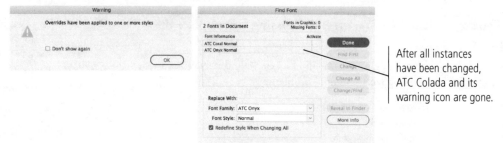

After all instances have been changed, ATC Colada and its warning icon are gone.

16. **Click Done to close the Find Font dialog box.**

Once you have replaced the missing font, the pink highlighting disappears.

17. **Choose File>Save to save your changes to the template file, and then continue to the next exercise.**

Because you used the Open Original option, you are editing the actual template file; this means you can simply use the regular Save command to save your changes to the template. If you used the Open Normal option to open and edit a template file, you would have to use the Save As command and save the edited file with the same name and extension as the original template to overwrite the original.

More about Managing Missing Fonts

It is important to understand that fonts are external files of data that describe the font for the output device. The fonts you use in a layout need to be available on any computer that opens the file. InDesign stores a reference to used fonts, but it does not store the actual font data.

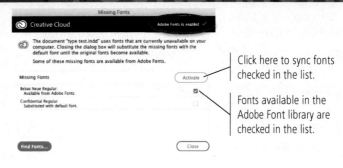

Click here to sync fonts checked in the list.

Fonts available in the Adobe Font library are checked in the list.

When you open a file that uses fonts you don't have installed on your computer, a Missing Fonts dialog box shows which fonts should be installed.

The software scans the Adobe Font library to locate missing fonts; missing fonts that exist in the Adobe Font library are automatically checked in the list. Clicking the Activate button syncs the required fonts in your Creative Cloud (CC) account, making them available in your desktop version of InDesign.

Using the Find Font Dialog Box

You can also use the Find Font dialog box (accessed by clicking the Find Font button in the Missing Fonts dialog box or by choosing Type>Find Font) to replace one font with another throughout a layout.

The top half of the dialog box lists every font used in the file; missing fonts are identified by a warning icon in the list. If a missing font is available in the Adobe Font library, it is automatically checked in the top list. You can click the Activate button to sync those fonts in your CC account.

Before changing a specific font, you can use the Find First button to locate the first instance where the font selected in the top list appears in the layout.

In the lower half of the dialog box, you can use the Replace With menus to choose any available font to use in place of the one selected in the top list.

The Change, Change All, and Change Find buttons affect only the font that is selected in the top list. If you click the Change/Find button, the first instance of the selected font will be changed, and the software identifies the next instance (if any).

If you check the Redefine Style When Changing All button, a missing font used in a style definition will also be replaced if you click the Change All button.

Replace Missing and Modified Graphics

Placed graphics can cause problems if those files aren't where InDesign thinks they should be. Placed graphics files can be either **missing** (they were moved from the location from which they were originally placed in the layout, or the name of the file was changed) or **modified** (they were resaved after being placed into the layout, changing the linked file's "time stamp" but not its location or file name). In either case, you need to correct these problems before the file can be successfully output.

Note:

The issue of missing and modified images is a common problem if you zip a job folder into an archive. When you unzip a job folder and open the InDesign file, you will often see a warning about missing/ modified images (especially on Windows).

To avoid this problem in the resource files for this book, we embedded most of the placed images into the layout files.

1. **With `araa-newsletter.indt` open in InDesign, display the Links panel (Window>Links).**

   The Links panel lists every file placed in your layout. Missing images show a red stop-sign icon; modified images show a yellow yield sign.

   If you don't see the Missing and Modified icons in the layout, choose View>Extras>Show Link Badge.

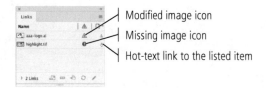

   Modified image icon
   Missing image icon
   Hot-text link to the listed item

2. **Click the hot-text page link for the modified aaa-logo.ai file in the panel.**

   You can also use the Go to Link button in the middle of the panel if the link information section is expanded or at the bottom of the panel if the link information section is collapsed.

   The Pages panel shows the A-Front master layout is now active because that is where the selected instance exists.

   This icon identifies a modified image.   This icon identifies a missing image.   Click the hot-text link to navigate to a specific instance.

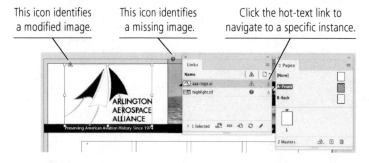

   You can easily use the Links panel to navigate to selected images.

3. **Using the Direct Selection tool or the Content Grabber, click the placed logo on the page.**

   As part of the Adobe Creative Suite, InDesign supports native Adobe Illustrator (AI) files (with the ".ai" extension) that have been saved to be compatible with the PDF format. Illustrator files can include raster and vector information, type and embedded fonts, and objects on multiple layers in a variety of color models (including spot colors, which are added to the InDesign Swatches panel when the AI file is imported).

The Links panel lists all files that have been placed into a layout.

A **Name** column shows the name of each linked file. If more than one instance of a file is placed in the same layout, they are grouped together by default; you can click the arrow button to expand the list and review individual instances.

B The **Status** column shows special icons to identify whether an image file is missing, modified, embedded, or linked from a CC Library.

C The **Page** column shows a hot-text link to the page where an image is placed. Letters in this column identify master page layouts; numbers identify regular document pages.

D **Show/Hide Link Information** expands or collapses the Link Information section of the panel, which shows details — file name, format, size, etc. — about the selected link.

E **Relink from CC Libraries** allows you to change a link to a file that is stored in a CC Library on your Creative Cloud account. (See Project 5: Folding Travel Brochure for more about CC Libraries.)

F **Relink** opens a navigation dialog box where you can locate a missing file or link to a different file.

G **Go to Link** selects and centers the file in the document window.

H **Update Link** updates modified links. If the selected image is missing, this button opens a navigation dialog box so you can locate the missing file.

I **Edit Original** opens the selected file in its native application. When you save the file and return to InDesign, the placed file is automatically updated.

You can click any column head in the panel to sort the list of links based on that column. For example, clicking the Status heading moves all missing and modified links to the top of the list so you can more easily find and address those issues.

When expanded, the Link Information section of the panel shows useful metadata related to the selected file.

Click this bar and drag to change the height of the Link Information area.

Click here and drag to resize the entire panel.

If you open the Panel Options dialog box (from the Links panel Options menu), you can change which information appears in each section of the panel.

• Use the **Row Size** menu to change the size of item thumbnails in the panel.

• Uncheck **Collapse Multiple Links to Same Source** to list multiple instances of the same file separately instead of grouped together (as they are by default).

• In the lower section of the dialog box, you can use the checkboxes to determine what information appears in the main Links panel (**Show Column**) and in the Link Information section of the panel (**Show in Link Info**). For example, you might want to include the Effective PPI as a column in the top half of the panel so you can easily monitor link resolution as you work.

Embedding Links

To avoid the problem of missing links, you can embed images directly into the layout file by Control/right-clicking an image in the Links panel and choosing Embed Link in the contextual menu.

This icon identifies an embedded link.

When links are embedded, there is no longer any relation to the original source file. This means the source files do not need to be included in the job package, and you will not see a missing-link error if the original source file is moved. It also means, however, that any changes in a source file will

not result in a modified link warning. To edit an image, you have to manually open the original source file in its native application, save it, then manually replace the embedded image with the edited file.

4. **Open the Transform panel (Window>Object & Layout>Transform).**

The options in the Transform panel are the same as those on the left side of the Control panel. As you can see, the selected graphic is placed at approximately 44%.

Note:

Make sure you use the Direct Selection tool or the Content Grabber to select the actual placed logo. If you select the frame instead, the Transform panel shows the values for the frame instead of the graphic placed in the frame.

5. **Click the Modified icon in the top-left corner of the image frame.**

The Missing and Modified icons provide an easy, on-screen method for identifying and correcting image-link problems.

You can also double-click the Modified icon in the Links panel, or select the file in the panel and click the Update Link button, to update selected modified files.

6. **Click the updated image with the Direct Selection tool.**

When you update or replace an existing placed image, the new file adopts the necessary scaling percentage to fit into the same space as the original. In this case, the new file is scaled to approximately 54%, which is the size necessary to fit the same dimensions as the original.

This icon identifies a linked image that is up-to-date.

7. **Click the Missing icon in the top-left corner of the grayscale image.**

You can also click the Relink button in the Links panel to replace a missing image link.

8. **In the resulting Locate dialog box, uncheck Show Import Options at the bottom of the dialog box.**

If the Search for Missing Links option is checked, InDesign will scan the selected folder to find other missing image files.

9. **Navigate to** `highlight-july.tif` **in the WIP>Aerospace folder, then click Open.**

After you identify a new source image, the graphics frame and the Links panel no longer show the Missing warning. The new image preview appears in the same frame.

The frame shows the new image, which replaced the missing image file.

10. **Save the file and continue to the next exercise.**

 # Edit Margin and Column Guides

Your client wants to make several changes to the layout, including fewer and wider columns on the front page. These changes will recur from one issue to the next, so you should change the template instead of changing the elements in each issue.

1. **With** `araa-newsletter.indt` **open, double-click the A-Front icon to show that layout in the document window.**

Every layout has a default setup, which you define when you create the file. Each master page has its own margin and column settings, which can be different than the default document settings.

2. **Choose Layout>Margins and Columns, and make sure the Preview option is checked in the resulting dialog box.**

Many InDesign dialog boxes have a Preview option, which allows you to see the effects of your changes before finalizing them.

3. **Change the Left and Right Margins fields to** `0.5 in`**, change the Columns field to** `3`**, and change the Gutter field to** `0.2 in`**.**

Notice that changing the margin and column guides has no effect on the text frame; you have to change the text frame settings independently.

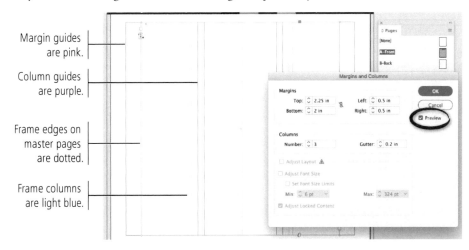

Margin guides are pink.

Column guides are purple.

Frame edges on master pages are dotted.

Frame columns are light blue.

Note:

You can change the default margins and columns for a layout by choosing File>Document Setup.

4. Click OK to apply the change and close the dialog box.

5. Using the Selection tool, click to select the four-column text frame in the layout.

6. Click and drag the outside-center handles to extend the frame edges to match the modified margin guides.

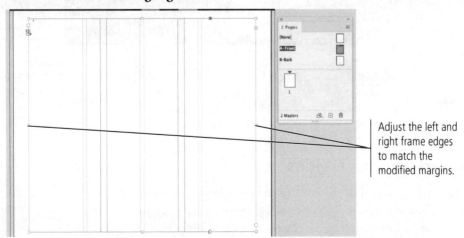

Adjust the left and right frame edges to match the modified margins.

7. With the text frame selected, locate the Text Frame options in the Properties panel.

8. Change the Number of Columns field to 3 and the Gutter field to 0.2 in to match the changes you made to the column guides.

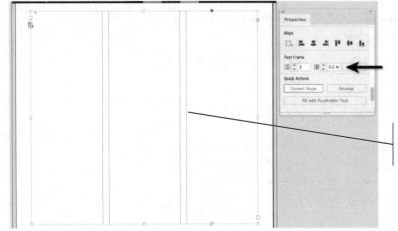

Text frame columns now match the adjusted margin and column guides.

Note:

The Columns options might also be available in the Control panel:

Number of Columns

Gutter

9. **With the same text frame selected, click the Options button in the Text Frame section of the Properties panel.**

   The Text Frame Options dialog box includes options for controlling a number text frame attributes, broken into five categories.

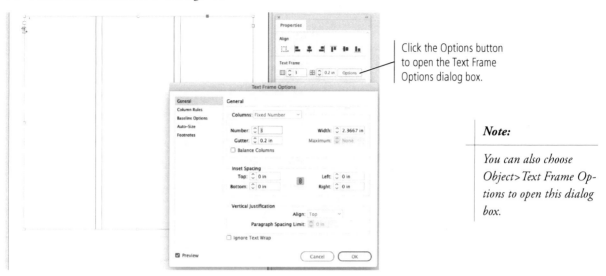

Click the Options button to open the Text Frame Options dialog box.

10. **Click Column Rules on the left side of the dialog box to show those options.**

11. **Click to activate the Insert Column Rules checkbox, then change the Stroke Weight field to 0.25 pt.**

   Column rules add lines between each column in the selected text frame. The rules extend from the ascent of the first line to the descent of the last line of text in the frame. You can change the Line Height to change the start and end position of the rules; negative lines extend the rules beyond the text, while positive values move the ends in from the start or end of the text.

   The rules are placed exactly in the center of the column gutter. You can change the Horizontal Position field to move the rules left (negative values) or right (positive values) in relation to the column gutters.

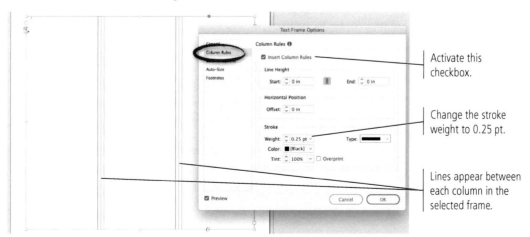

Activate this checkbox.

Change the stroke weight to 0.25 pt.

Lines appear between each column in the selected frame.

12. **Click OK to accept your changes and return to the document window.**

13. **Save the file and close it.**

There are two kinds of pages in InDesign:

- **Layout pages**, which appear in the bottom of the Pages panel, are the pages on which you place content.

- **Master pages**, which appear in the top of the Pages panel, are the pages on which you place recurring information such as running headers and footers (information at the top and bottom of the page, respectively).

Master pages are one of the most powerful features in page layout software. Think of a master page as a template for individual pages; anything on the master appears on the related layout page(s). Changing something on a master layout applies the same changes to the object on related layout pages (unless you already changed the object on the layout page or detached the object from the master).

The letter indicates which master is applied to the page.

Selected page (the icon is highlighted)

Active page (the page number is highlighted)

The Pages panel Options menu has a number of indispensable options for working with master pages:

- **New Master** opens a dialog box where you can assign a custom prefix, a meaningful name, whether the master will be based on another master page, the number of pages (from 1 to 10) to include in the master layout, and the size of the master layout (InDesign supports multiple page sizes within a single document).

- **Master Options** opens a dialog box with the same options you defined when you created a new master.

- **Apply Master to Pages** allows you to apply a specific master to selected pages. You can also apply a specific master to a layout by dragging the master icon onto the layout page icon in the lower half of the panel.

- **Override All Master Page Items** allows you to access and change master items on a specific layout page. (It's important to realize that this command functions on a page-by-page basis.) You can also override individual objects by pressing Command/Control-Shift and clicking the object you want to override.

In the Master Pages submenu:

- **Save as Master** is useful if you've built a layout on a layout page and want to convert that layout to a master. Instead of copying and pasting the page contents, you can simply activate the page and choose Save as Master.

- **Load Master Pages** allows you to import master pages from one InDesign file to another. Assets (styles, etc.) used on the imported masters will also be imported.

- **Select Unused Masters** highlights all master pages not associated with any layout page and not used as the basis of another master page. This can be useful if you want to remove extraneous elements from your layout.

- **Remove All Local Overrides** reapplies the settings from the master items to related items on the layout page. This option toggles to **Remove Selected Local Overrides** if you have an object selected in the layout.

- **Detach All Objects from Master** breaks the link between objects on a layout page and objects on the related master; in this case, changing items on the master has no effect on related layout page items. This selection toggles to **Detach Selection from Master** if you have a specific object selected in the layout.

- **Allow Master Item Overrides on Selection**, active by default, allows objects to be overridden on layout pages. You can protect specific objects by selecting them on the master layout and toggling this option off.

- **Hide/Show Master Items** toggles the visibility of master page items on layout pages.

Create a New File Based on the Template

Every issue of the newsletter has one front page and one back page. These layouts are already prepared as master pages, but you have to apply those master pages to the layout pages for individual issues. Since this occurs for every issue, it will remove a few more clicks from the process if you set up the layout pages as part of the template.

1. **Choose File>Open and navigate to your WIP>Aerospace folder. Select the araa-newsletter.indt template file and choose the Open [As] Normal option at the bottom of the dialog box.**

Macintosh   Windows

2. **Click Open to create a new file based on the template.**

   Opening a template using the Open [As] Normal option creates a new untitled document based on the template.

   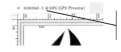 The result is a new, untitled document.

   If you double-click a template file on your desktop, the template opens as if you chose the Open [As] Normal option. To use the Open [As] Original or Open [As] Copy feature, you must choose File>Open from InDesign.

3. **Double-click the Page 1 icon in the Pages panel.**

4. **In the Pages panel, drag the A-Front master icon onto the Page 1 icon in the lower half of the Pages panel.**

   When a master page is applied to a layout page, everything on the master page is placed on the layout page.

Note:

You can change the size of page icons in the Pages panel by choosing Panel Options at the bottom of the panel Options menu.

Assign a master layout to a specific page by dragging the master icon onto the page icon.

Alternatively, you can choose Apply Master to Pages in the Pages panel Options menu. In the resulting dialog box, you can determine which master page to apply to specific layout pages. Some find this easier than dragging master page icons onto layout page icons in the panel; it is also useful if you want to apply a specific master layout to more than one page at a time.

5. **Click the B-Back icon and drag it into the bottom half of the Pages panel (below the Page 1 icon).**

   You can add new pages to your layout by dragging any of the master page icons into the lower half of the panel.

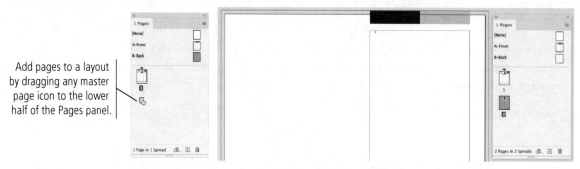

Add pages to a layout by dragging any master page icon to the lower half of the Pages panel.

You can also choose Insert Pages in the Pages panel Options menu. In the resulting dialog box, you can determine how many pages to add, exactly where to add the new pages, and which master page to apply to the new pages. This method makes it easier to add one page from a master page that includes spreads or add multiple pages at one time based on the same master.

6. **Choose File>Save As. Navigate to your WIP>Aerospace folder as the location for saving the template.**

   Because you opened the template to create a normal layout file, you have to use the Save As command to overwrite the edited template file.

7. **Change the file name to araa-newsletter. In the Format/Save As Type menu, choose InDesign 2020 Template.**

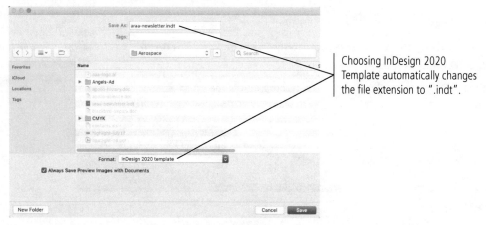

Choosing InDesign 2020 Template automatically changes the file extension to ".indt".

8. **Click Save, then read the resulting message.**

   Because you defined the same name as the original template, you have to confirm you want to overwrite the template file with the new version.

9. **Click Replace/Yes. When the save is complete, close the template file.**

Implement the Newsletter Template

By saving your work as a template, you eliminated a significant amount of repetitive work that would otherwise need to be redone for every issue. There are still some tasks that will need to be done for each issue, such as changing the issue date and adding images to the front and back pages. These elements will change in each issue, so they can't be entirely "templated." But if you review the layout, you'll see the template includes placeholders for these elements, so adding these elements is greatly simplified.

1. **Choose File>Open and navigate to your WIP>Aerospace folder. Select the araa-newsletter.indt template file, choose the Open [As] Normal option at the bottom of the dialog box, and click Open.**

   As in the previous exercise, opening the template file creates a new untitled document based on the template.

2. **Immediately choose File>Save As and navigate to your WIP>Aerospace folder. Change the file name to newsletter-july.indd and click Save.**

   The Format menu defaults to the InDesign 2020 Document option, so you do not have to change this menu to save the new file as a regular InDesign document.

3. **Navigate to Page 1 of the file.**

4. **Using the Selection tool, try to select the text frame that includes the date.**

   This step will have no effect, and nothing will be selected. By default, you can't select master page items on a layout page; changes have to be made on the master page.

   When you change an object on a master page, the same changes reflect on associated layout pages. For example, if you change the red box to blue on A-Front Page, the red box will turn blue on Page 1 as well. Because of this parent-child relationship, it's a good idea to leave objects attached to the master whenever possible.

Dotted frame edges indicate that a frame is attached to the related master page.

5. Command/Control-Shift-click the text frame that contains the issue date.

This method detaches an individual object from the master page. It is no longer linked to the master page, so changes to the same item on the master will not be reflected on the associated layout page.

If you look carefully, however, you might notice a problem. Detaching the single text frame from the master moves it in front of any object that exists only on the master page. The four colored rectangles are now hidden by the text frame's fill color.

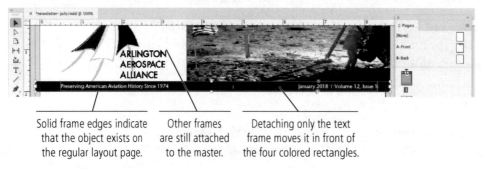

Solid frame edges indicate that the object exists on the regular layout page.

Other frames are still attached to the master.

Detaching only the text frame moves it in front of the four colored rectangles.

6. Choose Edit>Undo Override Master Page Items.

7. Control/right-click the Page 1 icon in the Pages panel and choose Override All Master Page Items from the contextual menu.

Overriding all items from the master page maintains the original stacking order of those objects. You can now see the colored rectangles on top of the text frame.

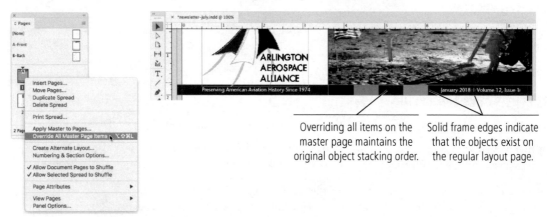

Overriding all items on the master page maintains the original object stacking order.

Solid frame edges indicate that the objects exist on the regular layout page.

8. Using the Type tool, change the date in the frame to July 2020, and change the issue number to 3.

Note:

You could have accomplished the same basic result by editing the text on the master page. However, we created these steps so you can understand the concept of detaching master page objects.

9. Save the file and continue to the next exercise.

Place a PDF File

PDF (Portable Document Format) files save layout, graphics, and font information in a single file. The format was created to facilitate cross-platform file-sharing so one file could be transferred to any other computer, and the final layout would print as intended. While originally meant for Internet use, PDF is now the standard in the graphics industry, used for submitting completed jobs to a service provider.

You can place a PDF file into an InDesign layout just as you would place any other image. You can determine which page to place (if the file contains more than one page), which layers are visible (if the file has more than one layer), and the specific file dimensions (bounding box) to use when placing the file.

1. **With newsletter-july.indd open, navigate to Page 1 of the newsletter.**

2. **Choose File>Place. In the Place dialog box, select spotlight-ad.pdf (in the WIP>Aerospace folder).**

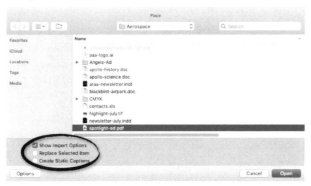

3. **Make sure Show Import Options is checked and Replace Selected Item is not checked, and then click Open.**

The options in the Place PDF dialog box are exactly the same as the options you saw when you placed the native Illustrator file. However, the options in the General tab are typically more important for PDF files than for Illustrator files.

PDF files can contain multiple pages; you can review the various pages using the buttons below the preview image. You can place multiple pages at once by choosing the All option, or you can select specific pages using the Range option. (Import multiple continuous pages by defining a page range, using a hyphen to separate the

Use these buttons to navigate the pages in the PDF file.

first and last pages in the range. Import non-continuous pages by typing each page number, separated by commas.) If you place multiple pages of a PDF file, each page is loaded into the cursor as a separate object.

The Crop To options are also significant when placing PDF files. If the file was created properly, it should include a defined bleed of at least 1/8″ and trim marks to identify the intended trim size.

4. **Choose Bleed in the Crop To menu and click OK.**

Note:

Before placing a PDF file in an InDesign job, make absolutely sure it was created and optimized for commercial printing. Internet-optimized PDF files typically do not have sufficient resolution to print cleanly on a high-resolution output device.

Note:

If you place an Illustrator file that contains multiple artboards, you have the same options for choosing which artboard (page) to place.

5. **Click the loaded cursor in the empty graphics frame at the bottom of Page 1 to place the loaded file.**

6. **Access the placed content by clicking the image with the Direct Selection tool or by clicking the Content Grabber with the Selection tool.**

   When you place the image into the frame, it is automatically centered in the frame; if you look carefully, you can see the text at the bottom of the frame appears very close to the bottom page edge.

   This file was created with 1/8″ bleeds on all four sides. In this context, however, the top bleed allowance is not necessary; the bleed area on the top causes the image to appear farther down than it should. You need to change the graphic's Y position to eliminate all unnecessary bleed at the top of the file.

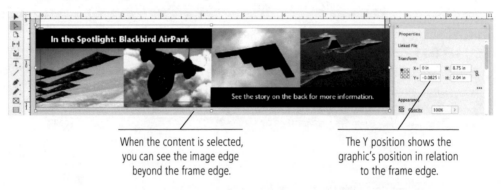

When the content is selected, you can see the image edge beyond the frame edge.

The Y position shows the graphic's position in relation to the frame edge.

7. **With the placed file still selected, make sure the top-left reference point is selected and then change the picture position (within the frame) to Y+: -0.125 in.**

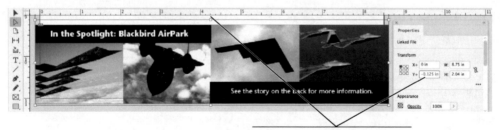

The image bounding box now shows the extra bleed allowance extending beyond the upper edge of the frame.

8. **Save the file and continue to the next exercise.**

Place an InDesign File

In addition to the different types of images, you can also place one InDesign layout directly into another. As with PDF files, you can determine which page is placed (if the file contains more than one page), which layers are visible (if the file has more than one layer), and the specific file dimensions (bounding box) to use when the file is placed.

1. **With newsletter-july.indd open, double-click the Page 2 icon in the Pages panel to navigate to Page 2 of the document. Make sure nothing is selected in the layout.**

2. **Choose File>Place. In the Place dialog box, select angels-ad.indd (in the WIP>Aerospace>Angels-Ad folder). With the Show Import Options box checked, click Open.**

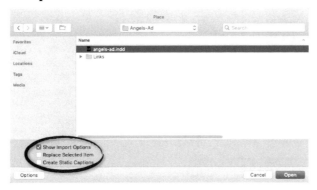

3. **In the General tab of the Place InDesign Document dialog box, choose Bleed Bounding Box in the Crop To menu.**

The options for placing an InDesign file are mostly the same as for placing PDF files; the only exception is the Crop To menu. When you place one InDesign file into another InDesign file, you can place the page(s) based on the defined page, bleed, or slug, as described in the Document Setup dialog box.

4. **Click OK. Read the resulting warning message and click OK.**

To output properly, image links need to be present and up-to-date. Images placed in nested InDesign layouts are still links, so the link requirements apply in those files. (You will fix these problems shortly.)

5. **Click the loaded cursor in the empty graphics frame on the left side of Page 2 to place the file.**

6. **Using the Content Grabber or the Direct Selection tool, click to select the new placed content inside the frame.**

As with PDF files, the bleed areas in an InDesign file might not exactly match the needs of the file where it is placed.

This frame is placed to include the required 1/8″ bleed area, but the placed file is centered in the existing frame area. This means the left edge of the placed content should align to the left edge of the frame.

The left bleed edge of the placed content does not match the left bleed edge of the document.

7. **Change the content's position inside the frame to X+: 0 in.**

The left bleed edge of the placed content now matches the left bleed edge of the document.

8. **Open the Links panel and click the arrow to the left of angels-ad.indd to show the nested images.**

When you place one InDesign file into another, the Links panel also lists images in the placed InDesign file, indented immediately below the placed InDesign file.

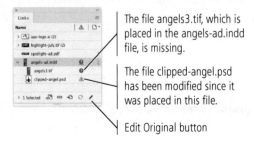

The file angels3.tif, which is placed in the angels-ad.indd file, is missing.

The file clipped-angel.psd has been modified since it was placed in this file.

Edit Original button

9. **Click angels-ad.indd in the Links panel, and then click the Edit Original button.**

   When you open any InDesign file, of course, you are warned if a necessary source file is missing or modified (which you already knew from the Links panel of the newsletter-july.indd file).

Note:

You can also Control/right-click a specific selected image in the layout and choose Edit Original from the contextual menu.

10. **Click Don't Update Links to dismiss the warning message.**

    Edit Original opens the file selected in the Links panel. Because angels-ad.indd is a placed InDesign file, that document opens in a new document window. When the file opens, you see the missing and modified image icons — the reason you are editing the file — in the document and in the Links panel.

The angels-ad.indd file is active.

This icon identifies the missing image.

This icon identifies the modified image.

Note:

If you don't see the Missing and Modified icons, choose View>Extras>Show Link Badge.

11. **Click the Modified icon for the placed image in the ad to update that file.**

12. **Click the Missing icon for the missing image in the layout. Navigate to angels-formation.tif in the WIP>Aerospace>Angels-ad>Links folder and click Open.**

13. **If the Image Import Options dialog box opens, click OK.**

The missing and modified links have now been fixed.

14. **Save the `angels-ad.indd` file and close it.**

    When you save and close the angels-ad.indd file, the Links panel for the newsletter file automatically reflects the new placed file.

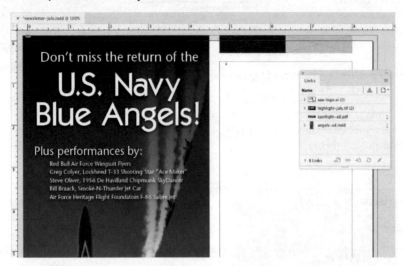

15. **Save `newsletter-july.indd` and continue to the next stage of the project.**

STAGE 2 / Working with Styles

The principles of good design state that headings, subheadings, body copy, and other editorial elements should generally look the same throughout a single job. In other words, editorial elements should be consistent from one page to another, whether the job is two pages or 200.

For any bit of text, there are dozens of character- and paragraph-formatting options, from the font and type size to the space above and below paragraphs. Whenever you work with longer blocks of copy, you'll apply the same group of formatting options to multiple pieces of text.

If you were to change each element manually, you would have to make hundreds of clicks to create a two-page newsletter. Fortunately, InDesign makes it easy to store groups of formatting options as **styles**, which can be applied with a single click.

The major advantages of using styles are ease of use and enhanced efficiency. Styles ensure consistency in text formatting throughout a publication; rather than trying to remember how you formatted a sidebar 45 pages ago, for example, you can simply apply a predefined Sidebar style. Changes can be made instantly to all text defined as a particular style (for example, changing the font in the Subhead style from Helvetica to Myriad); when a style definition changes, any text using that style automatically changes, too.

InDesign supports both character styles and paragraph styles. **Character styles** apply only to selected words; this type of style is useful for setting off a few words in a paragraph without affecting the entire paragraph. **Paragraph styles** apply to the entire body of text between two ¶ symbols; this type of style defines the appearance of the paragraph, combining the character style used in the paragraph with line spacing, indents, tabs, and other paragraph attributes.

In this project, the client's original template included a number of styles for formatting the text in each issue. Because the text frames already exist in the template layout, you only need to import the client's text and apply the existing styles.

Note:

Paragraph styles define character attributes and paragraph attributes; character styles define only the character attributes. In other words, a paragraph style can be used to format text entirely, including font information, line spacing, tabs, and so on.

Working with Microsoft Word Files

Microsoft Word files can include a fairly sophisticated level of formatting attributes, from basic text formatting to defined paragraph and character styles to automatically generated tables of contents. When you import a Word file into InDesign, you can determine whether to include these elements in the imported text.

You can use options in the **Include** section to import tables of contents, index text, footnotes, and endnotes that exist in the Word file.

If **Use Typographer's Quotes** is checked, quote marks in the Word file will be converted to typographically correct "curly" quotes in InDesign.

In the Formatting section, you can check the option to **Remove Styles and Formatting from Text and Styles** to import a file as plain text, with none of the Word-applied formatting maintained. When you place the file in InDesign, it is formatted with the [Basic Paragraph] style that defines the default appearance of text in a layout (12-pt black Minion Pro by default).

If **Preserve Styles and Formatting from Text and Tables** is active, you can choose a number of additional options related to translation between Microsoft Word and InDesign.

The **Manual Page Breaks** menu determines how page breaks in Word translate to InDesign. You can preserve them, convert them to column breaks, or ignore them.

If graphics have been placed into a Word file, **Import Inline Graphics** allows you to include those graphics as anchored objects in the InDesign story. It is important to understand that these graphics will likely be embedded into the story instead of linked to the original data file.

If you choose **Import Unused Styles**, all styles in the Word file will be imported into the InDesign layout. The most significant issue here is that styles might require fonts that you have not installed.

Word includes a collaboration tool called **Track Changes**, which allows one person to review another person's changes to a file. If you check the Track Changes option, any tracked changes from the Word file will be included in your InDesign layout. This can cause a lot of items to show up in your text that aren't supposed to be there (corrected typos, for example).

Convert Bullets & Numbers to Text allows you to convert automatically generated numbering and bullet characters into actual text characters.

The **Style Name Conflicts** area warns you if styles in the Word file conflict with styles in the InDesign file. In other words, they have the same style names but different definitions. You have to determine how to resolve these conflicts.

Import Styles Automatically allows you to choose how to handle conflicts in paragraph and character styles.

- **Use InDesign Style Definition** preserves the style as you defined it; text in the Word file that uses that style is reformatted with the InDesign definition of the style.

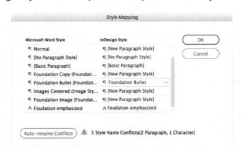

- **Redefine InDesign Style** replaces the layout definition with the definition from the Word file.

- **Auto Rename** adds the Word file to the InDesign file with "_wrd_1" at the end of the style name.

If you choose **Customize Style Import**, the Style Mapping button opens a dialog box where you can review and control specific style conflicts. Click an option in the InDesign Style column to access a menu where you can choose which InDesign style to use in place of a specific Word style.

If you always receive Microsoft Word files from the same source, you can save your choices (including Style Mapping options) as a preset or click the Set as Default button in the Import Options dialog box.

Apply Template Styles

Most InDesign jobs incorporate some amount of client-supplied text, which might be sent to you in the body of an email or saved in any number of text file formats. Many text files will be supplied from Microsoft Word, which includes fairly extensive options for formatting text (although not quite as robust or sophisticated as InDesign). Many Microsoft Word users apply **local formatting** (selecting specific text and applying character and/or paragraph attributes); more sophisticated Microsoft Word users build text formatting styles similar to those used in InDesign.

1. **With `newsletter-july.indd` open, double-click the Page 1 icon in the Pages panel to make that page active in the document window.**

2. **Choose File>Place and navigate to the file `apollo-history.doc`.**

   All text files for this project are in the WIP>Aerospace folder; we will not continue to repeat the entire path for each file.

3. **Check the Show Import Options box at the bottom of the dialog box and make sure Replace Selected Item is not checked. Click Open.**

4. **In the resulting dialog box, make sure the Preserve Styles and Formatting option is selected and the Import Styles Automatically radio button is selected. Choose Auto Rename in both conflict menus and then click OK.**

   When you import a Microsoft Word file into InDesign, you can either preserve or remove formatting saved in the Microsoft Word file (including styles defined in Microsoft Word).

Make sure this option is selected.

Choose Auto Rename in both of these menus.

5. **If you get a Missing Font warning, click Close.**

   You're going to replace the Microsoft Word formatting with InDesign styles, which will correct any problems of this sort.

6. **Click the loaded cursor in the empty three-column text frame.**

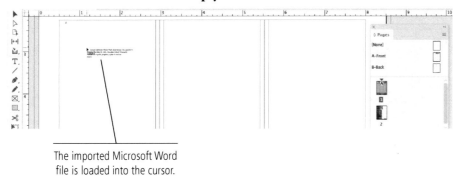

The imported Microsoft Word
file is loaded into the cursor.

At this point, the story does not fit into the frame because you haven't yet applied the
appropriate styles to the imported text.

Overset text icon

7. **Open the Paragraph Styles panel (Window>Styles>Paragraph Styles).**

8. **Place the insertion point in the first paragraph of the imported story (the
main heading) and look at the Paragraph Styles panel.**

The imported text appears to be preformatted, but the Paragraph Styles panel tells a
different story. This paragraph is formatted as "Normal+."

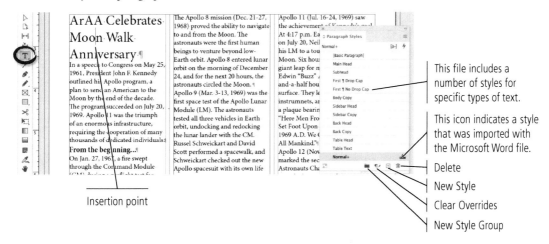

Insertion point

This file includes a
number of styles for
specific types of text.

This icon indicates a style
that was imported with
the Microsoft Word file.

Delete

New Style

Clear Overrides

New Style Group

When you imported the Microsoft Word file, you preserved the formatting in the file;
this is usually a good idea so you can see what the writer intended. Now that the text
is imported into your layout, however, you want to apply the template styles to make
the text in this issue consistent with other issues.

When you import text into InDesign, any number of new styles might appear in the
Styles panels; the most common imported style is Normal. Text in a Microsoft Word
file is typically formatted with the Normal style, even if you don't realize it; user-
applied formatting is commonly local (meaning it is applied directly to selected text
instead of with a defined style).

9. **With the insertion point still in place, click the Main Head style in the Paragraph Styles panel.**

A number of styles existed in the original newsletter template, so they also exist in any files based on that template. You should be able to guess the purpose of these styles from their names; it's always a good idea to use indicative names when you create styles or other user-defined assets.

Using styles, you can change all formatting attributes of selected text with a single click. Because you are working with paragraph styles, the style definition applies to the entire paragraph where the insertion point is placed.

The Main Head style has been applied to the active paragraph.

10. **Place the insertion point in the next paragraph of copy, then click the First ¶ Drop Cap style in the Paragraph Styles panel.**

11. **Format the next paragraph ("From the beginning...") with the Subhead style.**

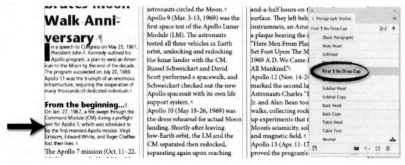

12. **Format the next paragraph with the First ¶ No Drop Cap style.**

13. **Select any part of the next four paragraphs (up to but not including the "Mission Accomplished" paragraph), then click the Body Copy style in the Paragraph Styles panel.**

Paragraph styles apply to any paragraph partially or entirely selected. You don't have to select an entire paragraph before applying a paragraph style.

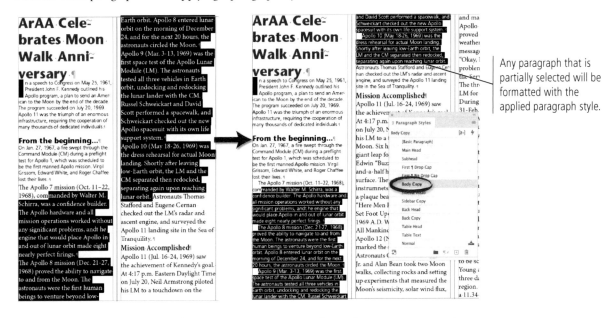

Any paragraph that is partially selected will be formatted with the applied paragraph style.

14. **Continue applying styles to the remaining copy; use the style names as a guide.**

Some text in the story will be overset until you apply the required paragraph styles; as you format each paragraph, more of the story will be visible. When all paragraphs are formatted, the entire story fits into the frame.

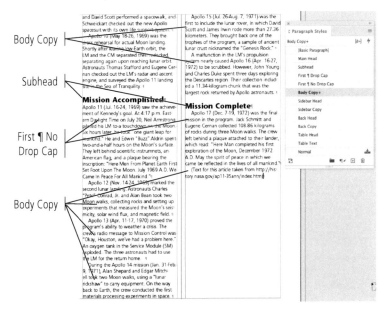

15. **Save the file and continue to the next exercise.**

Manage Local Formatting Overrides

Local formatting overrides — formatting outside the definition of the applied paragraph style — are common, especially when importing text from external sources such as Microsoft Word. This is usually caused by formatting options in the word-processing application not supported by InDesign. It is important to realize that if a paragraph includes local formatting, simply clicking a new style name might not work perfectly. You should be aware that you often need to clear overrides in the imported text before the InDesign style is properly applied.

1. **With newsletter-july.indd open, place the insertion point in the last paragraph of body copy on Page 1.**

2. **Look at the Paragraph Styles panel.**

   The Body Copy style, which you applied to the active paragraph, shows a + next to the style name. This indicates formatting other than what is defined in the style has been applied to the selected text (called a **local formatting override**).

   The insertion point should be in this paragraph.

   The plus sign indicates that some formatting other than the style definition has been applied.

3. **In the Paragraph Styles panel, click the Style Override Highlighter button.**

   In some cases, the override is fairly obvious (for example, a different applied font). In other cases, such as this one, the overrides are not always so easy to spot.

   Style Override Highlighter toggle

   All text with local formatting overrides is highlighted in the layout.

   The Style Override Highlighter button toggles this feature on and off, so you can quickly and visually identify text where formatting outside the style definition has been applied.

4. **With the insertion point in the last paragraph of body copy, click the Clear Overrides in Selection button at the bottom of the Paragraph Styles panel.**

   The **Clear Overrides in Selection** button removes local formatting not defined in the applied style. (As the name suggests, it only applies to *selected* text.)

   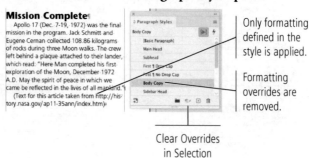

   Only formatting defined in the style is applied.

   Formatting overrides are removed.

   Clear Overrides in Selection

5. **Highlight the last paragraph of body copy, then change the Font Style menu to Italic.**

6. **Click to place the insertion point anywhere in the last paragraph, removing the highlighting.**

   In many cases, local formatting overrides are intentional. As you can see here, the Override Highlighting again appears in the layout as soon as you change the Font Style to something not defined in the Body Copy paragraph style.

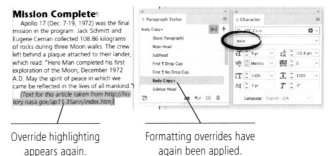

Override highlighting appears again.

Formatting overrides have again been applied.

7. **In the Paragraph Styles panel, click the Style Override Highlighter button to toggle the feature off.**

8. **Save the file and continue to the next exercise.**

 ## Edit a Paragraph to Span Columns

As a general rule, headlines in newsletters and newspapers extend across the top of the entire related story. In previous versions of the software, this required a separate frame spanning the width of the multicolumn body frame. InDesign includes a paragraph formatting option that makes it easy to span a paragraph across multiple columns *without* the need for a separate frame. This can be applied to individual paragraphs or defined as part of a paragraph style.

1. **With newsletter-july.indd open, make sure Page 1 is active.**

2. **Place the insertion point in the first paragraph of the story (the main head) and then open the Paragraph panel (Window>Type & Tables>Paragraph).**

3. **With the insertion point still in the same paragraph, open the Paragraph panel Options menu and choose Span Columns.**

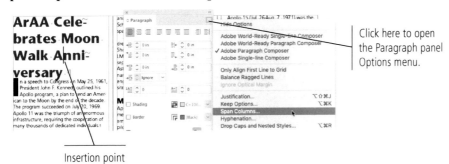

Insertion point

Click here to open the Paragraph panel Options menu.

4. **Click the Preview option on the right side of the dialog box, then choose Span Columns in the Paragraph Layout menu.**

   When the Preview option is active, you can see the result of your choices before you finalize them.

Note:

Items in the Paragraphs panel Options menu are also available in the Control panel Options menu when the insertion point is placed or when text is selected.

5. **Make sure the Span field is set to All.**

   You can use the Span field to extend a paragraph over only a certain number of columns.

6. **Click the Up Arrow button once for the Space After Span field.**

   The Space Before and Space After fields determine how much space is placed between the span paragraph and the paragraphs above or below. The arrow buttons increase or decrease the related values by 0.0625″. (This is the same concept used in the Space Above and Space Below options for regular paragraph formatting.)

Note:

The Split Column option can be used to divide a specific paragraph into multiple columns within a frame's defined column.

7. **Click OK to finalize your changes.**

8. **Save the file and continue to the next exercise.**

 ## Control Automatic Text Frame Size

Many page layouts have a primary story, as well as related stories called **sidebars**. These elements are not always linked to the main story and are often placed in their own boxes with different formatting to draw attention.

1. **On Page 1 of newsletter-july.indd, create a new text frame with the following dimensions (based on the top-left reference point):**

X: 5 in	W: 3.625 in
Y: 7 in	H: 2 in

   To create the new text frame, begin by clicking and dragging outside the boundaries of the existing frames. You can then select the new frame with the Selection tool and use the Control or Properties panel to define the frame's position and size.

2. **Fill the text frame with a 20% tint of Pantone 194 C.**

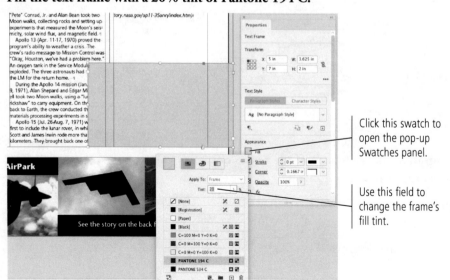

Click this swatch to open the pop-up Swatches panel.

Use this field to change the frame's fill tint.

3. **Choose File>Place. Select `apollo-science.doc`, uncheck the Show Import Options box, then click Open. Click Close if you get a Missing Font warning.**

4. **Click the loaded cursor inside the tinted frame you just created.**

Because you turned off the Show Import Options box in the Place dialog box, the file is imported with the last-used import options. In this case, the formatting is maintained, styles are imported, and conflicting styles are automatically renamed — resulting in the new Normal_wrd_1 style, which conflicted with the previously imported Normal style.

You should notice several problems with the imported text:

- The frame is not large enough to show all text in the story.
- Surrounding text runs under the sidebar frame.
- Placed text in the sidebar frame runs into the edge of the containing frame.

Amateur designers often create three separate elements to achieve the desired effect, which adds an unnecessary degree of complexity to the layout. You will fix each of these problems by changing the options for the single sidebar text frame.

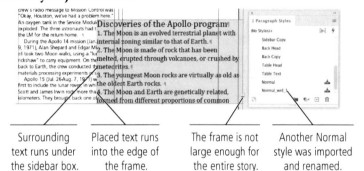

Surrounding text runs under the sidebar box.

Placed text runs into the edge of the frame.

The frame is not large enough for the entire story.

Another Normal style was imported and renamed.

5. **Select the sidebar frame with the Selection tool, then locate the Text Frame options in the Properties panel.**

6. **Click the Options button to open the Text Frame Options dialog box.**

You can also choose Object>Text Frame Options or press Command/Control-B to open the Text Frame Options dialog box. (If the Type tool is active, the Text Frame Options dialog box opens for the frame where the insertion point is placed.)

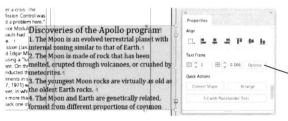

Click this button to open the Text Frame Options dialog box.

7. **On the left side of the dialog box, click Auto-Size to show those options. Make sure the Preview option is checked at the bottom of the dialog box.**

Auto-size options allow a text frame to expand or shrink as necessary to fit the contained text. You are going to use these options to dynamically change the sidebar box to fit the entire story, regardless of formatting options.

8. **On the right side of the dialog box, choose Height Only in the Auto-Sizing menu and choose the bottom-center reference point.**

   The reference points determine which point will remain fixed when the box changes size. In this case, you want the bottom edge to remain in place, so you are choosing the bottom reference point. Because you are only allowing the box's height to change, the left and right reference points are not available.

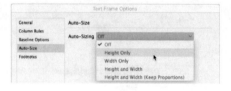

   You can also use the Constraints options to define a minimum height and width — in other words, the smallest possible size the frame can be. If you allow the frame to change width, you can check the No Line Breaks option to enlarge the frame as much as necessary to fit the entire text on one line.

The frame height increases to accommodate the entire story.

The bottom edge of the frame remains in place.

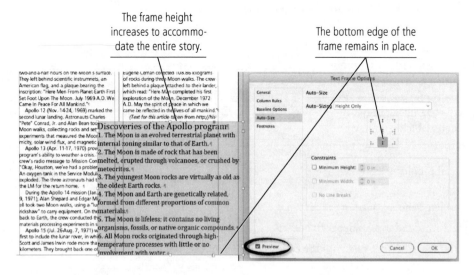

9. **Click OK to apply your changes.**

10. **Format the first line of the sidebar with the Sidebar Head style, and format the rest of the text in this frame using the Sidebar Copy style.**

    The type sizes in the applied styles are considerably smaller, which requires less space for the sidebar. As you can see, the Auto-Size feature shrinks the height of the frame as necessary to exactly fit the contained text.

The frame height shrinks because the new formatting requires less space.

11. **Save the file and continue to the next exercise.**

Edit Text Inset and Wrap Settings

A number of frame attributes can affect the appearance of text both within and around a text frame. In this exercise, you adjust the text inset and text wrap to force text into the proper position.

1. **With newsletter-july.indd open, select the sidebar box with the Selection tool and then open the Text Frame Options dialog box again.**

2. **With the Preview option checked and the General options visible in the dialog box, make sure the chain icon for the Inset Spacing fields is active.**

   Like the same chain icon in other dialog boxes, this forces all four inset values to the same value.

3. **Change the Top Inset field to 0.125 in, and then press Tab to move the highlight and apply the new Inset Spacing value to all four fields.**

   Text inset spacing is the distance text is moved from the inside edge of its containing frame. You can define different values for each edge, or you can constrain all four edges to a single value.

Note:

If you check the Ignore Text Wrap option in the Text Frame Options dialog box, the frame is not affected by wrap attributes of overlapping objects.

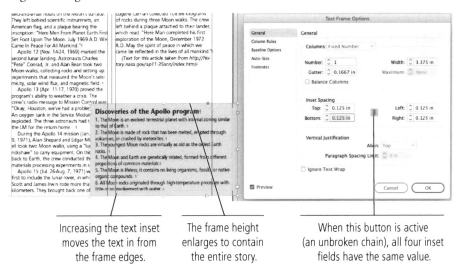

Increasing the text inset moves the text in from the frame edges.

The frame height enlarges to contain the entire story.

When this button is active (an unbroken chain), all four inset fields have the same value.

4. **Click the Chain icon in the Inset Spacing area to break the link, then change the Right field to 0.625 in.**

   The different right inset value accommodates for the right page margin.

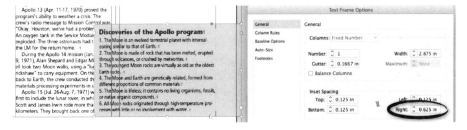

5. **Click OK to close the dialog box and apply your choices.**

6. **With the sidebar frame selected, click the second button from the left in the Text Wrap panel (Window>Text Wrap).**

   Text wrap is the distance around the edge of an object where surrounding text will flow.

7. **Make sure the chain icon is active so all four offset values are the same. Change the Top Offset field to 0.1875 in, then press Tab to apply the value.**

   Clicking the up- or down-arrow buttons changes the offset values by 0.0625″ for each click. Because the fields are linked, you could click the up-arrow button for any field to increase all four values by 0.1875″.

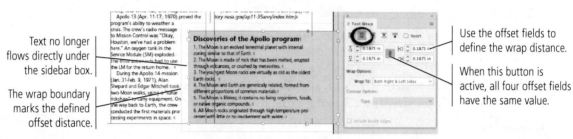

Text no longer flows directly under the sidebar box.

The wrap boundary marks the defined offset distance.

Use the offset fields to define the wrap distance.

When this button is active, all four offset fields have the same value.

8. **Save the file and continue to the next exercise.**

Understanding Text Wrap Options

InDesign provides five options for wrapping text around an object; wrap attributes are controlled in the Text Wrap panel.

A **No Text Wrap** allows text to run directly under the object.

B **Wrap Around Bounding Box** creates a straight-edged wrap around all four sides of the object's bounding box.

C **Wrap Around Object Shape** creates a wrap in the shape of the object. You can define which contour to use in the Contour Options menu:

- **Bounding Box** creates the boundary based on the object's bounding box.
- **Detect Edges** creates the boundary using the same detection options you use to create a clipping path.
- **Alpha Channel** creates the boundary from an Alpha channel saved in the placed image.
- **Photoshop Path** creates the boundary from a path saved in the placed image.
- **Graphic Frame** creates the boundary from the containing frame.
- **Same as Clipping** creates the boundary from a clipping path saved in the placed image.
- **User-Modified Path** appears by default if you drag the anchor points of the text wrap boundary.

D **Jump Object** keeps text from appearing to the right or left of the frame.

E **Jump to Next Column** forces surrounding text to the top of the next column or frame.

Regardless of which wrap you apply, you can define the offset value (the distance that any surrounding text will remain away from the object). If you use the Object Shape wrap, you can define only a single offset value; for the other types, you can define a different offset for each edge.

If you use the Bounding Box or Object Shape wrap option, you can also define the Wrap To options — whether the wrap is applied to a specific side (right, left, right and left, or the largest side) or toward or away from the spine.

By default, text wrap attributes affect all overlapping objects, regardless of stacking order; you can turn this behavior off by checking the Text Wrap Only Affects Text Beneath option in the Composition pane of the Preferences dialog box.

Format Numbered and Bulleted Lists

Many page-layout projects include lists, such as resources referenced in an article, people involved in planning an event, ingredients in a recipe, or steps to take in accomplishing a specific task. InDesign includes the ability to easily format both bulleted and numbered lists. You will use both of these options in this exercise.

1. **With newsletter-july.indd open, select all but the first paragraph in the sidebar on Page 1.**

2. **In the Properties panel, locate the Bullets and Numbering section and click the Numbered List button (the second one).**

    When you apply a numbered list, sequential numbers are automatically added to the beginning of each selected paragraph. The added number characters are not selected because they do not technically exist as characters in the text.

    Original numbers in the numbered paragraphs are still in place because they are simply characters in the imported text.

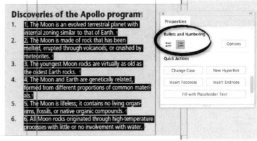

3. **Click the Options button in the Properties panel to open the Bullets and Numbering dialog box.**

    The Numbering Style section of the dialog box defines how numbers appear:

    • **Format** determines what type of numbers are used (Arabic numbers, Roman numerals, etc.).

    • **Number** defines the format of the list numbers; the default is "number, period, tab" (^# and ^t are the special character codes for the list number and the tab character, respectively.)

    • **Character Style** applies a defined style to characters in the paragraph number. Other characters in the paragraph are not affected.

    • **Mode** determines how a paragraph is numbered, whether it continues from the previous numbered paragraph or begins at a specific number.

    • If you have more than one level of list items, you can use the **Restart Numbers...** option to reset the numbering each time you begin a new list level.

In the Bullet or Number Position section, The **Alignment** menu defines how numbers in a list align to one another. This is especially useful for aligning the periods in a regular numbered list of more than nine items, or in a list using certain numbering formats with different numbers of characters in each number (such as Roman numerals):

Left	Center	Right	Left	Center	Right
8.	8.	8.	vii	vii	vii
9.	9.	9.	viii	viii	viii
10.	10.	10.	ix	ix	ix

The **Left Indent** and **First Line Indent** fields define the appearance of the bullet or number character in relation to the rest of the paragraph. A negative first-line indent moves the first line to the left of other lines in the same paragraph, sometimes called a **hanging indent**. When applied to a numbered list, the negative first-line indent defines the position of the number character(s) relative to the actual text in each list item.

When you define a negative first-line indent, the **Tab Position** field is cleared. The left-indent value becomes the default first tab position and the position of text immediately following the number character(s).

4. **In the Bullet or Number Position section, change the First Line Indent field to -0.125 in, then change the Left Indent field to 0.125 in.**

You have to change the First Line Indent field first because you cannot define a left indent smaller than the first-line indent.

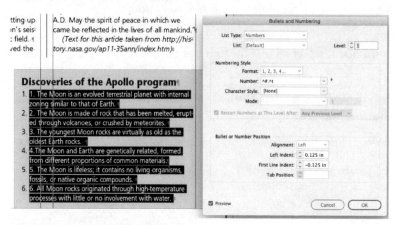

Note:

You can use the Level menu at the top of the dialog box to create nested lists. For example, you could create a list of departments in a business, then create secondary lists after each department to show the hierarchy of employees in each department:

1. Marketing
*   a. Harry*
*   b. Ron*
*   c. Julia*
2. Production
*   a. Roger*
*   b. Edward*
*   c. Caitlyn*
3. Administration
*   a. Stephanie*
*   b. Justin*
*   c. Betty*

5. **Click OK to finalize the list formatting and return to the layout.**

6. **Delete the extra numbers, periods, and spaces from the beginning of each list item.**

7. **Navigate to Page 2 of the layout and make sure nothing is selected.**

8. **Choose File>Place. Select blackbird-airpark.doc, uncheck the Show Import Options box, then click Open. Click Close if you get a Missing Font warning.**

9. **Click the loaded cursor within the margin guides on the right side of Page 2.**

10. **Format the first paragraph with the Back Head style, and format the remaining copy with the Back Copy style.**

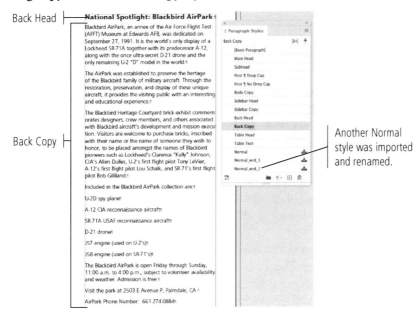

Back Head

Back Copy

Another Normal style was imported and renamed.

Note:

You can convert list characters (including bullets or paragraph numbers) by choosing Type>Bullets and Numbering>Convert Bullets and Numbering to Text.

11. **Select the six paragraphs as shown in the following image. In the Properties panel, click the Bulleted List button.**

12. **Click the Options button in the Properties panel to open the Bullets and Numbering dialog box.**

13. **In the Bullet Character section, choose the small star character.**

In addition to the options you saw for numbered lists, you can also choose the specific glyph to use as the bullet character. InDesign includes several common bullet characters by default; you can click the Add button to add different characters from any available font.

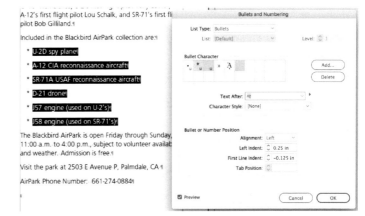

14. **In the Bullet or Number Position section, change the First Line Indent field to -0.125 in.**

Keep in mind that you can't define a negative First Line Indent unless the Left Indent field is greater than 0. Because the Left Indent field defaults to 0.25 in, you can simply change the First Line Indent field.

15. **Click OK to close the dialog box and return to the document window.**

16. **Save the file and continue to the next stage of the project.**

STAGE 3 / Working with Tables

Many page layouts incorporate tables of information, from basic tables with a few rows and columns to multipage catalog spreadsheets with thousands of product numbers and prices. InDesign includes a number of options for building tables directly in a page layout.

If the insertion point is placed in an existing text frame, you can create a new table by choosing Table>Insert Table. If the insertion point is not placed, you can choose Table>Create Table. These methods allow you to define your own table parameters, including the number of rows and columns, the number of header and footer rows (top and bottom rows appearing in every instance of the table if the table breaks across multiple columns or frames), and even a defined style for the new table (table styles store formatting options such as gridline weight and other attributes that you will learn about in this stage of the project). Using the Insert Table command, the new table is placed at the current insertion point. Using the Create Table command, the resulting table is loaded into the Place cursor; you can click and drag to create the text frame and place the loaded table.

You can also create a table by selecting a series of tab-delimited text in the layout and choosing Table>Convert Text to Table. (Tab-delimited means the content of each column is separated by a tab character.) Using this method, the new table becomes an inline object in the text frame that contained the original text.

Finally, you can create a new table by placing a file created in Microsoft Excel (the most common application for creating spreadsheets). You'll use this method to complete this stage of the newsletter project.

Working with the Tables Panel

The Table panel provides access to a number of options for formatting table cells.

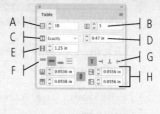

A **Number of Rows** is the existing number of rows in the table. You can change the value to add new rows to the bottom of the table or subtract rows from the bottom of the table. If you subtract rows, you will be asked to confirm the deletion.

B **Number of Columns** is the existing number of columns in the table. You can change the value to add new columns to the right side of the table or subtract columns from the right side of the table. If you subtract columns, you will be asked to confirm the deletion.

C **Row Height (type)** determines whether a row's height is exact or based on a minimum height. If At Least is chosen in the menu, a row's height can expand or shrink to the defined minimum to accommodate text in the cells.

D **Row Height (value)** is the numeric height of the table row. If At Least is selected in the related menu, this field defined the minimum possible row height.

E **Column Width** is the width of the active table column.

F **Vertical Cell Alignment** controls the top-to-bottom position of text in a table cell. From left to right:
 – Align Top
 – Align Center
 – Align Bottom
 – Justify Vertically

G **Text Rotation** rotates text clockwise within a cell. From left to right:
 – Rotate text 0°
 – Rotate text 90°
 – Rotate text 180°
 – Rotate text 270°

H **Cell Insets** have the same effect as Inset Spacing for a regular text frame; they move table text in from cell edges.

Place a Microsoft Excel Table

Microsoft Excel spreadsheets can be short tables of text or complex, multi-page spreadsheets of data. In either case, Microsoft Excel users tend to spend hours formatting their spreadsheets for business applications. Those formatting options are typically not appropriate for commercial printing applications, but they give you a better starting point in your InDesign file than working from plain tabbed text.

1. **With newsletter-july.indd open, navigate to Page 2. Click the pasteboard area to make sure nothing is selected.**

2. **Choose File>Place and navigate to the file contacts.xls in the WIP>Aerospace folder.**

3. **Uncheck the Replace Selected Item option, make sure Show Import Options is checked, and click Open.**

4. **Review the options in the resulting dialog box. Make sure your options match what is shown in the following image, and then click OK.**

Note:

If you see a warning about missing fonts, click OK; you're going to reformat the table text shortly.

5. **With the table loaded into the cursor, click in the pasteboard area to the right of Page 2 (near the top of the page edge).**

This table will eventually occupy the empty space in the bottom-right corner of Page 2. You are simply using the pasteboard as a temporary workspace.

When you place a table into a layout, a text frame is automatically created to contain the table. The new frame matches the width of the defined page margins, regardless of the actual table width. If the page has multiple columns defined, the frame matches the defined column width.

The pasteboard outside the page area is a good temporary workspace.

Imported tables are automatically placed in a text frame.

Obviously this table needs some significant modification to make it a cohesive part of the newsletter layout. Some placed tables require more work than others; be prepared to do at least some clean-up work whenever you place a spreadsheet or table.

6. **Select the Type tool and click in the top-left cell of the table.**

You can use the Type tool to select table cells individually or as entire rows/columns.

Note:

If you select the text frame containing a table, you can choose Object>Fitting>Fit Frame to Content to match the text frame dimensions to the table contained in the frame.

7. **Move the cursor to the top-left corner of the table. When you see a diagonal pointing arrow, click to select the entire table.**

The heavy diagonal arrow indicates that clicking will select the entire table.

The insertion point must be placed in the table to access the selection cursors.

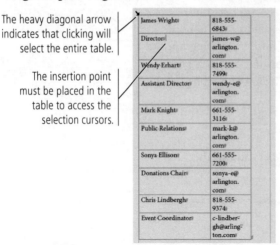

After clicking, all cells in the table are selected.

8. **Click Table Text in the Paragraph Styles panel to format all the text in the selected table cells.**

When you work with tables in InDesign, think of the table cells as a series of text frames. Text in a table cell is no different from text in any other text frame; it can be formatted using the same options you've already learned, including with paragraph and character styles.

9. **Click any cell to deselect all table cells.**

10. **Save the file and continue to the next exercise.**

 ## Format Cell Attributes

As we mentioned in the previous exercise, table cells are very similar to regular text frames. Individual cells can have different attributes such as height and width, text inset, vertical positioning, and text orientation.

1. **With newsletter-july.indd open, click in the top-left cell of the table with the Type tool.**

2. **Place the cursor over the top edge of the first column of the table. When you see a down-pointing arrow, click to select the entire column.**

You can also select rows by placing the cursor immediately to the left of a row and clicking when the cursor changes to a right-facing arrow.

The down-pointing arrow means clicking will select the entire column.

3. **Open the Table panel (Window>Type & Tables>Table).**

4. **With the left column selected, change the Column Width field to 1.25 in.**

   Resizing the width of a cell resizes the entire column; resizing the height of a cell resizes the entire row.

   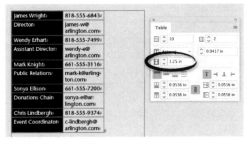

   You don't need to select the entire column to change its width. However, in the next step you are going to change the height of each row; you are selecting all cells in the column now, so they will all be affected by the height change in the next step.

5. **Choose Exactly in the Row Height menu, then change the field to 0.235 in.**

   Table row height uses the At Least method by default, which means they expand or shrink (down to the defined minimum) to accommodate whatever text exists in the cells.

   Because you defined a row height using the Exactly method, the row height is now a specific value; the email addresses in the right column no longer fit into the existing cell width, as you can see from the overset text icons in every other cell.

6. **Click to place the insertion point in any cell in the right column.**

   The column does not need to be selected to change its width by dragging or using the field in the Table panel.

7. **Place the cursor over the right edge of the second column until the cursor becomes a two-headed arrow.**

   When you see this cursor, you can drag the gridline to resize a column or row.

8. **Click and drag right until all of the overset text icons are gone.**

   You have to release the mouse button to see the results. If you still see the overset text icons after you release the mouse button, click and drag the edge again until the overset text icons are gone.

   The two-headed arrow means you can drag to resize a row or column.

Note:

When the insertion point is placed in a table cell, press the Escape key to select the active cell.

Note:

When working with tables in InDesign, pressing Tab moves the insertion point from one table cell to the next (from left to right, top to bottom). This means you can't press Tab to insert a tab character into text in an InDesign table; you have to choose Type>Insert Special Character>Other>Tab.

Note:

You can press the Shift key while dragging a gridline to resize a row or column without affecting the overall table size; only the rows or columns next to the gridline you drag are resized.

9. **Place the insertion point in any cell in the left column, then choose Table>Insert>Column.**

The insertion point should be placed in any cell in the first column.

10. **In the resulting dialog box, make sure the Number field is set to 1 and choose the Left option.**

11. **Click OK to return to the table.**

As you can see, one new column is added to the left of the previous selection.

12. **Place the insertion point in the top cell of the new column and type ArAA CONTACTS.**

13. **Click Table Head in the Paragraph Styles panel to format the new text.**

The overset text icon shows the text, with the Table Head formatting applied, does not fit into the cell.

14. **Select the entire first column in the table. In the Properties panel, locate the Cell Divisions options and click the Merge Cells button.**

This function extends the contents of a single cell across multiple cells. You can also choose Table>Merge Cells or use the same command in the Table panel Options menu.

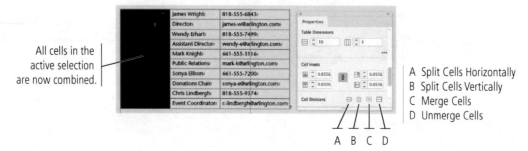

All cells in the active selection are now combined.

A Split Cells Horizontally
B Split Cells Vertically
C Merge Cells
D Unmerge Cells

A B C D

15. **Click to place the insertion point in the merged table cell. In the Table panel, click the Rotate 270° button.**

The Text Rotation buttons rotate text clockwise within a cell. Icons on each button indicate the resulting orientation of text in the selected cells.

16. **Click the top cell of the second column, hold down the mouse button, and drag down to also select the second cell in that column.**

You can use the click-and-drag method to select any range of consecutive cells, including cells in more than one row or column.

17. **Click the Merge Cells button in the Properties panel.**

When you merge cells, the content in each merged cell is combined into the merged cell. Each cell's content is separated by a paragraph return.

Click here...

...then drag to here.

18. **Repeat Steps 16–17 for the other name/title cells in the second column.**

19. **Select all cells in the table, then click the Align Center vertical alignment button in the Table panel.**

Because the text in the left column is rotated, this option actually aligns the text between the left and right cell edges. It is important to remember the vertical align options are based on the orientation of the text.

20. **Save the file and continue to the next exercise.**

Manage a Table as an Anchored Character

Tables in InDesign are always contained in a text frame. The table itself is an anchored object inside the story and is treated as a single character in the text frame's story. Rather than using multiple frames to contain different elements in the newsletter layout, you are going to move the table into the story on Page 2 of the existing layout.

1. **With newsletter-july.indd open, make sure the Type tool is active.**

2. **Click inside the text frame that contains the table; click below the actual table.**

   This places the insertion point in the frame but not in the table.

3. **Press Command/Control-A to select everything in the text frame.**

   The table is placed in the frame, but it exists as a single character in that frame (just like anchored graphics).

The character representing the table is selected.

4. **Press Command/Control-X to cut the selected element and store it in the clipboard.**

5. **Click with the Type tool to place the insertion point in the last paragraph on Page 2 of the newsletter layout.**

   The end-of-story character appears on its own line, indicating an empty paragraph exists after the paragraph with the phone number. You should place the insertion point in that empty paragraph

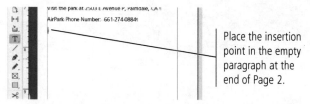

Place the insertion point in the empty paragraph at the end of Page 2.

6. **Press Command/Control-V to paste the table you cut in Step 4. If necessary, drag down the bottom-center handle of the containing text frame until the table is visible.**

If necessary, extend the containing frame's height to fit the table.

7. **Using the Type tool, click to place the insertion point in any cell in the table.**

8. **Place the cursor over the right edge of the left column, then click and drag until the right edge of the table matches the margin guide. If you see an overset text icon in the cell, drag the edge slightly right until the icon is gone.**

   It's a good idea to make a table fit into the overall layout. In this case you are adjusting the table to better match the margin guides on the page where it is placed.

Drag the right edge of the left column.

Watch the right edge of the table to see when it aligns to the margin guide.

9. **Place the cursor over the bottom edge of the bottom row, then click and drag until the bottom edge of the table matches the margin guide.**

   When you reduce the height of the final row, two things happen. First, the text in the bottom-right cell no longer fits into the adjusted cell height. Second, the rows are no longer the same height, which looks like an error.

Drag up the bottom edge of the last row.

The last row is no longer the same height as other rows.

Text no longer fits based on the adjusted row height.

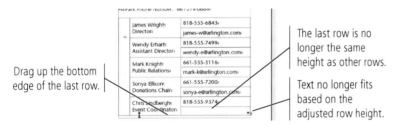

10. **Select the entire right column, then choose Table>Distribute Rows Evenly.**

    This command calculates the overall height of the selection, then divides that space evenly over all selected rows; the height of the overall table does not change. All rows in the selection now have the same height, and all text fits into the adjusted row height.

All rows are again the same height.

Text now fits into the adjusted row height.

    If more than one column is selected, you can choose Table>Distribute Columns Evenly to make multiple columns the same width.

11. **Using the Selection tool, click the empty frame on the pasteboard to select it, then press Delete/Backspace.**

    Although not strictly necessary, it's a good idea to remove unnecessary elements from the file, including the pasteboard around the actual layout pages.

12. **Save the file and continue to the next exercise.**

Define Table Fills and Strokes

Like text frames, table cells can have fill and stroke attributes. InDesign includes a number of options for adding color to tables, from changing the stroke and fill of an individual cell to defining patterns that repeat over a certain number of rows or columns.

1. **With newsletter-july.indd open, place the insertion point anywhere in the table on Page 2. Open the Table panel Options menu and choose Table Options>Table Setup.**

Note:

You can also choose Table>Table Options> Table Setup to access this dialog box.

2. **In the Table Setup tab, apply a 0.5-pt solid border of 100% Pantone 194 C.**

3. **In the Fills tab, choose Every Second Row in the Alternating Pattern menu. Set the First field to 2 rows and apply 20% Pantone 194 C. Set the Next field to 2 rows and apply None as the color.**

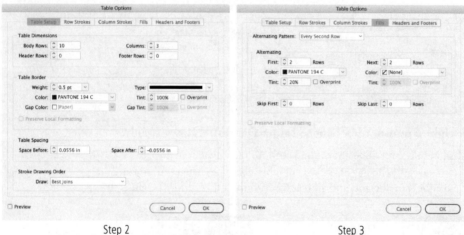

Step 2   Step 3

4. **Click OK to apply your choices.**

   When frame edges are visible, it's difficult (if not impossible) to see the table border and cell strokes.

5. **Select the left column in the table. Using the Swatches panel, change the cell fill tint to 100% of the Pantone 194 C swatch.**

   You can change the color of cell fills and strokes using the Swatches panel, and you can change the cell stroke attributes using the Stroke panel.

Cell fills can be changed in the Swatches panel just as you would change the fill of a text frame.

6. **Select all cells in the table. Open the Table panel Options menu and choose Cell Options>Strokes and Fills.**

7. **In the preview area of the dialog box, click to make sure all lines in the preview area are active.**

   The preview area shows what strokes you are affecting in the dialog box. When a line is blue, it is active, which means your changes will affect those lines in the selection. If a line is black, it is not active; your changes will not affect those lines.

   You can click any line in the preview to toggle it between active and inactive.

8. **Apply a 0.25-pt, 100% Pantone 194 C stroke value using the Solid stroke type.**

   These settings change the attributes of all gridlines for all selected cells.

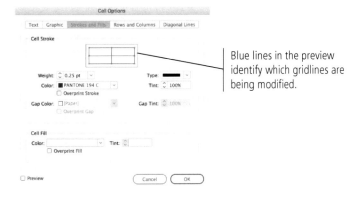

Blue lines in the preview identify which gridlines are being modified.

9. **Click OK to apply the stroke values to your table.**

10. **Click any cell in the table to deselect the previously selected cells.**

11. **Using the menu at the bottom of the Tools panel, activate the Preview option.**

    The Preview option hides all non-printing elements, including guides, invisible characters, and frame edges. This makes it easier to get an accurate preview of your table.

12. **Restore the file to the Normal view mode.**

13. **Save the file and continue to the next stage of the project.**

Moving Table Rows and Columns

When a table row or column is selected, moving the cursor over any cell in the selection shows a special Move cursor. You can click and drag the selection to reposition the selection somewhere else in the table. As you drag, a heavy blue line indicates where the moved selection will be placed when you release the mouse button.

Drag a selected
row or column.

Release the mouse button
to move the selection.

Managing Table Setup

The Table Setup tab of the Table Options dialog box defines the table dimensions, table border, spacing above and below the table, and how strokes are applied to the table. The **Stroke Drawing Order** option allows you to control behavior where gridlines meet. If Best Joins is selected, styled strokes such as double lines result in joined strokes and gaps.

Best Joins

Row Strokes in Front

Column Strokes in Front

Creating Graphic Cells

When you select one or more cells with no existing content (or the insertion point is placed in a cell with no content), you can choose Table>Convert Cell to Graphic Cell. The active cells become empty graphics cells, identified by crossed diagonal lines when frame edges are visible (View>Extras>Show Frame Edges).

Empty graphics cells show
crossed diagonal lines.

Controlling Cell Attributes

Basic attributes of table cells can be defined in the Text tab of the Cell Options dialog box. Most of these are exactly the same as for regular text frames; the only choice unique to tables is **Clip Contents to Cell**. If you set a fixed row height that is too small for the cell content, an overset text icon appears in the lower-right corner of the cell. (You can't flow text from one table cell to another.) If you check the Clip Contents to Cell option, any content that doesn't fit in the cell will be clipped.

As with any text frame, a table cell can have its own fill and stroke attributes. These attributes can be defined in the Strokes and Fills tab or by using the Swatches and Stroke panels. You can turn individual cell edges (strokes) on or off by clicking specific lines in the preview.

The Rows and Columns tab controls row height and column width. If **At Least** is selected in the Row Height menu, you can define the minimum and maximum possible row height; rows change height if you add or remove text or if you change the text formatting in a way that requires more or less space. If **Exactly** is selected, you can define the exact cell height.

If you're working with an extremely long table, you can break the table across multiple frames by threading (as you would for any long block of text). The **Keep Options** can be used to keep selected rows together after a break, and determine where those rows will go based on your choice in the Start Row menu.

You can add diagonal lines to specific cells using the Diagonal Lines tab. You can apply lines in either direction (or both) and choose a specific stroke weight, color, style, and tint. The Draw menu determines whether the line is created in front of or behind the cell's contents.

Working with Table Styles

If you've spent any amount of time refining the appearance of a table and you think you might want to use the same format again, you can save your formatting choices as a style. InDesign supports both table styles and cell styles, which are controlled in the Table Styles panel and Cell Styles panel.

Table and cell styles use the same concept as text-formatting styles. You can apply a cell style by selecting the cells and clicking the style name in the Cell Styles panel. Clicking a style in the Table Styles panel applies the style to the entire selected table.

Table styles store all options that can be defined in the Table Setup dialog box (except the options for header and footer rows). You can also define cell styles (called **nesting styles**) for specific types of rows as well as the left and right columns in the table.

Cell styles store all options that can be defined in the Cell Options dialog box, including the paragraph style that is applied to cells where that style is applied.

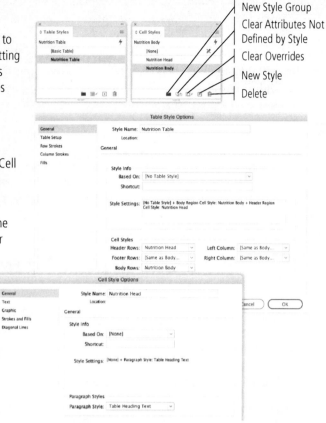

Creating Table Headers and Footers

You can break a table across multiple frames using repeating headers and footers for information that needs to be part of each instance of the table (for example, headings). Repeating headers and footers eliminate the need to manually insert the repeating information in each instance of the table.

Repeating header and footer rows are dynamically linked; this means that changing one instance of a header or footer — both content and its formatting — changes all instances of the same header or footer.

Finally, this capability also means the headers and footers remain at the top and bottom of each table instance even if other body rows move to a different instance.

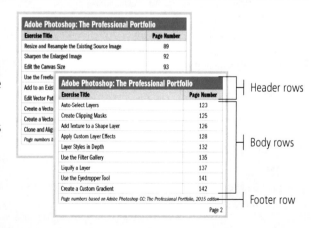

You can add new header and footer rows to a table when you create the table or by changing the options in the Headers and Footers tab of the Table Options dialog box. You can also convert existing rows to headers or footers by selecting one or more rows and choosing Table>Convert Rows>To Header or To Footer. You can also control these elements in the Headers and Footers dialog box.

STAGE 4 / Preflighting and Packaging the Job

Before you send a job to a commercial output provider, you should check to make sure the file is ready for commercial printing. When you opened the original template at the beginning of this project, you replaced missing fonts and graphics — two of the most common problems with layout files. However, successful output on a commercial press has a number of other technical requirements that, if you ignore them, can cause a file to output incorrectly or not at all. InDesign includes a **preflighting** utility that makes it easy to check for potential errors, as well as a **packaging** utility that gathers the necessary bits for the printer.

 ## Check Document Spelling

Many designers understand and carefully monitor the technical aspects of a job. It is all too common, however, to skip another important check: spelling errors. Misspellings and typos creep into virtually every job despite numerous rounds of proofing. These errors can ruin an otherwise perfect print job.

1. **With newsletter-july.indd open, navigate to Page 1 of the document. Place the insertion point at the beginning of the main story on Page 1.**

2. **Open the Dictionary pane of the Preferences dialog box.**

   InDesign checks spelling based on the defined language dictionary — by default, English: USA. You can choose a different language dictionary in the Language menu.

   The application also includes English: USA Legal and English: USA Medical dictionaries that will be of significant benefit to anyone working for either industry. If you work with foreign-language publishing, you can choose one of more than 40 different language dictionaries installed with InDesign.

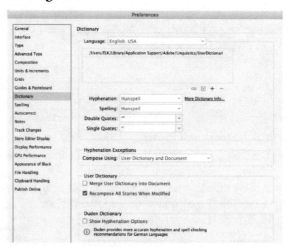

3. **Make sure English: USA is selected in the Language menu and click OK.**

4. **Choose Edit>Spelling>User Dictionary.**

   When you check spelling, you are likely to find words that, although spelled correctly, are not in the selected dictionary. Proper names, scientific terms, corporate trademarks, and other custom words are commonly flagged even though they are correct. Rather than flagging these terms every time you recheck spelling, you can add them to a custom user dictionary so InDesign will recognize them the next time you check spelling.

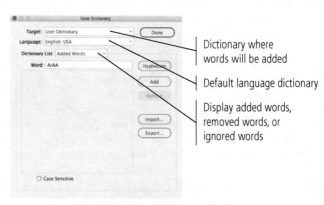

Dictionary where words will be added

Default language dictionary

Display added words, removed words, or ignored words

5. **In the Target menu, choose newsletter-july.indd.**

   By default, the user dictionary is associated with all documents. You can define custom words for a specific file using the Target menu; when you change the user dictionary for a specific file, words you add for that file will still be flagged in other files.

6. **Make sure ArAA appears in the Word field.**

   The active word (where the insertion point is placed) automatically appears in the Word field when you open this dialog box. If you placed the insertion point at the beginning of the Page 1 story (as instructed in Step 1), "ArAA" should already appear in the field.

   Your client's abbreviation is not a real word, so it will be flagged when you check the layout spelling. If you know certain words will be flagged, you can manually add those words to the user dictionary at any time.

7. **Check the Case Sensitive option at the bottom of the dialog box, and then click Add.**

   If Case Sensitive is not checked, InDesign will not distinguish between ArAA (which is correct) and ARAA (which is incorrect).

8. **Click Done to close the User Dictionary dialog box.**

9. **With nothing selected in the layout, choose Edit>Spelling>Check Spelling.**

10. **Choose Document in the Search menu at the bottom of the Check Spelling dialog box.**

    You can use the Search menu to check spelling in all open documents, the active document, the active story, to the end of the active story, or only the selected text.

    As soon as you open the Check Spelling dialog box, the first flagged word is highlighted in the layout. The same word appears in the Not in Dictionary field.

The suspect word is highlighted in the layout.

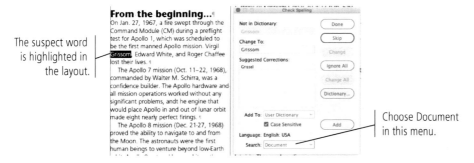

Choose Document in this menu.

The flagged word (Grissom) is a proper name, so it is not in the software's dictionary, but it is not misspelled. Never simply click Change when checking spelling. Review each flagged word carefully, and make the correct choices within the context of the layout.

11. Click Skip.

When you Skip a suspect word, the next suspect (Chaffee) is automatically highlighted in the layout. In this case, it is another proper name that is spelled correctly.

12. Click Ignore All in the Check Spelling dialog box.

When you click Ignore All, the word is added to a special list in the user dictionary, so it will not be flagged again.

Again, the next suspect (Schirra) is highlighted, and again, it is a proper name that is spelled correctly.

13. Click Ignore All again, then review the next error.

This is an example of a very common typo. The word "andt" is identified as an error, but if you look closely, you can see the next word is "he" — which the software will not identify as an error. You have to correct this problem manually.

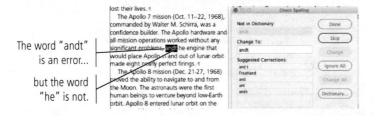

The word "andt" is an error...

but the word "he" is not.

14. Place the insertion point before the "t" in "andt", then press the Spacebar. Delete the space between the "t" and "he".

As soon as you click to place the insertion point in the story, the Check Spelling dialog box reverts to show the Start button. By interacting directly with the document to manually correct an error the software can't fix, you have to start the spell-check process over again.

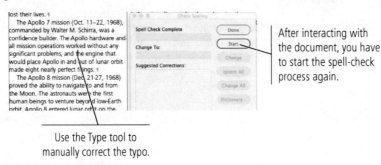

After interacting with the document, you have to start the spell-check process again.

Use the Type tool to manually correct the typo.

Note:

You might not (and probably won't) create the text for most design jobs, and you aren't technically responsible for the words your client supplies. However, you can be a hero if you find and fix typographical errors before a job goes to press; if you don't, you will almost certainly hear about it after it's too late to fix. Remember the cardinal rule of business: the customer is always right. You simply can't brush off a problem by saying, "That's not my job" — at least, not if you want to work with that client in the future.

Note:

Documents that have a lot of proper names can be time consuming to spell-check because many names are not in the user dictionary. This does not mean you should ignore this step.

15. Place the insertion point at the beginning of the active story, then click the Start button in the Check Spelling dialog box.

The process continues from the current insertion point; by moving it to the beginning of the story, you start the spell-check from the beginning of the text.

When the spell-check restarts, the first suspect is the same name you reviewed in Step 8. When you use the Skip option, the same suspect will be flagged every time you check spelling in the document.

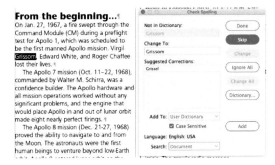

Note:

If you want a word to remain suspect each time you check the document spelling, use the Skip option instead of Ignore All.

16. Click Ignore All.

The other two names from Steps 10 and 11 (Chaffee and Schirra) are not highlighted because you used the Ignore All option the first time these were flagged.

The next suspect word (LM) is an abbreviation that reappears frequently in this story. Rather than ignore it, you are going to add it to the user dictionary for this file only.

17. Click the Dictionary button in the Check Spelling dialog box. Choose newsletter-july.indd in the Target menu, make sure the Case Sensitive option is checked, and click Add.

If you click the Add button in the Check Spelling dialog box, the words are added to the default user dictionary, which applies to all InDesign files on your computer. When you open the User Dictionary dialog box from the Check Spelling dialog box, you can choose the file-specific dictionary in the Target menu and click Add to add the word to the dictionary for the selected file only.

Note:

Be careful adding acronyms and abbreviations to the user dictionary; they often resemble words that are commonly misspelled. For example, adding TEH (without the case-sensitive option) could cause you to miss "teh" as a typo for "the".

Click Add to remember the abbreviation "LM" as a correct spelling in only this document.

18. **Click Done to close the User Dictionary dialog box and return to the Check Spelling dialog box. Click Skip.**

    When you return to the Check Spelling dialog box, LM still appears in the Word field. You have to click Skip to find the next suspect word.

19. **Continue checking spelling in the layout as follows:**

    - **Use the Skip button for words that are not misspelled but are not in the dictionary.**

    - **Use the Ignore All option for all proper names and web addresses.**

    - **Correct any actual misspellings by selecting the correct spelling in the list, then clicking Change.**

        instrumnets –> instruments

        hertage –> heritage

20. **When you see "Spell Check Complete" at the top of the dialog box, click Done to close the Check Spelling dialog box.**

Note:

In addition to mis-spellings, InDesign also identifies repeated words (such as "the the"), uncapitalized words it thinks should be capital-ized, and uncapitalized sentences. These options can be turned off in the Spelling pane of the Preferences dialog box.

21. **Using the Edit Original function in the Links panel, open angels-ad.indd and check spelling in the file. Correct any errors, then save and close the file.**

    The Check Spelling function only interacts with nested files if those files are already open and the All Documents option is selected in the Search menu.

    Review the suspects carefully before you decide to make a change. There is only one actual spelling error in the file that you should fix ("Foundatoin").

22. **Save newsletter-july.indd and then continue to the next exercise.**

FOUNDATIONS

You can turn on **Dynamic Spelling** (Edit>Spelling>Dynamic Spelling) to underline potential spelling and capitalization errors directly in a document layout. You can use the Spelling pane of the Preferences dialog box to assign a different-color underline for each of the four potential problems.

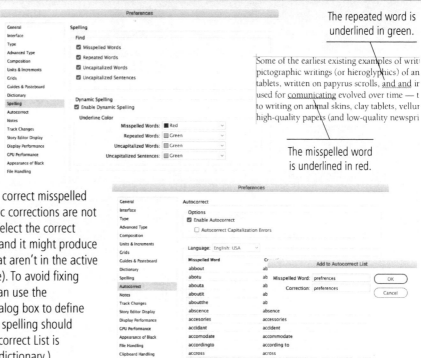

The repeated word is underlined in green.

The misspelled word is underlined in red.

If you type directly into InDesign, you can turn on the Autocorrect feature (Edit>Spelling>Autocorrect) to correct misspelled words as you type. Of course, automatic corrections are not always correct; software can't always select the correct word within the context of the layout, and it might produce some very strange results for words that aren't in the active dictionary (technical terms, for example). To avoid fixing "errors" that aren't really errors, you can use the Autocorrect pane of the Preferences dialog box to define what misspellings to replace and what spelling should replace those specific errors. (The Autocorrect List is maintained for the specified language dictionary.)

 ## Define a Preflight Profile

InDesign includes a built-in preflighting utility to check for common errors as you build a file. If you introduce a problem while building a file, the bottom-left corner of the document window shows a red light and the number of potential errors. In the following exercise, you define a profile to check for errors based on the information you have. This is certainly not an exhaustive check for all possible output problems. You should always work closely with your output provider to build responsible files that will cause no problems in the output workflow.

1. **With newsletter-july.indd open, look at the bottom-left corner of the document window.**

2. **Click the arrow to the right of the No Errors message and choose Preflight Panel from the menu.**

   The message currently shows no errors, but at this point you don't know exactly what is being checked. The Preflight panel provides an interface for defining preflight profiles as well as reviewing the specific issues identified as errors.

Note:

Ask your output providers if they have defined an InDesign preflight profile that you can load into your application to check for the problems that will interrupt their specific workflows.

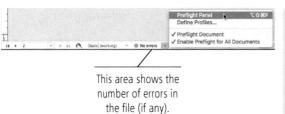

This area shows the number of errors in the file (if any).

Click this button to embed the current profile into the active document.

The Preflight panel shows which profile is being used to check for errors.

3. **Open the Preflight panel Options menu and choose Define Profiles.**

4. **In the Preflight Profiles dialog box, click the "+" button in the left side of the dialog box to create a new profile.**

   Rather than relying on generic built-in profiles, you should be aware of and able to control exactly what is (and is not) flagged as an error.

   You can use these buttons to create a new preflight profile (+) or delete an existing preflight profile (−). The preflight profile menu(≡) has options to load an external profile, export an existing profile, or embed a profile into the active document.

5. **Type ArAA Check in the Profile Name field, then click the empty area below the list of profiles to finalize the new name.**

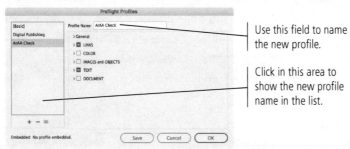

   Use this field to name the new profile.

   Click in this area to show the new profile name in the list.

6. **With the ArAA Check profile selected on the left side of the dialog box, expand the General category on the right. Highlight the existing text in the Description field, and then type Verify newsletter for 4c press.**

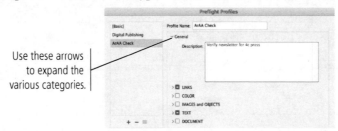

   Use these arrows to expand the various categories.

   Note:

   This description is simply a reminder of the profile's intent.

7. **Collapse the General category and expand the Links category. Check the Links Missing or Modified option, and uncheck all other options**.

   Image files placed in a layout need to be available when the job is output. By checking this option, you are warned if any placed image has been moved or modified since it was placed into the layout.

   Note:

   Some users have reported difficulty expanding various categories in the Preflight Profiles dialog box. Try clicking inside the arrow shape to work around this minor bug.

   Click inside the arrow shape.

8. **Collapse the Links category and expand the Color category. Uncheck all options in this category, then check and expand the Color Spaces and Modes Not Allowed option. Check only the RGB and Spot Color options.**

You know this newsletter is going to be output as a four-color job. Spot colors will create an extra separation, which can be a very costly error. By setting these options, you will receive a warning if you create a spot color in a job that should be output as four-color.

To achieve the best-quality, predictable output, it's a good idea to check for RGB images and control the conversion process in an image-editing application (i.e., Photoshop).

Note:

Some output processes use a method called in-RIP separation to convert RGB images to CMYK during the output process. However, the conversion process can cause significant color shift if it is not controlled.

9. **Collapse the Color category and expand the Images and Objects category. Uncheck all but the Image Resolution option, then expand the Image Resolution option. Check the three Minimum Resolution options. Change the Color and Grayscale minimums to 300 and change the 1-bit option to 1200.**

Remember, commercial output devices typically require at least 300 ppi to output raster images at good quality. By setting these minimum restrictions, you will receive a warning if your or your client's images do not have enough resolution to output at a good quality using most commercial printing processes.

Note:

Remember, required resolution is actually two times the line screen (lpi) used for a specific job. If possible, always ask your service provider what resolution to use for your job. If you don't know the lpi and can't find out in advance, 300 ppi resolution is a safe choice for most printing.

10. **Collapse the Images and Objects category and expand the Text category. Check only the Overset Text and Font Missing options.**

Overset text could simply be the result of extra paragraph returns at the end of a story. However, you should always check these issues to be sure some of the client's text has not been accidentally overset.

11. **Collapse the Text category and expand the Document category. Check the Number of Pages Required option. Expand that option, choose Exactly in the menu, and type 2 in the field.**

You know every issue of the newsletter should be exactly 2 pages. If your file has fewer or more than 2 pages, you will receive an error message.

12. **Click OK to save the profile and close the dialog box.**

13. **Continue to the next exercise.**

FOUNDATIONS

The Preflight Profiles dialog box includes a number of options for identifying potential errors. If you are going to build responsible files, you should have a basic understanding of what these options mean. The following is by no means an exhaustive list of all potential problems in digital page-layout files; it's a list of the problems Adobe included in the Preflight Profile dialog box. Other problems are beyond the scope of most graphic designers and are better left to prepress professionals to correct, given the specific equipment conditions in their workflows.

You should also realize that some of these issues are not necessarily errors but nonetheless should be reviewed before a job is output. For example, blank pages might be intentionally placed into a document to force a chapter opener onto a right-facing page; in this case, the blank page is not an error. In other cases, a blank page might be left over after text is edited; in this case, the blank page would be an error.

Links

- **Links Missing or Modified.** Use this option to receive a warning if a placed file has been moved (missing) or changed (modified) since it was placed into a layout. If a placed file is missing, the output will use only the low-resolution screen preview. If a placed file has been modified, the output will reflect the most up-to-date version of the placed file, which could be drastically different than the original.

- **Inaccessible URL Links.** Use this option to find hyperlinks that might cause problems if you are creating an interactive PDF document.

- **OPI Links.** OPI is a workflow tool that allows designers to use low-resolution FPO (for placement only) files during the design stage. When the job is processed for output, the high-resolution versions are swapped out in place of the FPO images. Although not terribly common anymore, some larger agencies still use OPI workflows.

Document

- **Page Size and Orientation.** Use this option to cause an error if the document size is not a specific size; you can also cause an error if the current document is oriented other than the defined page size (i.e., portrait instead of landscape or vice versa).

- **Number of Pages Required.** Use this option to define a specific number of pages, the smallest number of pages that can be in the document, or whether the document must have pages in multiples of a specific number.

- **Blank Pages.** Use this option to find blank pages in the document.

- **Bleed and Slug Setup.** Use this option to verify the document's bleed and slug sizes against values required by a specific output process.

- **All Pages Must Use Same Size and Orientation.** Because InDesign supports multiple page sizes in the same document, you can check this option to verify that all pages in the file have the same size.

Color

- **Transparency Blending Space Required.** Use this option to define whether CMYK or RGB should be used to flatten transparent objects for output.

- **Cyan, Magenta, or Yellow Plates Not Allowed.** Use this option to verify layouts that will be output with only spot colors or with black and spot colors.

- **Color Spaces and Modes Not Allowed.** Use this option to create errors if the layout uses RGB, CMYK, Spot Color, Gray, or LAB color models. (Different jobs have different defined color spaces. The option to flag CMYK as an error can be useful, for example, if you are building a layout that will be output in black only.)

- **Spot Color Setup.** Use this option to define the number of spot colors a job should include as well as the specific color model that should be used (LAB or CMYK) when converting unwanted spot colors for process printing.

- **Overprinting Applied in InDesign.** Use this option to create an error if an element is set to overprint instead of trap.

- **Overprinting Applied to White or [Paper] Color.** By definition, White or [Paper] is technically the absence of other inks. Unless you are printing white toner or opaque spot ink, white cannot, by definition, overprint. Use this option to produce an error if White or [Paper] elements are set to overprint.

- **[Registration] Applied.** The [Registration] color swatch is a special swatch used for elements such as crop and registration marks. Any element that uses the [Registration] color will output on all separations in the job. Use this option to find elements that are incorrectly colored with the [Registration] color instead of (probably) black.

Images and Objects

- **Image Resolution.** Use this option to identify placed files with too little or too much resolution. As you know, commercial output devices typically require 300 ppi to output properly. The maximum resolution options can be used to find objects that, typically through scaling, result in unnecessarily high resolutions that might take considerable time for the output device to process.

- **Non-Proportional Scaling of Placed Object.** Use this option to find placed files that have been scaled with different X and Y percentages.

- **Uses Transparency.** Use this option to find any element affected by transparency. You should carefully preview transparency flattening before outputting the job.

- **Image ICC Profile.** Use this option to find placed images that have embedded ICC profiles. Typically used in color-managed workflows, placed images often store information — in the form of profiles — about the way a particular device captured or created the color in that image. You can cause errors if the image profile results in CMYK conversion or if the embedded image profile has been overridden in the layout.

- **Layer Visibility Overrides.** Use this option to find layered Photoshop files in which the visibility of specific layers has been changed within InDesign.

- **Minimum Stroke Weight.** There is a limit to the smallest visible line that can be produced by any given output device. Use this option to find objects with a stroke weight smaller than a specific point size.

- **Interactive Elements.** Use this option to find elements with interactive properties (more on this in Project 6: Digital Layout Variations).

- **Bleed/Trim Hazard.** Use this option to find elements that fall within a defined distance of the page edge or spine for facing-page layouts (i.e., outside the live area).

- **Hidden Page Items.** Use this option to create an error if any objects on a page are not currently visible.

Text

- **Overset Text.** Use this option to find any frames with overset text.

- **Paragraph Style and Character Style Overrides.** Use this option to find instances where an applied style has been overridden with local formatting.

- **Font Missing.** Use this option to create an error if any required font is not available on the computer.

- **Glyph Missing.** Use this option to identify glyphs that aren't available.

- **Dynamic Spelling Detects Errors.** Use this option to cause an error if InDesign's dynamic spelling utility identifies any errors in the document.

- **Font Types Not Allowed.** Use this option to prohibit specific font types that can cause problems in modern output workflows.

- **Non-Proportional Type Scaling.** Use this option to identify type that has been artificially stretched or compressed in one direction (i.e., where horizontal or vertical scaling has been applied).

- **Minimum Type Size.** Use this option to identify any type set smaller than a defined point size. You can also identify small type that requires more than one ink to reproduce (a potential registration problem on commercial output devices).

- **Cross-References.** Use this option to identify dynamic links from one location in a file to another. You can cause errors if a cross reference is out-of-date or unresolved.

- **Conditional Text Indicators Will Print.** Use this option to create an error if certain visual indicators will appear in the final output. (You explore conditional text in Project 5: Folding Travel Brochure.)

- **Unresolved Caption Variable.** Use this option to find dynamic caption variables for which there is no defined metadata. (You will learn about creating captions in Project 5: Folding Travel Brochure.)

- **Span Columns Setting Not Honored.** Use this option to find paragraphs with a defined column-span setting that is prevented by other objects on the page.

- **Tracked Change.** Use this option to find instances of text that have been changed but not accepted when Track Changes is enabled. (You will explore this utility in Project 6: Digital Layout Variations.)

Evaluate the Layout

Now that you have defined the issues you know are errors, you can check your file for those issues and make the necessary corrections.

1. **With newsletter-july.indd open, click the Profile menu in the Preflight panel and choose ArAA Check as the profile to use.**

2. **In the bottom of the panel, make sure the All radio button is checked.**

   When the All option is active, the entire document is checked. You can use the other radio button to define a specific page or range of pages to preflight.

   As soon as you call the ArAA Check profile, the panel reports a number of errors.

This pane lists the problem categories that caused the errors.

The now-active profile results in a number of errors.

Use this option to check only certain pages.

Note:

Preflight profiles become part of the application but are not linked to or saved in a specific document unless you intentionally embed the profile.

3. **Expand the Info section of the Preflight panel.**

   This area offers information about a specific error and offers suggestions for fixing the problem.

4. **Click the arrow to expand the Color list, and then click the arrow to expand the Color Space Not Allowed list.**

5. **Click the first text frame listing to select it, and then click the hot-text page number for that item.**

   The hot-text link on the right side of the Preflight panel changes the document window to show the specific item causing the error.

Click the hot-text link to navigate to a specific instance of the problem.

6. **In the Swatches panel, Control/right-click the Pantone 534 C swatch and choose Swatch Options from the contextual menu.**

   You can also double-click the swatch name to open the Swatch Options dialog box for that swatch.

Note:

Spot colors are not always errors. Check the project's specifications carefully before you convert spot colors to process. Also, be aware that spot colors are often outside the CMYK gamut; converting a spot color to process can result in drastic color shift.

7. **In the Swatch Options dialog box, choose CMYK in the Color Mode menu and then change the Color Type menu to Process.**

   Because this swatch exists only in the layout file and not any of the placed images, you can change the swatch color mode, type, and name.

   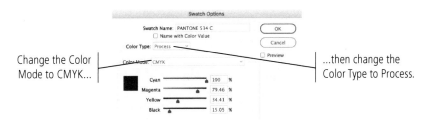

   Change the Color Mode to CMYK...   ...then change the Color Type to Process.

Note:

If a spot-color swatch was used in a placed file, you would only be able to change the Color Type menu in InDesign.

8. **Click OK to apply the new swatch options.**

   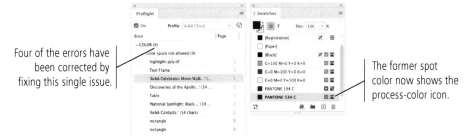

   Four of the errors have been corrected by fixing this single issue.

   The former spot color now shows the process-color icon.

9. **Repeat Steps 6–8 for the remaining spot color in the InDesign file.**

   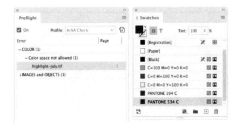

10. Select the remaining color problem instance in the Preflight panel and click the hot-text link to show that element in the layout.

When you overrode all master page items on Page 1, you created two instances of the placed highlight-july.tif file: the original one on the master page and the one on Page 1 of the layout. The Preflight panel shows only the item on Page 1 as an error because that file will be used for output.

The selected image is automatically highlighted in the Links panel.

The instance of the same image on the master page is not selected.

11. In the Links panel, click the Relink button. Navigate to `highlight-july-cmyk.tif` (in the WIP>Aerospace>CMYK folder) and click Open. If you see the Image Import Options dialog box, click OK to accept the default options.

After the image has been relinked, all color problems have been corrected. Because the preflight process only considers elements included in the actual output, the original highlight-july.tif file (which is still an RGB file) is not considered to be an error since it exists only on the master page. The Color listing no longer appears in the Preflight panel.

12. Expand the Images and Objects category, then expand the Image Resolution listing. Click the page link to navigate to the problem file.

This image is a placed PDF file supplied by your client. The Links panel shows the image is 280 ppi, which is lower than the minimum 300 that you defined for this file.

In this case, the 280 will probably be enough to produce good quality. But, in many instances, supplied-image resolution will be far below what you need for commercial printing. Low resolution is a common problem with client-supplied images. Because the placed image is a PDF file, you can't access the individual components and make changes; you would have to contact the client to resolve the problem.

The placed PDF file does not meet the minimum resolution that you defined in the profile.

13. Save the file and continue to the next exercise.

Create the Job Package

After you have corrected potential output problems, you can package it for the output provider. As we have already stated, the images and fonts used in a layout must be available on the computer used to output the job. When you send the layout file to the printer, you must also send the necessary components. InDesign includes a Package utility that makes this process very easy.

1. **With newsletter-july.indd open, choose File>Package.**

2. **Review the information in the Package dialog box and then click Package.**

    If you had not preflighted the file before opening the Package dialog box, you would see warning icons identifying problems with image color space or missing fonts. Because you completed the previous exercise, however, potential errors have been fixed, so this dialog box simply shows a summary list of information about the file you are packaging. (You can use the list on the left to review the specifics of individual categories.)

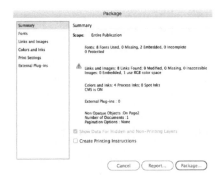

Note:

If you check the Create Printing Instructions option, clicking the Package button opens a secondary dialog box where you can define those instructions.

3. **If you see a message asking you to save, click Save.**

4. **In the resulting dialog box, navigate to your WIP>Aerospace folder as the target location.**

5. **Change the Save As/Folder Name field to Newsletter July Finished.**

    This field defines the name of the folder that will be created. All files for the job will be copied into this folder.

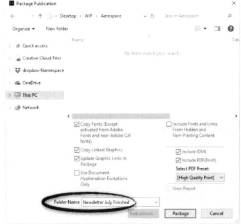

| Macintosh | Windows |

6. Review the options at the bottom of the dialog box.

These options determine what will be included in the packaged job folder.

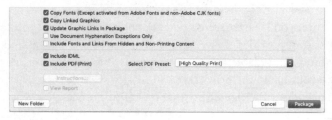

- **Copy Fonts (Except Activated from Adobe Fonts and non-Adobe CJK Fonts).** When checked, this option results in a secondary Document Fonts folder to contain the font files used in the InDesign file. If placed graphics require specific fonts, those will also be copied into the job package.

  If you hand off the job package folder to another user (or if someone sends you a job package), the fonts in the collected Document Fonts folder will be available in InDesign when you open the packaged INDD file — even if those fonts are not installed at the computer's system level. These **document-installed fonts** are installed when the related document is opened, and they are uninstalled when you close that file. These fonts supersede any existing font of the same PostScript name within the document. Document-installed fonts are not available to other documents or in other applications.

  As the name of this item suggests, Adobe and non-Adobe CJK (Chinese/Japanese/Korean) fonts are not copied into the job package. If you send a file to other InDesign users, they will have to sync the required Adobe fonts using their own Creative Cloud subscriptions or license the required CJK fonts.

- **Copy Linked Graphics.** When checked, all linked files are copied into a Links folder in the job package folder. If you have placed InDesign files in your main layout, any graphics used in those files will also be copied into the job package.

- **Update Graphic Links in Package.** When checked, links in the InDesign file are changed to refer to the new copied link files (in the job package Links folder). If this option is not checked, the links still point to the original placed file, which might cause a missing-file warning when you send the job package to another user or open the file at a later time.

- **Use Document Hyphenation Exceptions Only.** If another user opens your InDesign file, hyphenation exceptions in that user's version of InDesign will automatically apply to the file. If you have defined custom hyphenation exceptions, you can check this option to prevent another user's settings from overriding the ones you define in a specific layout.

- **Include Fonts and Links from Hidden and Non-Printing Content.** This option packages elements that either are not visible or have been set to not print (for example, content in hidden conditional text or on a layer for which the Print option has been disabled).

- **Include IDML.** IDML, which stands InDesign Markup Language, is a special format that allows a file created in the current release of InDesign to be opened in older versions of the software. Keep in mind that features added in later versions will not be available in earlier software, so the document might lose elements of the design.

- **Include PDF (Print).** You can check this option to automatically create a PDF at the same time you create the job package. When this option is checked, you can also choose the specific PDF Preset containing the export settings you want to use.

Note:

Conditional text and PDF Presets are explained in Project 5: Folding Travel Brochure.

Non-printing layers are explained in Project 6: Digital Layout Variations.

7. **At the bottom of the dialog box, make sure the Copy Fonts, Copy Linked Graphics, and Update Graphic Links options are checked.**

8. **Uncheck the Include IDML and Include PDF options, then click Package.**

   When you create a job package, InDesign automatically creates a new folder for the job.

9. **Read the resulting warning and click OK.**

   As with any software, you purchase a license to use a font. You do not own the actual font. It is illegal to distribute fonts freely, as it is illegal to distribute copies of your software. Most (but not all) font licenses allow you to send your copy of a font to a service provider as long as the service provider also owns a copy of the font. Always verify you are not violating font copyright before submitting a job.

   When the process is complete, the necessary job elements appear in the job folder (in your WIP>Aerospace folder).

10. **Close the InDesign file.**

PROJECT REVIEW

fill in the blank

1. An image file that has been renamed since it was placed into an InDesign layout shows a status of _____.

2. The _____ is used to monitor the status of images that are placed into a layout.

3. _____ is the distance between the edge of a frame and the text contained within that frame.

4. _____ is the distance between the edge of an object and text in other overlapping frames.

5. _____ apply only to selected text characters; this is useful for setting off a few words in a paragraph without affecting the entire paragraph.

6. _____ apply to the entire body of text between two ¶ symbols.

7. While working in a table, the _____ key has a special function; pressing it does not insert the associated character.

8. When the _____ row height method is selected, table rows change height if you add or remove text from the table cells or if you change the text formatting in a way that requires more or less space.

9. A(n) _____ is a special kind of table row that repeats at the top of every instance of the same table.

10. _____ is the process of checking a layout for errors before it goes to print.

short answer

1. Briefly explain the significance of a Missing Font warning.

2. List three advantages to using templates.

3. Briefly define "styles" in relation to text formatting.

PORTFOLIO BUILDER PROJECT

Use what you learned in this project to complete the following freeform exercise.
Carefully read the art director and client comments, then create your own design to meet the needs of the project.
Use the space below to sketch ideas; when finished, write a brief explanation of your reasoning behind your final design.

Your client is a local food market that sells gourmet and specialty products. To help promote the business, the owners have hired you to create a series of flyers that can be handed out at art festivals and farmers markets.

To complete this project, you should:

❏ Design an 8.5″ × 11″ template that can be reused to feature different sections of the store. The flyer can be printed on both sides of the paper but should not include bleeds.

❏ Include some type of category identifier that will change for each flyer in the series.

❏ Use the content that has been provided in the **CenterMarket_ID20_PB.zip** archive on the Student Files web page. You can use some or all images provided by the client.

Center Market includes an artisanal cheese market, an old-world bakery with craft breads and desserts, a butcher shop featuring wild game, and a large international section with hard-to-find ingredients for just about any type of cuisine.

Our target customers are the home-gourmet "foodie" types, so we want the flyers to speak to the higher-end market. We definitely prefer a classier approach than the "Sale! Sale! Sale!" flyers you see in regular weekly grocery ads.

We already have text and images for the artisanal cheese, so start with that one. Once we've approved what you come up with, we'll gather everything you will need for the other pieces.

Other than the text we already provided you, be sure to include the store name, address, and phone number prominently on the flyer:

4127 West Alton Drive, Los Angeles, CA 90016
800-555-3663

PROJECT SUMMARY

This project introduced a number of concepts and tools that will be very important as you work on more complex page-layout jobs. Importing text content from other applications — specifically, Microsoft Word and Microsoft Excel — is a foundational skill you will use in most projects; this newsletter showed you how to control content on import and then re-format it as appropriate in the InDesign layout.

Templates, master pages, and styles are all designed to let you do the majority of work once and then apply it as many times as necessary; virtually any InDesign project can benefit from these tools, and you will use them extensively in your career as a graphic designer. This project provided a basic introduction to these productivity tools; you will build on these foundations as you complete the remaining five projects of this book.

Correct missing and modified graphics

Replace or locate missing fonts

Edit master page layouts

Import formatted text from a Microsoft Word file

Apply style sheets from the template

Control text wrap to move surrounding text away from frame edges

Control text frame inset to move contained text away from frame edges

Place PDF and INDD files as images

Format bulleted and numbered lists

Check for and correct spelling errors

Import and format a table from Microsoft Excel

Preflight a file, and make corrections based on four-color printing requirements

Museum Exhibits Booklet

4

Your client is the special exhibits director at the Getty Foundation, which oversees a group of museums in Los Angeles. She has hired you to create a booklet to highlight the special exhibits that will be featured this year at the museum's public venues.

This project incorporates the following skills:

❑ Understanding and controlling facing-page layouts

❑ Designing master pages to apply repetitive layout elements

❑ Working with text that flows across multiple frames and pages

❑ Controlling advanced text formatting options such as automatic hyphenation, widow and orphan control, and bulleted lists

❑ Printing a booklet using built-in imposition options

❑ Exporting a PDF file with animated page transitions

PROJECT MEETING

client comments

We produce a special exhibits catalog twice a year to feature the ongoing and new displays that are being hosted at The Getty Villa and The Getty Center.

The text for this issue was created in Microsoft Word, using a custom template with all the text formats we use in a number of similar collateral pieces.

The Getty recently decided to make available, free of charge, all digital images to which the Getty holds the rights or that are in the public domain to be used for any purpose. We call it the Getty Open Content Program.

You can download whatever images you think work best for this catalog from the Getty Search Gateway or the museum's Collection web page.

art director comments

This booklet was originally specified as 16 pages with a separate cover, but the client decided that a self-cover will work just as well. We had already designed the front and back covers for the initial pitch, so you can import the cover layouts into the main booklet file.

Consistency is important for any document with more than a few pages; the same basic grid should be used for most internal pages in the booklet. Completing this project will be much easier if you take the time to build the basic layout on master pages.

This project, like most documents with a lot of text, will require tight control over the text flow. Long documents like this one require special attention to detail to prevent problems such as bad line and page breaks.

We were able to download the images we need from the Getty Search Gateway (http://search.getty.edu/gateway/landing).

project objectives

To complete this project, you will:

❏ Convert layout pages to master pages, and import them into the main booklet file.

❏ Build master pages with placeholders for the different elements of the layout.

❏ Define styles based on other styles to improve consistency and facilitate changing multiple styles at once.

❏ Control paragraph positioning using Keep options in applied styles.

❏ Control automatic hyphenation to prevent bad line breaks.

❏ Format paragraphs as bulleted lists to improve readability.

❏ Print a sample booklet for client approval.

❏ Export a PDF version with page transitions.

As a general rule, you should use facing pages any time a design will be read like a book: left to right, Page 2 printed on the back of Page 1 and facing Page 3, and so on. For facing-page layouts, the left page mirrors the right page of each **spread**. The side margins are referred to as "inside" (near the spine) and "outside" (away from the spine) instead of "left" and "right."

 ## Create the Booklet File

Multi-page documents, such as the booklet you build in this project, typically require special layout considerations so the pages will appear in the correct arrangement when the job is finished. You'll deal with output considerations in Stage 3. For now, however, you need to understand two issues related to setting up this type of file:

- Books and booklets usually have facing pages, which means opposing left and right pages of a spread mirror each other.

- Files with facing pages can have different margin values on the inside (near the spread center) and outside (away from the spread center) edges.

1. Download **Museum_ID20_RF.zip** from the Student Files web page.

2. Expand the ZIP archive in your WIP folder (Macintosh), or copy the archive contents into your WIP folder (Windows).

   This creates a folder named **Museum**, which contains the files you need for this project. You should also use this folder to save the files you create in this project.

3. In InDesign, choose File>New>Document. Choose the Print option at the top of the dialog box, and choose the Letter-Half document preset.

4. Define the following settings in the Preset Details section:

Name: **exhibits**	Columns: 2
Units: Inches	Gutter: 0.25″
Facing Pages: Checked	Margins: 0.5″ (constrained)
Primary Text Frame: Checked	Bleeds: 0.125″ (constrained)

Note:

If a setting isn't mentioned, leave it at the default value.

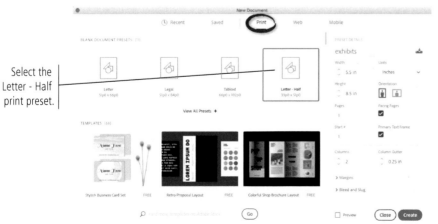

Select the Letter - Half print preset.

5. **Click Create to create the new document.**

6. **If rulers are not visible, choose View>Rulers.**

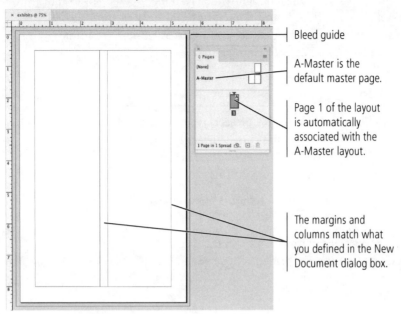

Bleed guide

A-Master is the default master page.

Page 1 of the layout is automatically associated with the A-Master layout.

The margins and columns match what you defined in the New Document dialog box.

7. **Save the file as exhibits.indd in your WIP>Museum folder, then continue to the next exercise.**

Understanding Master Page Icons

When you work with facing pages, the default master page is actually a spread. In the Pages panel, the A-Master layout icon shows two pages, representing the two pages in the master page spread. Depending on your needs, you can also create master pages with a single page instead of a spread.

If you double-click the name of a master page in the Pages panel, you select the entire page or spread that makes up that master layout. You can select only one page of a master page spread by clicking the left or right page icon for that master.

In a facing-page document, the default A-Master has two pages (a spread).

You can add a single-page master layout to a facing-page document.

Double-click the master page name to select all pages in that layout.

If an entire master page spread is already selected (both page icons are highlighted), you have to first deselect the spread before you can select only one page of the spread. You can do this by simply clicking any other master-page or regular-icon page icon in the panel.

Single-click either page icon in a master page spread to select only that page.

Create Master Pages from Layout Pages

This project was originally defined by the client as a 16-page booklet "plus cover." In other words, the main booklet file would have 16 pages, but the cover would be created and printed as a separate file. Once printed, the two pieces would be combined and bound together into a single finished piece.

Based on the amount of text they created, your clients have decided to create the booklet as 16 pages "including self cover," which means the first and last pages of the main booklet file will be the front and back covers, respectively. The first step in completing this project is to bring the cover pages into the main layout.

1. **Open the file cover.indd from the WIP>Museum folder.**

   If you get a warning about missing or modified images, correct the links as necessary using the files in the WIP>Museum>Links folder.

   This file includes two page layouts — the front cover and the back cover. Like many projects, however, these pages were not created using master pages.

   Although you could simply copy the page contents from this file into your main file, it is a better idea to work with master pages whenever possible. Once you develop master pages, you can easily import those layouts into other files and apply the layouts to specific layout pages as necessary. Fortunately, it is very easy to create a master page layout from a regular page layout.

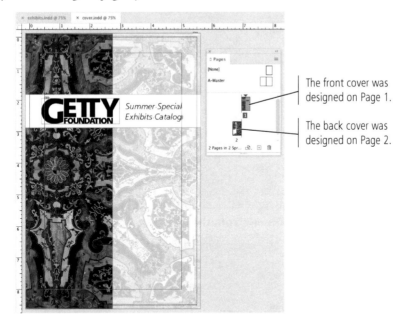

The front cover was designed on Page 1.

The back cover was designed on Page 2.

Note:

You can create a new master page from scratch by choosing New Master in the Pages panel Options menu.

2. **In the Pages panel, click the Page 1 icon and drag it to the top section of the panel (where the A-Master appears).**

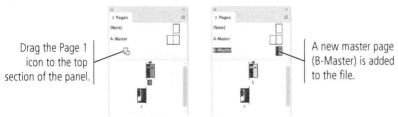

Drag the Page 1 icon to the top section of the panel.

A new master page (B-Master) is added to the file.

3. **Control/right-click the new B-Master icon (in the top section of the Pages panel) and choose Master Options for "B-Master" from the contextual menu.**

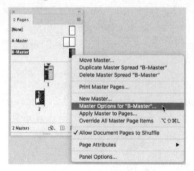

4. **In the resulting Master Options dialog box, change the name to Front Cover and click OK.**

5. **Repeat this process to convert the Page 2 layout to a master page layout named Back Cover.**

6. **In the top section of the Pages panel, Control/right-click the A-Master layout name and choose Delete Master Spread "A-Master" from the contextual menu.**

The default master layout in this file was never used, so you can simply delete it.

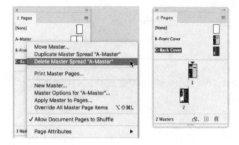

7. **Save the file as cover-masters.indd in your WIP>Museum folder, and then close the file.**

8. **Continue to the next exercise.**

Import Master Pages

Now that the front and back covers are saved as master pages, you can easily import and apply them in the booklet file.

1. **With `exhibits.indd` open, choose Master Pages>Load Master Pages from the Pages panel Options menu.**

2. **In the resulting dialog box, navigate to the file `cover-masters.indd` in your WIP>Museum folder and click Open.**

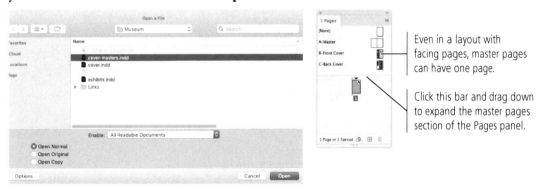

Even in a layout with facing pages, master pages can have one page.

Click this bar and drag down to expand the master pages section of the Pages panel.

3. **Open the Swatches and Paragraph Styles panels.**

Loading master pages from one file to another is an all-or-nothing process. Both master pages from the cover-masters.indd file are now part of the new file.

When you load a master page from one file to another, all required assets (styles, swatches, etc.) are also imported. One color swatch has been added to the Swatches panel; four paragraph styles have been added to the Paragraph Styles panel.

Note:

There is no dynamic link between the master pages now in the booklet file and the master pages in the original cover file. Changing one version of the Page Head style, for example, will not affect the other version.

One new color swatch was imported from the cover-masters.indd file.

Four paragraph styles were imported.

4. In the Pages panel, drag the B-Front Cover icon onto the Page 1 icon.

By default, Page 1 of any new file is associated with the A-Master layout. You can change this by simply dragging a different master onto the page icon.

5. Make sure frame edges are visible (View>Extras>Show Frame Edges).

Several objects now appear on Page 1. The frame edges appear as dotted lines instead of solid lines, indicating the objects are from the associated master; you can't select them on the layout page unless you override master items for that layout page.

Note:

You can Control/right-click a page icon in the lower section of the Pages panel and choose Apply Master to Page from the contextual menu.

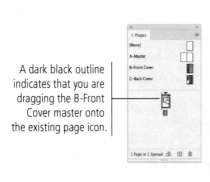

A dark black outline indicates that you are dragging the B-Front Cover master onto the existing page icon.

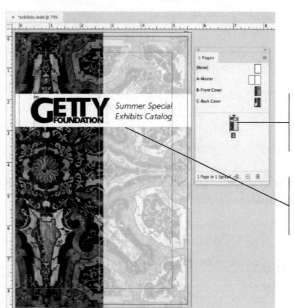

After releasing the mouse button, Page 1 is associated with the B-Front Cover master.

Dotted lines indicate that objects are placed on the associated master page.

6. In the Pages panel, drag the C-Back Cover icon below the Page 1 icon.

Using facing pages, new pages are added to the left and right of the spread center. When you release the mouse button, the new Page 2 is automatically added on the left side of the spread center. All of the elements on the C-Back Cover master are now visible on the Page 2 layout.

Drag the C-Back Cover master below the Page 1 icon.

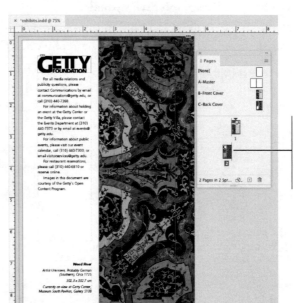

Page 2, which is associated with the C-Back Cover master, is added to the left side of the spread.

7. **In the Pages panel, select only the left page of the A-Master spread and drag it to the left of the Page 2 icon.**

Note:

*Pages on the left side of the spread center are called **left-facing** or **verso** pages.*

*Pages on the right side of the spread center are called **right-facing** or **recto** pages.*

If both pages of the master spread are highlighted, dragging the selected icons into the lower half of the panel will add the entire master page spread. If only one page of the master spread is selected, you can add a single page to the layout.

Before you release the mouse button, a vertical black bar indicates the potential position of the new page.

Only the left page of the spread is selected.

This line shows you are adding the page before the existing Page 2.

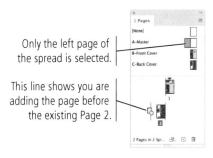

After you release the mouse button, the new page is automatically added before Page 2. Because this is a facing-page layout, the new Page 2 becomes the left-facing page, and the old Page 2 — now Page 3 — moves to the right side of the spread.

Note:

By convention, odd-numbered pages are right-facing and even-numbered pages are left-facing.

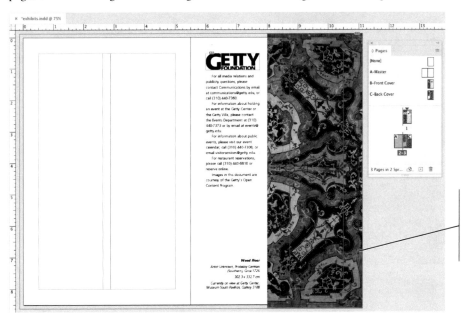

Objects from the C-Back Cover master still appear in the same position relative to the page.

8. **Save the file and continue to the next exercise.**

You need to understand the differences between spread master pages and single-page master pages, especially when working with facing pages.

When you work with a master page spread, objects on the master-page layout are positioned relative to the entire spread. Objects on regular layout pages, however, are positioned relative to the page on which they exist.

This concept is particularly important if you work with objects that bleed off the left or right side of a page or if you override the master page items on a specific page.

When you move a page from one side of a spread to the other (e.g., from left to right), bleed objects will continue to bleed past the same edge of the page's new position — possibly interfering with the other page of the spread.

Solid frame edges identify objects created on a regular page.　　Dotted frame edges identify master-page objects.

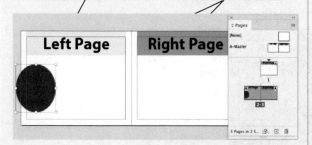

After adding a new A-Master page in front of Page 2:

The regular page object (the pink circle) is in the same position relative to the page where it was created, which is now Page 3. Master-page objects that have not been detached are unchanged.

A related problem occurs when you override and change master-page items on regular layout pages. When you override master-page items, they become regular layout page items. Adding pages to the middle of a layout moves those items relative to their new page position; the original master-page objects are added directly behind the overridden objects. (If necessary, you can eliminate the overridden objects by choosing Remove All Local Overrides from the Pages panel Options menu, or you can select specific objects and choose Remove Selected Local Overrides.)

We overrode master page items for Page 2, then changed the object fill color from yellow to green.　　This frame is still a master page object.

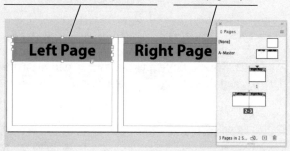

We added a new A-Master page in front of Page 2. Because overriding master-page items converts them into regular page items, the overridden object moves relative to the page on which it is placed (the moved Page 2):

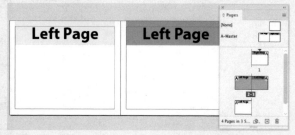

Moving the overridden object shows that the correct master-page object has been added to the page behind the overridden object:

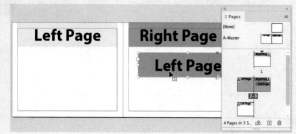

Edit the Default Master Page

The main body of the booklet will be 14 pages in seven spreads; each spread will have the same basic layout, so it makes sense to create the required frames on a master page layout rather than on each individual page. You could either create a new master page for the body spread or simply edit the existing default master page.

1. **With exhibits.indd open, double-click the words "A-Master" in the top section of the Pages panel.**

   Double-clicking a master page navigates to that master layout in the document window. Each page of the A-Master spread has the margin and column settings you defined in the New Document dialog box.

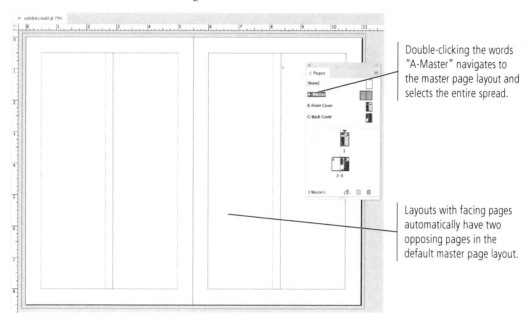

Double-clicking the words "A-Master" navigates to the master page layout and selects the entire spread.

Layouts with facing pages automatically have two opposing pages in the default master page layout.

   Each page in this spread has different margin requirements. Fortunately, InDesign allows you to modify those settings for individual pages in the spread.

2. **Click once on any page other than the A-Master spread in the Pages panel.**

   When you double-click the master page name in the Pages panel, the entire spread is selected (highlighted) in the panel. To change a setting for only one page of the spread, you first have to deselect the spread (by selecting some other page), and then select only the specific page you want to modify.

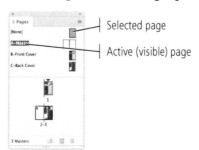

Selected page

Active (visible) page

Note:

You can click a regular page or a master page icon; the important point is to deselect the A-Master spread.

3. **In the Pages panel, click once on the left page icon of the A-Master spread.**

   Clicking a page icon once selects that page without changing the visible (active) page in the document window.

4. **With the left page of the A-Master layout selected, choose Layout>Margins and Columns.**

5. **With the Preview option checked, make sure the four margin fields are not linked. Change the bottom margin to 3.5 in.**

   To define different values for each margin, make sure you see the broken chain links between the fields; you do not want all four margins to be constrained to the same value.

6. **In the lower half of the Margins and Column dialog box, uncheck the Adjust Layout option.**

   When you make changes to the layout — page size, margins, etc. — you can use the Adjust Layout option to allow the software to change page elements as necessary to match the new settings.

   When this option is not checked, you simply change the margins and columns without affecting elements on the page.

   In this case, the primary text frame on the left page of the spread, which was created based on the settings you defined in the New Document dialog box, did not change to match the new bottom margin.

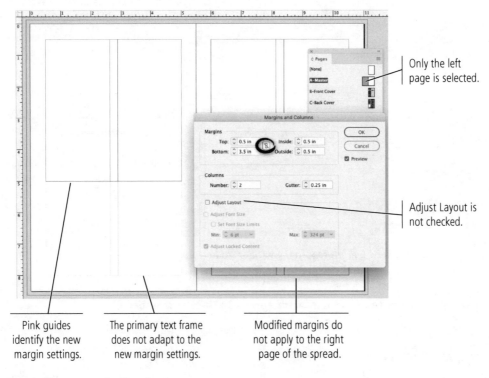

Only the left page is selected.

Adjust Layout is not checked.

Pink guides identify the new margin settings.	The primary text frame does not adapt to the new margin settings.	Modified margins do not apply to the right page of the spread.

7. **Click OK to apply the changes.**

8. **Choose the Gap tool in the Tools panel. Place the cursor in the bottom margin area of the left-facing page.**

The Gap tool allows you to actively manipulate white space on a page. When you place the cursor between existing objects or between an object and the page edge, the gray highlight shows which space you are editing; the arrow indicator behind the cursor icon shows what can be moved by clicking and dragging.

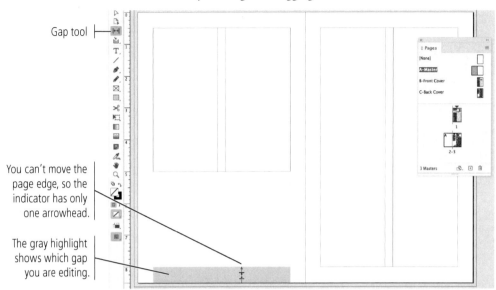

Gap tool

You can't move the page edge, so the indicator has only one arrowhead.

The gray highlight shows which gap you are editing.

Understanding the Gap Tool

The Gap tool is designed to let you actively manipulate the white space on a page. Using one or more modifier keys, the Gap tool can also resize or move objects that touch the gap you edit.

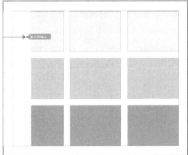

Click and drag a margin to change the space between the page edge and nearby objects and to affect other objects that touch the margin.

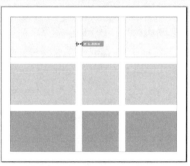

Click and drag a gap between objects to move the gap and affect the size of adjacent objects.

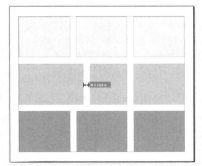

Shift-click and drag to move the gap only between immediately adjacent objects.

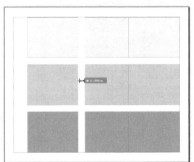

Option/Alt-click and drag to move the white space and adjacent objects without affecting the objects' size.

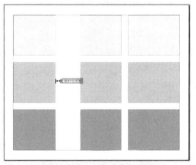

Command/Control-click and drag to resize the gap and change the size of adjacent objects.

9. **Click in the margin area below the left page of the spread. Drag up until the cursor feedback shows a height of 3.5 in.**

When you edit the gap between a page edge and an object, you resize the object in the direction you drag. When you drag near the adjusted margin guide, the frame edge snaps to align with the guide.

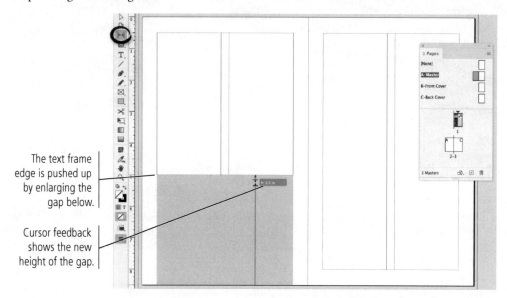

The text frame edge is pushed up by enlarging the gap below.

Cursor feedback shows the new height of the gap.

10. **In the Pages panel, select only the right page of the A-Master spread. Choose Layout>Margins and Columns and change the bottom margin to 6.5 in.**

11. **In the lower half of the Margins and Columns dialog box, check the Adjust Layout option.**

When the Adjust Layout is active, the primary text frame automatically adjusts to match the new margin settings. You will not have to manually adjust the frame later.

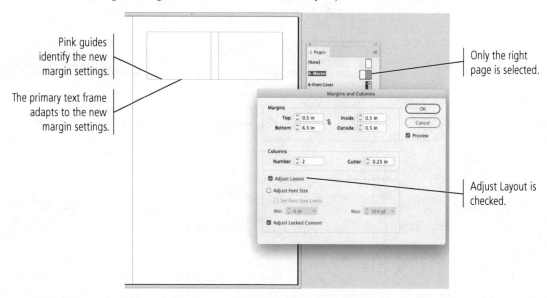

Pink guides identify the new margin settings.

The primary text frame adapts to the new margin settings.

Only the right page is selected.

Adjust Layout is checked.

12. **Click OK to finalize the changes to the right side of the layout.**

13. **Save the file and continue to the next exercise.**

Add Common Elements to a Master Page Layout

In addition to the primary text frame, you need several other elements to appear on every spread in the booklet: a callout box on the left page of the spread, a text frame with supporting copy on the right page of the spread, a large graphics frame, a text frame for the image caption, and a page footer on the right page of the spread. Again, it makes sense to create master page placeholders for these objects rather than recreating the objects on every individual layout page.

1. **With exhibits.indd open, make sure the A-Master layout is showing in the document window.**

2. **Create a new text frame with the following dimensions (based on the top-left reference point):**

   > X: –0.125 in W: 3 in
   > Y: 5.25 in H: 2.5 in

3. **Fill the new text frame with the C=36 M=59 Y=94 K=24 swatch.**

4. **Click to select the new frame with the Selection tool, then open the Text Frame Options dialog box for the selected frame.**

   Remember, to open this dialog box, you can

   - Click Options in the Text Frame section of the Properties panel.
   - Choose Object>Text Frame Options.
   - Control/right-click the frame and choose Text Frame Options from the contextual menu.

5. **In the General pane of the resulting dialog box, change the Top, Bottom, and Right Inset Spacing fields to 0.125 in, and change the Left Inset Spacing field to 0.625 in. Click OK.**

   Again, to define different values for each inset, make sure you see the broken chain links between the fields.

   Because the frame bleeds off the page edge, you need to adjust the frame inset on only the bleed side to match the rest of the layout. Instead of overlaying two frames — one with the fill color and one with the text frame — you can use uneven inset spacing to achieve the same goal.

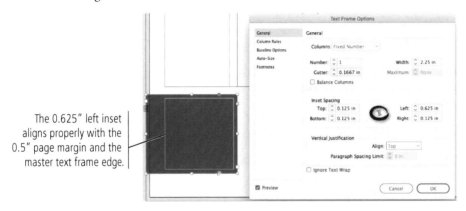

The 0.625" left inset aligns properly with the 0.5" page margin and the master text frame edge.

6. **Create another new text frame with the following dimensions (based on the top-left reference point):**

> X: 8.375 in   W: 2.125 in
> Y: 6.25 in   H: 1.5 in

By default, InDesign measurements reflect an object's position relative to the entire spread; the X: 8.375″ position is actually 2.875″ from the left edge of the right page (aligned to the left column edge in the text frame at the top of the page).

Note:

You can change this behavior by changing the Ruler Units origin in the Units & Increments pane of the Preferences dialog box.

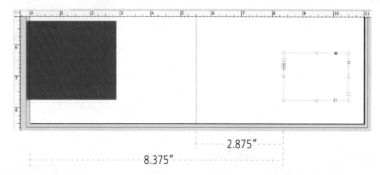

7. **Open the Text Frame Options dialog box for the new frame. Define a 0.125 in Inset value for all four sides, and choose Bottom in the Vertical Justification Align menu. Click OK to apply the changes.**

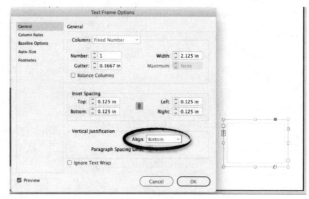

8. **Make sure you can see the entire spread in the document window.**

9. **Using the Selection tool, click to select the primary text frame on the left page of the spread.**

When a text frame is selected in the layout, the icon in the top-left corner identifies whether the frame is a primary text frame or a standard text frame.

This icon identifies the primary text frame.

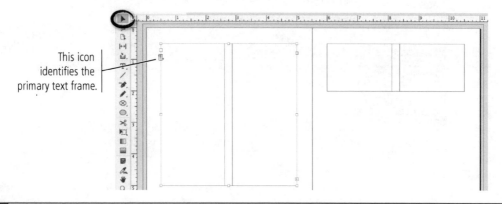

10. Click to select the color-filled frame at the bottom of the page.

New text frames are not automatically part of the primary text thread. If you want a frame to be a part of the primary thread, you have to manually add it.

This icon identifies a regular text frame.

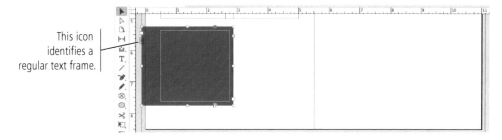

11. Select the primary text frame on the left page and click the frame's Out port. Immediately click the color-filled text frame to link the two frames.

Clicking the colored frame adds it to the primary text thread; text will flow from the top frame into the bottom one. Keep in mind that you can only have one primary text thread on each master page, but that thread can have multiple linked frames.

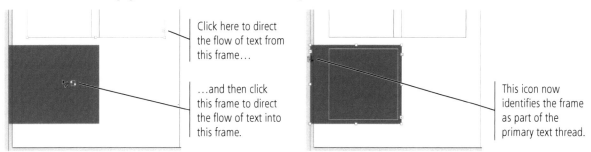

Click here to direct the flow of text from this frame...

...and then click this frame to direct the flow of text into this frame.

This icon now identifies the frame as part of the primary text thread.

12. Choose View>Extras>Show Text Threads.

This command makes it possible to visualize the way text will flow throughout the document. The primary text frames on each page are automatically linked, so the thread automatically runs from the colored frame to the primary text frame on the right page of the spread.

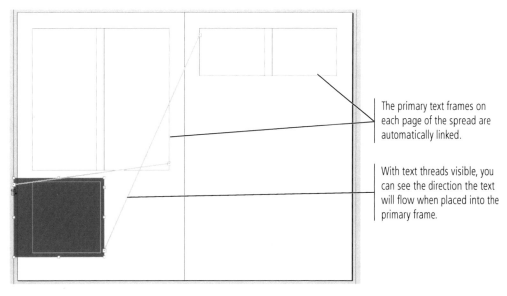

The primary text frames on each page of the spread are automatically linked.

With text threads visible, you can see the direction the text will flow when placed into the primary frame.

13. **Repeat Steps 9–11 to link from the primary text frame on the right page of the spread to the bottom text frame on the same page.**

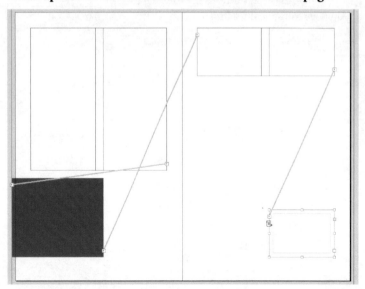

14. **Turn off the text threads (View>Extras>Hide Text Threads).**

15. **Using the Rectangle Frame tool, create an empty graphics frame using the following dimensions (based on the top-left reference point):**

   X: 2.875 in   W: 8.25 in
   Y: 2.1875 in   H: 5.75 in

16. **Fill the frame with a 20% tint of the C=36 M=59 Y=94 K=24 saved swatch.**

17. **Choose Object>Arrange>Send to Back to move the graphics frame behind the text frame on that page.**

   Placing the graphics frame on the master layout eliminates the need to manually draw or adjust the frame on each spread. The fill color simply serves as a visual reference.

18. **Select the bottom text frame on the right page of the spread. Change its fill color to Paper and change its Opacity value to 85%.**

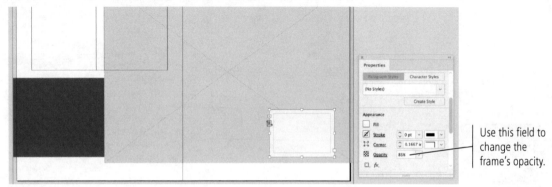

Use this field to change the frame's opacity.

19. **Save the file and continue to the next exercise.**

Place Automatic Page Number Markers

The next item to add to the master page layout is the page footer information, which is the page number and the name of the booklet. Rather than manually numbering each page in the booklet, which can be time consuming and invites human error, you can use special characters to automatically number the pages in any layout.

1. **With exhibits.indd open, make sure the A-Master layout is showing.**

2. **Create a new text frame with the following dimensions (based on the top-left reference point):**

    X: 6 in   W: 4.5 in
    Y: 8.15 in   H: 0.2 in

Special Characters and White Space

A number of special characters can be accessed in the Type submenus.
Use the following chart as a guide for accessing these characters.

Menu			What it's used for
Insert Special Character	Markers	Current Page Number	Places the current page number
		Next Page Number	Places the page number of the next frame in the same story
		Previous Page Number	Places the page number of the previous frame in the same story
		Section Marker	Places a user-defined text variable that is specific to the current layout section. (You'll learn about section numbering in Project 8.)
		Footnote Number	Inserts a number character based on the options defined in the Footnote Options dialog box
	Hyphens and Dashes	Em Dash	Places a dash that has the same width as the applied type size
		En Dash	Places a dash equivalent to one-half of an em dash
		Discretionary Hyphen	Allows you to hyphenate a word in a location other than what is defined by the current dictionary or hyphenate a word when automatic hyphenation is turned off; only appears if the word is hyphenated at the end of a line
		Nonbreaking Hyphen	Places a hyphen character that will not break at the end of a line; used to keep both parts of a phrase on the same line of the paragraph
	Quotation Marks	Double Left Quotation Marks	"
		Double Right Quotation Marks	"
		Single Left Quotation Mark	'
		Single Right Quotation Mark	'
		Straight Double Quotation Marks	"
		Straight Single Quotation Mark	'
	Other	Tab	Forces following text to begin at the next defined or default tab stop
		Right Indent Tab	Forces following text to align at the right indent of the column or frame
		Indent to Here	Creates a hanging indent by forcing all following lines in the paragraph to indent to the location of the character
		End Nested Style Here	Interrupts nested style formatting before the defined character limit
		Non-joiner	Prevents adjacent characters from being joined in a ligature or other alternate character connection

3. Inside the frame, type Getty Foundation Summer Special Exhibits Catalog. Change the formatting to 8-pt ATC Coral Normal with right alignment.

4. Place the insertion point immediately after the word "Catalog" and press the Spacebar once.

   Because the text is right-aligned, the Space character is not visible; a space at the end of a line is not considered in the line length or position when InDesign aligns paragraphs.

5. With the insertion point flashing after the space character (which you can't see), choose Type>Insert Special Character>Markers>Current Page Number.

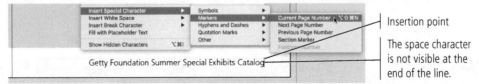

Insertion point

The space character is not visible at the end of the line.

Special Characters and White Space (continued)

Menu		What it's used for
Insert White Space	Em Space	Space equivalent to a capital M in the applied font and type size
	En Space	1/2 of an em space
	Nonbreaking Space	Places a space character the same width as pressing the Spacebar; prevents a line break from occurring, keeping related words together on the same line
	Nonbreaking Space (Fixed Width)	Same as the regular nonbreaking space but does not change size when a paragraph uses justified alignment
	Hair Space	1/24 of an em space
	Sixth Space	1/6 of an em space
	Thin Space	1/8 of an em space
	Quarter Space	1/4 of an em space
	Third Space	1/3 of an em space
	Punctuation Space	Same width as a period in the applied font
	Figure Space	Same width as a number in the applied font
	Flush Space	Variable space in a justified paragraph placed between the last character of the paragraph and a decorative character (a "bug") used to indicate the end of a story
Insert Break Character	Column Break	Forces text into the next available column (or frame, if used in a one-column frame or the last column of a multicolumn frame)
	Frame Break	Forces text into the next available frame
	Page Break	Forces text into the first available frame on the next page, skipping any available frames or columns on the same page
	Odd Page Break	Forces text into the first available frame on the next odd-numbered page
	Even Page Break	Forces text into the first available frame on the next even-numbered page
	Paragraph Return	Creates a new paragraph (same as pressing Return/Enter)
	Forced Line Break	Creates a new line without starting a new paragraph (called a "soft return")
	Discretionary Line Break	Creates a new line if the character falls at the end of the line only

6. If the hidden characters are not visible, choose Type>Show Hidden Characters.

The Current Page Number command inserts a special character that reflects the correct page number of any page where it appears. Because you placed this character on the A-Master page, the character shows as "A" in the text frame.

Now that the Space character is no longer the last character in the line, you can see it.

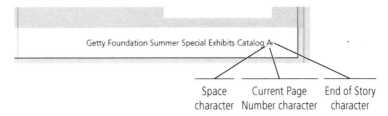

In this case, the single, regular Space character is not enough to separate the booklet name from the page number. InDesign provides a number of options for increasing and decreasing white space without simply pressing the Spacebar numerous times.

Keyboard Shortcuts for Special Characters

Character	Keyboard Shortcut	
	Macintosh	**Windows**
Current Page Number	Command-Option-Shift-N	Control-Alt-Shift-N
Em Dash	Option-Shift-Hyphen (-)	Alt-Shift-Hyphen (-)
En Dash	Option-Hyphen	Alt-Hyphen
Discretionary hyphen	Command-Shift-Hyphen	Control-Shift-Hyphen
Nonbreaking hyphen	Command-Option-Hyphen	Control-Alt-Hyphen
Double Left Quotation Marks	Option-[	Alt-[
Double Right Quotation Marks	Option-Shift-[	Alt-Shift-[
Single Left Quotation Mark	Option-]	Alt-]
Single Right Quotation Mark	Option-Shift-]	Alt-Shift-]
Straight Double Quotation Marks	Control-Shift-'	Alt-Shift-'
Straight Single Quotation Mark	Control-'	Alt-'
Tab	Tab	Tab
Right Indent Tab	Shift-Tab	Shift-Tab
Indent to Here	Command-\	Control-\
Em Space	Command-Shift-M	Control-Shift-M
En Space	Command-Shift-N	Control-Shift-N
Nonbreaking Space	Command-Option-X	Control-Alt-X
Thin Space	Command-Option-Shift-M	Control-Alt-Shift-M
Column Break	Enter (numeric keypad)	Enter (numeric keypad)
Frame Break	Shift-Enter (numeric keypad)	Shift-Enter (numeric keypad)
Page Break	Command-Enter (numeric keypad)	Control-Enter (numeric keypad)
Paragraph Return	Return	Enter
Forced Line Break	Shift-Return	Shift-Enter

7. **Highlight the Space character before the Page Number character.**

8. **Choose Type>Insert White Space>Em Space.**

   An **em** is a typographic measure equivalent to the applied type size. An em space is white space equal to one em.

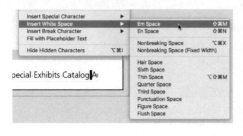

Em Space character

9. **Type a forward slash, then add a second Em Space character immediately after the slash.**

10. **Save the file and continue to the next stage of the project.**

STAGE 2 / Controlling the Flow of Text

The time you spent building effective master pages will enable you to more quickly place the content and create a multi-page document; you significantly reduced development time because you don't have to recreate these elements on each page.

You are building a document with 16 facing pages. You could manually insert the necessary pages, and then manually link the text from one page to the next. But anytime you see the word "manually," you should look for ways to automate some or all of the process. The ability to automate work is one of the defining characteristics of professional page-layout software such as InDesign.

Import and Auto-Flow Client Text

By applying styles, you can apply multiple formatting attributes — both character and paragraph — with a single click. InDesign is not the only software that supports text-formatting styles; Microsoft Word does as well.

Many clients will submit text with local formatting (changed font, different type size, and so on) that you will strip out and replace with the proper InDesign translations. Some, however, will send files formatted with Microsoft Word styles. In this case, you can import the styles from Microsoft Word directly into your InDesign layout to use as the basis for your work.

1. **With `exhibits.indd` open, use the Pages panel to navigate to Page 2 of the layout.**

2. **Open the Type pane of the Preferences dialog box.**

   Remember, preferences are accessed in the InDesign menu on Macintosh and the Edit menu on Windows.

3. **Make sure the Smart Text Reflow option is checked, choose End of Story in the Add Pages To menu, and check the Delete Empty Pages option. Click OK.**

When Smart Text Reflow is active, InDesign automatically adds pages to accommodate an entire story placed in a primary text frame. This option applies to adding text within a story and to changing formatting in a way that affects the number of required pages, which you will do in a later exercise.

- You can use the **Add Pages To** menu to determine where pages are added to the file (at the end of the current story, the current section, or the current document).

- If **Limit To Primary Text Frames** is not checked, you can add or remove pages when editing text in frames other than a primary text frame. This option only applies if the existing frame is already part of a text thread with at least one other frame. (New pages added when the text frame is not a primary text frame have a single-column text frame matching the default page margins for the file.)

- If **Preserve Facing-Page Spreads** is active, pages added to the middle of a document are added as document spreads based on the applied master layout. When unchecked, only the necessary pages will be added; subsequent existing pages are reshuffled (left-facing to right-facing) if necessary.

- If **Delete Empty Pages** is active, unnecessary pages are removed from the layout if you delete text or format text to require less space.

4. **Choose File>Place. Navigate to the file exhibits.docx in the WIP>Museum folder. Make sure the Show Import Options box is checked and click Open.**

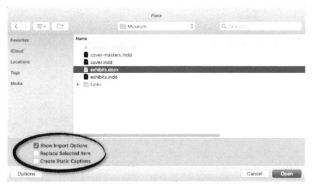

Note:

If Smart Text Reflow is not active, you can press Shift and click the loaded text cursor in a primary text frame on a layout page to automatically flow the entire story; InDesign adds pages as necessary to accommodate the entire story. (In this case, new pages are always added at the end of the document, regardless of the position of the text box where you first click to place the text. The Smart Text Reflow preference is not activated.)

5. **In the Import Options dialog box, make sure the Preserve Styles and Formatting from Text and Tables option is selected.**

6. **In the Manual Page Breaks menu, choose No Breaks.**

This command removes any page and section breaks in the client's Microsoft Word file.

7. **Select the Import Styles Automatically option, choose Use InDesign Style Definitions in both conflict menus, then click OK.**

8. **Click the loaded text cursor inside the margin guides on Page 2.**

Because of your choices in the Smart Text Reflow preferences, new pages are added at the end of the story to accommodate all the text in the placed story. The previous Page 3, which was the back cover of the booklet, is still the last page in the document because you chose to add new pages at the end of the story instead of the end of the document.

If your text does not automatically flow onto multiple pages, undo the placement. Make sure you are looking at the Page 2–3 spread —not the A-Master spread — and click again to place the loaded text.

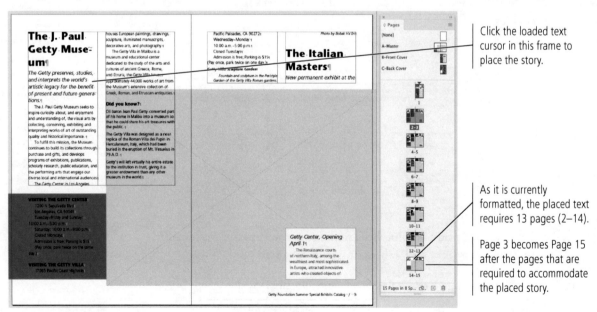

Click the loaded text cursor in this frame to place the story.

As it is currently formatted, the placed text requires 13 pages (2–14).

Page 3 becomes Page 15 after the pages that are required to accommodate the placed story.

9. **Save the file and continue to the next exercise.**

Understanding the Primary Text Frame

It is important to understand how the primary text frame affects placed text. If you change the master-page layout that is associated with a specific page, text inside the primary text frame reflows based on the dimensions of the primary text frame on the newly applied master page.

To illustrate this point in the examples here, we added a new facing-page master page layout named D-Master, with text frames in different properties than the frames on the A-Master in the booklet file (position, size, and number of columns).

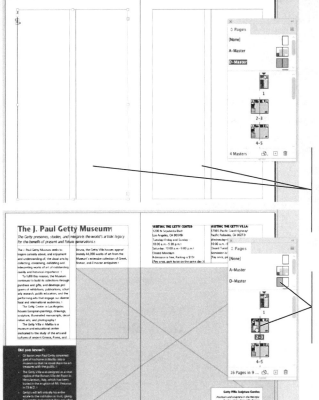

The primary text frames on the D-Master have different dimensions and parameters than the primary text frames on the A-Master layout.

We dragged the left page of the D-Master onto the Page 2 icon to change the master that is applied to the page.

Frames on the right page of the spread are not affected because we did not change the master layout associated with that page.

Text in the primary frame reflows into the primary text frame dimensions that are defined on the newly applied master page.

The colored frame does not exist on the D-Master layout, so it is no longer on the regular page.

The graphics frame is placed on Page 3, so it remains in place.

Keep the following in mind when you work with primary text frames:

- When you work on the master-page layout, you can click the Primary Text Frame icon to convert a frame to a standard text frame or click the Standard Text Frame icon to convert a frame to the primary text frame.

- You can only have one primary text frame (or series of threaded frames) per page.
- If you convert one frame in the primary text thread, all frames in the thread are converted to regular frames.
- If you convert a different frame to the primary text frame, the existing primary text frame is automatically converted to a standard text frame.

Review and Replace Imported Styles

As you can see in the current booklet file, the text is just a single long block running throughout the threaded text frames on seven spreads. Formatting has been applied to various elements, so the first step in this type of project is to evaluate any styles that might have been imported into the document and make necessary adjustments based on the styles that already exist in your InDesign file.

1. **With Page 2 of exhibits.indd showing, click with the Type tool to place the insertion point in the first paragraph.**

2. **Look at the Paragraph Styles panel (Window>Styles>Paragraph Styles).**

   The first paragraph is formatted with the Heading style. (You can assume other text with the same basic appearance is also a heading.) The plus sign (+) next to the style name indicates some formatting other than what is defined for the style has been applied to the active text. This is very common with text imported from Microsoft Word because some formatting options in Word do not accurately map to formatting choices in InDesign.

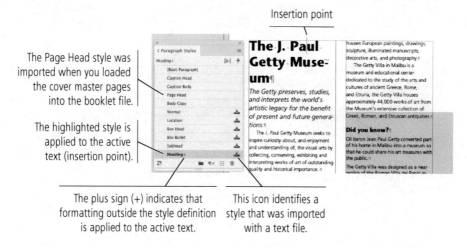

The Page Head style was imported when you loaded the cover master pages into the booklet file.

The highlighted style is applied to the active text (insertion point).

Insertion point

The plus sign (+) indicates that formatting outside the style definition is applied to the active text.

This icon identifies a style that was imported with a text file.

3. **Choose Edit>Select All to select all text in the story, then click the Clear Overrides in Selection button at the bottom of the Paragraph Styles panel.**

   This button removes any formatting that is not part of the actual style definition. It is a good idea to perform this step whenever you import a file that includes stored styles.

   You can clear overrides for any selected text, whether for a single character or an entire story. In this case, all overrides were created in the original Microsoft Word file; rather than manually clearing overrides in each paragraph, you can simply select the entire story and clear all overrides at once.

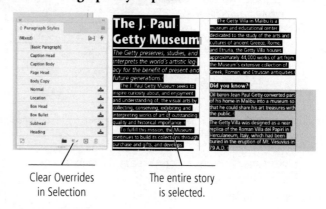

Clear Overrides in Selection

The entire story is selected.

4. **Click to place the insertion point back in the first paragraph of the story.**

5. **In the Paragraph Styles panel, Control/right-click the Heading style and choose Delete Style from the contextual menu.**

The Page Head style was imported with the cover pages; you should use that style instead of the one imported with the text.

6. **In the Delete Paragraph Style dialog box, choose Page Head in the Replace With menu and click OK.**

If you delete a style that's being used, you have to determine what to do with text that uses the style you want to delete. If you want to maintain the formatting of that text without applying a different style, you can choose [No Paragraph Style].

After the Heading style has been replaced with the Page Head style, the associated text in the layout changes in appearance to match the new style definition. (The Page Head style definition changes the text fill color and calls for the paragraph to span all columns in the frame.)

Text that was formatted with the Heading style is now formatted with the Page Head style.

7. **In the Paragraph Styles panel, drag Normal to the panel's Delete button.**

It's a good idea to remove unnecessary styles from the InDesign document.

Dragging a style to the panel's Delete button is the same as choosing Delete from the style's contextual menu.

Drag a style to the panel's Delete button to remove it.

8. **In the resulting dialog box, choose [No Paragraph Style] in the Replace With menu. Make sure the Preserve Formatting option is selected, then click OK.**

InDesign's default [No Paragraph Style] is not a style. In fact, it is the express lack of a defined style. Anytime you choose [No Paragraph Style] in the Replace With menu, the Preserve Formatting option becomes available in the Delete Paragraph Style dialog box.

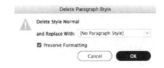

9. **Save the file and continue to the next exercise.**

Styles can store a very large number of settings, which you'll see as you complete the next exercises. Use the following chart as a reminder of exactly what can be stored in a paragraph style definition.

Character styles include a subset of these same options: General, Basic Character Formats, Advanced Character Formats, Character Color, OpenType Features, Underline Options, and Strikethrough Options.

Category	Options		
General	Based On Style Settings	Next Style Reset to Base	Shortcut Apply Style to Selection
Basic Character Formats	Font Family Leading Case	Style Kerning Position	Size Tracking Styles
Advanced Character Formats	Horizontal Scale Skew	Vertical Scale Language	Baseline Shift
Indents and Spacing	Alignment Left & Right Indent Space Before	Balance Ragged Lines First Line Indent Space After	Ignore Optical Margin Last Line Indent Align to Grid
Tabs	X position	Leader	Align On
Paragraph Rules	Rule Above On Offset Gap attributes	Rule Below On Left & Right Indents	Width Rule Weight/Style/Color
Paragraph Border	Stroke Weight/Style/Color	Corner Size and Shape	Offsets
Paragraph Shading	Shading Color/Tint	Corner Size and Shape	Offsets
Keep Options	Keep with Previous Start Paragraph Location	Keep with Next [N] Lines	Keep Lines Together
Hyphenation	Hyphenate On/Off (and all related options)		
Justification	Word Spacing Auto Leading	Letter Spacing Single Word Justification	Glyph Scaling Composer
Span Columns	Single Column	Span Columns	Split Column
Drop Caps and Nested Styles	Number of Lines Align Left Edge Nested Line Styles	Number of Characters Scale for Descenders	Character Style Nested Styles
GREP Style	New GREP Style	Apply [Style]	To Text Pattern
Bullets and Numbering	List Type Text After Bullet	List Style Character Style	Bullet Character Bullet/Number Position
Character Color	Fill Color, Tint, Overprint attributes Stroke Color, Tint, Weight, Overprint attributes		
OpenType Features	Titling, Contextual, & Swash Alternates Ordinals, Fractions, Discretionary Ligatures, Slashed Zero, Figure Style, Positional Form Stylistic Sets		
Underline Options	Underline On	Stroke attributes	Gap attributes
Strikethrough Options	Strikethrough On	Stroke attributes	Gap attributes
Export Tagging	EPUB and HTML Tag, Class	PDF Tag	

Edit a Style Definition

In most cases, styles imported with a text file need at least some modification, if for no other reason than InDesign has more sophisticated options relevant to commercial printing. Editing styles is both easy and efficient; when you change the options in a style definition, any text formatted with that style is reformatted.

1. **With Page 2 of exhibits.indd visible in the document window, place the insertion point in the second paragraph of the story.**

   This paragraph is formatted with the Location style. It should extend across both columns of the text frame, just as the Page Head does.

2. **Control/right-click the Location style and choose Edit "Location" in the contextual menu.**

   You can also edit a style by double-clicking the style in the panel. However, double-clicking a style in the panel applies the style to the current text and opens the Paragraph Style Options dialog box.

   By Control/right-clicking the style in the panel, you can edit the style without applying it to the currently selected text.

Note:

You can edit the default type settings for a layout by editing the [Basic Paragraph] style. You can edit the default type settings for all new InDesign layouts by editing the [Basic Paragraph] style when no file is open.

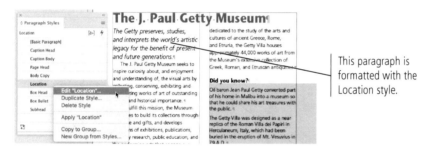

This paragraph is formatted with the Location style.

The Paragraph Style Options dialog box provides access to all the formatting options that can be stored in a paragraph style. In the left side of the dialog box, clicking a category name shows settings related to that category.

In the General category of options:

- **Based On** can be used to base one style on another, applying the same formatting options as those defined in the Based On style (the "parent" style). This menu defaults to [No Paragraph Style] if you do not choose another specific parent style.

- **Next Style** determines which style will be applied when you press Return/Enter to start a new paragraph.

- **Shortcut** can be used to define a keyboard shortcut that will apply the style.

- **Reset To Base** removes all formatting not defined in the parent style.

- **Style Settings** summarizes all formatting options in the style. If a style is based on another style, options different from the parent style appear after the + sign.

- **Apply to Selection** is available when you create a new style. If checked, the style you are defining is automatically applied to the active paragraph when you click OK to close the Paragraph Style Options dialog box.

3. **Make sure the Preview option is checked at the bottom of the dialog box.**

When the Preview option is checked, you can see the effect of your changes before you click OK.

4. **In the Span Columns options, choose Span Columns in the Paragraph Layout menu, and change the Space After Span value to 0.125 in.**

When the Preview option is active, you can see the effect of the change on text that is formatted with the style you are editing.

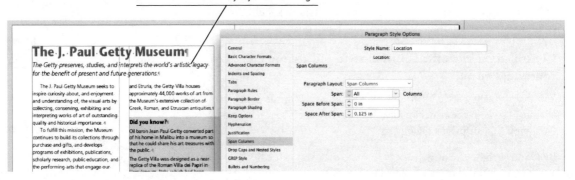

5. **Click Paragraph Rules in the list of categories.**

6. **Choose Rule Below in the primary menu.**

You can define a rule to appear above or below a paragraph (or both).

7. **With Rule Below showing in the menu, check the Rule On box.**

8. **Change the Weight field to 3 pt and choose White Diamond in the Type menu.**

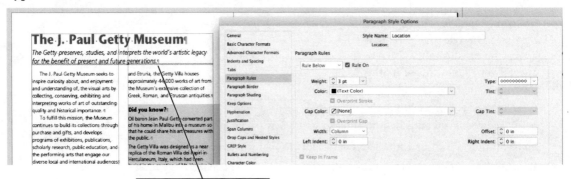

The rule below sits immediately below the text baseline.

Understanding Paragraph Rules and Borders

Many of the options for paragraph rules are the same as those for any other stroke. **Weight**, **Color**, and **Tint** define the basic appearance of the rule. The **Type** menu, which defaults to solid, includes a number of predefined line styles, such as dotted or dashed.

Gap Color and **Gap Tint** define the appearance of empty spaces in line styles that include white space.

HEADLINE HERE

HEADLINE HERE

HEADLINE HERE

HEADLINE HERE

HEADLINE HERE

HEADLINE HERE

Rules with no gap color   Rules with red gap color

The **Width** menu defaults to Column, which extends the rule across the entire column where the paragraph exists. If the frame has only one column, the rule extends across the entire frame width; if the paragraph spans more than one column, the rule extends across the width of whatever columns the paragraph spans. If you choose Text in this menu, the paragraph rule extends only the width that is occupied by the text in the paragraph.

HEADLINE HERE

Rule with width set to Column

HEADLINE HERE

Rule with width set to Text

Paragraph rules begin at the baseline of the paragraph where they are applied. In the image shown below, we applied a cyan rule above the paragraph and a red rule below the paragraph; you can see that the bottom of the Rule Above (cyan) and the top of the Rule Below (red) rests on the paragraph baseline.

The **Offset** value moves the rule away from the text baseline. For a Rule Above, increasing the Offset moves the line up; for a Rule Below, increasing the Offset moves the line down.

HEADLINE HERE   Rules have their origins at the paragraph baseline

HEADLINE HERE   Increasing Offset moves rules away from the baseline

Left Indent and **Right Indent** move the ends of the rule away from the edges of the defined width.

HEADLINE HERE   Rule with no Indent values

HEADLINE HERE   Rule with increased Indent values

In addition to paragraph rules, you can also use **Paragraph Borders** to define lines on all four sides of a paragraph. Checking the Paragraph Borders box in the Control panel applies default borders to the active paragraph. Option/Alt-clicking the Paragraph Border icon in the Control panel opens the Paragraph Borders and Shading dialog box, where you can change the settings for applied borders.

Most of the options (stroke attributes and offset) for paragraph borders are the same as those for paragraph rules. In fact, there is little difference between a top and bottom paragraph border and the paragraph rules above and below. Depending on the sides where you choose to apply borders, you can also use the Corner Size and Shape options to define the appearance of connecting borders.

Option/Alt-click this icon to open the Paragraph Borders and Shading dialog box.

This paragraph has borders defined on the left and ride sides.

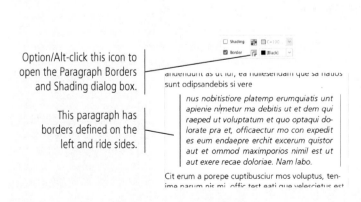

9. **Change the Offset value to 0.0625 in.**

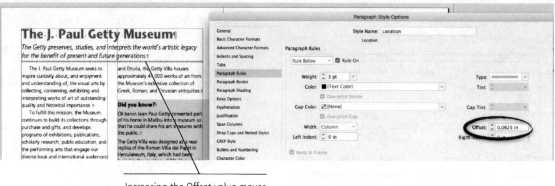

Increasing the Offset value moves the rule away from the baseline.

10. **Click OK to change the style definition.**

11. **Save the file and continue to the next exercise.**

Control Page and Frame Breaks

In the completed booklet, each spread will feature one exhibit in the museum. The layout defines specific spaces for specific elements of the story:

- The exhibit name begins the story on each spread. These are all formatted with the Page Head style.

- The "Did You Know" list of facts will appear in the color-filled box. The first line of the fact list is formatted with the Box Head style.

- The secondary heading and following text will appear in the two-column text frame on the right page of the spread. Each secondary heading is formatted with the Subhead style.

- The caption will appear in the frame on top of the large graphics frame. The first line of each caption is formatted with the Caption Head style.

Rather than manually placing page and frame breaks, you can use styles and paragraph formatting options to automatically place text in the correct frames.

1. **With exhibits.indd open, zoom out if necessary to show the entire Page 2–3 spread.**

Each spread should have only one instance of the Page Head style, in the first text frame on the left page of the spread.

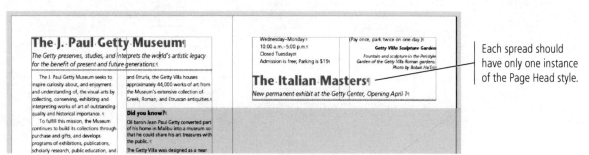

Each spread should have only one instance of the Page Head style.

2. **Control/right-click Page Head in the Paragraph Styles panel and choose Edit "Page Head" from the contextual menu.**

3. **Display the Keep Options pane. In the Start Paragraph menu, choose On Next Even Page.**

   Each section heading should appear on the left page of a spread, and left-facing pages are even-numbered.

Note:

These same options can be applied to any specific paragraph by choosing Keep Options from the Paragraph panel Options menu.

4. **Click OK to change the style definition.**

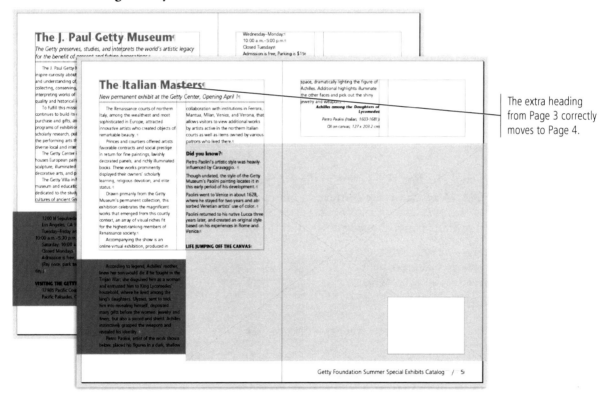

The extra heading from Page 3 correctly moves to Page 4.

5. **Save the file and continue to the next exercise.**

   You will use additional techniques in the next exercise to force each type of subhead into the appropriate location on the spread.

Define Parent-Child Style Relationships

When designing long documents, it is important to format text consistently from one page to the next throughout the entire document; body copy (for example) should use the same basic font throughout the entire layout. If you change the main body font, you should also change any related styles that are variations of the main body text, such as bulleted or numbered lists.

The best way to manage this type of situation is to create secondary styles based on the main style. This way, changes to the main style (called the **parent style**) are reflected in styles based on that style (the **child styles**).

1. **With `exhibits.indd` visible, navigate to and review the Page 4–5 spread.**

This file includes three different types of subheadings. All three have a similar (but not exact) appearance, so three separate styles are used to format these various elements. You are going to create parent/child relationships between these headings so that later changes to one will affect all three.

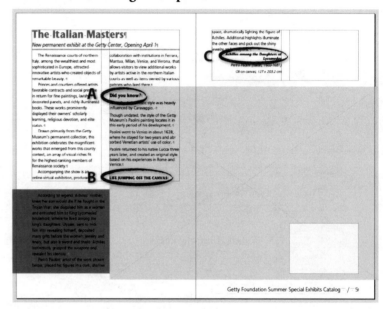

A   Box Heads should begin in the frame in the bottom-left corner of the spread.

B   Subheads should begin in the two-column frame at the top of the right page.

C   Caption Heads should begin in the frame in the bottom-right corner of the spread.

2. **Control/right-click the Box Head style in the Paragraph Styles panel and choose Edit "Box Head" from the contextual menu.**

3. **In the General options pane, choose Subhead in the Based On menu.**

When you base one style on another, the settings area lists the formatting options that differ between the two styles. When you redefine an existing style to be based on another style, InDesign tries to maintain the original formatting of the style you are editing instead of the one it is based on. In the Style Settings area, you can see the style will be Subhead +. Everything after the plus sign is different than the settings defined for the style in the Based On menu.

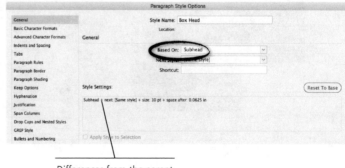

Differences from the parent style are listed after the +.

4. **Make the following changes to the Box Head style definition:**

Basic Character Formats:	**Case: Normal**
Advanced Character Formats:	**Horizontal Scale: 100%**

5. **Click the General tab and review the Style Settings area.**

You can see the style now uses the same settings as the Subhead style but with four exceptions: the two that existed when you changed the Based On style menu and the two that you defined in Step 4.

Note:

You can click the Reset to Base button to remove any formatting options that are not part of the Based On style.

6. **Click OK to apply the changes.**

You won't see any obvious changes yet in the layout because you are not actually changing the style formatting. You are only changing the relationship between styles so that later changes will be easier.

7. **Control/right-click the Caption Head style in the Paragraph Styles panel and choose Edit "Caption Head" from the contextual menu.**

8. **In the General options pane, choose Subhead in the Based On menu.**

If you review the Style Settings description, you might see a number of options listed that do not technically apply to the style. In this case, the default Paragraph Shading and Paragraph Borders settings are different in the child style than they are in the parent style — even though those features are not actually turned on for either style. This is a minor bug in the software but one to be aware of.

Note:

Changes to the parent will not override formatting options that have already been overridden in the child style. For example, the type size of the Box Head and Caption Head child styles is already different than the type size of the Subhead style; changing the type size of the parent (Subhead) would not affect the two child styles.

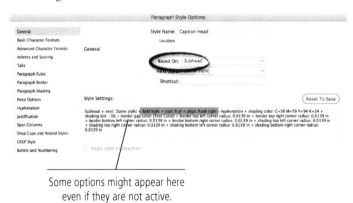

Some options might appear here even if they are not active.

9. **Click the Reset To Base button above the style description.**

The Reset To base button removes *all* formatting different from what is defined in the parent style.

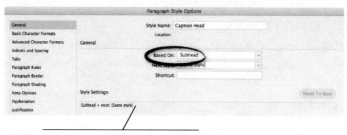

Reset To Base removes all formatting
not defined in the parent style.

10. **Make the following changes to the Caption Head style settings:**

Basic Character Formats:	**Style: Bold Italic**
	Size: 8 pt
	Leading: Auto
	Case: Normal
Advanced Character Formats:	**Horizontal Scale: 100%**
Indents and Spacing:	**Alignment: Right**

11. **Click OK to close the dialog box and apply the changes.**

12. **Control/right-click the Subhead style in the Paragraph Styles panel. Choose Edit "Subhead" in the contextual menu.**

Now that the Box Head and Caption Head styles are based on the Subhead style, you can change the settings of all three styles by changing only the parent.

13. **In the Keep Options, choose In Next Column in the Start Paragraph menu.**

The In Next Column option moves a paragraph to the next column in the same frame or to the next frame if the text is already in the last or only column of a frame.

14. Click OK to apply the change.

You can see the Caption Head on the active spread correctly moved to start a new column. The overall layout, however, is obviously wrong. It is important to understand that changes to styles can have significant impact on your overall layout, especially in the early stages of implementation. Changes in the next few exercises will correct the remaining problems with text position in various frames.

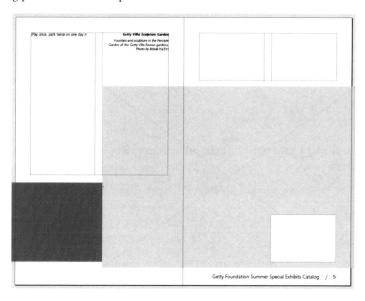

15. Save the file and continue to the next exercise.

 ## Control Widows and Orphans

Widows (single lines of a paragraph at the top of a column or a very short last line of a paragraph) and **orphans** (single lines of a paragraph at the end of a column) are considered bad typography and can sometimes ruin your intended layout. In this exercise you will use a number of techniques to correct these problems.

When working through a multipage document, it is important to understand that changes on early pages can affect text flow later in the document. It is a good idea to start at the beginning and work forward; this allows you to better see how changes early in the booklet might affect the layout in later spreads.

1. With exhibits.indd open, navigate to the Page 2–3 spread and place the insertion point in the third paragraph on Page 2.

The active paragraph text is currently formatted with the Body Copy style. However, the first paragraph after each Location and Subhead paragraph should have no first-line indent. You will create a secondary style to easily apply the correct formatting to each paragraph that needs no first-line paragraph indent.

2. **Control/right-click the Body Copy style in the Paragraph Styles panel and choose Duplicate Style.**

   The new style name defaults to the original style name plus the word "copy." The new style also defaults to the same formatting options as the one you chose to duplicate.

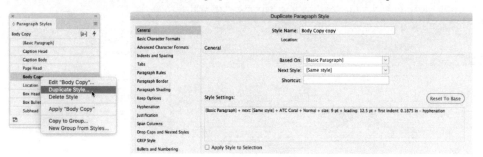

3. **Change the new style name to Body Copy No Indent, and choose Body Copy in the Based On menu.**

   The first-line indent value should be the only difference between this new style you are creating and the existing one.

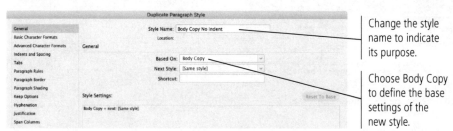

   Change the style name to indicate its purpose.

   Choose Body Copy to define the base settings of the new style.

Note:

Because you are basing the new style of the existing one, changes you make to the original Body Copy style will also affect this new Body Copy No Indent style.

4. **In the Indents and Spacing options, change the First Line Indent field to 0 in.**

5. **Click General in the category list and review the Style Settings window.**

   You can see the style has only one difference ("First Indent: 0") from the original Body Copy style.

6. **Check the Apply Style to Selection option, then click OK.**

When Apply Style to Selection is active, the new style you are defining is automatically applied to the active selection in the layout.

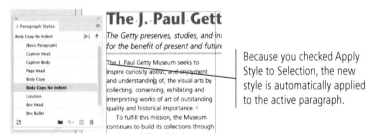

Because you checked Apply Style to Selection, the new style is automatically applied to the active paragraph.

7. **Zoom out to view the entire spread.**

The single word at the top of the right Page 3 column is both a widow and an orphan. Not only is it considered to be bad form, but it does not leave room in the column for the next subheading. You can use the style you just created to correct this problem.

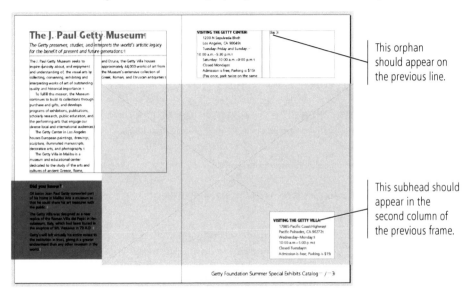

This orphan should appear on the previous line.

This subhead should appear in the second column of the previous frame.

8. **On the right side of the Page 2–3 spread, apply the Body Copy No Indent style to all body paragraphs after the "Visiting the Getty Center" subhead.**

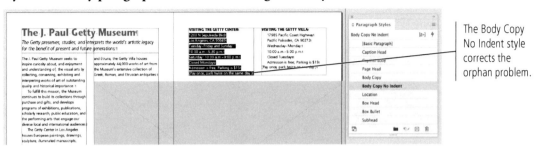

The Body Copy No Indent style corrects the orphan problem.

9. **Apply the Body Copy No Indent style to the seven paragraphs immediately following the second subhead.**

10. **Navigate to and review the Page 4–5 spread.**

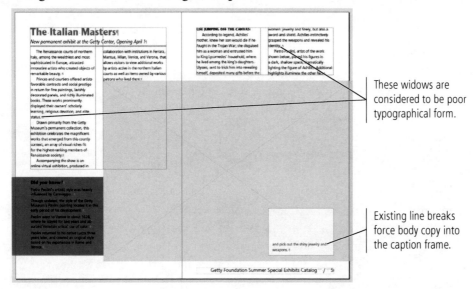

These widows are considered to be poor typographical form.

Existing line breaks force body copy into the caption frame.

11. **Apply the Body Copy No Indent style to the first regular paragraphs on Page 4 and Page 5.**

All the subheadings now appear in the correct positions, but the second paragraph of body copy on Page 4 has a bad widow, and the last line of body copy on the same page runs very close to the edge of the graphics frame. Allowing hyphenation can often fix problems created by widows.

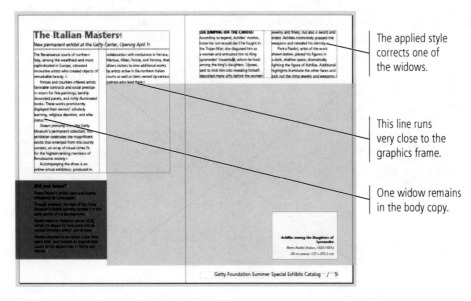

The applied style corrects one of the widows.

This line runs very close to the graphics frame.

One widow remains in the body copy.

12. In the Paragraph Styles panel, Control/right-click the Body Copy style and choose Edit "Body Copy" from the contextual menu.

Remember, the Body Copy No Indent style is based on the Body Copy style; by changing the hyphenation options for this style, you change the options for both styles.

13. In the Paragraph Style Options dialog box, show the Hyphenation options.

14. Check the Hyphenate option.

The Hyphenation options control the way InDesign hyphenates text. If the Hyphenate box is unchecked, InDesign will not hyphenate text in the paragraph.

- **Words With At Least _ Letters** defines the minimum number of characters that must exist in a hyphenated word.

- **After First _ Letters** and **Before Last _ Letters** define the minimum number of characters that must appear before and after a hyphen.

- **Hyphen Limit** defines the maximum number of hyphens that can appear on consecutive lines. (Remember, you are defining the limit here, so zero means there is no limit, allowing unlimited hyphens.)

- **Hyphenation Zone** defines the amount of white space allowed at the end of a line of unjustified text before hyphenation begins.

- **Hyphenate Capitalized Words** allows capitalized words (proper nouns) to be hyphenated.

- **Hyphenate Last Word** allows the last word in a paragraph to be hyphenated.

- **Hyphenate Across Column** allows the last word in a column or frame to be hyphenated.

Note:

Typographic conventions recommend no hyphenation in headings, no more than three hyphens in a row, and at least three characters before or after a hyphen. Some designers follow stricter rules, such as not hyphenating proper nouns; others prefer no hyphenation at all.

15. Change the After First and Before Last fields to 3.

Overriding Automatic Hyphenation

InDesign applies automatic hyphenation based on the defined language dictionary. You can override the hyphenation as defined in the dictionary by choosing Edit>Spelling>User Dictionary.

If you highlight a word before opening the dictionary, it automatically appears in the Word field. Clicking the Hyphenate button shows the possible hyphenation locations as defined in the dictionary. You can override the automatic hyphenation by adding or deleting the consecutive tilde characters in the Word field. When you change the hyphenation of a word, you have to click the Add button to add the new hyphenation scheme to the dictionary.

Default hyphenation locations

If you add the exception to the list, the word "photography" will only hyphenate between the "o" and the "g".

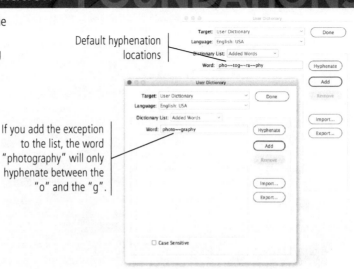

16. Click OK to change the style definition.

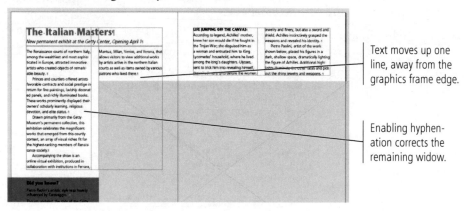

Text moves up one line, away from the graphics frame edge.

Enabling hyphenation corrects the remaining widow.

Note:

Hyphenation options can be applied to any specific paragraph by choosing Hyphenation from the Paragraph panel Options menu.

17. Navigate through the layout and apply the Body Copy No Indent style to the first regular paragraph on each page of each spread.

18. Show the Page 10–11 spread in the document window.

Typographic conventions suggest that at least two lines of a paragraph should be kept together at the beginning and end of a column or frame. (Headings at the end of a frame or column are also sometimes considered orphans.) You should correct this problem.

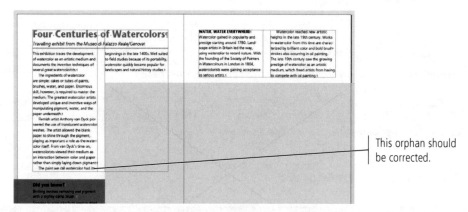

This orphan should be corrected.

19. Place the insertion point in the last line of the left column. Open the Paragraph panel Options menu and choose Keep Options.

You can use the options in this menu to change paragraph formatting settings for only the selected text.

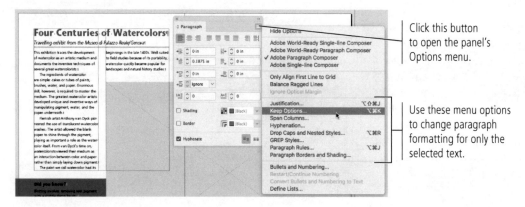

Click this button to open the panel's Options menu.

Use these menu options to change paragraph formatting for only the selected text.

20. **Activate the Keep Lines Together check box, and choose the At Start/ End... option. Leave the Start and End fields set to the default 2.**

21. **Click OK to return to the document.**

The orphaned first line moves into the second column because the first column does not have enough space to fit two lines at the beginning of the paragraph, as you defined in the step.

A plus sign (+) appears next to the applied style name, indicating that formatting other than the style definition has been applied to the active selection. You edited only this paragraph and not the style definition, so the local formatting override is intentional.

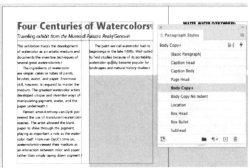

22. **Save the file and continue to the next exercise.**

Understanding Paragraph Composition Options

InDesign offers two options for controlling the overall flow of text (called **composition**) within a paragraph: **Adobe Paragraph Composer** (the default) and **Adobe Single-line Composer**. Both methods create breaks based on the applied hyphenation and justification for a paragraph.

You can change the composition method for an individual paragraph in the Paragraph panel Options menu or the Justification dialog box, or you can change the composition method for a paragraph style in the Justification pane of the Paragraph Style Options dialog box.

The Adobe Paragraph Composer evaluates the entire paragraph as a unit; changing one line of a paragraph might alter other lines in the paragraph (including earlier lines) to create what the software defines as the "best" overall composition. For example, adding a line break on Line 6 to eliminate a hyphen might also cause Lines 2 through 5 to reflow if InDesign determines the shift will create a "better" overall paragraph.

The Adobe Single-line Composer is a good choice if you prefer exact control over your text flow. Using Single-line Composer, adding a manual line break on Line 6, for example, will not affect preceding lines in the paragraph.

Define Bullets and Numbering Options

The paragraphs in the color-filled boxes should be bulleted lists, as suggested by the style name ("Box Bullet"). You could manually type the bullets at the beginning of each line, but it is easier and more efficient to use the Bullets and Numbering options in the style settings to automatically format all the bulleted list items at one time.

1. **With exhibits.indd open, zoom in to the color-filled frame on Page 2.**

2. **Control/right-click the Box Bullet style in the Paragraph Styles panel and choose Edit "Box Bullet" from the contextual menu.**

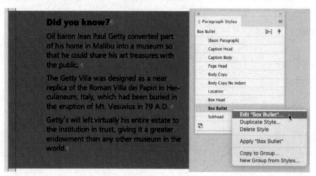

3. **In the Paragraph Style Options dialog box, display the Bullets and Numbering pane. In the List Type menu, choose Bullets.**

   By default, you can apply the Bullets or Numbers type of list. You can also define custom lists by choosing Type>Bulleted & Numbered Lists>Define Lists. If you've defined a custom list type, it will be available in the List Type menu of the Paragraph Style Options dialog box.

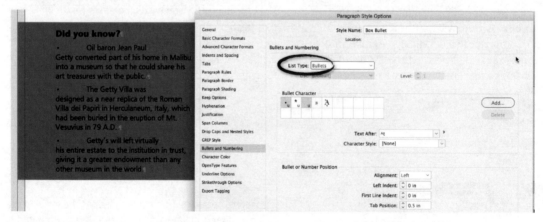

4. **Click the Add button to the right of the Bullet Character list.**

   The Add Bullets dialog box allows you to choose a character for the bullet. This character defaults to the same font used in the style, but you can choose any font and font style from the menus at the bottom of the dialog box.

5. **Open the Font Family menu in the Add Bullets dialog box and choose a font that includes dingbat characters.**

   For the bullet character, try the Zapf Dingbats (Macintosh) or Wingdings (Windows) fonts. If you don't have one of these fonts, use any character from any font you think works well as a bullet character in this layout.

6. **In the table of glyphs at the top of the dialog box, select any character you feel works well with the theme of a museum exhibit catalog.**

   We used the character of an old-fashioned ink pen tip.

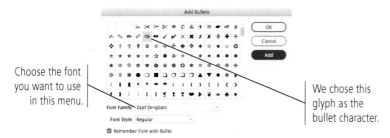

Choose the font you want to use in this menu.

We chose this glyph as the bullet character.

7. **Make sure the Remember Font with Bullet option is checked, and then click OK to return to the Paragraph Style Options dialog box.**

   The Remember Font with Bullet option is important if you use extended characters or decorative or dingbat fonts as bullet characters. If you select the solid square character (■) in the Zapf Dingbats font, for example, changing to a different font would show the letter "n" as the bullet character.

8. **In the grid of available characters, click to select the gylph you just added.**

9. **Leave the Text After field at the default (^t, the code for a Tab character).**

10. **In the Bullet or Number Position area, change the Left Indent value to 0.2 in, and change the First Line Indent value to -0.2 in. Leave the Tab Position value blank.**

    The Tab Position field defaults to the first available half-inch mark; if you define a 0.6″ left-indent, for example, the default tab position would be 1″. When you define a negative first-line indent (called a **hanging indent**), the Tab Position field is cleared; the first tab is the defined left-indent value.

Note:

Changing these fields also changes the same fields in the Indents and Spacing options.

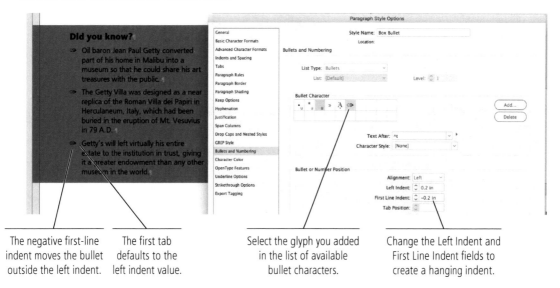

The negative first-line indent moves the bullet outside the left indent.

The first tab defaults to the left indent value.

Select the glyph you added in the list of available bullet characters.

Change the Left Indent and First Line Indent fields to create a hanging indent.

11. **Click OK to change the style definition and return to the layout.**

12. **Save the file and continue to the next exercise.**

ASCII is a text-based code that defines characters with a numeric value between 001 and 256. The standard alphabet and punctuation characters are mapped from 001 to 128. **Extended ASCII characters** are those with ASCII numbers higher than 128; these include symbols (bullets, copyright symbols, etc.) and some special characters (en dashes, accent marks, etc.). Some of the more common extended characters can be accessed in the Type>Insert submenus.

Unicode fonts include two-bit characters that are common in some foreign language typesetting (e.g., Cyrillic, Japanese, and other non-Roman or pictographic fonts).

OpenType fonts can store more than 65,000 **glyphs** (characters) in a single font — far beyond what you could access with a keyboard. In many cases, these extra glyphs are alternative formatting for other characters (such as ligatures and fractions). This large glyph storage capacity means that a single OpenType font can replace the multiple separate "Expert" fonts that contain variations of fonts. Minion Swash, for example, is no longer necessary when you can access the Swashes subset of the Minion Pro font. The OpenType format also enables you to use the same font files on both Macintosh and Windows computers.

OpenType features are a character-formatting attribute. You can apply OpenType features to specific text using the OpenType menu in the Character panel Options menu.

OpenType attributes can be applied even if they aren't available for the font you are currently using. For example, you can apply the Fractions attribute to a list of ingredients; as you experiment with different fonts, the Fractions attribute will be applied if it's available in the applied font.

OpenType attributes are bracketed if they are unavailable for the currently selected font.

It's also important to realize that OpenType attributes change the appearance of glyphs but do not change the actual text in the layout. When the Fractions attribute replaces "1/2" with "½", the text still includes three characters; the OpenType Fractions attribute has simply altered the glyphs that represent those characters to display a styled fraction. You can turn off OpenType attributes by toggling off the option in the Character panel Options menu. With OpenType attributes turned off, the styled characters return to their basic appearance.

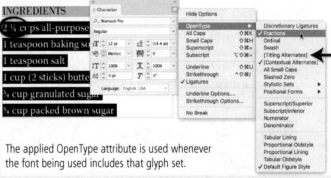

The applied OpenType attribute is used whenever the font being used includes that glyph set.

When a text frame is selected, clicking the OpenType badge on the bottom edge of the frame displays the OpenType properties that are available for text in the frame.

The same options are available when specific text is highlighted. Clicking the OpenType badge opens a menu of attributes and stylistic sets that can be applied to the selected text.

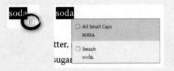

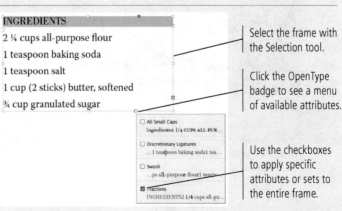

Select the frame with the Selection tool.

Click the OpenType badge to see a menu of available attributes.

Use the checkboxes to apply specific attributes or sets to the entire frame.

Working with Alternate Glyphs

The Glyphs panel (Window>Type & Tables>Glyphs or Type>Glyphs) provides access to all glyphs in a font. Using the panel is simple: place the insertion point where you want a character to appear, then double-click the character you want to place. By default, the panel shows the entire active font, but you can show only specific character sets using the Show menu.

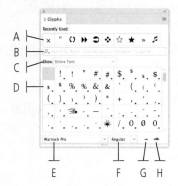

A — Access recently used glyphs, regardless of the active font.

B — Search for a specific glyph by name, unicode value, or glyph ID.

C — Show a specific character set for the selected font.

D — Double-click a glyph in the chart to add it at the current insertion point.

E — Change the font family that is displayed in the panel.

F — Change the font style that is displayed in the panel.

G — Zoom out (make glyphs in the panel grid smaller).

H — Zoom in (make glyphs in the panel grid larger).

You can also use the Glyphs panel to explore the different character sets available for a specific font. The Show menu allows you to access different character sets, including extended character sets such as symbols and OpenType alternative character sets.

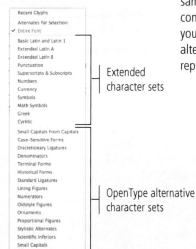

Extended character sets

OpenType alternative character sets

When text set with an OpenType font is selected in the layout, InDesign offers an on-screen menu of alternates for the first character in the selection (indicated by a blue bar below that character). Move your cursor over the indicated character to see the contextual menu, then simply click one of those alternates to replace the glyph.

The Type tool cursor is over the highlighted glyph.

Alternates for the selection appear in a contextual pop-up menu.

In addition to alternate characters for a single glyph, the in-context menus also support fractions, ordinals, and ligatures when more than one relevant character is selected.

Fractions   Ordinals   Ligatures

You can turn this behavior off by unchecking the Show for Alternates option in the Advanced Type pane of the Preferences dialog box.

If you choose Alternates for Selection in the Glyphs panel Show menu, you can see the same options you would in the contextual menu. In this case, you have to double-click the alternate glyph in the panel to replace it in the text.

Redefine Styles Based on Local Formatting Overrides

You might have noticed the black text in the color-filled boxes is difficult to read because the boxes have a dark fill color. Although you are going to change the box color on each spread, you are going to use other dark colors that still make the black text difficult to read.

In addition to changing the style definitions in the dialog box, you can experiment with formatting options directly in the layout. When you're satisfied with your results, you can use what you define in the layout to redefine the style definition.

1. **With exhibits.indd open, make sure the color-filled box on Page 2 is visible.**

2. **Select the entire first bullet paragraph in the box. Using the Swatches panel, change the text color to Paper.**

3. **Move the insertion point to the end of the paragraph and review the results.**

   The Paper swatch removes or knocks out the color of the text frame (hence the term **knockout text**); the text is now much more readable.

The Paper color is not defined in the Box Bullet style.

4. **Control/right-click Box Bullet in the Paragraph Styles panel and choose Redefine Style in the contextual menu.**

   This option makes it easy to experiment with formatting within the context of the layout and change a style definition to match what you created with local formatting. In this case you are redefining the Box Bullet style based on the changes you made in Step 2.

   Because more than one Box Bullet paragraph appears on this page, you can see how redefining the style based on local formatting affects all text where that style is applied.

Note:

Changing the color of text in the paragraph also changes the color of the bullet character in that paragraph.

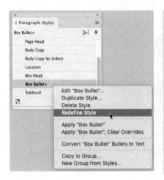
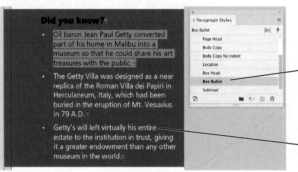

After redefining the style, the style no longer shows local overrides.

Other Box Bullet paragraphs also show the redefined color.

5. Select the heading paragraph in the box ("Did You Know?") and change the text fill color to Paper.

6. With the same paragraph selected, open the Paragraph Styles panel Options menu and choose Redefine Style.

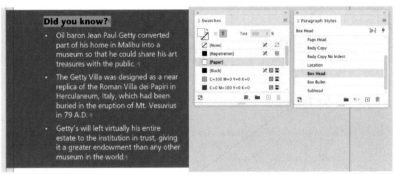

7. Save the file and continue to the next exercise.

Make Manual Layout Adjustments

Despite all the available automation and productivity options, some things simply must be resolved manually. There is no way to tell InDesign, for example, "Add a line break if the paragraph is visually unbalanced." Resolutions to issues such as these, which add polish to a professional layout, must be determined and applied manually.

1. With **exhibits.indd** open, zoom in to the caption text frame on the Page 2–3 spread.

   You created this frame on the master page layout at a specific size, but the size you defined was simply an estimation. You want the frame on each page to be only as large as necessary to contain the caption text.

2. Select the text frame with the Selection tool, then Control/right-click the active text frame and choose Fitting>Fit Frame to Content in the contextual menu.

   Unfortunately, the Auto-Height text frame option does not work well for text frames that are part of the primary text thread. Instead you have to manually adjust the frame height. You could simply drag the frame handles to change its size, but InDesign's frame-fitting capabilities make the process much more exact.

When working with a text frame, this command shrinks the frame to the smallest possible height based on the text inside the frame. The top edge of the frame remains in place regardless of the selected reference point in the Control panel.

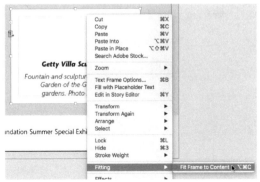

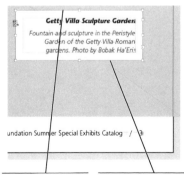

The top edge of the frame remains in its original position.

The frame shrinks to the minimum height required to contain the text.

3. With the frame selected, choose one of the bottom reference points in the Properties panel and change the frame's Y position to 7.75 in.

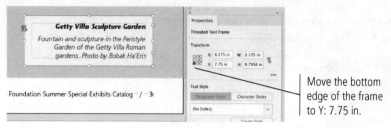

Move the bottom edge of the frame to Y: 7.75 in.

4. Navigate to the caption frame on the Page 4–5 spread.

5. Place the insertion point before the word "Daughters" in the caption head and press Shift-Return/Enter.

This character, called a **soft return**, forces a new line without starting a new paragraph.

There is some subjective element to balancing lines of copy, especially headings. The forced line break makes this caption heading appear better balanced.

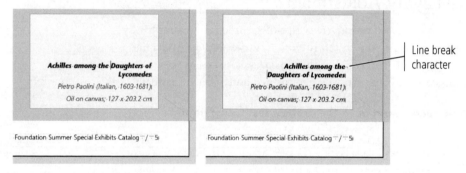

Line break character

6. Repeat Steps 2–3 to adjust the text frame size to fit the text, and reposition its bottom edge at Y: 7.75 in.

7. Navigate through the layout and add soft returns as necessary to balance the caption headings and caption text. Adjust each frame to fit its content and then reposition its bottom edge at Y: 7.75".

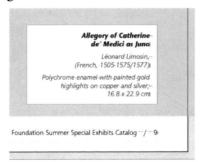

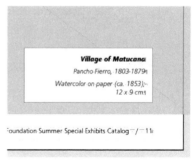

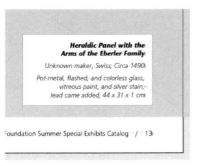

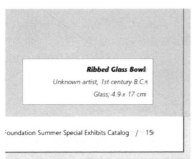

8. Save the file and continue to the next exercise.

 ## Place Images into Master Frames

For all intents and purposes the booklet text is finished. The next task is to place the images. Because you placed the graphics frame on the master page layout, you can simply place these images into the existing frames without any additional intervention.

1. With **exhibits.indd** open, navigate to the Page 2–3 spread. Deselect all objects in the layout, then choose File>Place.

2. In the resulting dialog box, uncheck the Show Import Options box. Navigate to the WIP>Museum>Links folder, then Command/Control-click to select the following images:

achilles.jpg

battle.jpg

bowl.jpg

herald.jpg

juno.jpg

villa.jpg

watercolor.jpg

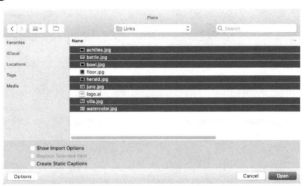

Note:

When multiple images are selected in the Place dialog box, the Replace Selected Item option is grayed out (unavailable). All selected images are loaded into the Place cursor.

3. **Click Open to load the selected images into the cursor, then review the Links panel.**

When more than one image is loaded in the Place cursor, the cursor shows the number of images currently loaded. The Links panel shows "LP" for the active image in the Loaded Place cursor.

LP identifies the active image in the Loaded Place cursor.

The cursor shows that 7 images are loaded in the Place cursor.

4. **Press the Right Arrow key five times to make villa.jpg active in the Loaded Place cursor.**

The Right Arrow key moves to the next unplaced item in the list; the Left Arrow key moves to the previous unplaced item.

The villa.jpg file is active in the Loaded Place cursor.

5. **Click inside the graphics frame on Page 3 to place the image.**

Don't click inside the frame area on Page 2 of the spread. InDesign only recognizes the frame as existing on the right page of the spread; the process won't work if you click in the frame area on the left page of the spread.

As with placing text into the primary text frame, you don't have to override the master page to place the image into the graphics frame. InDesign assumes that clicking inside an existing frame — even one from the master page — means you want to place the image inside that frame. Once you place the image, the frame is automatically detached from the master page.

After placing the image, the next image in the Links panel list automatically becomes active in the Loaded Place cursor.

The villa.jpg file is now placed on Page 3 in the layout.

The watercolor.jpg file is now active in the Loaded Place cursor.

6. Using the Pages panel, navigate to the Page 4–5 spread.

7. Use the arrow keys to make achilles.jpg active in the Loaded Place cursor.

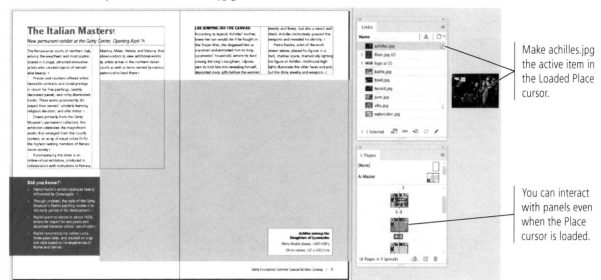

Make achilles.jpg the active item in the Loaded Place cursor.

You can interact with panels even when the Place cursor is loaded.

8. Click inside the empty graphics frame on the Page 4–5 spread to place the loaded image.

9. **Use the same method from Steps 6–8 to place the remaining images in the layout.**

Pages 6–7 **battle.jpg**

Pages 8–9 **juno.jpg**

Pages 10–11 **watercolor.jpg**

Pages 12–13 **herald.jpg**

Pages 14–15 **bowl.jpg**

10. **Zoom in to the caption text frame on Page 13.**

If you look carefully at the text frame, you might notice the underlying images are slightly visible behind the text. Because you defined the frame's opacity as 85% on the master page, all attributes of the frame are 85% opaque, including text inside the frame.

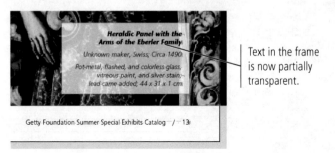

Text in the frame is now partially transparent.

11. **Navigate to the A-Master layout. Select the text frame on the right page of the spread, then open the Effects panel.**

As you can see, the entire object is 85% opaque. The Stroke, Fill, and Text are listed separately, however, which means you can change each of those values independently.

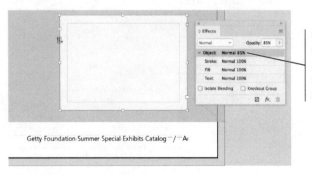

When you use the Opacity field in the Control or Properties panel, you change the opacity of the entire object, including any contents.

12. **With Object selected in the panel, change the Opacity field to 100%.**

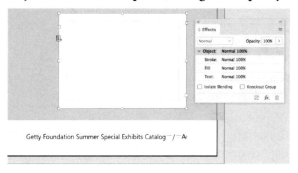

Note:

The Stroke, Fill, and Text opacity percentages are applied as a percentage of the object's opacity.

13. **Select Fill in the Effects panel, then change the Opacity field to 85%.**

Use the options in this panel to change the opacity of individual frame attributes.

14. **Navigate to Page 13 of the layout and review the caption text frame.**

You can still see the graphic behind the frame, but the text in the frame is now 100% opaque.

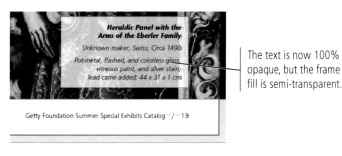

The text is now 100% opaque, but the frame fill is semi-transparent.

15. **Save the file and continue to the next exercise.**

Unify Spreads with Color

Using similar or complementary colors on each page of a spread is one way to help unify a design. When you created the master pages, you applied a dark brown fill to the text frame on the lower-left part of the spread. Now that the images are in place, it would be better to use colors from each spread's image on the associated frame. The Eyedropper tool, which you can use to **sample** colors from existing objects, makes it easy to apply image colors to native object fills.

You can use the Eyedropper tool to copy a number of formatting options, including stroke and fill settings, character and paragraph settings, and object settings. By default, the Eyedropper tool copies all formatting attributes. You can change that behavior by double-clicking the tool in the Tools panel to access the Eyedropper Options dialog box. Simply uncheck the options you don't want to copy (including individual options in each category), and then click OK.

1. **With exhibits.indd open, navigate to the Page 2–3 spread.**

2. **Click the pasteboard area with the Selection tool to make sure nothing is selected in the file.**

   If anything is selected when you sample with the Eyedropper tool, the selected element is automatically reformatted with the sampled settings. If nothing is selected, the Eyedropper tool "loads" with the formatting attributes.

3. **Choose the Eyedropper tool. Using whatever method you prefer, change the Stroke color to None and then make sure the Fill color is the active attribute.**

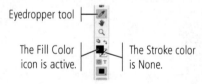

Eyedropper tool

The Fill Color icon is active.   The Stroke color is None.

4. **Click a dark red area in the image on the right side of the spread.**

   We are using a reddish color as the complement to the predominant green and blue in this image.

Empty Eyedropper tool cursor

We sampled this color from the image.

5. **Move the filled Eyedropper cursor over the brown-filled text frame and click to change the frame's fill color to the sampled color from Step 4.**

Sampling the color in Step 4 changes the active fill color.

Filled Eyedropper tool cursor

Clicking with the Eyedropper tool changes the active attribute (the fill) to the sampled color.

6. **Move the cursor over the Page Head paragraph at the top of Page 2. When you see a "T" icon in the tool cursor, click and drag to highlight the entire Page Head paragraph.**

The T in the tool cursor indicates you can click and drag to change the color attributes of text. Because the fill color is still the active attribute, this step changes the fill color of the text you highlight.

Click and drag to highlight the entire Page Head paragraph.

The highlighted text adopts the fill color that is loaded in the Eyedropper tool.

7. **Navigate to the Page 4–5 spread. With the Eyedropper tool still active, press Option/Alt and click to sample a medium gray-green color from the shield in the painting.**

As long as the Eyedropper tool remains selected, it retains the last-sampled color, so you can continuously apply the sampled attributes to multiple objects. Pressing Option/Alt allows you to sample a new color.

Press Option/Alt and click to sample a new color.

8. **Click the brown-filled frame on Page 4 to fill it with the new sampled color.**

Click inside the frame to fill it with the new sampled color.

9. **Repeat Step 6 to change the fill color of the Page Head paragraph on Page 4.**

10. **Repeat the same basic process from Steps 7–9 to change the box and Page Head color on each spread of the layout.**

11. **Activate the Preview screen mode and review the results.**

Activating Preview mode turns off all the guides, hidden characters, and other non-printing elements. This allows you to better review your results.

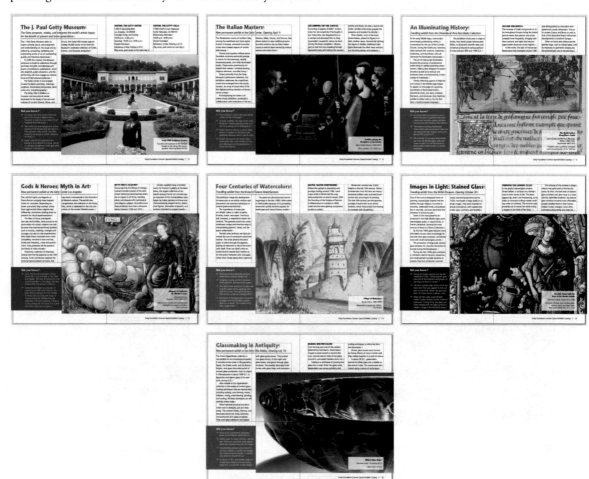

12. **Save the file, and then continue to the final stage of the project.**

Working with Color Themes

The Color Theme tool, grouped with the Eyedropper tool in the Tools panel, is used to sample sets ("themes") of colors based on the colors in existing layout objects.

When you move the cursor over different areas of the layout, the tool identifies different regions from which you might want to sample colors.

Clicking with the tool creates a five-color theme from the region you sample. The Color Theme widget appears and shows the color theme that was created.

The tool cursor is automatically loaded with the center color in the theme. You can use the Right and Left Arrow keys to change the active color in the cursor.

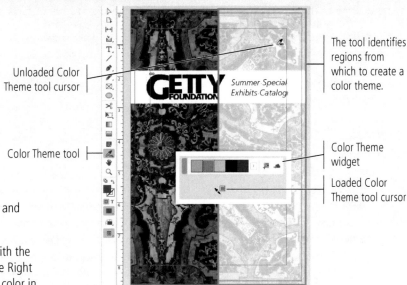

Unloaded Color Theme tool cursor

Color Theme tool

The tool identifies regions from which to create a color theme.

Color Theme widget

Loaded Color Theme tool cursor

When you sample a color theme, you can use the widget to access several variations of the active theme.

Click to open the menu of alternate color themes.

Clicking the Add Theme to Swatches button saves a new color group in the Swatches panel. Option/Alt clicking the button adds only the active color as a new swatch in the Swatches panel.

STAGE 3 / Outputting Variations of Files

The final stage of this project requires creating two versions of final output:

- A desktop proof for your client, showing the spreads as they will appear in the final bound booklet.

- A low-resolution PDF file that prospective clients can download from the organization's website.

InDesign includes a number of tools that make it easy to create both versions without destroying the integrity of the original layout file.

Create a Folding Dummy

Multipage documents with facing pages have special output requirements. When multipage books and booklets are produced, they are printed in signatures of four or more pages at a time. A **signature** consists of multiple document pages, all printed on the same press sheet, which is later folded and cut to the final trim size.

Layouts are designed in reader's spreads but arranged into printer's spreads on the printing plate. A **reader's spread** is a set of two pages that appear next to each other in a printed document — Page 2 faces Page 3, and so on. A **printer's spread** refers to the way pages align on a press sheet so, after a press sheet is folded and cut, the reader's spreads will be in the correct locations.

Imposition refers to the arrangement of a document's pages on a press sheet to produce the final product. If you fold a piece of paper in half twice, number the pages, and then unfold the paper, you will see the basic imposition for an eight-page signature. If you look at your unfolded piece of paper, you can see the tops of all the pages are folded together. If elements bleed to the top of a page, that ink would appear on the edge of the page it abutted on the signature (for example, Pages 12 and 13 in the illustration to the right).

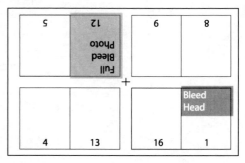

The pages of a signature must be cut apart at the top, which requires at least 1/8″ at the top of the page for the trim. The outside edge of half the pages also must be cut apart (this is called a **face trim**) so the pages of the finished piece can be turned. This face trim also requires 1/8″ around the page edge. That trim would shorten an 8.5″ × 11″ book to 8.375″ × 10.875″. This shorter size might be fine, but it could also ruin a design.

On the press-sheet layout, space is added between the tops of the printer's spreads to allow room for bleed and trimming. This separation is probably all that's required for a 16-page saddle-stitched booklet printed on a 70# (70-pound) text-weight paper. If you use a heavier paper, or if you have more than one 16-page signature, you need to allow room for **creep**, which is the progressive extension of interior pages of the folded signature beyond the trim edge of the outside pages.

If you have questions about folds or imposition, you should always call your service provider. Somebody there will be able to advise you on the best course to take. In most cases, these issues will be handled entirely by the service provider, often using software specifically designed for the prepress workflow. If you try to do too much, you might cause them extra work (and yourself extra expense).

1. **Fold a piece of paper in half lengthwise, and then in half widthwise.**

2. **While the paper is still folded, write the sequential page numbers 1 through 8 on the folded sections.**

3. **Unfold it so you can see the printer's spreads for an eight-page document.**

   The dummy unfolds to show how an eight-page signature is laid out. Page 8 and Page 1 create a single printer's spread.

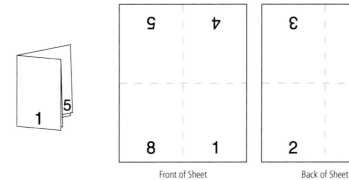

Front of Sheet   Back of Sheet

Print a Booklet Proof

You generally don't need to think about creating full impositions for a press. At times, however, you might want to print proofs in printer's spreads to show clients. You could work through a complicated manual process of rearranging pages, but the InDesign Print Booklet command is far easier — and it's non-destructive.

1. **With exhibits.indd open, choose File>Print Booklet.**

   This dialog box shows only the output options related to printing printer's spreads. These options are set; you can't directly change the printer used for output in this dialog box.

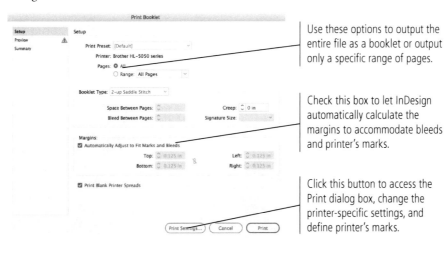

Use these options to output the entire file as a booklet or output only a specific range of pages.

Check this box to let InDesign automatically calculate the margins to accommodate bleeds and printer's marks.

Click this button to access the Print dialog box, change the printer-specific settings, and define printer's marks.

Note:

In printer's spreads, the sum of pairs of page numbers always totals the number of pages in the signature, plus 1. For example, in a 16-page signature, Page 1 faces Page 16, Page 2 face Page 15, and so on.

2. **In the Setup pane of the dialog box, make sure 2-up Saddle Stitch is selected in the Booklet Type menu.**

In the Booklet Type menu, you can choose what kind of imposition to create.

- **2-up Saddle Stitch** creates two-page printer's spreads from the entire layout or selected page range. If the layout doesn't contain enough pages to create the necessary printer's spreads, InDesign automatically adds blank pages at the end of the layout.

- **2-up Perfect Bound** creates two-page printer's spreads that fit within the specified signature size (4, 8, 12, 16, or 32 pages). If the number of layout pages to be imposed is not divisible by the selected signature size, InDesign adds blank pages as needed at the end of the finished document.

- **Consecutive** creates a two-, three-, or four-page imposition appropriate for a foldout brochure.

You can also define settings to adjust for imposition issues related to printer's spreads versus reader's spreads.

- **Space Between Pages** defines the gap between pages in the printer's spread. This option is available for all but saddle-stitched booklet types.

- **Bleed Between Pages** defines the amount page elements can bleed into the space between pages in a printer's spread (from 0 to half the defined space between the pages) for perfect-bound impositions.

- **Creep** defines the amount of space necessary to accommodate paper thickness and folding on each signature.

- **Signature Size** defines the number of pages in each signature for perfect-bound impositions.

- **Print Blank Printer Spreads** determines whether any blank pages added to a signature will be printed.

3. **Click the Print Settings button. In the resulting Print dialog box, choose the printer and PPD you will use to output the booklet (if possible).**

4. **In the Setup options, choose US Letter/Letter in the Paper Size menu and choose landscape orientation.**

5. **In the Marks and Bleed options, uncheck the All Printer's Marks and Use Document Bleed Settings options, and change all four Bleed values to 0 in.**

6. **Click OK to return to the Print Booklet dialog box.**

7. **In the Print Booklet dialog box, uncheck the Automatically Adjust to Fit Marks and Bleeds option. With the Chain icon active, change all four Margin fields to 0 in.**

You're only printing a client proof on letter-size paper, so you do not need bleeds or printer's marks.

Note:

If you have a printer with tabloid-paper capability, you could output the file with marks and bleeds, and then trim the proof to size. Doing so would eliminate any issue with the margins required by some desktop printers, which would prevent the pages from printing the outer edges of the layout.

8. **Click Preview in the list of options.**

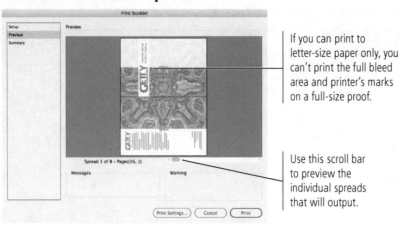

If you can print to letter-size paper only, you can't print the full bleed area and printer's marks on a full-size proof.

Use this scroll bar to preview the individual spreads that will output.

9. **Click Print.**

10. **When the file is finished spooling to the printer, continue to the next exercise.**

 ## Create a PDF with Page Transitions

In addition to the printed job, your client requested a low-resolution PDF file that can be posted on the organization's website. To add interest to the digital version, you are going to add interactive page transitions that affect the way new pages appear when users navigate through the PDF file.

1. **With exhibits.indd open, open the Page Transitions panel (Window>Interactive>Page Transitions).**

2. **In the Pages panel, double-click the Page 2–3 spread numbers (below the page icons) to select the entire spread.**

   Remember, there can be a difference between the active and selected pages. Double-clicking the targeted page or spread ensures the spread you want is the one selected.

3. **Open the Page Transitions panel Options menu and select Choose.**

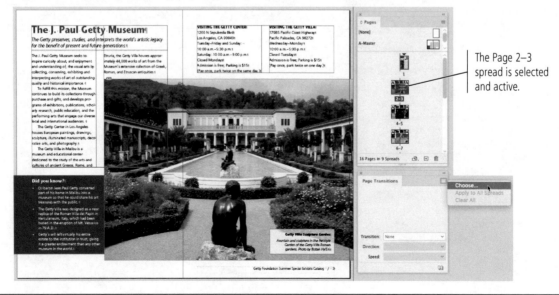

The Page 2–3 spread is selected and active.

4. **In the resulting Page Transitions dialog box, activate the Comb radio button and make sure the Apply to All Spreads option is unchecked.**

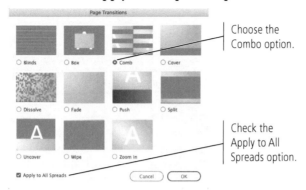

Choose the Combo option.

Check the Apply to All Spreads option.

5. **Click OK to apply the transition to the selected spread.**

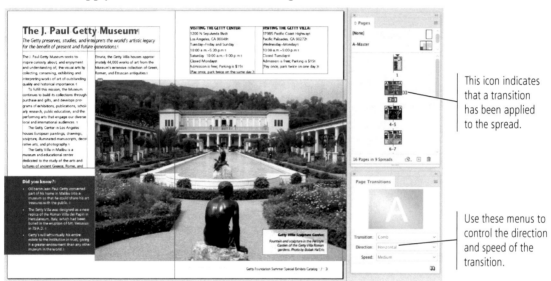

This icon indicates that a transition has been applied to the spread.

Use these menus to control the direction and speed of the transition.

6. **With the Page 2–3 spread active, open the Transition menu in the Page Transitions panel and choose Wipe.**

You can use this menu to apply a transition to the active page or spread or change the transition that is already applied.

Use this menu to apply a specific transition to the active page or spread.

Note:

Different spreads can have different transitions (although this is not typically a good idea).

7. **With the Page 2–3 spread selected, click the Apply to All Spreads button at the bottom of the Page Transitions panel.**

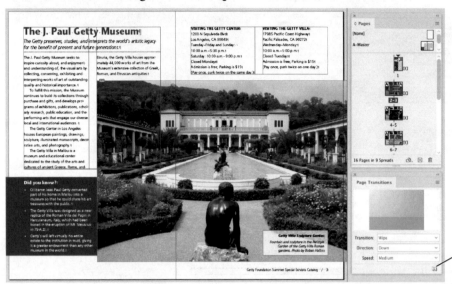

Clicking this button applies the selected transition to all spreads in the layout.

8. **Choose File>Export. Choose Adobe PDF (Interactive) in the Format/Save As Type menu and then click Save.**

9. **Review the options in the General pane of the resulting Export to Interactive PDF dialog box.**

The Adobe PDF (Interactive) option opens a dialog box with settings relevant to PDF files for digital distribution.

- **Pages** determines which pages will be included in the resulting PDF file. You can export All pages or select the Range option and define a specific page range to include.

- The **Pages** and **Spreads** radio buttons determine how pages are treated in the resulting PDF file. When the Spread option is checked, facing-page spreads result in a single PDF page.

- **Create Separate PDF Files** can be used to create individual PDFs of each page included in the Pages section above. When you check this option, you can define the suffix added to the end of the file name to distinguish each exported PDF:

  - **Incremental Numbers** (sequential, beginning with 01 for the first exported page)
  - **Page Number** (the default option, including a preceding "_" character)
  - **Page Size** (useful if you use a single layout to design multiple versions of the same content).

- **View** determines the default view percentage of the exported PDF. You can cause the file to open at actual size, fit the page into the Acrobat window based on a number of dimensions, or choose a specific percentage (25, 50, 75, or 100).

- **Layout** determines how spreads appear in the resulting PDF file.

  - The **Single Page** options export each page or spread separately.
  - The **Continuous** options export files so users can scroll through the document and view parts of successive pages at the same time.
  - The **Two-Up Facing** options export two pages or spreads side-by-side.
  - The **Two-Up Cover Page** options export the first spread as a single page and then the remaining spreads two at a time side-by-side.

> **Note:**
>
> *The default view and layout options open the file based on the reader application's default options.*

- **Presentation Opens In Full Screen Mode** opens the resulting PDF without showing Acrobat's menus or panels. You can then use the **Flip Pages Every** field to automatically change pages after a defined interval.

- **Page Transitions** defaults to the From Document option, which maintains the settings you define in the Transitions panel. You can choose None to export the PDF without transitions or choose one of the methods in the menu to override document settings.

- **Forms and Media** options can be used to include movies, sounds, buttons, and form fields placed in the InDesign file. If you choose Appearance Only, the PDF will show only a static version of interactive objects.

- **Embed Page Thumbnails** creates a thumbnail preview for every exported page.

- **View After Exporting** automatically opens the file in your system's default PDF application.

- **Create Acrobat Layers** maintains InDesign layers as Acrobat layers in the PDF file.

- **Create Tagged PDF** automatically tags elements in the story based on a subset of the Acrobat tags supported by InDesign (basic text formatting, lists, tables, etc.).

10. **Define the following settings in the General pane:**
    - **Make sure the All [Pages] radio button is selected.**
    - **Choose the [Export As] Spreads radio button.**
    - **Choose Fit Height in the View menu.**
    - **Choose Single Page in the Layout menu.**
    - **Check the Open in Full Screen Mode option.**
    - **Leave the Flip Pages Every option unchecked.**
    - **Check the View After Exporting option.**
    - **Choose From Document in the Page Transitions menu.**
    - **Check the Embed Page Thumbnails option.**

11. **Click Compression in the list of options on the left, then review the available settings.**

    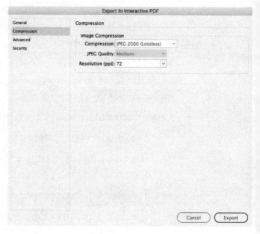

    - **Compression** determines how images in the resulting PDF are managed to reduce file size for digital distribution. JPEG (Lossy) removes data and can result in poor image quality. JPEG 2000 (Lossless) reduces file size without discarding image data but can result in larger file size than JPEG (Lossy). Automatic allows the software to determine the best quality for images.
    - **JPEG Quality** defines how much compression is applied if you choose JPEG (Lossy) or Automatic compression. Higher quality settings result in larger files.
    - **Resolution** defines the resolution of raster images in the exported PDF. High resolution is important if you want users to be able to zoom in close to an image, but higher resolution settings mean larger file sizes.

12. **Define the following settings in the Compression pane:**

    - **Choose JPEG 2000 (Lossless) in the Compression menu.**
    - **Define the target Resolution as 72 ppi.**

13. **Click Export to create the PDF file.**

14. Read the resulting warning message, and then click OK.

If you get a Full Screen warning message when Acrobat opens, click Yes to allow the file to switch to Full Screen mode.

Note:

If you have some other application set as your default PDF reader, full-screen mode and page transitions might not work.

15. When the PDF file opens, press the Down Arrow button to see the interactive page transitions.

    You have to view the file in full-screen mode to see the page transitions.

16. Press the Escape key to exit Full-Screen mode, then close the PDF file. Return to InDesign, then save and close the InDesign file.

PROJECT REVIEW

fill in the blank

1. _____ have inside and outside margins instead of left and right margins.

2. When _____ is active, InDesign automatically adds pages to accommodate an entire story placed in a primary text frame.

3. A local formatting override is indicated by _____ next to the style name in the Paragraph Styles panel.

4. A negative first-line indent is called a(n) _____.

5. A(n) _____ is a single line of a paragraph at the end of a column.

6. A(n) _____ is a single line of a paragraph at the top of a column or a very short last line of a paragraph.

7. _____ in the Paragraph Style Options dialog box can be used to force a paragraph to begin in the next linked frame.

8. _____ fonts can store more than 65,000 glyphs in a single font file; the same font file works on both Macintosh and Windows.

9. You can use the _____ option to create a parent/child relationship between two styles; changes made to the parent style reflect in the child style, as well

10. _____ is the process of arranging pages on a press sheet so, when folded and trimmed, the pages appear in the correct order.

short answer

1. Briefly explain the difference between facing pages and non-facing pages.

2. Briefly explain the difference between reader's spreads and printer's spreads.

3. Briefly explain the advantages and disadvantages of nesting text-formatting styles.

PORTFOLIO BUILDER PROJECT

Use what you learned in this project to complete the following freeform exercise.
Carefully read the art director and client comments, then create your own design to meet the needs of the project.
Use the space below to sketch ideas; when finished, write a brief explanation of your reasoning behind your final design.

art director comments

Your clients are very happy with the finished exhibits catalog. One of the museum board members is also on the local historical society executive committee, and she would like you to create a booklet featuring various historical landmarks in the local community. The booklet will be featured at local events throughout the year in an effort to promote tourism.

To complete this project, you should:

❏ Create a 16-page booklet using the same document size as the museum catalog.

❏ Design a facing-page layout featuring one landmark on each spread.

❏ Find or create images for each spread to support the overall theme of the project.

❏ Use placeholder text to design the various elements of the layout.

client comments

This booklet should be a visual centerpiece for our current promotional efforts. We will provide the copy for each landmark in a few weeks, but for now we would like you to plan out the overall design.

The text for each spread will include similar content as the museum booklet:

- A primary head and subhead
- Main body copy (but no secondary subheads)
- A callout box with a separate head
- A caption (but without a separate heading)

Even though we are going to use a similar structure for the copy, we want the booklet to use a very different layout from the museum catalog.

Finally, we would like you to create a cover with images and text that clearly identifies our city. Maybe include the town motto and logo if possible?

project justification

PROJECT SUMMARY

Controlling the flow of text in a document, especially for documents with more than one or two pages, is just as important as controlling the appearance of the different type elements. InDesign provides powerful tools that let you control virtually every aspect of document design, from the exact position of individual paragraphs and entire blocks of text to automatic page numbers based on the location of special characters in the layout.

Changing the master page settings for this booklet allowed you to automatically flow a single story across multiple pages. Using the Keep options for the applied styles, you were able to position each element in the appropriate frame on the appropriate spread, which significantly reduced the amount of manual evaluation and adjustment that would have been required without these features.

Using effective master pages also allowed you to place repeating elements on every spread in the layout. Combining that functionality with special characters, you also eliminated a number of unnecessarily repetitive tasks, such as manually numbering the pages.

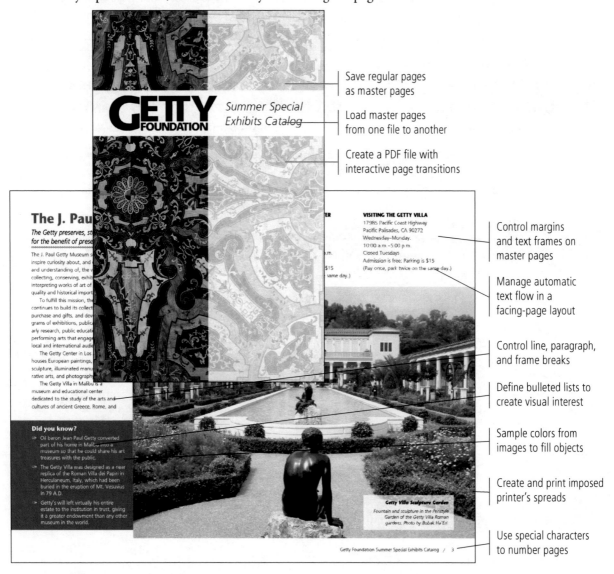

Save regular pages as master pages

Load master pages from one file to another

Create a PDF file with interactive page transitions

Control margins and text frames on master pages

Manage automatic text flow in a facing-page layout

Control line, paragraph, and frame breaks

Define bulleted lists to create visual interest

Sample colors from images to fill objects

Create and print imposed printer's spreads

Use special characters to number pages

Folding Travel Brochure

5

Your client is a travel agency that is creating a set of brochures to promote a series of travel packages. The client wants to create a letterfold rack brochure for Australian tourism. The job includes a relatively small amount of copy, a number of images, and a basic form that people can fill out and enter to win a free trip — a common technique for gathering potential clients' contact information.

This project incorporates the following skills:

❑ Building a template for specific folding requirements

❑ Defining slug information using static and variable text

❑ Using libraries and object styles to reduce repetitive tasks

❑ Managing advanced frame options such as embedded clipping paths, Alpha channels, and irregular text wraps

❑ Creating image captions using stored file metadata

❑ Controlling tabs to format columns of text

PROJECT MEETING

client comments

We are planning a new series of promotional brochures that need to fit into standard rack holders, which means the finished size should be 4″ wide by 9″ high. A letterfold gives us three panels on each side, which should be plenty of space for the information we want to include.

The brochures will mostly be hand-outs for people who walk into our office or visit our booth at trade shows, but some will be mailed, so we want the brochure to be a self-mailer.

These brochures will be mostly visual, with a little bit of descriptive copy. We're sending you the text and images for the Australian brochure first because that's the only one that's been finalized.

We went back and forth for weeks over the styles for our other collateral, and we were all finally happy with the results on other pieces your agency designed. We want to use the same formatting in these brochures that you used in all our other jobs.

art director comments

A lot of people design folding documents incorrectly. Some use a six-page layout with each page the size of the final folded job; others use two pages, each divided into three equal "columns." In both cases, all panels on the job are the exact same width, which is wrong.

For a letterfold, the job needs to have one panel narrower than the others. Plus, each side of the brochure has to mirror the other so the narrow panel is in the correct location when the job is printed, trimmed, and folded.

The last item to remember is that the brochure will be a self-mailer; the back panel needs to be blank with only the return address in the upper-left corner.

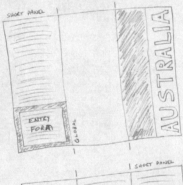

project objectives

To complete this project, you will:

- ❏ Create a folding layout template on master page spreads.

- ❏ Use the slug area to mark folding panels.

- ❏ Define a custom text variable to track file status.

- ❏ Use InDesign library files to store and access frequently used objects and groups.

- ❏ Use object styles to apply consistent formatting to multiple frames.

- ❏ Apply an Alpha channel that is embedded in a Photoshop file.

- ❏ Control text wraps around basic frames and irregular shapes.

- ❏ Import text styles from a Microsoft Word file.

- ❏ Add dynamic captions based on image metadata.

There are several common types of folds:

Letterfolds have two folds and three panels to a side. These are often incorrectly called "trifold" because they result in three panels. The panel that folds in should be 1/16" to 1/8" narrower than the two outside panels; ask your service provider how much allowance is required for the paper you're using.

Accordion folds can have as many panels as you prefer. When it has six panels (three on each side), it's often referred to as a **Z-fold** because it looks like the letter Z. Because the panels don't fold into one another, an accordion-fold document has panels of consistent width.

Double-parallel folds are commonly used for eight-panel rack brochures, such as those you often find in a hotel or travel agency. Again, the panels on the inside are narrower than the outside panels. This type of fold uses facing pages because the margins need to line up on the front and back sides of the sheet.

Barrel folds (also called **roll folds**) are perhaps the most common fold for 14" × 8.5" brochures. The two outside panels are full size, and each successive panel is narrower than the previous one. You can theoretically have as many panels as you want, but at some point the number of fold-in panels becomes unwieldy.

Gate folds result in a four-panel document; the paper is folded in half, and then each half is folded in half toward the center so the two ends of the paper meet at the center fold. The panels that fold in are narrower than the two outside panels. This type of brochure allows two different spreads: the first is revealed when you open the outer panels, and the second is revealed when you open the inner flaps.

It's important to consider the output process when planning a job with documents that are not just a single sheet of standard-size paper, such as documents with multiple pages folded one or more times or other non-standard page sizes. The mechanics of commercial printing require specific allowances for cutting, folding, and other finishing processes. There are two basic principles to remember when designing documents that fold:

- Folding machines are mechanical devices, and paper sometimes shifts as it flows through the machine's paper path. Most are accurate to about 0.0125".

- Paper has thickness; thicker paper requires more allowance for the fold.

Because of these two principles, any panel that folds into the other panels needs to be smaller than the other panels. You should note that the issues presented here have little to do with the subjective elements of design. Layout and page geometry are governed by specific variables, including mechanical limitations in the production process. These principles are rules, not suggestions. If you don't leave adequate margins, for example, design elements will be cut off or won't align properly from one page to the next.

Create the Outside Master Pages

When working with folding documents, the trim size is actually the size of the flat sheet *before* it's folded. Once you know the flat trim size of a job, you have to calculate the size of individual panels before you set up the layout.

For example, imagine you're printing a letterfold brochure on a laser printer that can only print to letter-sized paper. The flat trim size, then, is 11" wide by 8.5" high. The first required calculation is the base size of each panel:

$$11'' \div 3 = 3.6667''$$

But remember, the fold-in panel has to be narrower than the other two panels; you also have to factor the required folding variance, which your service provider can tell you, into the panel size. Half the difference is removed from the fold-in panel, and one-fourth of the difference is added to each outer panel. Assuming a folding variance of 1/8" (0.125), here are the necessary calculations:

Fold-in panel = 3.6667" − 1/16" = 3.6042"

Outer panel 1 = 3.6667" + 1/32" = 3.698"

Outer panel 2 = 3.6667" + 1/32" = 3.698"

You can safely round these values to 3.6" and 3.7", resulting in a panel variance of 0.1", which is enough for most papers that can be run through a desktop laser printer. This seems like a complicated series of calculations, and it is only relevant when printing to a defined flat trim size.

In other cases, however, you might know the finished size of your folding brochure. For example, a rack card or brochure is commonly 4" × 9", which fits into standard display racks (hence the name). If you know the final target size, it is easy to calculate the size of individual panels used to build the folding document. This example uses the 4" × 9" rack card with a required 1/8" panel variance:

Outer Panel 1 = 4"

Outer Panel 2 = 4"

Fold-in Panel = 4" − 0.125" = 3.875"

Because the different panels in a folding document are different sizes, earlier versions of the software required you to define each side of a folding document as a separate page. You had to use page guides to define the folds and margins of individual panels. Fortunately, InDesign supports multiple page sizes in a single document, which makes it far easier to set up the basic document layout for items such as folding brochures.

1. Download **Australia_ID20_RF.zip** from the Student Files web page.

2. Expand the ZIP archive in your WIP folder (Macintosh), or copy the archive contents into your WIP folder (Windows).

   This results in a folder named **Australia**, which contains the files you need for this project. You should also use this folder to save the files you create in this project.

3. **Choose File>New>Document. In the New Document dialog box, choose the Print option at the top and then define the following parameters:**

Name:	**letterfold**
Units:	**Inches**
Page Size:	**Width: 4″**
	Height: 9″
Facing Pages:	**Not Checked**
Primary Text Frame:	**Checked**
Columns:	**1**
Margins:	**0.25″ (constrained)**
Bleed:	**0.125″ (constrained)**
Slug:	**0.5″ on the top and bottom**
	0″ on the left and right

Note:

If an option isn't listed, leave it at the default value.

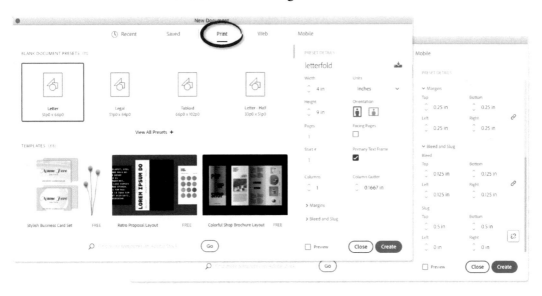

4. **Click Create to create the new file.**

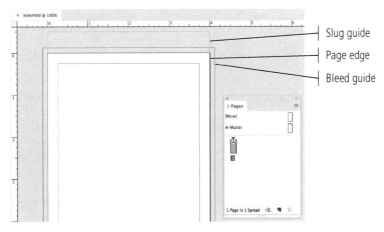

Slug guide

Page edge

Bleed guide

5. **In the Pages panel, Control/right-click the A-Master page name and choose Master Options for "A-Master" in the contextual menu.**

6. **In the resulting dialog box, type** `Outside` **in the Name field and type 3 in the Number of Pages field. Click OK to return to the layout.**

The outside of the brochure has three panels, so you are defining three pages in the master page spread — one page for each panel.

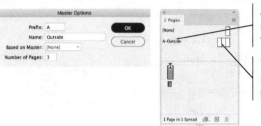

After you click OK, the new name appears in the Pages panel.

The master page icon now shows all three pages in the spread.

Note:

It's always a good idea to use a meaningful name for any element you define in InDesign, including a master page.

7. **In the Pages panel, double-click the A-Outside layout to display the master page in the document window.**

The master page spread now has three pages, as you defined in Step 6. All three pages have 0.25″ margins, as you defined when you created the file. The bleed area surrounds the entire spread because each page abuts the other pages in the spread.

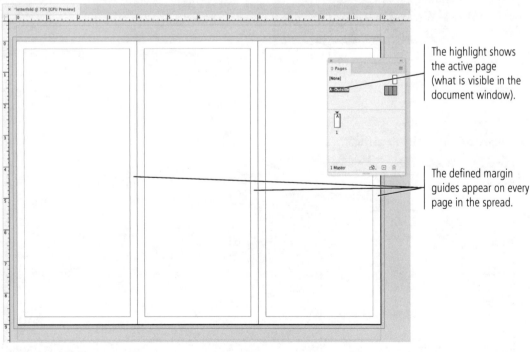

The highlight shows the active page (what is visible in the document window).

The defined margin guides appear on every page in the spread.

8. **Using the Selection tool, click inside the margin area on the left page of the spread to select the primary text frame.**

Adding pages to a master page does not automatically place a primary frame on each new page. You have to manually create the frames on the two new pages.

9. **Option/Alt-click the primary text frame and drag right to clone it. Drag until the cloned frame snaps to the margins on the center page.**

When you release the mouse button, the icon in the top-left corner of the frame identifies the cloned frame as a regular text frame. A master layout can have only one primary text frame or thread. The text on each panel will not always be a single story, so you are not going to link these frames into a primary thread.

The frame is the
primary text frame.

The cloned frame is
a regular text frame.

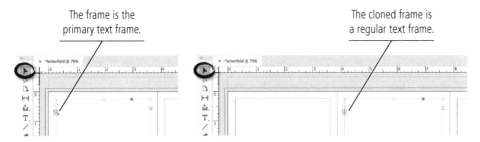

10. **Repeat Step 9 to add a text frame to the right page in the spread.**

11. **Choose the Page tool in the Tools panel, then click the left page of the spread to select that page.**

The Page tool makes it possible to change the dimensions of a single (selected) page in the document.

Page tool

Click to select
the left page in
the spread.

Handles at the
edges identify
the selected page.

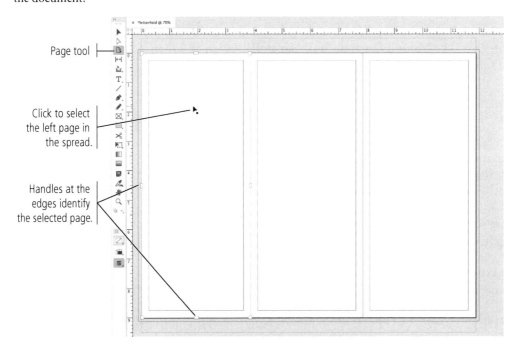

12. **In the Control panel, choose Object-based in the Liquid Page Rule menu, and check the Objects Move with Page option.**

You will work in depth with liquid page rules in Project 6: Digital Layout Variations.

13. **Choose the right-center reference point. Click in the W field after the existing value, then type -.125 and press Return/Enter to apply the change.**

InDesign understands mathematical operators in most dialog box and panel fields. Because you know you need to remove 1/8″ from the fold-in panel width, it is very easy to simply subtract that amount from the existing value.

Choose the right-center reference point.　　Type after the existing value.　　Choose this option to resize the text frame along with the page.

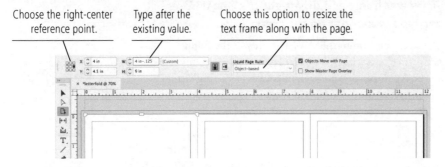

The margins on the selected page are still 0.25″ from the adjusted page edges. Because you activated the Object-based liquid page rule, the text frame on the page adjusted to remain snapped to the adjusted margins.

The left page is 1/8″ narrower than the other two pages in the spread.　　The margins on the adjusted page are still 1/4″ from each edge.

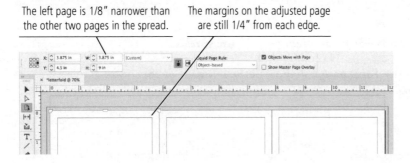

14. **Save the file as letterfold.indd in your WIP>Australia folder, and then continue to the next exercise.**

Add Slug Information and Fold Marks

When you work with folding grids, it's easy to forget which panel goes where. You can use the layout slug area to add nonprinting elements as self-reminders and place folding marks the output provider can use for reference. These elements should be placed on the master page layout.

1. **With letterfold.indd open, make sure the A-Outside master page layout is showing in the document window.**

2. **Select the Type tool and create a text frame above the left panel of the spread, between the bleed and slug guides.**

3. **Type Outside Left Panel - Fold In in the frame, and then apply centered paragraph alignment.**

Placing objects outside the bleed but inside the slug area prevents them from interfering with the layout elements.

4. **Choose Window>Output>Attributes to open the Attributes panel.**

5. **Select the text frame in the slug area with the Selection tool, and then check the Nonprinting box in the Attributes panel.**

   These objects are for your information only; they should not be included in the output.

Note:

If you want to print these frames, you can override this setting using the Print Non-printing Objects option in the General print settings.

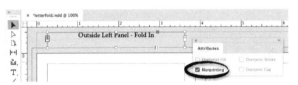

6. **Control/right-click the text frame and choose Allow Master Item Overrides to deactivate the option and protect this object on associated layout pages.**

   This item should be unchecked.

7. **Using the Selection tool, press Option/Alt, then click and drag to clone the text frame to the right.**

   Like the original frame from which they are cloned, these text frames are also set as nonprinting objects.

8. **Position the clone above the center page in the spread, and then change the text in the frame to** `Outside Center Panel - Mailing Area`.

9. **Repeat Steps 7–8 to place a text frame over the right page of the spread, with the text** `Outside Right Panel - Front`.

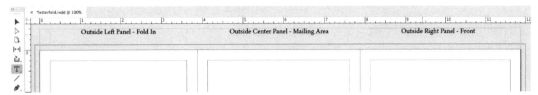

10. **Using the Line tool, click the slug guide above the line that separates the left and center pages in the spread. Press Shift and drag down to the top page edge.**

    Pressing Shift constrains the line to a multiple of a 45° angle (45, 90, 135, 180, etc.).

11. **Define the line stroke as** `0.5 pt`, **and set the stroke color to Black.**

12. **In the Stroke panel (Window>Stroke), choose Dashed in the Type menu. After applying the Dashed line type, type 3 pt in the first Dash field at the bottom of the panel and then press Return/Enter to finalize the change.**

If you don't see the Type menu in the Stroke panel, open the panel Options menu and choose Show Options.

When you only define the first dash value, that number will also be used for the gap values.

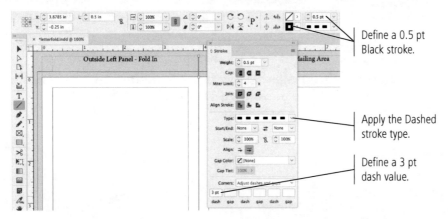

Define a 0.5 pt Black stroke.

Apply the Dashed stroke type.

Define a 3 pt dash value.

13. **Using the Control panel, select one of the horizontal-center reference points and then position the line at X: 3.875 in (the same as the left page's width).**

In general, lines have thickness; you have to first select one of the horizontal-center reference points for the line to be correctly centered over the panel edges.

Select one of the horizontal-center reference points to position the center of the line over the center of the panel edge.

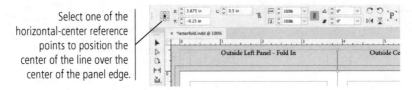

14. **Using the Selection tool, Control/right-click the dashed line and toggle off the Allow Master Item Overrides option.**

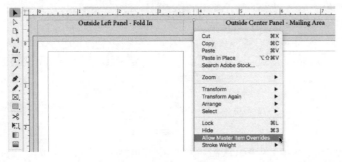

15. **Clone the line and place the copy centered above the line separating the center and right pages in the spread (X: 7.875 in).**

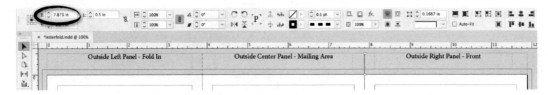

16. **Select the two lines and clone them down, placing the cloned lines in the bottom slug area.**

    Press Shift while cloning the lines to constrain them to be in the same X position as the original lines.

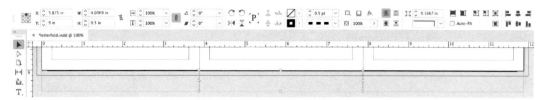

17. **Save the file and continue to the next exercise.**

 Place Text Variables

The final item to add on the master page is a custom slug containing information about the file's development status. You can use text variables to place the same information on each of the three master pages in the layout.

1. **With letterfold.indd open, make sure the A-Outside layout is showing.**

2. **Create a new text frame in the slug area below the left page of the spread.**

3. **With the insertion point flashing in the new text frame, choose Type>Text Variables>Insert Variable>File Name.**

    The resulting string of text is treated as a single anchored object in the slug text frame.

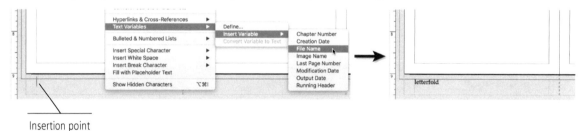

Insertion point

    Although you can't select the actual characters within the text variable instance, you can still change the formatting of variables by highlighting the instance in the layout and making whatever changes you want.

4. **With the insertion point after the File Name variable, press the Spacebar, type / Modified:, then press the Spacebar again.**

5. **Choose Type>Text Variables>Insert Variable>Modification Date.**

6. **If necessary, adjust the frame width so the entire footer slug fits on one line, but remains only under the left page of the spread.**

7. **Save the file and continue to the next exercise.**

> **Note:**
>
> *You can convert a particular instance of a text variable to regular text by selecting an instance in the layout and choosing Type>Text Variables>Convert Variable to Text.*

Define a Custom Text Variable

In this exercise, you will add a custom variable to track the status of the project. This information should appear on both spreads, which means it needs to be placed on both master page layouts. (You will create the second spread in the next exercise.) By defining a text variable, you can simply change the variable definition and all placed instances of the variable will reflect that change.

1. **With letterfold.indd open, choose Type>Text Variables>Define.**

Note:

Click New to create a new custom text variable, or click Edit to edit the definition of an existing variable.

2. **In the Text Variables dialog box, click the New button.**

3. **In the Name field of the New Text Variable dialog box, type Project Status.**

4. **In the Type menu, choose Custom Text.**

   Your choice in the Type menu of the New/ Edit Text Variable dialog box determines what options are available.

Note:

If you delete a variable that is used in the layout, you can choose to replace placed instances with a different variable, convert the instances to regular text, or simply remove the placed instances.

5. **Click the menu to the right of the Text field, and choose Ellipsis from the attached menu.**

   Using the Custom Text option, you can determine what text appears in the variable. The menu provides access to common special characters. These are the same characters you can access in the Type>Insert Special Character submenus.

6. **With the insertion point after the code for the Ellipsis character, press the Spacebar and then type Work in Progress.**

Understanding Text Variable Options

For all but the Custom Text variable, you can define the characters that precede (Text Before) or follow (Text After) the variable information. You can type specific information in either of these fields, or you can use the associated menus to place symbols, em or en dashes, white-space characters, or typographer's quotation marks.

The **Chapter Number** variable inserts the chapter number based on the file's position in a book document. The Style menu formats the chapter number as lowercase or uppercase letters, lowercase or uppercase Roman numerals, or Arabic numbers.

The **Creation Date** variable inserts the time the document is first saved. The **Modification Date** variable inserts the time the document was last saved. The **Output Date** variable inserts the date the document was last printed, exported to PDF, or packaged. You can use the **Date Format** menu to modify the date format for all three of these variables. You can either type a format directly into the field or use the associated menu to choose the options to include. (If you type the format into the field, you have to use the correct abbreviations.)

The **File Name** variable inserts the name of the open file. You can use the check box options to include the entire folder path and file extension. (The path and extension will not appear until you save the file at least once.)

The **Last Page Number** variable creates a "Page x of y" notation. This can indicate the last page number of the entire document or the current section in the Scope menu. You can also determine the numbering style with the same options as the Chapter Number variable.

The **Metadata Caption** option is the same as the Live Caption option in the Object>Captions submenu. (You will use this option later in this project.)

The **Running Header** variables can be used to find content on the page based on applied paragraph or character styles. In the Style menu, you choose the paragraph or character style to use as the variable content. The Use menu identifies which instance of the defined style (first or last on the page) to use. For example, say you have a glossary page, and all the terms are formatted with the Glossary Term character style. You could define two Running Header (Character Style) variables: one that identifies the first use of the Glossary Term style and one that identifies the last use of the Glossary Term style on the current page. You can then place the two variables in a text frame to create a running header that shows the first and last terms on the page (i.e., [First Term] – [Last Term]).

Abbreviation	Description	Example
M	Month number	1
MM	Month number (two digits)*	01
MMM	Month name (abbreviated)	Jan
MMMM	Month name (full)	January
d	Day number	3
dd	Day number (two digits)*	03
E	Weekday name (abbreviated)	Wed
EEEE	Weekday name (full)	Wednesday
yy	Year number (last two digits)	13
yyyy	Year number (four digits)	2013
G	Era (abbreviated)	AD
GGGG	Era (full)	Anno Domini
h	Hour	1
hh	Hour (two digits)*	01
H	Hour (24-hour format)	16
HH	Hour (two digits, 24-hour format)*	16
m	Minute	9
mm	Minute (two digits)*	09
s	Second	2
ss	Second (two digits)*	02
a	AM or PM	AM
z	Time zone (abbreviated)	PST
zzzz	Time zone (full)	Pacific Standard Time

*The two-digit formats force a leading zero in front of numbers less than than 10. For example, 9/25/19 would appear as 09/25/19 if you use the two-digit Month format).

The Delete End Punctuation option identifies the text without punctuation. For example, you can identify a Bold Run-In character style that is applied to text that always ends with a period. When the style is identified as the variable, the period will not be included in the variable text.

The Change Case options determine capitalization for the variable text:

- Upper Case capitalizes the entire variable.
- Lower Case removes all capitalization.
- Title Case capitalizes the first letter in every word.
- Sentence Case capitalizes only the first word.

The **Custom Text** variable inserts whatever text you define in the associated field.

7. Click OK to close the New Text Variable dialog box, then click Done to close the Text Variables dialog box.

8. Create a new text frame in the slug area under the right page of the spread.

9. With the insertion point flashing in the new frame, type `Project Status`, press the Spacebar, and then choose Type>Text Variables>Insert Variable>Project Status.

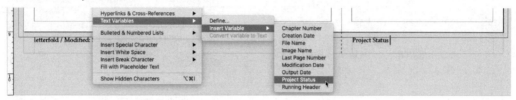

The variable text you defined is placed immediately after the space.

10. Select both text frames in the bottom slug area. Control/right-click either frame and choose Allow Master Item Overrides to deactivate the option and protect both objects on associated layout pages.

11. Save the file and then continue to the next exercise.

 Create the Inside Master Pages

When you plan a folding document layout, it is also important to understand how the two sides of the document relate to one another. Fold marks on the front and back should line up; this means if one panel is a different size than the others, the back side of the sheet must be laid out as a mirror image of the front side.

In the illustration to the right, a document has one fold — a smaller panel that folds over to cover half of the inside of the brochure. Fold marks on the outside layout must mirror the inside of the brochure so, when folded, the two sides line up properly.

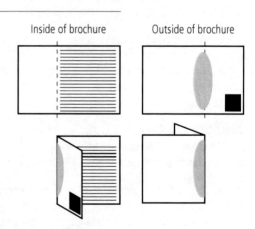

Inside of brochure   Outside of brochure

1. With **letterfold.indd open**, Control/right-click the A-Outside master page name and choose Duplicate Master Spread "A-Outside" in the contextual menu.

2. **Control/right-click the resulting B-Master layout name and choose Master Options for "B-Master" in the contextual menu.**

3. **Type Inside in the Name field and then click OK to apply the new name to the B master page layout.**

   The new B-Inside master page spread is automatically displayed in the document window. All the elements you created on the A-Inside master are in place because you duplicated the existing master page.

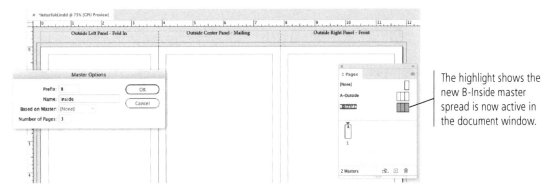

The highlight shows the new B-Inside master spread is now active in the document window.

4. **Zoom out so you can see the entire pasteboard area around the master page spread.**

5. **Choose the Page tool in the Tools panel. In the Control panel, make sure the Objects Move with Page option is checked.**

   Because the inside of the brochure needs to be a mirror image of the outside of the brochure, you need to move the shorter panel to the other side of the spread.

6. **Click the left page in the spread to select it. Click again outside the text frame area on the page and drag right until the reduced panel snaps to the right edge of the spread.**

   To move the page, you must click outside the boundaries of the text frame; click in the page's margin area to complete this step.

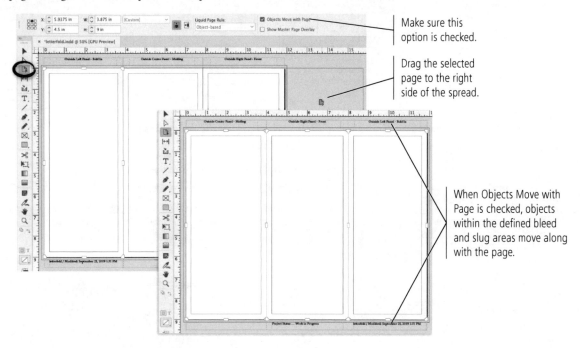

Make sure this option is checked.

Drag the selected page to the right side of the spread.

When Objects Move with Page is checked, objects within the defined bleed and slug areas move along with the page.

7. **In the text frames in the top slug area, change the text to**

Left page:	Inside Left Panel
Center page:	Inside Center Panel
Right page:	Inside Right Panel – Fold In

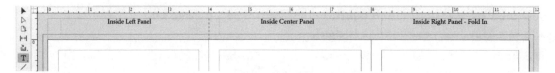

8. **Choose the Selection tool, then deselect everything in the layout.**

9. **Click to select the slug guide over the right edge of the right page.**

   The folding guide that was over the right page edge is still over the right page edge, which is incorrect. You need to move this guide into place over the line between the center and right pages of the spread.

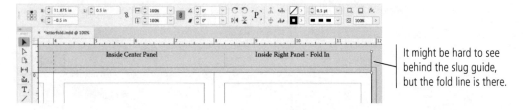

It might be hard to see behind the slug guide, but the fold line is there.

10. **Drag the fold line left until it is centered over the line between the center and right pages of the spread (X: 8 in).**

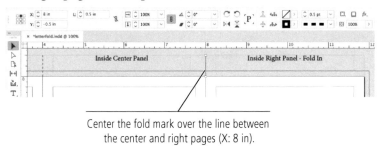

Center the fold mark over the line between
the center and right pages (X: 8 in).

11. **In the bottom slug area, make the following adjustments:**

- **Drag the text frame with the file name and modification date below the left page of the spread.**

- **Drag the frame with the project status (with the "Work in Progress" message) below the right page of the spread.**

- **Move the right fold mark into place between the center and right pages of the spread (X: 8 in).**

letterfold / Modified: September 21, 2019 1:31 PM   Project Status ... Work in Progress

12. **Save the file and continue to the next exercise.**

 ## Save a Template

As the previous exercises demonstrated, setting up a brochure properly can be time-consuming. Once you have set up a folding layout, it's a good idea to save the layout as a template so the same structure can be applied to any similar type of layout. Every time you want to create a rack card with the same folded size, you can open this template and begin with an empty file containing the correct guides and marks.

1. **With letterfold.indd open, click the A-Outside master page layout name to select the entire spread.**

   Clicking a master page name selects all pages in that spread. If you wanted to select actual layout pages instead of master pages, you could click the page number sequence below a spread in the lower half of the panel to select all pages in that spread.

2. **Click and drag the A-Outside master page layout into the lower half of the Pages panel, below the existing Page 1.**

   Because all three pages in the master layout are selected, releasing the mouse button adds a three-page spread below the existing Page 1.

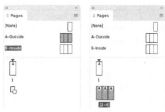

Note:

You can also use the Layout>Pages>Insert Pages option to add multiple pages to a layout.

3. **Click the Page 1 icon in the Pages panel, and drag it to the panel's Delete button. When asked if you want to delete the page, click OK.**

4. **Click the B-Inside master page layout name to select the entire spread.**

5. **Click and drag the B-Inside layout into the lower half of the Pages panel, below the spread you added in Step 2.**

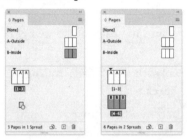

Note:

You can Shift-click to select multiple pages in the Pages panel and override master page items for all selected pages at one time.

6. **In the lower half of the Pages panel, double-click the [1-3] page numbers below the first spread to navigate to that spread.**

7. **Choose View>Fit Spread in Window.**

   This command shows the entire spread of Pages 1–3, including the defined bleed areas. The slug areas, however, are not entirely visible.

8. **If necessary, reduce your view percentage so the slug areas are visible.**

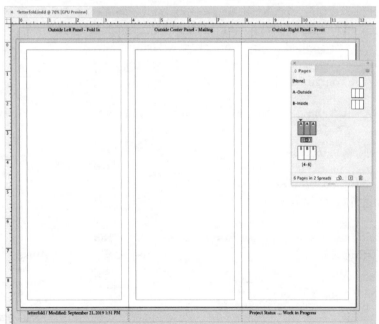

9. **Control/right-click the selected spread and choose Override All Master Page Items in the contextual menu.**

This command allows you to access the text frames you created on the master layout. You won't be able to access the fold marks or nonprinting slug items, which you protected by toggling off the Allow Master Item Overrides option.

10. **Control/right-click the page numbers under the 4–6 spread and choose Override All Master Page Items.**

By Control/right-clicking the page numbers under the spread thumbnails, you are applying this command to all three pages in the spread. If you want to affect only one page in a spread, you can Control/right-click a specific thumbnail in the panel.

11. **Open the Type pane of the Preferences dialog box. Uncheck the Smart Text Reflow option and then click OK.**

If this option is already unchecked, simply click Cancel to close the Preferences dialog box.

Because you know this type of brochure will have only the specific number of pages you already defined, you don't want the software to automatically add pages to fit long blocks of text.

Uncheck this option.

12. **Choose File>Save As and navigate to your WIP>Australia folder. Choose InDesign 2020 Template in the Format/Save As Type menu and click Save.**

These pages and settings will be available whenever you implement the layout. Remember, every click you can save by adding template elements will save that much more time whenever you reuse the same template.

Choosing the template option automatically changes the extension to "indt".

13. **Close the file and continue to the next stage of the project.**

Understanding Pages Panel Options

In addition to features you have already used in this and earlier projects, the Pages panel Options menu has a number of other choices for working with document pages. (Options related to alternate and liquid layouts are explained in Project 7: Repurposed Content Layouts.)

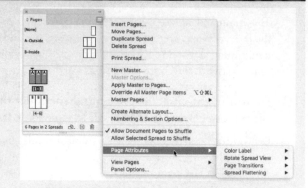

- **Insert Pages** allows you to insert 1 to 9999 pages before or after a specific page, or at the start or end of the document. You can also determine which master page to base the new pages on.

- **Move Pages** allows you to reposition specific pages anywhere in the current file or in another open file.

- **Duplicate Page/Spread** allows you to replicate the selected page or spread, including all elements on that page or spread.

- **Print Page/Spread** opens the Print dialog box with settings predefined to output the active page or spread.

- **Delete Page/Spread** removes the page or spread.

- **Allow Document Pages to Shuffle** is checked by default. You can toggle off this option if you want to create spreads of more than two pages (called an **island spread**) in a facing-page layout.

- **Allow Selected Spread to Shuffle** is checked by default. If you toggle this option off, adding pages before an island spread maintains the island spread pages as you created them. Brackets around the page numbers indicate that Allow Selected Spread to Shuffle is turned off for that spread.

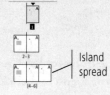

Island spread

- **Color Label** applies a colored bar below the selected page icon(s), which provides an additional visual indicator of a specific, user-defined status.

- **Rotate Spread View** changes the orientation of the page on screen. This does not affect the physical dimensions of the page but is useful for working with a page that is oriented differently than the overall document.

- **Page Transitions** are visual effects that apply when a document is exported as a PDF or SWF file that will be distributed digitally.

- **Spread Flattening** allows you to apply flattener settings to individual spreads in a document, overriding the document flattener settings. Default uses the document settings. None (Ignore Transparency) eliminates any function that requires transparency. Custom opens the Custom Spread Flattener settings.

- The **View Pages** submenu can be used to view alternate layouts in a file.

STAGE 2 / **Advanced Frame Options**

You've already learned how to place graphics and control them within their frames. InDesign, of course, offers many more functions that provide control over graphics. Some of these, such as libraries and object styles, improve your productivity by automating repetitive tasks; others, such as creating a custom frame from formatted text, enhance your creative capabilities when designing a page layout.

Convert Text to Outlines

1. **Create a new file by opening your letterfold.indt template (WIP>Australia).**

   Remember, to create a new file from a template, you have to open the template file using the Open [As] Normal option.

2. **Save the new file as aussie-fold.indd in your WIP>Australia folder.**

3. **In the Pages panel, double-click the [1-3] page numbers below the page icons to show that spread in the document window.**

4. **Using the Type tool, click inside the empty text frame on Page 3.**
   Type AUSTRALIA in the frame, and format it as 80-pt ATC Onyx Bold.

5. **Press Command/Control to temporarily access the Selection tool and reveal the frame's handles. Drag the frame handles until the frame is large enough to show the entire word you just typed on a single line.**

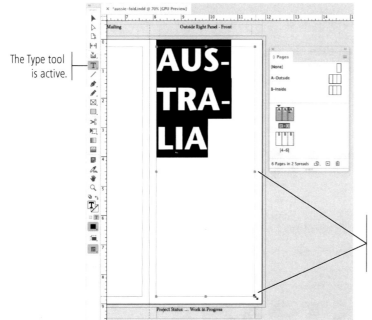

The Type tool is active.

Note:

You can convert individual characters to inline objects by selecting specific characters before you choose Type>Create Outlines.

Press Command/Control to temporarily access the Selection tool and the frame's handles.

When you release the Command/Control key, the Type tool is still active.

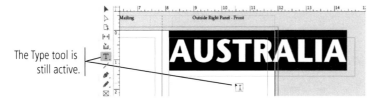

The Type tool is still active.

6. **Click with the Type tool between the A and the U to place the insertion point. Using the Character panel, change the kerning to -80 to reduce the space between these two letters.**

Place the insertion point
between two letters.

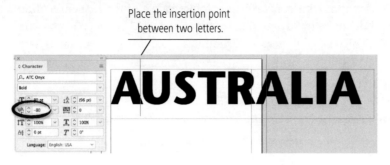

7. **Continue adjusting the kerning in this word as necessary.**

Kerning is largely a matter of personal preference. Our choices are shown here.

−80   −70   +20 −20 −30 −10

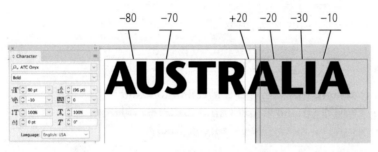

8. **Choose the Selection tool in the Tools panel.**

9. **Click the text frame to select it, and then choose Type>Create Outlines.**

By converting the text to outlines, you eliminate the potential problem of a missing font file. You also create a group of letter-shaped objects that can contain other objects, such as a picture of Australia's iconic kangaroo.

The text frame is gone; it is
replaced by a bounding box for
the group of letter shapes.

Note:

When you drag a specific handle, the X and Y fields in the Control panel show the position of the handle you drag. The selected reference point is not relevant.

10. **With the new frame selected, use the Control panel to rotate the group counterclockwise by 90°.**

11. **Drag the rotated group until the top-right corner snaps to the top-right bleed guide on Page 3.**

12. **Drag the bottom-center handle until it snaps to the bottom bleed guide.**

    Because the group is rotated, dragging the bottom handle actually changes the object *width* rather than height.

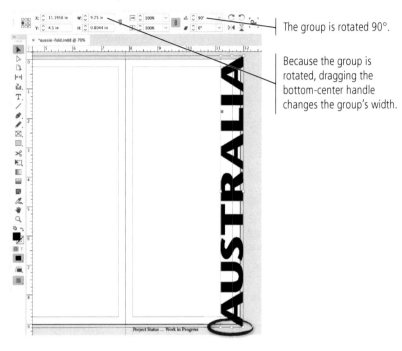

The group is rotated 90°.

Because the group is rotated, dragging the bottom-center handle changes the group's width.

13. **Drag the left-center handle until the group's height is 1.625 in.**

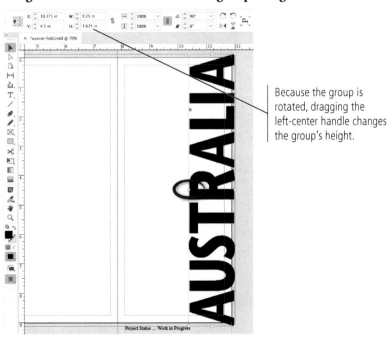

Because the group is rotated, dragging the left-center handle changes the group's height.

14. **Choose File>Place. Navigate to kangaroo.psd in your WIP>Australia>Links folder, activate the Replace Selected Item option, then click Open.**

The image is placed directly into the shape of the letters.

15. **Move the cursor over the frame until you see the Content Grabber, then click to select the image inside the frame.**

Remember, you rotated the group of letters in Step 10. The placed image is also rotated because it is placed in the rotated container.

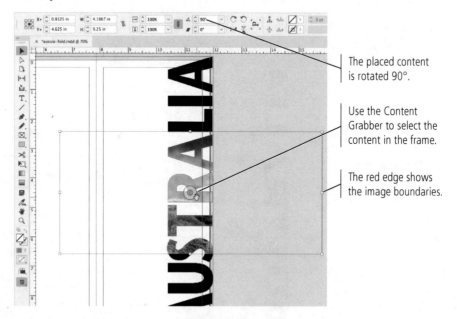

The placed content is rotated 90°.

Use the Content Grabber to select the content in the frame.

The red edge shows the image boundaries.

16. **With the placed image selected, choose the center registration point, then rotate the image 0°.**

Choose the center registration point.

Change the content rotation to 0°.

17. **Save the file and continue to the next exercise.**

Control Object Stacking Order

When you create a compound path out of multiple shapes, attributes and contents of the topmost selected shape are applied to the resulting combined shape. Even when objects do not technically overlap, the concept of stacking order still applies. Objects created later are higher in the stacking order than older objects unless you manually rearrange those objects. You can always use the Layers panel listings to monitor and control the stacking order of objects.

1. **With `aussie-fold.indd` open, use the Rectangle tool to create a frame filling the left half of Page 3, extending to the top and bottom bleed guides and leaving 1/8″ between the new frame and the group of lettershapes.**

   Use the image after Step 3 as a positioning guide.

2. **Apply a fill color of Black and stroke color of None to the new rectangle.**

3. **Open the Layers panel and expand the Layer 1 listing.**

   As you know, you created the rectangle after the AUSTRALIA group; that means the rectangle is higher in the stacking order than the kangaroo.psd image.

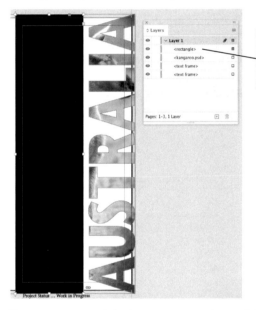

Because <rectangle> was created after <kangaroo.psd>, it exists higher in the stacking order.

You want to extend the kangaroo image beyond the letter-shaped frames into the rectangle. You can easily combine the rectangle and letter-shaped frames using the Pathfinder functions. Most Pathfinder operations, however, apply attributes of the topmost object to the entire resulting shape. This means you have to rearrange object stacking order before you can combine the two shapes into a single compound path.

4. **In the Layers panel, click the <rectangle> item and drag it below the <kangaroo.psd> item.**

Note:

Depending on how you created the frames on your master pages, your kangaroo.psd object might appear in a different stacking position relative to the two <text frame> objects.

The important point here is the position of the <rectangle> object relative to the <kangaroo.psd> object.

5. **Using the Selection tool, Shift-click the rectangle and the AUSTRALIA frame to select both objects in the layout.**

6. **Choose Object>Pathfinder>Add.**

   This command combines the selected objects into a single compound path. The image placed in the lettershapes now extends into the rectangle.

After being combined, a single bounding box surrounds the rectangle and the group.

Attributes of the top object (the group) are applied to the back object (the rectangle).

7. **Move the cursor over the frame until you see the Content Grabber, then click to select the image inside the frame.**

8. **Drag the placed image to fill the entire combined frame.**

9. **Save the file and continue to the next exercise.**

Work with an InDesign Library

In many cases, you might need to use the same content (such as a logo) or the same group of objects (such as a logo with a grouped text frame containing contact information) on multiple pages throughout a single document or even in multiple documents. In these situations, you can use an InDesign library to speed the process.

An InDesign **library** is a special type of file that stores objects (including the objects' content) for use in any InDesign file. Library files are not linked or specific to any individual layout (.indd) file, so you can open and use items from any existing library in any layout.

1. **With `aussie-fold.indd` open, make the inside spread (Pages 4–6) visible in the document window.**

2. **Choose File>Open. Select the `australia-assets.indl` library file from your WIP>Australia folder and click Open.**

   You can open a library file using the same File>Open command (Command/Control-O) you use to open a regular InDesign file. This library contains two items that will be part of the Australia tourism brochure.

Note:

You can choose File>New>Library to create a new InDesign library file.

If extensions are not visible in Windows, use the icon to identify the library file.

3. **Move your mouse over the right item in the library panel and read the description.**

   If a library item includes descriptive text, that text appears in the tool tip when you move your mouse over that item. This description provides useful information about what you should do with the item.

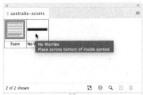

4. **Click the right library item and drag it into the active layout.**

5. **If you see a Missing Font warning, click Close.**

   Library items do not store fonts. If a library item uses a specific font, that font must be active on whatever system uses the library item. You probably don't have the Dragoon font used in this library item, so InDesign shows a missing Font warning that lists the fonts required by the library item.

6. **Position the object at the bottom of the spread aligned to the bleed guides.**

   Assuming you don't have Dragoon installed on your computer, the text should appear highlighted in pink — the indication of a missing font.

7. **Open the Swatches panel.**

   If a library item uses styles or other assets (including defined color swatches), those required assets are placed in any file where you place the library item.

8. **Highlight all text in the frame, then change the font to ATC Onyx Bold.**

   When the missing-font highlight is gone, you can see the dark blue fill color of the text frame you placed from the library.

9. **Click to place the insertion point in the text, which will remove the highlight, and review the results.**

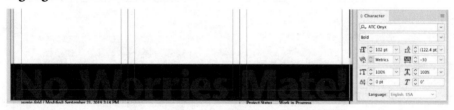

10. **Move your mouse over the Form item in the Library panel and read the description.**

11. **Navigate to the outside spread (Pages 1–3).**

12. **Click the Form item in the library and drag into the open file. Position the placed instance aligned to the bottom-left bleed guide on the spread.**

   Library items store the links to placed graphics files; if a library item contains a placed image or graphic, the placed file must be available in the same location as when it was added to the library. You have to make sure the links are up-to-date before output.

Note:

If a library item uses a style (text or object) that conflicts with a style in the document where you're placing an instance, the style definition from the document overrides the style definition from the library item.

13. **Click the Missing Image icon in the top-left corner of the image. Navigate to `coastline.tif` in your WIP>Australia>Links folder and click Open.**

The title bar of the Locate dialog box identifies the file you want to find.

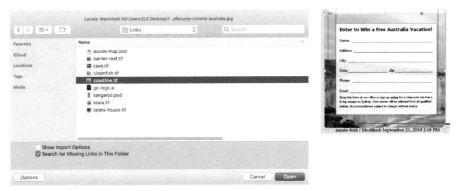

14. **Open the file `ge-assets.indd` from the WIP>Australia folder.**

This file includes a single group, with your client's logo and address information. It has been used with this same alignment in many other projects, and the client wants to maintain consistency from document to document.

Rather than copying and pasting the group from one document to another, you can use an InDesign Library file to make the group easily accessible in any InDesign file.

15. **In the ge-assets layout, select the group on the page and drag it into the australia-assets library panel.**

You can also click the New Library Item button at the bottom of the Library panel to add the selected object as a new library item.

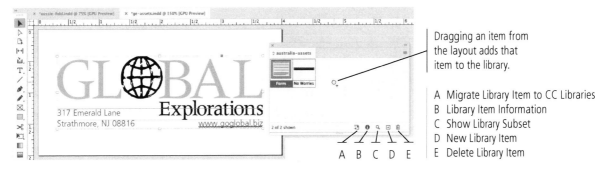

Dragging an item from the layout adds that item to the library.

A Migrate Library Item to CC Libraries
B Library Item Information
C Show Library Subset
D New Library Item
E Delete Library Item

Dragging an object from the layout into the Library panel has no effect on the object already placed in the layout. When you release the mouse button, the new library item appears in the panel, and the original item in the layout is exactly the same as it was before you dragged it into the library.

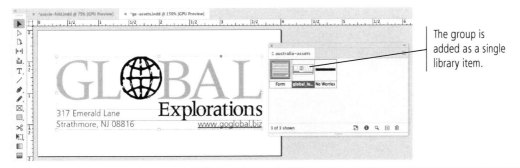

The group is added as a single library item.

16. **With the new library item selected, click the Library Item Information button at the bottom of the panel.**

17. **In the resulting Item Information dialog box, change the Item Name field to** `Logo with Address`.

18. **In the Description field, type** `Use this group wherever the logo and address are required`, **then click OK.**

19. **Close the ge-assets.indd file without saving.**

    Library files are not linked to a specific InDesign file; you can use them to access common styled elements from any InDesign file.

20. **With the outside spread of** `aussie-fold.indd` **visible, drag the Logo With Address item from the Library panel into the layout.**

21. **Rotate the placed group 90° counterclockwise, and align it to the bottom-left margin guide on Page 2 (the center page in the spread).**

    Rotating the placed instance has no effect on the item in the library.

22. **Drag a second copy of the library item into the layout, and position the new instance on Page 1, immediately above the form. Leave approximately 1/8″ between the bottom edge of the logo and the top edge of the form.**

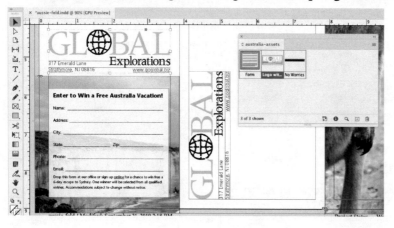

Note:

Choose Add Items On Page [N] As Separate Objects in the Library panel Options menu to add all objects on the page as separate library items.

Choose Add Items On Page [N] in the panel Options menu to add all objects on the page as a single library item.

Note:

Deleting an object from the library has no effect on placed instances in the layout. Deleting a placed instance has no effect on the item in the library.

Note:

You can show a subset of the library by clicking the Show Library Subset button at the bottom of the panel. Use the resulting dialog box to define what you want to find based on the item name, creation date, object type, or description text. You can always restore the entire library by choosing Show All in the Library panel Options menu.

23. **Using the Selection tool, double-click the text frame below the logo on Page 1 to select only that frame in the group. Press Delete/Backspace to remove the selected frame.**

There is no dynamic link between items in the library and instances placed in a layout. Changing one placed instance has no effect on the original library item or on other placed instances of the same item.

Double-click the frame to access only one piece of the group.

Placed instances of the same library item are not dynamically linked.

24. **Click the Close button on the Library panel to close the library file.**

25. **Save the InDesign file and continue to the next exercise.**

Working with Adobe CC Libraries

If you have an individual-user subscription to the Adobe Creative Cloud, you have access to CC Library functionality, which allows you to easily share assets across various Adobe CC applications. This technology makes it very easy to maintain consistency across a design campaign — for example, using the same color swatches for all pieces, whether created in Illustrator, InDesign, or Photoshop.

A Library list
B Show Items as Icons
C Show Items in a List
D Add Content
E Create Group
F Libraries Sync Status
G Delete

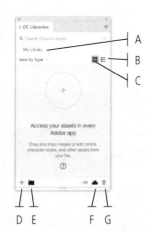

Once you create a CC library, it is stored in your Creative Cloud account so you can access the same assets in other Adobe applications. In InDesign, you can use the menu at the top of the CC Libraries panel (Window>CC Libraries) to create new libraries or to access existing ones.

Regardless of which application you use to create a library, you can use those libraries in any Adobe CC application. In the image below, we created the Portfolio Elements library in InDesign and used Illustrator to add a graphic element for use throughout the Portfolio books.

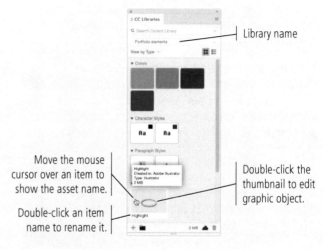

Library name

Move the mouse cursor over an item to show the asset name.

Double-click an item name to rename it.

Double-click the thumbnail to edit graphic object.

Working with Adobe CC Libraries (continued)

Creating Library Items

You can add new items to a CC library by using the Add Content button at the bottom of the CC Libraries panel, or by simply dragging and dropping items from the layout into the panel.

The Swatches, Paragraph Styles, Character Styles panels also provide an easy method for adding existing assets to the active library. Clicking the Add Selected... button adds the selected assets to the active CC Library.

You can also add new elements to a CC Library when you define a new color swatch, paragraph style, or character style by checking the Add to CC Library option at the bottom of the dialog boxes.

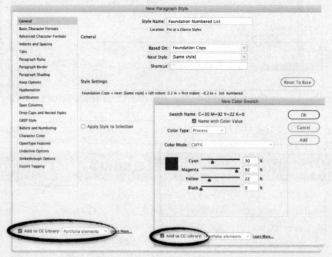

Working with Library Items

Unlike regular InDesign library items, graphics in CC Libraries maintain a dynamic link between the library item and placed instances of that library item.

If you double-click a graphic in the CC Libraries panel, the object opens in the application where it was created. After editing the library item and saving it, placed instances in the InDesign layout automatically reflect the changes.

There are cases in which changes to a placed library item are not automatically reflected in placed instances. Instead, the Links panel shows a "modified" icon, which you can choose to update as you would any other placed image or graphic.

This badge identifies a link to a CC Library item.

This icon identifies a link to a CC Library item.

Relink from CC Libraries

Changes in the library item automatically reflect in placed instances.

In the top image to the right, you can see that the placed object is an instance of highlight.ai, which is stored in a CC Library. We double-clicked the highlight.ai item in the CC Libraries panel to edit it. After changing the object's stroke color in Illustrator, the placed object in InDesign reflects the new red stroke color.

Working with Synced Text

If a text frame is selected, or if specific text is highlighted in the layout, you can use the Add Content menu button at the bottom of the CC Libraries panel to add the actual text in the frame as a new library item. (The original frame text, from which you make the synced text object, is NOT linked to the new library item.)

Double-clicking a text item in the CC Libraries panel opens a file with the synced text. Any text and/or formatting changes you make in this file will automatically be reflected in placed instances of that object. If you had made changes to a placed instance, those changes will be overwritten with the edited text.

If you drag a text item from the CC Libraries panel, text in the synced item is loaded into the Place cursor. Clicking in an empty space creates a new text frame that contains the synced text, including applied formatting. Clicking inside an existing empty text frame places the text into the existing frame.

Double-clicking the item in the library opens the text in a separate file.

You can also place the text at the current insertion point by Control/right-clicking the item in the CC Libraries panel and choosing Place Inline from the contextual menu. In this case, the placed text is not actually linked to the synced text object; changes to the object will not be reflected in these instances.

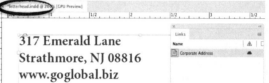

Changes in the linked text file are reflected in placed instances.

Sharing and Collaboration

Libraries also offer a powerful opportunity to communicate assets with other users.

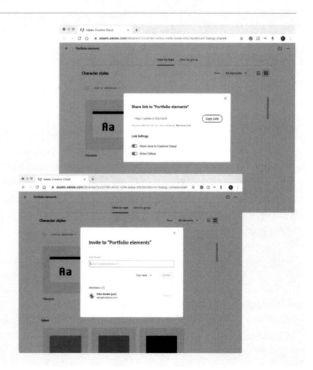

- If you invite others to collaborate, authorized users can edit assets in the library.
- If you share a link to a library, invited users can view a library's contents but not edit those assets.

The options in the Libraries panel submenu navigate to your Adobe CC account page and automatically ask you to invite users for collaborating or create a public link for sharing.

Edit the Basic Graphics Frame Style

An object style stores multiple frame formatting options so you can apply all settings with one click. Object styles can include virtually any attribute that can be applied to a frame in the layout. Like paragraph styles, object styles are dynamic, which means changing an object style automatically changes the appearance of any object using that style.

Object styles are accessed and managed in the Object Styles panel (Window>Styles>Object Styles). Every layout includes a default [Basic Graphics Frame] and a default [Basic Text Frame] style. You can also use the [None] option to separate a specific frame from the [Basic] default settings.

In this exercise, you apply and change the Basic Graphics Frame style so a number of frames will have the same basic settings (i.e., no stroke value and a defined text wrap attribute).

What's in an Object Style?

Use the following chart as a reminder of exactly what can be stored in an object style definition, as well as where to find the equivalent in the application interface for a selected object.

Category	Options
General	Based on Shortcut Reset to base
Fill	Color and Tint
Stroke	Color and Tint Weight Type Gap attributes
Stroke & Corner Options	Stroke alignment Join End cap Miter limit End treatment (arrowheads) Corner Options (Size and Shape)
Size and Position Options	Width, Height, or Width and Height X position, Y position, or X and Y position X and Y offset from page edge or margin
Paragraph Styles	Default paragraph style for frame
Text Frame General Options	Columns Inset spacing Vertical justification Ignore text wrap
Text Frame Baseline Options	First baseline Custom baseline grid options

Category	Options
Text Frame Auto Size Options	Auto-size by height, width, or both
Text Frame Footnote Options	Span footnotes across columns Spacing before and between footnotes
Story Options	Optical margin alignment
Text Wrap & Other	Text wrap type Offset value Wrap options Contour options Nonprinting attribute
Anchored Object Options	Position (Inline, Above Line, Custom) Prevent manual positioning
Frame Fitting Options	Crop amount Alignment reference point Fitting on empty frame
Export Tagging	EPUB/HTML tag User-defined CSS class
Effects	Effect (including Transparency) for object, fill, stroke, or text
Export Options	Alt Text Tagged PDF EPUB and HTML

1. **With `aussie-fold.indd` open, make the inside spread visible in the document window.**

2. **Using the Rectangle Frame tool, click the left margin guide on Page 4 and drag to the right margin guide on Page 6. Do not release the mouse button.**

Note:

Choose Load Object Styles in the Object Styles panel Options menu to copy an object style from one file to another. Any assets required by the object style (paragraph styles, swatches, etc.) will also be copied into the file where you add the object styles.

3. **While holding down the mouse button, press the Right Arrow key three times.**

   If you press the arrow keys while creating a frame, you can create a grid of frames within the area you drag. This method of creating multiple frames, called **gridified tools**, works with any of the frame or basic shape tools.

   - Press the Right Arrow key to add columns.
   - Press the Left Arrow key to remove columns.
   - Press the Up Arrow key to add rows.
   - Press the Down Arrow key to remove rows.

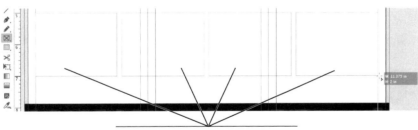

Pressing the Right Arrow key splits the area you draw into four equal-sized frames.

4. **Release the mouse button.**

   The resulting frames are equal in size and have the same amount of space between each.

5. **With the four frames still selected, use the Control panel to position the frames' top edges at 5.8 in and change their height to 2.35 in.**

6. **With all four frames selected, Control/right click any of the frames and choose Fitting>Frame Fitting Options in the contextual menu.**

7. **In the resulting dialog box, check the Auto-Fit option and choose Fill Frame Proportionally in the Fitting menu. Click OK to apply the change.**

    By setting this option for the empty frames, you ensure the images you place later will entirely fill the frames without leaving white space inside any frame edge.

8. **Open the Object Styles panel (Window>Styles>Object Styles). With the four frames selected in the layout, click [Basic Graphics Frame] in the Object Styles panel.**

    All four frames now show the 1-pt black frame that is the default setting for the [Basic Graphics Frame] style.

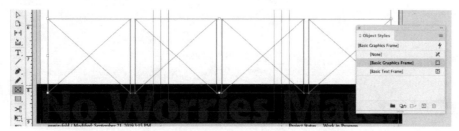

9. **In the Object Styles panel, Control/right-click [Basic Graphics Frame] and choose Edit "[Basic Graphics Frame]".**

    You can also double-click an object style in the panel to open the Object Style Options dialog box for that style. In this case, the first click would apply the selected style to any object selected in the layout.

10. **Click Fill in the Basic Attributes list and choose Paper as the Fill color.**

Note:

By default, object styles do not store the dimensions or position of a frame. You can change that setting in the Size and Position Options pane of the Objects Style Options dialog box.

11. **Click Text Wrap & Other in the Basic Attributes list and apply a text wrap based on the object bounding box with a 0.0625 in offset on all four sides.**

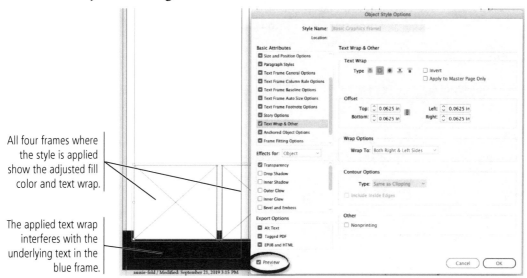

All four frames where the style is applied show the adjusted fill color and text wrap.

The applied text wrap interferes with the underlying text in the blue frame.

12. **Click OK to return to the layout.**

13. **Using the Selection tool, click to select the blue text frame under the empty frames. Control/right-click the blue frame and choose Text Frame Options from the contextual menu.**

14. **In the Text Frame Options dialog box, check the Ignore Text Wrap option and then click OK.**

    This option allows the text to reappear in the frame because the frame is no longer affected by the text wrap attributes of the four overlying empty graphics frames.

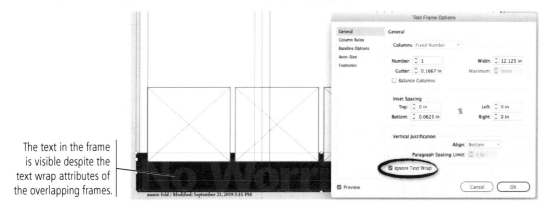

The text in the frame is visible despite the text wrap attributes of the overlapping frames.

15. **Save the file and continue to the next exercise.**

Create a New Object Style

As you saw in the previous exercise, you can edit the default styles for new text and graphics frames. When you need to define the same options for multiple frames but don't want to affect every new object you create, you can create a new object style to minimize repetitive work.

1. **With aussie-fold.indd open, select the empty graphics frame on the left side of the inside spread.**

2. **In the Appearance section of the Properties panel, click the *fx* button and choose Drop Shadow to open the Effects dialog box.**

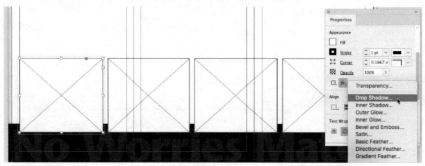

3. **In the Effects dialog box, change the Opacity setting to 45%. Change the X Offset and Y Offset to 0.04 in to reduce the strength of the effect, and then click OK to return to the document.**

When you define specific X and Y Offset values, the Distance is automatically calculated. In this case, the resulting Distance value is 0.0566 in.

4. **With the frame selected, Option/Alt-click the Create New Style button in the Object Styles panel.**

Option/Alt-clicking the Create New Style button automatically opens the Object Style Options dialog box for the new style, where you can name the style and change its settings. If you simply clicked the Create New Style button, you would have to Control/right-click the new style and choose the Edit option in the contextual menu to rename the new style.

Create New Style button

If you simply click the Create New Style button, a new style (named by default as "Object Style [N]" where "N" is a sequential number) is added to the file. The new style has the same settings as the currently selected object, but it is not automatically applied to the selected object.

5. **In the New Object Style dialog box, change the style name to Image with Shadow. At the bottom of the dialog box, check the Apply Style to Selection option.**

Note:

You can use the Effects For menu in the left side of the dialog box to define effects to the object, stroke, fill, and/ or text.

6. **Click Stroke in the Basic Attributes list and choose None as the Stroke color.**

7. **Click OK to rename the style and return to the document.**

Because you checked the Apply Style to Selection option in Step 6, the new style is automatically applied to the selected graphics frame.

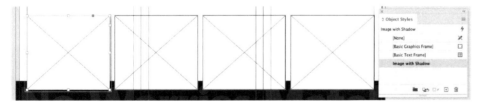

8. **Select the three remaining empty frames, and then apply the Image with Shadow style to those frames.**

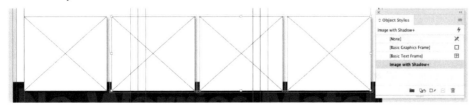

9. **Save the file and continue to the next stage of the project.**

STAGE 3 / **Advanced Text Formatting**

If you completed the first four projects in this book, you have already learned about many options for formatting text, both locally and using styles. And yet, there are still more options, including more complex ones that meet very specific needs (such as formatting tabbed text), improving consistency from one document to another (such as importing styles from another InDesign document), and even automatically generating text from stored image data. This stage of the project introduces some of the more sophisticated options for working with text.

Import and Flow Client-Supplied Text

In the previous project you learned the basics of importing user-defined styles from a Microsoft Word file. When your clients use more sophisticated styles in their layouts, you need to understand what to do with those styles when you import the files into your InDesign layout.

1. **With `aussie-fold.indd` open, make the Page 4–6 spread visible in the document window with nothing selected.**

   Remember, you can double-click the page numbers below the page icons to show the entire spread in the document window.

2. **Choose File>Place. Navigate to `brochure_copy.doc` in your WIP>Australia folder. Make sure the Show Import Options box is checked and click Open.**

   The Formatting section of the resulting Import Options dialog box shows two conflicts exist between the styles in the Microsoft Word file and the styles in the InDesign file.

3. **Under Preserve Styles and Formatting from Text and Tables, make sure the Import Styles Automatically option is selected. Choose Auto Rename in the Paragraph Style Conflicts and Character Style Conflicts menus, then click OK.**

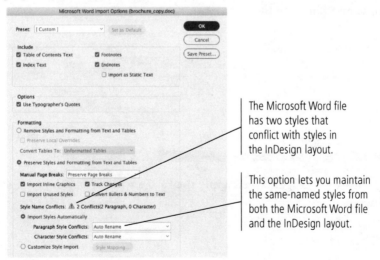

The Microsoft Word file has two styles that conflict with styles in the InDesign layout.

This option lets you maintain the same-named styles from both the Microsoft Word file and the InDesign layout.

4. **If you see a Missing Font warning, review the information and click Close.**

   You will replace the fonts from the Word file in the next exercise; you are including the formatting so you can more clearly see the editorial priority of various text elements. This is a common problem with client-supplied text files.

5. In the document window, press Option/Alt and move the cursor over the text frame on Page 4.

Normally, clicking with the loaded text cursor fills the current frame and leaves overset text as overset text. By pressing Option/ Alt before clicking, however, you can keep overset text loaded in the cursor so you can choose the next frame where the story will thread; this is called **semi-automatic text flow**.

Pressing Option/Alt converts the loaded cursor to the semi-auto flow cursor.

Note:

You can automatically flow an entire story by Shift-clicking with the loaded cursor. In this case, pages are added as necessary to accommodate the entire story. (This method works even when the Smart Reflow option is turned off in the Type preferences.)

6. While holding down the Option/Alt key, click once to place the loaded text into the frame on Page 4.

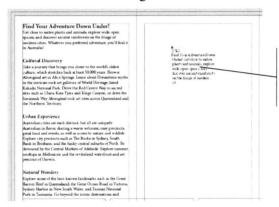

By Option/Alt-clicking the first text frame, the rest of the story remains loaded in the cursor.

Note:

Semi-automatic text flow works on one frame at a time, so you have to Option/Alt-click each frame to keep overset text loaded in the cursor.

7. While holding down the Option/Alt key, click in the text frame on the middle page of the spread to place more of the story.

8. Click the third frame to place the rest of the story.

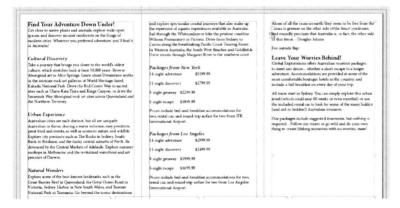

Note:

Remember, the loaded place cursor always shows the first part of the story even when the first part has already been placed.

9. Highlight all text beginning with "For outside flap:" and ending at the end of the story.

In some cases, you might want to thread text across multiple frames (as you just did for the inside of the brochure). In other cases, it is better to break a single story into multiple stories to prevent text from accidentally flowing into the wrong place.

Note:

This kind of notation is common in client-supplied text.

10. Cut the text from the frame (Edit>Cut or Command/Control-X).

As in many applications, when you cut text from a story, the text is stored in the Clipboard so you can paste it somewhere else.

11. **Using the Type tool, click the empty text frame on Page 1 (on the outside spread) to place the insertion point and then paste the text you just cut (Edit>Paste or Command/Control-V).**

12. **Highlight the entire first paragraph in the frame (beginning with "For outside flap:", including the paragraph-return character), and press Delete/Backspace.**

    Pressing Delete/Backspace removes the selected text from the story; the deleted text is not stored in the Clipboard.

13. **Save the file and continue to the next exercise.**

 ## Import InDesign Styles

In many instances, the styles you need for a particular job have already been created for another job. For example, a particular client likes to use 12-pt Garamond with 14-pt leading for the main body copy in every job. If you've already spent the time to create styles once, you can simply import them into your current file instead of repeatedly redefining the same styles.

1. **With `aussie-fold.indd` open, choose Load All Text Styles from the Paragraph Styles panel Options menu.**

    You could also choose Load Paragraph Styles, but the Load All Text Styles allows you to access both character and paragraph styles in a single pass instead of requiring two steps to import the two different types of styles.

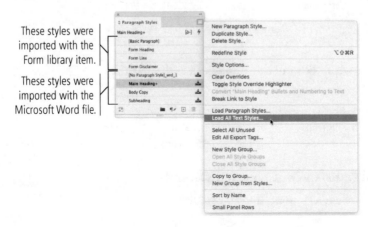

2. **Navigate to the file `ge-assets.indd` in the WIP>Australia folder and click Open.**

   This file contains several styles that were used when your agency created other printed products for the client; for consistency, the client would like to use the same styles in this brochure.

   The Load Styles dialog box shows all styles available in the ge-assets.indd file. Any listed style with an option in the Conflict with Existing Style column conflicts with a style already in InDesign.

   By default, the incoming style definitions will override the existing style definitions. You can choose Auto-Rename in the menu to maintain both versions of a same-named style.

3. **Click the box to the left of [Basic Paragraph] to uncheck that style.**

   By unchecking the style, it will not be imported into the active InDesign file.

   Uncheck this style to exclude it from the import process.

4. **Click OK to import the selected styles (six paragraph and three character).**

   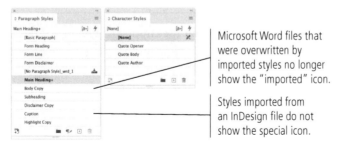

   Microsoft Word files that were overwritten by imported styles no longer show the "imported" icon.

   Styles imported from an InDesign file do not show the special icon.

5. **Select all the text in the frame on Page 1 and then click the Clear Overrides in Selection button in the Paragraph Styles panel.**

   When you have conflicts between styles imported from Microsoft Word and styles in InDesign, it is fairly common to see the + indicator next to style names, indicating something other than the style definition is applied. Clearing overrides solves this problem.

   Clear Overrides in Selection

   Note:

   Clearing overrides could also remove intentional formatting such as a bold or italic word. Carefully review client-supplied text before making sweeping changes.

6. On Page 4, place the insertion point in the first text frame and then choose Edit>Select All.

7. Click the Clear Overrides in Selection button in the Paragraph Styles panel.

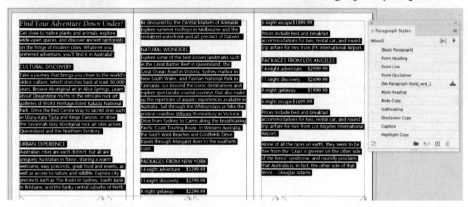

8. Save the file and continue to the next exercise.

Create a Custom Text Wrap

At times, you might want to show a specific part of an image instead of the entire image. You can accomplish this task in a number of ways, but the two most common methods involve using either Alpha channels or clipping paths stored in the image.

A **clipping path** is a vector-based path used to mask (cover) specific parts of an image; areas inside the path are visible, and areas outside the path are hidden. Because the clipping path is vector-based, it always results in hard edges on the clipped image.

An **Alpha channel** is a special type of image channel that masks specific parts of an image by determining the degree of transparency in each pixel. In other words, a 50% value in the Alpha channel means that particular spot of the image will be 50% transparent. The soft edge created by a blended Alpha channel means you can blend one image into another, blend one layer into another, or blend an entire image into a background in a page-layout application.

1. With `aussie-fold.indd` open, make the inside spread visible and make sure nothing is selected in the layout.

2. Choose File>Place. Select `aussie-map.psd` in the WIP>Australia>Links folder. Make sure Show Import Options is checked and then click Open.

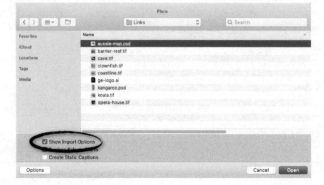

3. **In the resulting Image Import Options dialog box, click the Image tab and review the options.**

If the Photoshop file includes transparent areas, the Alpha Channel menu defaults to "Transparency", which refers to the actual transparent areas in the file. You can use this menu to choose another saved alpha channel, which will define the transparent areas in the file placed into the layout.

If the Photoshop file includes a saved clipping path, you can activate the Apply Photoshop Clipping Path option to make that clipping path active in the placed image.

Note:

Unless you know what the different layers contain, it is difficult to decide what you want to place based on the very small preview image.

Note:

After you place a Photoshop file into the layout, you can change the visible layers by choosing Object>Object Layer Options.

4. **Click the Layers tab, review the options, then click OK.**

Photoshop files can include multiple layers and layer comps. You can turn off specific layers by clicking the Eye (visibility) icon for that layer. If the file includes layer comps, you can use the Layer Comp menu to determine which comp to place.

If you change the visible layers in the file, you can use the Update Link Options to determine what happens if you relink or update the link to the image file. Using the Keep Layer Visibility Overrides option, InDesign remembers which layers you defined as visible in the layout. If you choose Use Photoshop's Layer Visibility, the file reverts to the actual saved state when you relink or update the link.

5. **Click to place the loaded image on the inside spread. Place the image, based on the top-left reference point, at X: 5.8 in, Y: 1.7 in.**

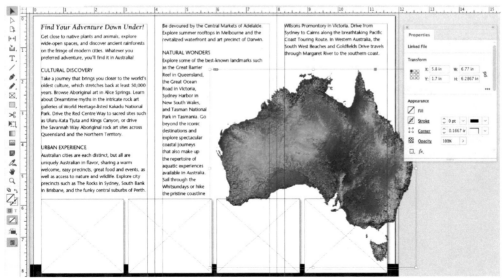

6. **In the Text Wrap panel, click the Wrap Around Object Shape option, and then choose Alpha Channel in the Contour Options Type menu. Change the Top Offset field to 0.125 in.**

There are no "sides" to the non-standard shape, so you can only define a single offset value (using the Top Offset field).

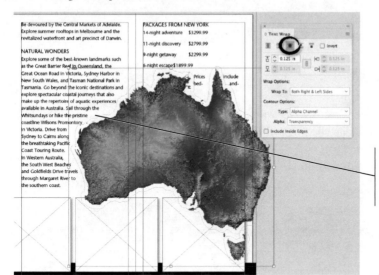

Applying the Alpha Channel contour type allows text to flow around the shape.

Note:

You can use the Direct Selection and Pen tool variants to manually edit the text wrap in the document window. If you manually edit the clipping path, the Contour Options Type menu changes to show "User-Modified Path" and the Offset field becomes unavailable.

7. **In the Properties panel, reduce the placed image opacity to 50%.**

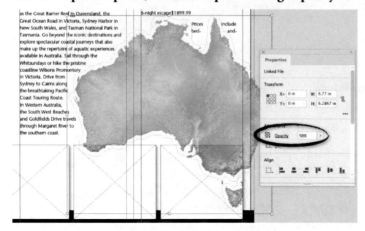

8. **Using the Layers panel, click the <aussie-map.psd> item and drag it below the four <rectangle> items.**

The empty graphics frames are now entirely visible on top of the placed Australia image. Always remember that the Layers panel makes it easy to rearrange the stacking order of objects without worrying about manually selecting anything in the layout.

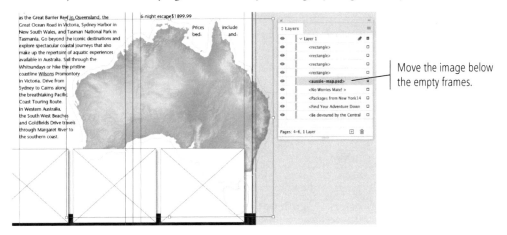

Move the image below the empty frames.

9. **Save the file and continue to the next exercise.**

 ## Create a Style for Pull Quotes

Your client asked you to include a **pull quote**, which is a special visual treatment for text that either is pulled from the story (hence the name) or somehow supports the surrounding text.

You could simply format these elements in the layout, but nested styles allow you to create the structure once and apply it anywhere. For the pull quote in this layout, you will use three character styles to define various aspects of the quote.

1. **With aussie-fold.indd open, click the text frame on Page 6 to select it.**

2. **Using the Selection tool, click the overset text icon to load the rest of the story into the cursor.**

3. **Click the pasteboard area to the right of the spread near the top of the page to place the remaining text in a new text frame.**

4. **Highlight the last paragraph in the story and cut it (Edit>Cut or Command/Control-X).**

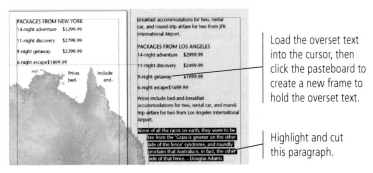

Load the overset text into the cursor, then click the pasteboard to create a new frame to hold the overset text.

Highlight and cut this paragraph.

5. **Create a new text frame with the following dimensions:**

> X: 6.6 in   W: 5 in
>
> Y: 3.125 in   H: 2.5 in

6. **Use the Type tool to place the insertion point in the new frame, then paste the text you cut in Step 4.**

   You applied a text wrap to the map image in the previous exercise, so that wrap applies to the new frame.

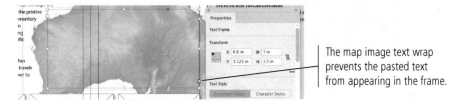

The map image text wrap prevents the pasted text from appearing in the frame.

7. **Select the new frame with the Selection tool and open the Text Frame Options dialog box. Check the Ignore Text Wrap option and then click OK.**

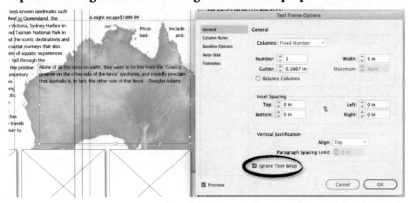

8. **Place the insertion point anywhere in the pasted text, and apply right paragraph alignment to the paragraph.**

9. **With the insertion point anywhere in the quote paragraph, Option/Alt-click the Create New Style button in the Paragraph Styles panel.**

   As with object styles, Option/Alt-clicking the Create New Style button automatically creates a new style and opens the New Paragraph Style dialog box. The new style adopts the settings of the current insertion point or selection.

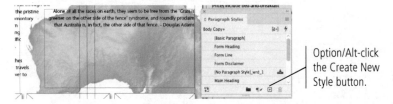

Option/Alt-click the Create New Style button.

10. **In the resulting New Paragraph Style dialog box, change the style name to Pull Quote.**

11. **Check the Apply Style to Selection option.**

   When this option is active, the new style is automatically applied to the active (selected) paragraph in the layout.

12. **At the bottom of the dialog box, uncheck the Add to CC Library option and check the Preview option.**

Because you activated Apply Style to Selection, you will be able to immediately see the effect of your choices in the layout while the dialog box is open.

Check this option.
Uncheck this option.
Check this option.

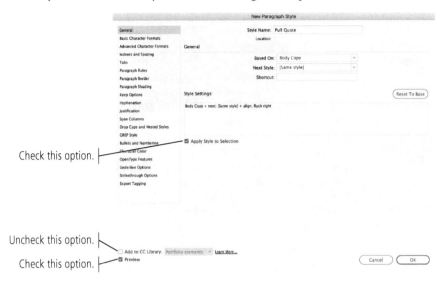

13. **Click Drop Caps and Nested Styles in the list of categories to display those options, then click the New Nested Style button.**

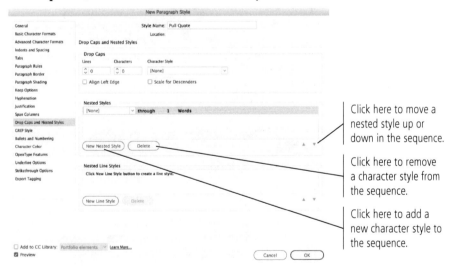

Click here to move a nested style up or down in the sequence.

Click here to remove a character style from the sequence.

Click here to add a new character style to the sequence.

14. **Click the first menu (the one that says "[None]") and choose Quote Opener in the list of available character styles.**

When you imported the styles from the ge-assets.indd file, you imported three character styles that should be used to format pull quotes. In the next few steps, you will create a nested style that automatically applies those styles to the appropriate parts of the quote.

15. Click the Words menu and choose Characters from the list.

Nested styles can be applied up to or through a specific character sequence; if you choose the Through option, the character(s) you specify will be formatted with the character style you define. For this layout, the first character in any pull quote will be formatted with the Quote Opener style; you can leave the default Through 1 option.

Note:

You might need to click away from the Characters menu to see the change in the document window.

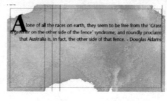

16. Add another nested style to the list, applying the Quote Body character style and using the Up To option instead of the Through option. Highlight the contents of the fourth menu and type a hyphen (-).

You can define a specific character by highlighting the field and typing the character. In this case, you're formatting all text up to the hyphen preceding the author's name.

Nested Style Character Options

- **Sentences** applies the style up to or through the defined number of sentences. InDesign recognizes the end of a sentence as the location of a period, question mark, or exclamation point. (Quotation marks following punctuation are included as part of the sentence.)

- **Words** applies the style up to or through the defined number of words. InDesign recognizes the division of individual words by space characters.

- **Characters** applies the style up to or through the defined number of characters. Nonprinting characters (tabs, spaces, etc.) are included in the character count.

- **Letters** applies the style up to or through the defined number of letters.

- **Digits** applies the style up to or through the defined number of Arabic numerals (0–9).

- **End Nested Style Character** applies the style up to or through a placed End Nested Style Here character (Type> Insert Special Character>Other>End Nested Style Here).

- **Tab Characters** applies the style up to or through a nonprinting tab character. (Choose Type>Show Hidden Characters to see tab characters in the text.)

- **Forced Line Break** applies the style up to or through a nonprinting, forced line break character.

- **Indent to Here Character** applies the style up to or through a nonprinting Indent to Here character.

- **Non-Breaking Spaces**, **Em Spaces**, and **En Spaces** apply the style up to or through these space characters.

- **Anchored Object Marker** applies the style up to or through an inline frame.

- **Auto Page Number** and **Section Marker** apply the style up to or through page or section markers.

17. **Add a third nested style to the list, applying the Quote Author character style up to 1 Tab Characters.**

    In this case, you want the style to go through the end of the paragraph. The Up To 1 Tab Characters option means the Quote Author style will apply until the application encounters a Tab character; because the author information is the end of the text frame, there will never be a Tab character to interrupt the style.

18. **Click OK to return to the document.**

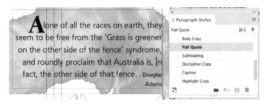

19. **Place the insertion point before the hyphen and press Shift-Return/Enter to force the author information onto a new line without starting a new paragraph.**

    Remember, Shift-Return/Enter is the key command for a forced line break (soft return), which starts a new line without starting a new paragraph.

20. **Add another soft return before the words "in fact" in the last line of the quote.**

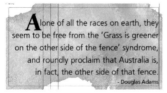

21. **Save the file and continue to the next exercise.**

InDesign supports three basic kinds of nested styles. The first is the basic parent/child relationship, in which one style is based on another. When you base one style on another, you change all related styles by changing the parent style.

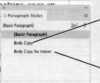

Body Copy uses 12-pt Minion Pro with a 0.25" first-line indent.

Body Copy No Indent is based on Body Copy with the first-line indent changed to 0".

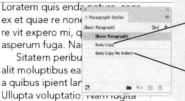

Changing Body Copy to use Avenir…

…applies the same change to Body Copy No Indent.

The second type of nested style incorporates different character styles for specific parts of a paragraph, as you do to create the Pull Quote style in this project. You can also use nested character styles to format drop caps, bulleted lists, and numbered lists.

The drop cap character created in the Body Copy No Indent paragraph style is formatted with the Red Drop Cap character style.

The Blue Typewriter character style is applied to the numbers created by the Numbered List paragraph style.

Nested Line Styles (at the bottom of the dialog box) affect the appearance of entire lines of text. You can define specific character styles to apply to a specific number of lines; the Repeat option allows you to continue a sequence of defined styles throughout the paragraph. In this example, the applied paragraph style defines two Nested Line Styles, which tell InDesign to apply the Green Text character style to the first line of the paragraph and then apply the Red Text character style to the second line of the paragraph. The third item — [Repeat] — determines what to do with the remaining lines of the paragraph; in this example, InDesign will *repeat* the *last 20 lines* of the Nested Line Styles list.

The applied paragraph style defines a sequence of two character styles that will be applied to every other line in the paragraph.

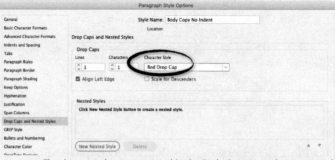

Control Tab Formatting

Some people incorrectly rely on the Spacebar for aligning columns of text, or they rely on the default tab stops (usually every half-inch in InDesign and Microsoft Word), adding multiple tab characters to align text. Both methods can be time consuming, and both are unnecessary to properly format tabbed text.

1. **With the inside spread of `aussie-fold.indd` visible, make sure hidden characters are showing (Type>Show Hidden Characters).**

2. **Click with the Type tool to place the insertion point in the first paragraph after the Packages from New York heading.**

3. **Using the Control or Paragraph panel, change the Space After value to `0 in`.**

4. **If possible, make the top of the selected frame visible in the document window.**

5. **Choose Type>Tabs.**

   This is the only InDesign panel not accessed in the Window menu. If the top edge of the active text frame is visible, the Tabs panel will automatically appear at the top of the frame. If the top edge of the frame is not visible, the panel floats randomly on the screen.

6. **Click the Align to Decimal tab marker in the Tabs panel and then click the bar above ruler to add a tab stop.**

   Remember that tab settings are a paragraph formatting option. Adding the tab stop affects only the selected paragraph(s).

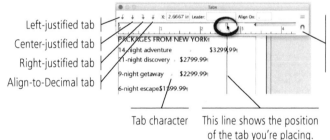

Left-justified tab
Center-justified tab
Right-justified tab
Align-to-Decimal tab

If the top of the frame is visible, the Tabs panel automatically snaps to the top of the frame.

Tab character

This line shows the position of the tab you're placing.

7. **With the stop you added in Step 6 selected on the ruler, change the X field to `3.125 in`.**

   You can either drag markers on the ruler to adjust tab-stop positions, or you can use the X field to define a precise location. If you drag an existing stop to a new position, make sure you drag straight across the tab ruler; if you drag too high or too low, you might delete the tab stop when you release the mouse button.

8. **Type ". " (a period followed by a space) in the Leader field, then press Return/Enter to apply the change.**

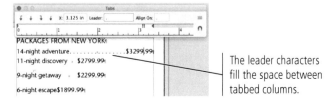

The leader characters fill the space between tabbed columns.

9. **With the insertion point still in the first price line, Option/Alt-click the Create New Style button at the bottom of the Paragraph Styles panel.**

The new style automatically adopts the settings of the current insertion point. In this case, it has all of the formatting defined in the paragraph you just edited, including the reduced space after and the tab with its leader characters.

10. **Type** `Price Line` **in the Style Name field. Check the Apply Style to Selection option, then click OK to return to the document window.**

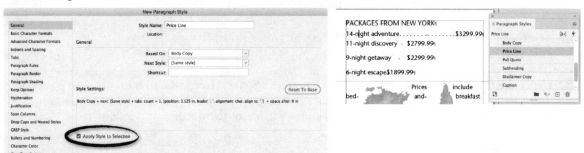

11. **Select the remaining three lines of prices, then click the new Price Line style to apply it to those paragraphs.**

Note:

Many client files will have multiple tab characters separating one bit of text from another. You should almost always remove extra tab characters and use tab-formatting options to create the appropriate columns.

12. **Place the insertion point in the last paragraph of the story and then click the Disclaimer Copy style to apply it.**

13. **In the text frame on the pasteboard (to the right of Page 6), apply the Price Line style to the four paragraphs after the Packages from Los Angeles heading. Apply the Disclaimer Copy style to the last paragraph.**

Don't worry if the price lines don't fit onto one line in the overset frame. In a later exercise, you will use conditional text to move those lines into the Page 6 frame; because you know the lines currently on Page 6 fit into the frame width, the overset lines, which are formatted with the same styles, will also fit in that frame.

Note:

You will fix the problem of the overset text in the next exercise.

14. **Save the file and continue to the next exercise.**

Create Variations with Conditional Text

The concept of **versioning** is a growing segment of graphic design. Clients are using a single base document, adding varying content for different users based on specific demographics such as geographic region, age, or gender. Other reasons for versioning include producing special editions of documents with content that does not appear on all copies; customization based on known information about past purchases or preferences; and even individual personalization using variable data to target specific users.

To complete this project, you will use conditional text to create two variations of this brochure: one for East Coast clients and one for West Coast clients.

1. **With `aussie-fold.indd` open, make sure the inside spread is visible.**

2. **Open the Conditional Text panel (Window>Type & Tables>Conditional Text).**

3. **Click the New Condition button at the bottom of the panel.**

New Condition

4. **In the New Condition dialog box, type `East Coast Text` in the Name field and then click OK.**

   Options in the dialog box determine how conditional text appears in the page layout:

   - Use the Method menu to change the style of indicators from an underline to a highlight.

   - Use the Appearance menu to change the conditional indicator from the default Wavy style to the Solid or Dashed style.

   - Use the Color menu to change the color of indicators for the specific condition.

5. **Click the New Condition button again. In the New Condition dialog box, type `West Coast Text` in the Name field and then click OK.**

6. **In the text frame on Page 6, highlight all text related to packages from New York. Make sure you include the paragraph return at the end of the disclaimer copy as part of the selection.**

7. Click East Coast Text in the Conditional Text panel.

Applying a condition is as simple as selecting the targeted text and choosing the appropriate condition in the panel. The selected text is part of the condition, which you can turn off when you need to display the West Coast packages.

Click the condition to apply it to the selected text.

8. Place the insertion point at the end of the active selection and review the text.

The wavy lines below the previously selected text are the conditional-text indicators. The color of the indicators matches the color of the item in the panel.

These lines are conditional-text indicators.

9. Click the Eye icon to the left of the East Coast Text condition.

When you have multiple conditions in a file, only the visible conditions will be included in the output. By default, the conditional indicators do not appear on the output.

When the East Coast conditional text is hidden, the "Packages from Los Angeles" list, which is part of the existing text thread, moves into place on Page 6.

Click this column to toggle the visibility of specific conditions.

This character identifies hidden conditional text.

10. Highlight all text related to the Los Angeles packages then click the West Coast Text condition.

11. Place the insertion point at the end of the active selection and review the text.

Note:

Conditional text indicators do not appear in the output unless you choose "Show and Print" in the Indicators menu of the Conditional Text panel.

12. In the Conditional Text menu, choose Hide in the Indicators menu.

Hiding the conditional-text indicators affects only what you see in the layout; the indicators are still present but do not interfere with the layout's appearance on screen.

Use this menu to hide the conditional-text indicators in the layout.

13. Save the file and continue to the next exercise.

Define Paragraph Shading

The brochure layout is almost complete with only a few remaining issues to address. In this exercise, you are going to use paragraph shading to add more visual weight to the subheadings in the body copy. Paragraph shading is a simple way to apply color behind the text of a specific paragraph.

1. With **aussie-fold.indd** open, make sure the inside spread is visible. Using the Selection tool, click an empty area of the pasteboard to deselect all objects.

2. In the Paragraph Styles panel, double-click the Subheading style to open the Paragraph Style Options dialog box for that style.

3. Click Paragraph Shading in the list of formatting categories and make sure the Preview option is checked.

4. Check the Shading box. Open the Color menu and choose the Corporate Blue swatch, then change the tint field to 15%.

   This swatch is used by one of the styles you imported from another InDesign file in a previous exercise. When you import a style from one InDesign file to another, any other required assets — such as color swatches — are also imported into the current file.

   Shading is applied by default between the ascent (the top of the highest ascender) and the descent (the bottom of the lowest descender) of the applied font. You can change those values in the Top Edge and Bottom Edge menus, respectively. Alternatively, you can change the Offset values to move the shading away from the edges of type.

Note:

Check the Do Not Print or Export to show the shading in the layout but not in any printed or exported file (such as a PDF created from the layout).

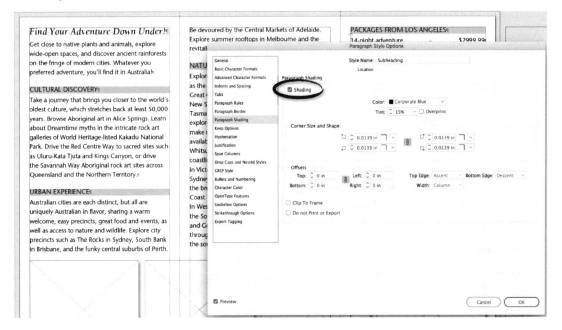

5. **Unlink the Offset fields, then change the Top Offset field to 0.04 in.**

   This adds slightly more shading above the top edges of the text.

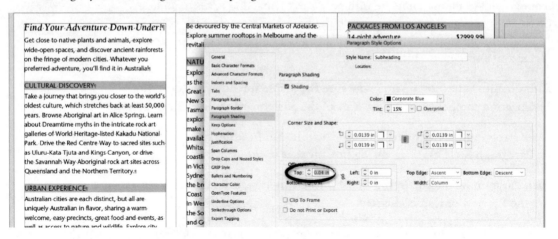

6. **Click OK to close the dialog box and return to the layout.**

   By editing the style definition, you simultaneously changed the appearance of all four paragraphs formatted with the Subheading style.

7. **Choose Type>Hide Hidden Characters.**

8. **Save the file and continue to the next exercise.**

 ## Create Dynamic Captions

The client wants to include captions to identify images but did not send any specific text for those captions; instead, the client added titles to the image files as metadata. In this exercise, you will place the client's images and generate captions directly in the layout based on the metadata defined for the placed images.

1. **With aussie-fold.indd open, make the inside spread visible in the document window.**

2. **With nothing selected in the document, choose File>Place. In the resulting dialog box, navigate to WIP>Australia>Links (if necessary). Press Command/Control and click to select the following images:**

   cave.tif

   clownfish.tif

   koala.tif

   opera-house.tif

3. **Uncheck the Show Import Options box, then click Open to load the four selected images into the cursor.**

4. **Click in each of the four empty frames at the bottom of the spread to place the four loaded images in the following positions.**

5. **Click the left image to select it, and then open the Links panel. Review the information in the lower half of the panel.**

Files can include a wide range of metadata, including information about how and when the image was captured, file dimensions and resolution, and color mode. You can also define custom metadata for a file, including a title, keywords, and descriptive text that make searching easier. These images have all been assigned unique titles to identify the location shown in the image. You are going to use those titles to automatically generate captions in the layout.

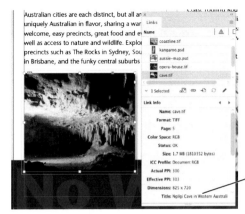

The Link Info shows that the client identified each picture in the Title metadata field.

6. **Choose Object>Captions>Caption Setup. In the resulting dialog box**

- **Choose Title in the Metadata menu.**

  You can use the empty text fields to define specific text before and after the selected metadata.

- **Choose Below Image in the Alignment menu.**

  You can align the caption to the left, right, top, or bottom edge of the image frame.

- **Change the Offset field to 0.0625 in.**

  The offset determines how far the caption text appears from the image frame; it is applied as a text inset within the resulting caption frame.

- **Choose Caption in the Paragraph Style menu.**

  You can use any existing paragraph style to automatically format the resulting caption.

- **Check the Group Caption with Image option.**

  When this option is checked, the resulting caption frame is automatically grouped with the related image frame. When Group Caption with Image is *not* checked, you can use the Layer menu to choose a specific layer where the resulting caption frames will be placed. This is useful, for example, if you want to add captions that you can see during development (file name, color mode, etc.), but that should not be included in client proofs or final output.

7. **Click OK to close the Caption Setup dialog box.**

Nothing yet appears in the layout because you haven't yet created the captions.

8. **With the left image selected, choose Object>Captions>Generate Live Caption.**

The resulting caption frame is added to the frame, and the caption appears below the image.

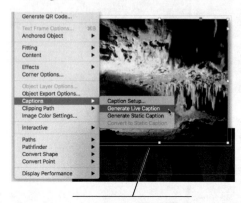 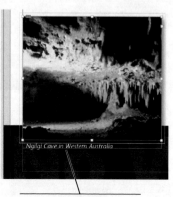

The caption does not appear until you generate it.

The caption, based on the Setup you just defined, is created in a new text frame.

9. **Select the other three image frames and choose Object>Captions>Generate Live Caption.**

Once you have defined the caption setup in a file, you can apply the same setup to other images, including multiple selected images at once.

The second image caption shows a placeholder that indicates the placed image has no defined Title metadata. This is referred to as an **unresolved caption variable** and can be flagged as an error using the Preflight panel.

The caption shows that the placed file does not include the necessary metadata.

10. **Select only the image frame within the second group.**

You can either use the Layers panel or double-click the graphics frame with the Selection tool to select it within the group.

11. **Choose File>Place. Select `barrier-reef.tif` in the dialog box, check the Replace Selected Item option, and click Open.**

Because you used the Live Caption option, the existing caption automatically changes to show the Title metadata for the replacement image. If you used the Static Caption option, the caption would not change when you replace the image.

Ngilgi Cave in Western Australia   The Great Barrier Reef   Frankie, the blue-eyed koala   Sydney Opera House

12. **Save the file and continue to the next exercise.**

 ## Clean and Finish the File

Almost every job requires some amount of clean-up work at the end, even if only to optimize your file. In this exercise, you perform this last check before creating a PDF file for the output provider.

1. **With `aussie-fold.indd` open, make the inside spread visible in the document window.**

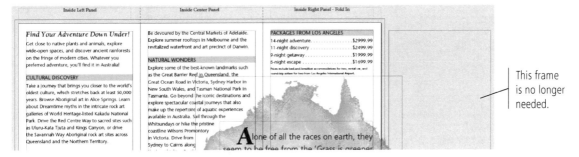

This frame is no longer needed.

2. **Select the empty text frame on the right side of the pasteboard and press Delete/Backspace to remove it.**

Leaving extraneous text and graphics on the pasteboard can trigger false alarms for missing fonts and graphics. It's a good idea to delete these objects to avoid unnecessary potential problems. As a general rule, objects on the pasteboard should be removed before the file is considered "final."

3. **Choose Type>Text Variables>Define.**

The Project Status variable you defined in an earlier exercise allows you to monitor the status of the project while you work. As you finalize the project, you should change the variable to reflect the new status.

4. **Select Project Status in the list and click Edit. In the Text field, change "Work in Progress" to** Finished.

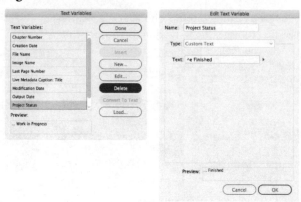

5. **Click OK, and then click Done to return to the layout.**

Because you placed the Project Status variable on each master page layout, changing the variable definition changes all placed instances on the associated layout pages.

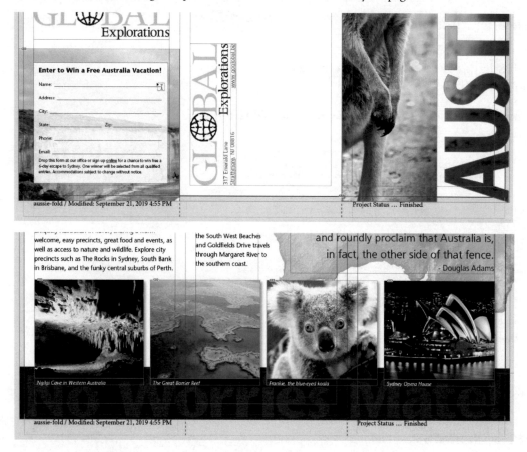

6. **Save the file and continue to the final exercise.**

Export Variations as PDF Files

The file is now complete and ready for output. To create the various versions of the file, you have to output the same file a number of times, selecting different conditions for each version.

1. With **aussie-fold.indd** open, open the Conditional Text panel.

2. In the Conditional Text panel, show the East Coast Text and hide the West Coast Text condition.

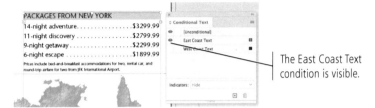

The East Coast Text condition is visible.

3. Choose File>Export. Change the file name to **aussie-fold-east.pdf**, and choose Adobe PDF (Print) in the Format/Save As Type menu. Click Save.

4. In the resulting dialog box, choose Press Quality in the Preset menu.

5. In the General pane, make the following changes:

   - In the Pages area, check the Spreads option.

   - In the Viewing area, choose Fit Page in the View menu.

   - In the Viewing area, check the View PDF after Exporting option.

   Because you created each panel as a separate page, you need to export each spread as a single page in the resulting file.

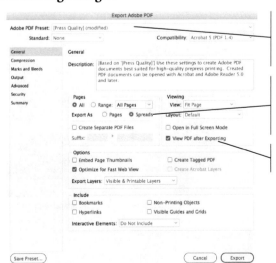

Start with the [Press Quality] preset; the (modified) indicator appears when you change the Spreads option.

Check the Spreads option to output each side of the brochure as a single page in the PDF file.

Check this option to open the PDF when it is complete.

6. **In the Marks and Bleeds pane, turn on Crop Marks with a 0.125 in offset. Activate the Use Document Bleed Settings and Include Slug Area options.**

7. **Click the Save Preset button at the bottom of the Export Adobe PDF dialog box. In the resulting Save Preset dialog box, name the preset Australia Brochure and click OK.**

You're going to export this file again; creating a preset means you need to make your export choices only once.

8. **Click Export to create the PDF file. Review the PDF file when it appears in Acrobat or your default PDF reader application.**

Text frames in the upper slug areas are not included because you checked the Nonprinting option in the Attributes panel when you created them.

9. **Close the PDF file and return to InDesign.**

10. **In InDesign, hide the East Coast Text condition and show the West Coast Text condition.**

11. **Choose File>Export. With Adobe PDF (Print) still selected in the Format/Save As Type menu, change the file name to `aussie-fold-west.pdf` and then click Save.**

12. **Make sure Australia Brochure is selected in the Adobe PDF Preset menu and click Export.**

    When you reopen the Export Adobe PDF dialog box, the Australia Brochure preset should be already selected; the menu remembers the last-used settings. The preset calls all the same options you already defined.

13. **Review the PDF file, close it, and return to InDesign.**

14. **Save and close the `aussie-fold` file.**

PROJECT REVIEW

1. A(n) _____ folds three times, resulting in four panels on each side of the sheet. The paper is folded in half, and then each half is folded in half toward the center so the two ends of the paper meet at the center fold.

2. A(n) _____ can be used to place information such as creation/modification date, file name, or custom text.

3. A(n) _____ is a spread with more than two pages.

4. You can use the _____ panel to define whether certain objects are printed when the job is output.

5. The _____ is used to modify the dimensions of a master page.

6. A(n) _____ is a special visual treatment for text that either is pulled from the story or somehow supports surrounding text.

7. A(n) _____ caption will not change if you replace one image with another in a layout.

8. A(n) _____ can be used to define multiple styles that will be used for different portions of the same paragraph based on specific sequences of characters or markers.

9. A(n) _____ is used to format entire lines of text within a single paragraph.

10. A(n) _____ can be used to apply the same attributes, such as text wrap and stroke weight, to multiple text frames.

1. Briefly explain the rules of page geometry regarding panels that fold into other panels in a folding document.

2. Explain three different ways text formatting styles might appear in an InDesign file.

3. Describe two scenarios in which multiple page sizes in a document might be useful.

PORTFOLIO BUILDER PROJECT

Use what you learned in this project to complete the following freeform exercise.
Carefully read the art director and client comments, then create your own design to meet the needs of the project.
Use the space below to sketch ideas; when finished, write a brief explanation of your reasoning behind your final design.

art director comments

Your client, the owner of Blue Moon Café, has hired you to redesign the look of the café's menus. The new menu design should reflect the gourmet style of the ocean-front bistro.

❏ Determine the best size and shape to present the menu content. The menu should be contained on a single sheet, but it can be printed on both sides of the sheet.

❏ Design a template you can reuse to create the bistro's new breakfast, lunch, and dinner menus once the layout is approved.

❏ Use the client's provided text (in the **BlueMoon_ID20_PB.zip** archive on the Student Files web page) to design the catering menu and present the new layout.

❏ You must use the client's supplied logo. You can use some or all of the photos provided by the client, or you can find or create your own images to illustrate the menu.

client comments

We used to have a huge menu with more than 100 options listed on eight pages. The menu included all three meals at once, and it was a nightmare for our customers to decide what they wanted.

We've decided to simplify both the meals we offer and the way the options are presented. We're going to separate out our menus for each meal — breakfast, lunch, and dinner — and we want each menu to be on a single sheet of paper.

We also need a fourth menu to present our breakfast catering options. We actually want you to start with that one and then move on to the bistro offerings once we've settled on a basic design.

We would like to be able to print and reprint the menus at the local quick-print shop. The owner advised using standard-size paper (letter- or tabloid-size) with no bleeds to keep down printing cost. He also suggested the paper not be cut, although it can be folded in halves or thirds at little extra cost.

project justification

_____

_____

_____

_____

_____

_____

_____

_____

_____

_____

_____

_____

_____

_____

This project built on the skills you learned in previous projects. To begin the letterfold layout, you built a technically accurate folding guide by taking advantage of InDesign's ability to incorporate multiple page sizes into a single layout. You also incorporated dashed fold guides and nonprinting text frames into the slug area. To speed up the process when you next need to build one of these common jobs, you saved your initial work as a template.

You also learned about several more options for improving workflow. Object styles allow you to store and apply multiple frame-formatting options, including nested paragraph styles, with a single click. Libraries store entire objects or groups of objects, including their formatting and contents, so you can place as many instances as necessary on any page of any file.

Finally, you learned about a number of advanced text-formatting options, including importing styles from another InDesign document, creating a complex text wrap, converting text to frames, building a nested paragraph style, formatting tabs and paragraph rules, and adding dynamic image captions based on information stored in a placed image.

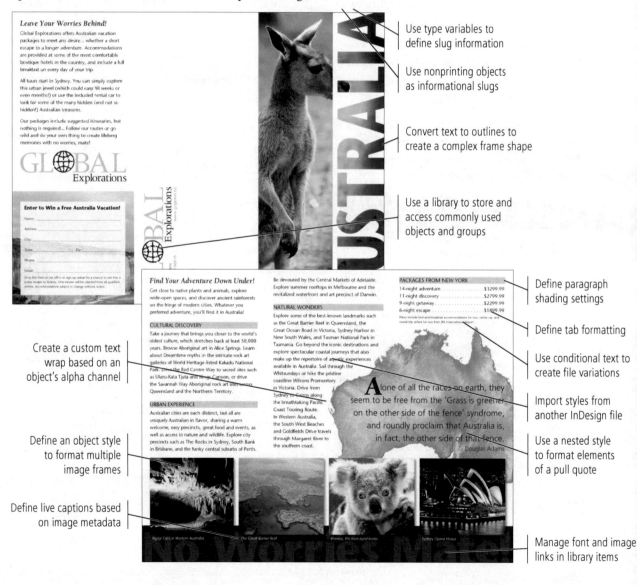

Use type variables to define slug information

Use nonprinting objects as informational slugs

Convert text to outlines to create a complex frame shape

Use a library to store and access commonly used objects and groups

Create a custom text wrap based on an object's alpha channel

Define an object style to format multiple image frames

Define live captions based on image metadata

Define paragraph shading settings

Define tab formatting

Use conditional text to create file variations

Import styles from another InDesign file

Use a nested style to format elements of a pull quote

Manage font and image links in library items

Digital Layout Variations

6

You have been hired to create four different versions of a brochure for a local organization to promote the group's rebranding. You need to create a color-managed print brochure with a metallic spot color, a digitally distributed PDF with an interactive slideshow and form, an e-book that can be used on popular e-reader devices, and an HTML file that can be fed into the client's website.

This project incorporates the following skills:

- ❏ Managing color in a print layout
- ❏ Searching for and replacing text and object attributes
- ❏ Defining hyperlinks for digital output
- ❏ Creating PDF form fields
- ❏ Exporting an interactive PDF file
- ❏ Preparing files for e-book and web publishing
- ❏ Creating an interactive slideshow
- ❏ Exporting EPUB and HTML files

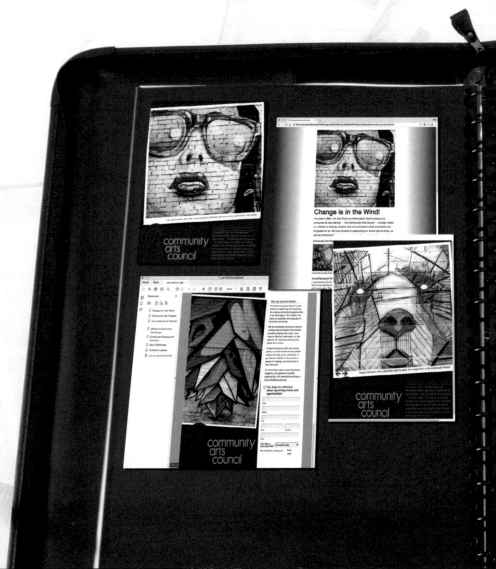

PROJECT MEETING

client comments

We just heard from the printer that we can only use one spot color. The logo uses two, and each is used throughout the layout as well. We decided to keep the metallic silver, but we need you to change the other one.

Now that it's official, we'd also like to use the actual name "Community Arts Council" rather than just "City Parks and Recreation Guild."

Once you've finalized the print file, we need you to use the same content to create a PDF we can email, an e-book we can distribute, and an HTML file that we can add into our website.

We have a lot of great photos of the local mural project. We weren't able to use them all in the print version, but we'd like to show as much as we can in the digital PDF and on the website.

We'd also like the form on the final page to be fully functional in the file we email to people. There's no point making people print something when they can just submit the form by email.

art director comments

You have a lot of work to do, but InDesign has the tools to make all of this possible in the same layout. Of course, so many different versions do require some careful planning and attention to detail.

The only thing you won't be able to establish in InDesign is the form distribution settings. We'll have to set that up in Acrobat, but you can still define the necessary form fields right in the layout.

Layers are a great choice for managing interactive content that won't work in the print layout. If you set everything up properly, you'll be able to accomplish all four versions without saving separate files for different output media.

project objectives

To complete this project, you will:

- ❏ Review the colors in the existing file.
- ❏ Search for and change specific content and attributes.
- ❏ Export a color-managed PDF file for printing.
- ❏ Prepare layers to manage static and animated content in the same file.
- ❏ Define hyperlinks and other interactive elements as necessary for digital document delivery.
- ❏ Create PDF form fields.
- ❏ Export an interactive PDF file.
- ❏ Define a table of contents for PDF and EPUB navigation.
- ❏ Anchor images to text for HTML and EPUB export.
- ❏ Export the document to HTML for web publishing.
- ❏ Create an interactive slideshow for EPUB export.

You can't accurately reproduce color without some understanding of color theory, so we present a very basic introduction in the following pages. Be aware that there are entire, weighty books written about color science; we're providing this highly condensed version of what you absolutely must know to work effectively with color.

While it's true that color management science can be extremely complex and beyond the needs of most graphic designers, applying color management in InDesign is more intimidating than difficult. We believe this foundational knowledge of color theory and color management will make you a more effective and practically grounded designer.

Additive vs. Subtractive Color Models

The most important thing to remember about color theory is that color is light, and light is color. Without light, you can't see — and without light, there is no color.

The **additive color** model (RGB) is based on the idea that all colors can be reproduced by combining pure red, green, and blue light in varying intensities. These three colors are considered the additive primaries. Combining any two additive primaries at full strength produces one of the additive secondaries: red and blue light combine to produce magenta, red and green combine to produce yellow, and blue and green combine to produce cyan. Although usually considered a "color," black is the absence of light and, therefore, of color. White is the sum of all colors, produced when all three additive primaries are combined at full strength. Additive color theory is practically applied in computer monitors, which are black when turned off; when the power is turned on, light in the monitor illuminates at different intensities to create the range of colors you see.

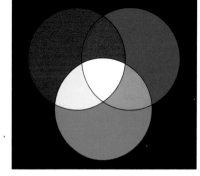

Additive color model

Printing pigmented inks on a substrate is a very different method of reproducing color. Reproducing color on paper requires **subtractive color** theory, which is essentially the inverse of additive color theory. Instead of adding red, green, and blue light to create the range of colors, subtractive color begins with a white surface that reflects red, green, and blue light at equal and full strength. To reflect (reproduce) a specific color, you add pigments that subtract or absorb only certain wavelengths from the white light. To reflect only red, for example, the surface must subtract (or absorb) the green and blue light.

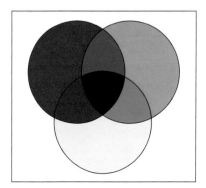

Subtractive color model

Remember that the additive primaries (red, green, and blue) combine to create the additive secondaries (cyan, magenta, and yellow). Those additive secondaries are also called the subtractive primaries because each subtracts one-third of the light spectrum and reflects the other two-thirds:

- Cyan absorbs red light, reflecting only blue and green light.

- Magenta absorbs green light, reflecting only red and blue light.

- Yellow absorbs blue light, reflecting only red and green light.

A combination of two subtractive primaries, then, absorbs two-thirds of the light spectrum and reflects only one-third. As an example, a combination of yellow and magenta absorbs both blue and green light, reflecting only red.

Color printing is a practical application of subtractive color theory. The pigments in the cyan, magenta, yellow, and black inks are combined to absorb different wavelengths of light. To create the appearance of red, the green and blue light must be subtracted or absorbed, thus reflecting only red. Magenta absorbs green light, and yellow absorbs blue light; combining magenta and yellow inks on white paper reflects only the red light. By combining different amounts of the subtractive primaries, it's possible to produce a large range (or gamut) of colors.

Because white is a combination of all colors, white paper should theoretically reflect equal percentages of all light wavelengths. However, different papers absorb or reflect varying percentages of some wavelengths, thus defining the paper's apparent color. The paper's color affects the appearance of ink colors printed on that paper.

Understanding Gamut

Different color models have different ranges or **gamuts** of possible colors. A normal human visual system is capable of distinguishing approximately 16.7 million different colors. Color reproduction systems, however, are far more limited. The RGB model has the largest gamut of the output models. The CMYK gamut is far more limited; many of the brightest and most saturated colors that can be reproduced using light cannot be reproduced using pigmented inks.

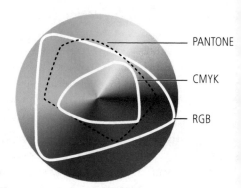

This difference in gamut is one of the biggest problems graphic designers face when working with color images. Digital image-capture devices (including scanners and digital cameras) work in the RGB space, which, with its larger gamut, can more closely mirror the range of colors in the original scene. Printing, however, requires images to be first converted or separated into the CMYK color space.

The usual goal in color reproduction is to achieve a color appearance equivalent to the original. Depending on the images, it is likely that at least some colors in the RGB model cannot be reproduced in the more limited gamut of the CMYK color model. These out-of-gamut colors pose a challenge to faithfully reproducing the original image. If the conversion from RGB to CMYK is not carefully controlled, color shift can result in drastic differences between the original and the printed images.

Color Management in Brief

Color management is intended to preserve color consistency as a file is moved from one color mode to another in the reproduction process. Color management can also eliminate ambiguity when a color is specified by only some numbers. For example, you might create a royal purple in the Swatches panel; without color management, that same set of RGB numbers might look more lilac or gray when converted to CMYK for printing. A well-tuned color management system can translate the numbers defining a color in one space to numbers that better represent that same color in another space.

It is, however, important to have realistic expectations of color management. Color management is not a replacement for a thorough understanding of the color-reproduction process. Even at its best, color management can't fix bad photos; all it can do is provide consistency and predictability to a process that often has neither.

Color management relies on color profiles, which are data sets defining the reproduction characteristics of a specific device. A **profile** is basically a recipe that contains the ingredients for reproducing a specific color in a given color space. The color recipes in profiles are known as Look-Up Tables (LUTs), which are essentially cross-reference systems for finding matching color values in different color spaces.

Note:

Color shift can also result when converting from one CMYK profile to another (e.g., a sheetfed press profile to a web press profile) or (though less likely) from one version of RGB to another. Whatever models are being used, color management gives you better control over the conversion process.

Note:

Color profiles are sometimes called "ICC profiles," named after the International Color Consortium (ICC), which developed the standard for creating color profiles.

Source profiles are the profiles of the devices (scanners, digital cameras, etc.) used to capture an image. **Destination profiles** are the profiles of output devices. LAB (or L*a*b* or CIELAB) is a device-independent, theoretical color space that represents the entire visible spectrum. The color management engine uses LAB as an intermediate space to translate colors from one device-dependent space to another.

The mechanics of color-managed conversions are simple. Regardless of the specific input and output spaces in question, the same basic process is followed for every pixel in the image:

1. The color-management engine looks up the color values of a pixel in the source (input-space) profile to find a matching set of LAB values.

2. The color-management engine looks up the LAB values in the destination (output-space) profile to find the matching set of color values that will display the color of that pixel as accurately as possible in the output space.

When you need to convert an image from an RGB space to a more limited CMYK space, you need to tell the color-management engine how to handle any colors outside the CMYK space. You can do this by specifying the **rendering intent** that will be used when you convert colors.

Note:

Most professional-level devices come with profiles you can install when you install the hardware; a number of generic and industry-specific destination profiles are also built into InDesign.

Color Management in Theory and Practice

RGB and CMYK are very different entities. The two color models have distinct capabilities, advantages, and limitations. There is no way to exactly reproduce RGB color using the CMYK gamut because many of the colors in the RGB gamut are simply too bright or too saturated. Rather than claiming to produce an exact, but impossible, match from your monitor to a printed page, the true goal of color management is to produce the best possible representation of the color using the gamut of the chosen output device.

A theoretically ideal color-managed workflow looks like this:

- Image-capture devices (scanners and digital cameras) are profiled to create a look-up table that defines the device's color-capturing characteristics.
- Images are acquired using a profiled device. The profile of the capturing device is tagged to every image captured.
- You define a destination (CMYK) profile for the calibrated output device that will be used for your final job.
- InDesign translates the document and embedded image profiles to the defined destination profiles.

This ideal workflow mentions the word "calibrate," which means to check and correct the device's characteristics. **Calibration** is an essential element in a color-managed workflow; it is fundamentally important to consistent and predictable output.

Taking this definition a step further, you cannot check or correct the color characteristics of a device without having something to compare the device against. To calibrate a device, a known target — usually a sequence of distinct and varying color patches — is reproduced using the device. The color values of the reproduction are measured and compared to the values of the known target. Precise calibration requires adjusting the device until the reproduction matches the original.

As long as your devices are accurately calibrated to the same target values, the color acquired by your RGB scanner will match the colors displayed on your RGB monitor and the colors printed by your CMYK desktop printer. Of course, most devices (especially consumer-level desktop devices, which are gaining a larger market share in the commercial graphics world) are not accurately calibrated, and very few are calibrated to the same set of known target values.

Keeping in mind these ideals and realities, the true goals of color management are to

- Compensate for color variations in the different devices.
- Accurately translate one color space to another.
- Compensate for limitations in the output process.
- Better predict the final outcome when a file is reproduced.

One final note: It's important to realize that color perception is a function of the human visual system. Many people perceive color differently, and some have deficiencies in one or more ranges of the spectrum. Despite your best efforts at color management, your client might perceive color differently than what you see.

Define Application Color Settings

There are two primary purposes for managing color in InDesign: previewing colors based on the intended output device and converting colors to the appropriate space when a file is output (whether to a PDF or an output device for commercial printing). The process begins with defining the color settings for your current workflow.

1. **With no file open in InDesign, choose Edit>Color Settings.**

   The Color Settings dialog box defines default working spaces for RGB and CMYK colors, as well as general color management policies.

   The RGB working space defines the default profile for RGB colors and images that do not have embedded profiles. The CMYK working space defines the profile for the device or process that will be used to output the job.

2. **Choose North America Prepress 2 in the Settings menu.**

   InDesign includes a number of common option groups, which you can access in the Settings menu. You can also make your own choices and save those settings as a new preset by clicking Save, or you can import settings files created by another user by clicking Load.

   The Working Spaces menus identify exactly which version of each space defines color within that space. Using Adobe RGB (1998), for example, means new RGB colors in the InDesign file and imported RGB images without embedded profiles will be described by the values in the Adobe RGB (1998) space.

3. **In the CMYK menu, choose U.S. Sheetfed Coated v2.**

   There are many CMYK profiles; each output device has a gamut unique to that individual device. U.S. Sheetfed Coated v2 is an industry-standard profile for a common type of printing (sheetfed printing on coated paper). In a truly color-managed workflow, you would actually use a profile for the specific press/paper combination being used for the job. We're using one of the default profiles to show you how the process works.

Note:

The Adobe RGB (1998) space is a neutral color space that isn't related to a specific monitor's display capabilities. Using this space assumes you are making color decisions on numeric values, not by what you see on your monitor.

4. **In the Color Management Policies, make sure Preserve Embedded Profiles is selected for RGB, and Preserve Numbers (Ignore Linked Profiles) is selected for CMYK.**

   These options tell InDesign what to do when you open existing files or if you copy elements from one file to another.

   • When an option is turned off, color is not managed for objects or files in that color mode.

   • **Preserve Embedded Profiles** maintains the profile information saved in the file; files with no profile use the current working space.

   • If you choose **Convert to Working Space**, files automatically convert to the working space defined at the top of the Color Settings dialog box.

   • For CMYK colors, you can choose **Preserve Numbers (Ignore Linked Profiles)** to maintain raw CMYK numbers (ink percentages) rather than adjusting the colors based on an embedded profile.

5. **Check all three options under the Color Management Policies menus.**

The check boxes control InDesign's behavior when you open an existing file, paste an element from a document with a profile other than the defined working space (called a profile mismatch), or open a file that does not have an embedded profile (called a missing profile).

6. **If it is not already checked, activate the Advanced Mode check box (below the Settings menu).**

The Engine option determines the system and color-matching method for converting between color spaces:

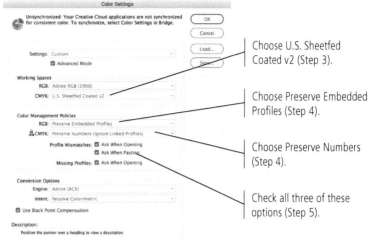

Choose U.S. Sheetfed Coated v2 (Step 3).

Choose Preserve Embedded Profiles (Step 4).

Choose Preserve Numbers (Step 4).

Check all three of these options (Step 5).

- **Adobe (ACE)**, the default, stands for Adobe Color Engine.

- **Apple CMM** (Macintosh only) uses the Apple ColorSync engine.

- **Microsoft ICM** (Windows only) uses the Microsoft ICM engine.

The **Intent** menu defines how the engine translates source colors outside the gamut of the destination profile:

- **Perceptual** presents a visually pleasing representation of the image, preserving visual relationships between colors. All colors in the image, including those available in the destination gamut, are shifted to maintain the proportional relationship within the image.

- **Saturation** compares the saturation of colors in the source profile and shifts them to the nearest-possible saturated color in the destination profile. The focus is on saturation instead of actual color value, which means this method can produce drastic color shift.

- **Relative Colorimetric** maintains any colors in both the source and destination profiles; source colors outside the destination gamut are shifted to fit. This method adjusts for the whiteness of the media and is a good choice when most source colors are in-gamut.

- **Absolute Colorimetric** maintains colors in both the source and destination profiles. Colors outside the destination gamut are shifted to a color within the destination gamut without considering the white point of the media.

When the **Use Black Point Compensation** option is selected, the full range of the source space is mapped into the full-color range of the destination space. This method can result in blocked or grayed-out shadows, but it is most useful when the black point of the source is darker than that of the destination.

7. **Click OK to apply your settings, then continue to the next exercise.**

Assign Color Settings to an Existing File

This project requires working on a file that has already been started, so some work has been completed before the file was handed off to you. To manage the process throughout the rest of this project, you need to make sure the existing file has the same color settings you just defined.

1. **Download CACouncil_ID20_RF.zip from the Student Files web page.**

2. **Expand the ZIP archive in your WIP folder (Macintosh), or copy the archive contents into your WIP folder (Windows).**

   This results in a folder named **CACouncil**, which contains the files you need for this project. You should also use this folder to save the files you create in this project.

3. **Open the file cac-brochure.indd from the WIP>CACouncil folder.**

4. **If you get a warning about missing or modified images, update the links once the file opens.**

   All the required images are available in the WIP>CACouncil>Links folder.

5. **In the Profile or Policy Mismatch dialog box, select the second option (Adjust the document to match current color settings).**

   The existing file has neither a defined RGB nor CMYK profile. Because you activated the Ask When Opening option in the Color Settings dialog box, InDesign asks how you want to handle RGB color in the file.

   "None" means that the file you're opening does not have a defined RGB profile.

   This option assigns the existing RGB color settings, which you defined in the previous exercise, to the existing file.

6. **Leave the remaining options at their default values and click OK.**

   Again, your choice in the Color Settings dialog box was to Ask When Opening if a file was missing a CMYK profile. Because the file does not have a defined CMYK profile, you see that warning now.

7. **In the second warning message, choose the second radio button (Adjust the document to match current color settings).**

   "None" means that the file you're opening does not have a defined CMYK profile.

8. **Click OK to open the file.**

This file contains the layout for a four-page brochure.

9. **Save the file and continue to the next exercise.**

Assigning and Converting Color Profiles

If you need to change the working RGB or CMYK space in a document, you can use either the Assign Profiles (Edit>Assign Profiles) or Convert to Profile (Edit>Convert to Profile) dialog box. Although these two dialog boxes have slightly different appearances, most of the functionality is exactly the same.

In the Assign Profiles dialog box:

- **Discard (Use Current Working Space)** removes the current profile from the document. This option is useful if you do not want to color manage the document. Colors will be defined by the current working space, but the profile is not embedded in the document.

- **Assign Current Working Space** embeds the working profile in the document.

- **Assign Profile** allows you to define a profile other than the working profile. However, colors are not converted to the new space, which can dramatically change the appearance of colors as displayed on your monitor.

You can also define different rendering intents for solid colors, placed raster images, and transparent elements that result from blending modes, effects, or transparency settings. (All three Intent menus default to use the intent defined in the Color Settings dialog box.)

In the Convert to Profile dialog box, the menus can be used to change the RGB and CMYK destination spaces. This is basically the same as using the Assign Profile options in the Assign Profiles dialog box. You can also change the color management engine, rendering intent, and black point compensation options.

Preview Separations

To be confident in color output, you should check the separations that will be created when your file is output for commercial printing. InDesign's Separations Preview panel makes this easy to accomplish from directly within the application workspace.

1. **With cac-brochure.indd open, choose Window>Output>Separations Preview.**

2. **In the View menu of the Separations Preview panel, choose Separations.**

   When Separations is selected in the View menu, the display automatically switches images to their high-resolution previews. Extras, such as frame edges and invisible characters, are automatically hidden.

   All separations in the current file are listed in the panel. You can turn individual separations on and off to preview the different ink separations that will be created:

   - To view a single separation and hide all others, click the name of the separation you want to view. By default, areas of coverage appear in black; you can preview separations in color by toggling off the Show Single Plates in Black command in the panel Options menu.

   - To view more than one separation at the same time, click the empty space to the left of the separation name. When viewing multiple separations, each separation is shown in color.

   - To hide a separation, click the eye icon to the left of the separation name.

   - To view all process plates at once, click the CMYK option at the top of the panel.

   As you can see, the file includes two spot-color inks. You can't simply delete the extra spot color from the layout because it is used in the placed logo file.

3. **Click Pantone 8863 C in the Separations Preview panel to see where that color is used.**

   As your client stated, the brochure should use a single spot color — the dark magenta color in the new logo. The Separations Preview shows this color is used for headings throughout the brochure, as well as for background frames on Pages 1 and 4.

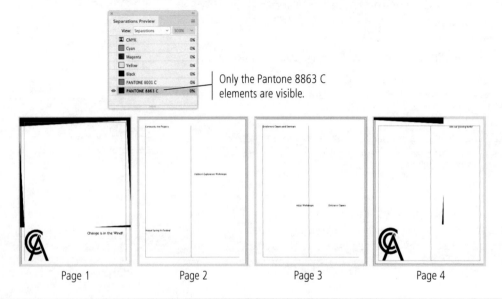

Only the Pantone 8863 C elements are visible.

Page 1   Page 2   Page 3   Page 4

4. **Click Pantone 8001 C in the Separations Preview panel to review where that color is used in the layout.**

   By reviewing the separation, you can see that the gray from the logo is used for the text on Page 1 of the brochure, as well as for a number of frame edges on Page 4.

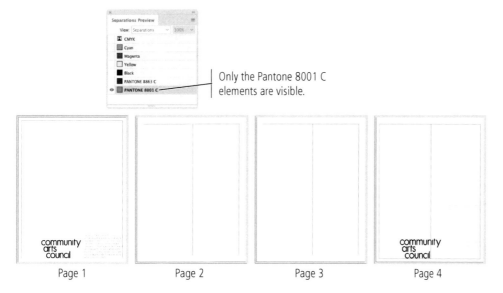

   Only the Pantone 8001 C elements are visible.

   Page 1   Page 2   Page 3   Page 4

5. **Click the empty space to the left of CMYK in the Separations Preview panel to view the CMYK separations in addition to the Pantone 8001 C separation.**

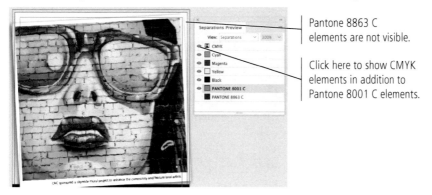

   Pantone 8863 C elements are not visible.

   Click here to show CMYK elements in addition to Pantone 8001 C elements.

6. **Choose Off in the View menu at the top of the Separations Preview panel.**

   When you turn off the separations preview, you again see the frame edges.

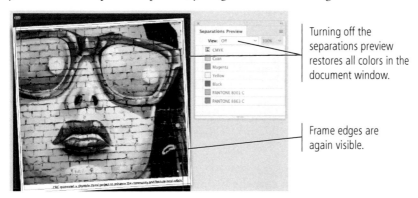

   Turning off the separations preview restores all colors in the document window.

   Frame edges are again visible.

7. **Continue to the next exercise.**

Enable Track Changes

In many cases, multiple users collaborate on a single document; designers, editors, content providers, and clients all go back and forth throughout the design process. Each person in the process will request changes, from changing the highlight color in a document to rewriting the copy to fit in a defined space. Because the words in a design are a vital part of the client's message, tracking text changes can be useful to make sure all changes are accurate and approved before the job is finalized.

1. **With `cac-brochure.indd` open, use the Type tool to place the insertion point in any story.**

2. **Choose Type>Track Changes>Enable Tracking in All Stories.**

   The Track Changes feature can help monitor text editing during development. This allows multiple users to edit the text without permanently altering that text until the changes have been reviewed and approved or rejected. (After you have made all the changes in this stage of the project, you will review and finalize those changes.)

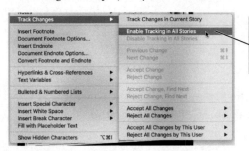

These options are not available unless the insertion point is currently placed.

3. **Open the Track Changes pane of the Preferences dialog box. Make sure the Added Text, Deleted Text, and Moved Text options are checked.**

4. **Choose Underline in the Added Text Marking menu.**

   The Marking options add a visual indicator (strikethrough, underlining, or outlining) so you can more easily identify text affected by the Track Changes function.

5. **Choose Red in the Deleted Text Background menu.**

   The Text Color options define the color of highlighting that will identify each type of change. All three options default to the same color; changing the color for Deleted Text will make it easier to identify this type of change when you review the corrections at the end of this stage of the project.

6. **Click OK to return to the document, then save the file and continue to the next exercise.**

Note:

Some text issues, however, have little to do with typography and more to do with "user malfunction" — common errors introduced by the people who created the text (most often, your clients). Regardless of how knowledgeable or careful you are, some problems will inevitably creep into the text elements of your layouts.

Note:

Remember, preferences are accessed in the InDesign menu on Macintosh or in the Edit menu on Windows.

Note:

It is very easy to make a mistake when spellchecking, so it's a good idea to check the Include Deleted Text When Spellchecking option at the bottom of the Preferences dialog box.

Find and Change Text

You will often need to search for and replace specific elements in a layout — a word, a phrase, a formatting attribute, or even a specific kind of object. InDesign's Find/Change dialog box allows you to easily locate exactly what you need, whether your layout is two pages or two hundred. For this brochure, you can use the Find/Change dialog box to correct the name of the client's project.

1. **With** `cac-brochure.indd` **open, navigate to Page 1.**

2. **Using the Type tool, place the insertion point at the beginning of the story on that page.**

3. **Choose Edit>Find/Change. If necessary, click the Text tab to show the options for searching the file text.**

4. **Place the insertion point in the Find What field and type** `City Parks and Recreation Guild`**.**

5. **Press Tab to highlight the Change To field, then type** `Community Arts Council`**.**

6. **In the Search menu, choose Document.**

    When the insertion point is placed, you can choose to search the entire Document, All [open] Documents, only the active Story, or only text following the insertion point in the selected story (To End of Story).

    If the insertion point is not currently placed, you can only choose to search the active Document or All Documents.

7. **Choose the Forward Direction option, then click Find Next.**

    Using the Forward Direction option (the default), the search identifies the first instance of the Find What text after the location of the insertion point. If you use the Backward Direction option, the search would identify the first instance preceding the current insertion point.

Note:

Two consecutive spaces after a period and two consecutive paragraph returns are common typing errors that are relics from the days before digital typeset- ting, when people were taught to type with manual typewriters. Although many people have never even seen an actual typewriter, these conventions still persist. When you import client-supplied text files into an InDesign document, you should immediately check for these issues and use the Find/Change dialog box to fix them.

Note:

The Find/Change dialog box is one of the few dialog boxes that allow you to interact directly with the document even while the dialog box is still open.

As you have seen, the Text tab allows you to search for and change specific character strings, with or without specific formatting options. The Object tab identifies specific combinations of object formatting attributes such as fill color or applied object effects. In addition to the tools you use in this project, the Find/Change dialog box has a number of options for narrowing or extending a search beyond the basic options. The buttons below the Search menu are toggles for specific types of searches (from left to right):

A When **Include Locked Layers and Locked Objects** is active, the search locates instances on locked layers or individual objects that have been locked; you can't replace locked objects unless you first unlock them.

B When **Include Locked Stories** is active, the search locates text that is locked; you can't replace locked text unless you first unlock it.

C When **Include Hidden Layers and Hidden Objects** is active, the search includes frames on layers that are not visible.

D When **Include Master Pages** is active, the search includes frames on master pages.

E When **Include Footnotes** is active, the search identifies instances within footnote text.

F When **Case Sensitive** is active, the search only finds text with the same capitalization as the text in the Find What field. For example, a search for "InDesign" will not identify instances of "Indesign," "indesign," or "INDESIGN."

G When **Whole Word** is active, the search only finds instances where the search text is an entire word (not part of another word). For example, if you search for "old" as a whole word, InDesign will not include the words "gold," "mold," or "embolden."

The GREP tab is used for pattern-based search techniques such as finding phone numbers in one format (e.g., 800.555.1234) and changing them to the same phone number with a different format (e.g., 800/555-1234). Adobe's video-based help system (www.adobe.com) provides some assistance in setting up an advanced query.

The Glyph tab allows you to search for and change glyphs using Unicode or GID/CID values. This is useful for identifying foreign and pictographic characters as well as characters from extended sets of OpenType fonts.

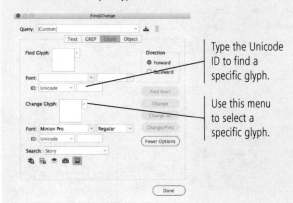

Type the Unicode ID to find a specific glyph.

Use this menu to select a specific glyph.

You can also save specific searches as queries, and you can call those queries again using the Query menu at the top of the Find/Change dialog box. This option is useful if you commonly make the same modifications such as changing Multiple Return to Single Return, which is so common that this particular search and replacement query is built into the application.

Click this button to save a custom query.

8. **Click the Change/Find button.**

   The next instance of the Find What text is highlighted in the document. Because you selected the option to search the entire document, the search finds the next instance in the second story.

The Change/Find button changes the previously selected instance and highlights the next instance in one click.

9. **Click Change All.**

10. **When you see the message that 5 replacements were made, click OK.**

11. **Save the file and continue to the next exercise.**

Find and Change Text Formatting Attributes

In addition to finding and replacing specific text, you can also find and replace formatting attributes for both text and objects. For this project, you need to remove the gray spot color from various layout elements. You can't simply delete the spot color from the Swatches panel, however, because that color is used in the placed logo file. The Find/Change dialog box makes this kind of replacement a relatively simple process.

1. **With cac-brochure.indd open, click anywhere on the pasteboard to deselect everything in the file.**

2. **Choose Edit>Find/Change (if the dialog box is not already open).**

3. **Delete all text from the Find What and Change To fields.**

4. **Choose Wildcards>Any Character in the menu to the right of the Find What field.**

   Wildcards allow you to search for formatting attributes, regardless of the actual text. In addition to searching for Any Character, you can also narrow the search to Any Digit, Any Letter, or Any White Space characters.

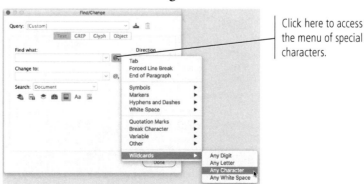

Click here to access the menu of special characters.

5. **Click the More Options button to show the expanded Find/Change dialog box.**

When more options are visible, you can find and replace specific formatting attributes of the selected text.

^? is the special code for a wildcard character.

Specify Attributes to Find/Change

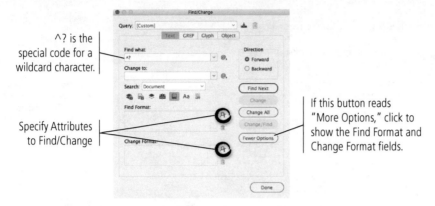

If this button reads "More Options," click to show the Find Format and Change Format fields.

6. **Click the Specify Attributes to Find button to open the Find Format Settings dialog box.**

You can search for and replace any character formatting option (or combination of options) that can be applied in the layout.

7. **Show the Character Color options and click the Pantone 8001 C swatch.**

8. **Click OK to return to the Find/Change dialog box.**

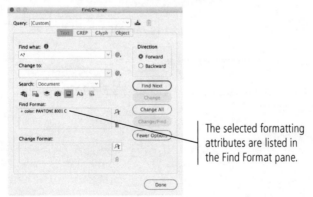

The selected formatting attributes are listed in the Find Format pane.

9. **Click the Specify Attributes to Change button to open the Change Format Settings dialog box.**

10. **In the Character Color options, choose the Black swatch and type 35% in the Tint field.**

11. **Click OK to return to the Find/Change dialog box.**

12. **Make sure Document is selected in the Search menu and click Change All. Click OK to close the message about the number of replacements.**

13. **In the Find/Change dialog box, delete the special-character code from the Find What field, then click the Delete buttons to remove the formatting options from the Find Format and Change Format fields.**

It can be easy to forget to remove these formatting choices. However, if you leave them in place, your next search will only find the Find What text with the selected formatting. It's a good idea to clear these formatting choices as soon as you're done with them.

Click the Delete buttons for both Find Format and Change Format to clear these choices.

14. **Save the file and continue to the next exercise.**

You can enter special characters in InDesign dialog boxes using the following special codes, called metacharacters. (Note that these metacharacters are case specific; for example, "^n" and "^N" refer to different special characters.)

Character	Code (Metacharacters)	Character	Code (Metacharacters)
Symbols		**Break Characters**	
Bullet (•)	^8	Paragraph return	^p
Caret (^)	^^	Forced line break (soft return)	^n
Copyright (©)	^2	Column break	^M
Ellipsis (…)	^e	Frame break	^R
Paragraph	^7	Page break	^P
Registered trademark (®)	^r	Odd page break	^L
Section (§)	^6	Even page break	^E
Trademark (™)	^d	Discretionary line break	^j
Dashes and Hyphens		**Formatting Options**	
Em dash (—)	^_	Tab character	^t
En dash (–)	^=	Right indent tab character	^y
Discretionary hyphen	^-	Indent to here character	^i
Nonbreaking hyphen	^~	End nested style here character	^h
White Space Characters		Nonjoiner character	^k
Em space	^m	**Variables**	
En space	^>	Running header (paragraph style)	^Y
Third space	^3	Running header (character style)	^Z
Quarter space	^4	Custom text	^u
Sixth space	^%	Last page number	^T
Flush space	^f	Chapter number	^H
Hair space	^| (pipe)	Creation date	^S
Nonbreaking space	^s	Modification date	^o
Thin space	^<	Output date	^D
Figure space	^/	File name	^l (lowercase L)
Punctuation space	^.	**Markers**	
Quotation Marks		Section marker	^x
Double left quotation mark	^{	Anchored object marker	^a
Double right quotation mark	^}	Footnote reference marker	^F
Single left quotation mark	^[	Index marker	^I
Single right quotation mark	^]	**Wildcards**	
Straight double quotation mark	^"	Any digit	^9
Straight single quotation mark	^'	Any letter	^$
Page Number Characters		Any character	^?
Any page number character	^#	White space (any space or tab)	^w
Current page number character	^N	Any variable	^v
Next page number character	^X		
Previous page number character	^V		

Find and Change Object Attributes

In addition to searching for specific text formatting attributes, you can also find and replace specific object formatting attributes. In this exercise you will replace all gray spot-color frame edges with the dark magenta spot color.

1. **With cac-brochure.indd open, open the Find/Change dialog box if it is not already open.**

2. **Click the Object tab to display those options.**

3. **Choose Document in the Search menu and choose All Frames in the Type menu.**

   The Document menu lets you search all documents, only the active document, or only the active selection. In the Type menu, you can limit your search to specific kinds of frames, or you can search all frames.

Specify Attributes to Find/Change

4. **Click the Specify Attributes to Find button to open the Find Object Format Options dialog box.**

   You can find and change any formatting attributes that can be applied to a frame.

5. **Display the Stroke options and click the Pantone 8001 C swatch.**

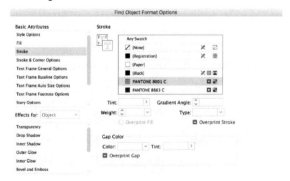

6. **Click OK to return to the Find/Change dialog box.**

7. **Click the Specify Attributes to Change button to open the Change Object Format Options dialog box.**

8. Choose the Pantone 8863 C swatch in the Stroke options.

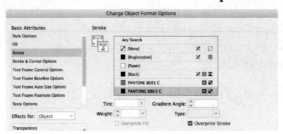

9. Click OK to return to the Find/Change dialog box.

10. Click Change All, then click OK to dismiss the message about the number of changes.

11. Click the Delete buttons for both the Find Object Format and Change Object Format options to clear your choices.

12. Click Done to close the Find/Change dialog box.

13. Click anywhere on the pasteboard to deselect everything in the file.

14. Open the Separations Preview panel (Window>Output>Separations Preview). Choose Separations in the View menu at the top of the panel.

15. Click Pantone 8863 C in the panel and review each page of the layout.

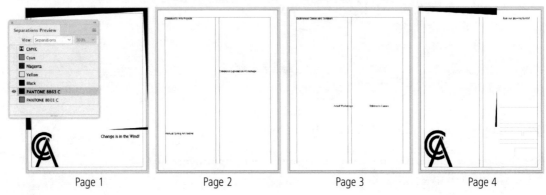

Page 1   Page 2   Page 3   Page 4

16. Click Pantone 8001 C in the panel and review each page of the layout.

The only thing now set with the second spot color is the three words in the placed logo file. Because you can't change the logo in InDesign, you will use other options to convert that spot color to process when you output the file.

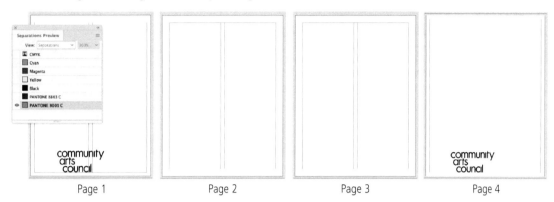

| Page 1 | Page 2 | Page 3 | Page 4 |

17. Choose Off in the View menu of the Separations Preview panel, then close the panel.

18. Save the file and continue to the next exercise.

 # Review Tracked Changes

Earlier in this project, you enabled the Track Changes feature for all stories in this document. You might have noticed, however, there is no visual indication of those changes in the layout. Tracking editorial changes is useful for monitoring changes in the text, but displaying those changes in the layout would make it impossible to fit copy and accurately format the text in a layout. To avoid this confusion, changes are tracked in a special utility called the Story Editor, which more closely resembles a word processor screen.

1. With cac-brochure.indd open, place the insertion point at the beginning of the text frame on Page 1.

2. Choose Edit>Edit in Story Editor.

The Story Editor opens in a separate window, showing only the current story. (A **story** in InDesign is the entire body of text in a single frame or string of linked frames.)

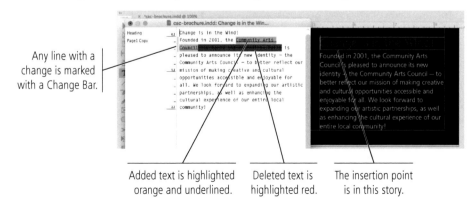

Any line with a change is marked with a Change Bar.

Added text is highlighted orange and underlined. Deleted text is highlighted red. The insertion point is in this story.

Note:

If your deleted text is not highlighted red, you missed a step in the earlier exercise where you enabled the Track Changes feature (see page 376). You can open the Track Changes pane of the Preferences dialog box and change the highlight options now.

3. **Open the Track Changes panel (Window>Editorial>Track Changes).**

When the Story Editor window is active, you can use the Track Changes panel to review the tracked changes.

A Enable/Disable Track Changes in Current Story toggles the track changes function on and off.

B Show/Hide Changes toggles the visibility of tracked changes in the Story Editor window.

C Previous Change highlights the first change before the current location of the insertion point.

D Next Change highlights the first change after the current insertion point.

E Accept Change makes the highlighted change permanent.

F Reject Change restores the original text for deleted text or removes added text.

G Accept All Changes in Story applies the same result as the Accept Change button, but for all tracked changes in the active story. The option does not allow you to individually review each change.

H Reject All Changes in Story applies the same result as the Reject Change button, but for all tracked changes in the active story. Again, the option does not allow the opportunity to individually review each change.

Note:

You can also Option/Alt click the Accept or Reject Change button to apply the change and then automatically highlight (find) the next change.

4. **Click the Next Change button in the Track Changes panel.**

If you read the text, you can see this instance refers to the client as the City Parks and Recreation Guild. The sentence goes on to explain that it was rebranded as "Community Arts Council," so it wouldn't make logical sense to use the term before it is defined.

The first change in the story is highlighted.

Next Change button

5. **Click the Reject Change button, then click the Next Change button.**

The added text is removed because you rejected that change.

The next tracked change is highlighted.

Note:

This type of decision is usually the client's to make; in this exercise, we are assuming the client would agree.

6. **Click the Reject Change button again.**

Because you did not keep the replacement text, you need to keep the deleted text.

7. **Click the Next Change button in the Track Changes panel.**

Because there were no more changes in the first story, clicking the Next Change button opens the next story where a change is located. Each story appears in a separate Story Editor window.

As you can see, the only change in this story is the replacement of the old client name with the new one. Rather than reviewing each instance separately, you can simply accept all changes in the story at one time.

Each story opens in its own window.

8. **Click the Accept All Changes in Story button at the top of the Track Changes panel.**

9. **When asked to confirm the change, click OK.**

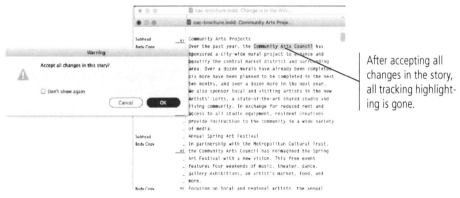

After accepting all changes in the story, all tracking highlighting is gone.

10. **Click the Next Change button.**

    The third story has a number of changes, but they are all the same text replacement you saw in the first two stories.

    In Step 8 you only accepted all changes in the active story; the third story in the layout still has tracked changes that should be reviewed.

11. **Open the Track Changes panel Options menu and choose Accept All Changes>In This Document.**

    The In This Document option affects all stories in a file, even if they are not currently open in a Story Editor window.

    Accepting all changes without reviewing them essentially defeats the purpose of tracking changes; in a professional environment you should be sure to carefully review all tracked changes before finalizing the job. We are telling you, in this case, it is safe to simply accept all the changes.

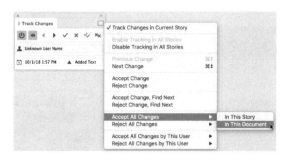

12. **Click OK to dismiss the Warning dialog box and accept the changes.**

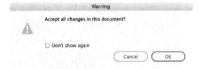

13. **Close all three Story Editor windows.**

14. **Save the file and continue to the next exercise.**

Export a Color-Managed PDF File

InDesign allows you to convert image data to the defined output profile when you create a PDF file for print while still maintaining the RGB images for the digitally distributed formats (PDF, EPUB, and HTML). However, because the RGB model allows a much greater gamut than CMYK, some color shift might occur when you export the PDF file for print. It's a good idea to review the potential color shift before you create the final print PDF.

Note:

RGB images in a layout are extremely common, especially when you work with files created by non-professionals. Be prepared to either correct the images in Photoshop and replace them or convert them to CMYK when you export the PDF file for print.

1. **With cac-brochure.indd open, navigate to Page 1.**

2. **Choose View>Proof Setup>Working CMYK.**

   Remember from the beginning of this project, the working CMYK profile is what you defined as the color characteristics of the intended output device — in this case, a standardized sheetfed press.

3. **Choose View>Proof Colors.**

   This toggle provides an on-screen preview of what will happen when the image is converted to the CMYK working-space profile, which won't affect the actual file data. This option, called **soft proofing**, is more valuable with an accurately calibrated monitor. Even with an uncalibrated monitor, you should be able to see any significant trouble areas.

   When Proof Colors is active, the document tab shows the profile being used for soft proofing.

Soft Proofing to Custom Profiles

You can soft proof to any profile — not just the working profile — by choosing View>Proof Setup>Custom. In the resulting dialog box, choose a profile in the Device to Simulate menu.

InDesign also allows soft proofing and export to grayscale profiles, which are included near the bottom of the various device profile menus. This is particularly useful if you are creating a file that might be placed in a newspaper or other document that prints only with black ink.

Using the Dot Gain 10% (grayscale) profile, you can see the rather drastic effect on the placed images.

4. **Navigate through the layout and review the differences. Toggle the Proof Colors option on and off for each page to look for significant color shift.**

   In many instances, the color shift will be subtle; most obvious changes will be visible in the brightest colors, such as the blue tarp in the image on the lower half of Page 3.

   We do not include images of the differences here because they do not reproduce well in print. However, you should be able to see the differences on your screen when you toggle the Proof Colors option on and off.

5. **Turn off the Proof Colors option, then choose File>Export.**

6. **At the bottom of the dialog box, uncheck the Use InDesign Document Name as the Output Filename option.**

7. **Change the file name to `cac-brochure-print.pdf` and choose Adobe PDF (Print) in the Format menu. Click Save.**

Uncheck this option.

8. **In the Export Adobe PDF dialog box, choose Press Quality in the Adobe PDF Preset menu.**

9. **In the Marks and Bleeds options, check the Crop Marks option and change the Offset value to `0.125 in`. In the lower half of the dialog box, check the option to Use Document Bleed Settings.**

10. **In the Output options, choose Convert to Destination in the Color Conversion menu.**

    You have several options for converting colors when you output a file:

    - **No Color Conversion** maintains color data, including that in placed images, in its current space.

    - **Convert to Destination** converts colors to the profile in the Destination menu.

    - **Convert to Destination (Preserve Numbers)** converts colors to the destination profile if the applied profile does not match the defined destination profile. Objects without color profiles are not converted.

    The Destination menu defines the gamut for the output device that will be used. This menu defaults to the active destination working space. Color information in the file and placed images is converted to the selected Destination profile.

Note:

Spot-color information is preserved when colors are converted to the destination space.

11. **Choose Don't Include Profiles in the Profile Inclusion Policy menu.**

    The **Profile Inclusion Policy** menu determines whether color profiles are embedded in the resulting PDF file. Different options are available, depending on what you selected in the Color Conversion menu.

12. **Click the Ink Manager button.**

    As you already know, this file is only allowed to use one spot color — Pantone 8001 C (metallic silver) — when it is printed.

    The Ink Manager, which lists all separations in the job, offers control over specific ink separations at output time. Changes here affect the current output, not how the colors are defined in the document.

13. **Click the Spot Color icon to the left of the Pantone 8863 C ink.**

    This converts the individual ink to a process color for the current output. Keep in mind that spot colors are often outside the CMYK gamut; there will almost always be color shift in the resulting CMYK build. (You can also access this dialog box by clicking the Ink Manager button in the Output pane of the Print dialog box.)

    Click this icon to convert a specific spot color to a process build.

    Check this option to convert all spot colors to process builds.

    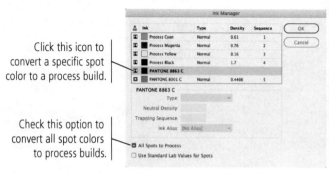

14. **Click OK to return to the Export Adobe PDF dialog box, then click Export.**

15. **If the PDF file opens, close it and then return to InDesign.**

16. **Save the InDesign file, then continue to the next stage of the project.**

STAGE 2 / Creating Interactive PDF Elements

Now that the print file is complete, you need to repurpose the content into several different versions for digital distribution — a common assignment in the professional market.

You already know the PDF format can contain all of the elements — fonts, images, etc. — required to create high-quality printing. Digitally distributed PDF files also support interactive elements and multimedia, which are not possible in static print jobs.

In this stage of the project, you are going to create interactive bookmarks, hyperlinks, a slideshow of images, and a form users can fill out directly in Adobe Acrobat. InDesign allows you to create all of these elements directly in the layout, without the need for additional software.

Define Interactive Bookmarks

The PDF format supports interactive tables of contents, which appear separate from the main document in the Acrobat document window. If you use styles to format the text in an InDesign layout, you can define a table of contents based on those styles. That table of contents can be automatically converted into the PDF bookmarks.

1. **With cac-brochure.indd open, choose Layout>Table of Contents Styles.**

Don't choose this option.

The Table of Contents Styles dialog box stores groups of settings that define different lists. If you choose the basic Table of Contents option in the Layout menu, you can define settings for a table of contents without saving it as a style, then generate the list and place it in the layout.

2. **Click New in the Table of Contents Styles dialog box.**

You can use this dialog box to define the styles that will appear in the resulting table of contents. All available styles appear in the Other Styles list by default.

3. **At the top of the dialog box, type PDF Contents in the TOC Style field. Delete the contents of the Title field.**

The TOC Style field is simply an internal way to identify the style you are defining; this name does not appear anywhere in the compiled table of contents. Text in the Title field appears at the top of the resulting table of contents in the document.

Type the style name here.

Delete the text from this field.

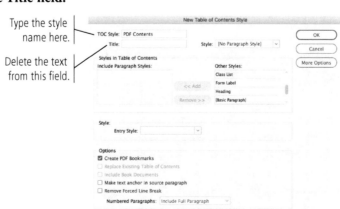

4. **In the Other Styles list, select the Heading style and click the Add button.**

5. **In the Other Styles list, select the Subhead style and click the Add button.**

Successive styles are automatically indented from the preceding style.

Note:

You are defining this table of contents style to create bookmarks in the interactive PDF file. Since you are not including the table of contents in the actual layout, most of the other options in this dialog box are not relevant. You will work with tables of contents in greater detail in Project 8: Multi-Chapter Booklet.

6. **Click the More Options button on the right side of the dialog box.**

7. **With Subhead selected in the list, change the Level field to 1.**

   The Level of a style automatically defaults to the next level after the previously selected style in the Include Paragraph Styles list.

   The designer correctly used a separate style for the larger heading on Page 1 of the layout, but, in this case, the nested levels of headings are not necessary. By changing the Level field for the Subhead style, all items in the PDF table of contents will appear at the same level of editorial priority.

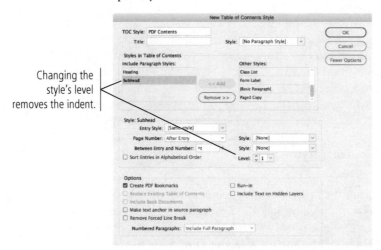

Changing the style's level removes the indent.

8. **At the bottom of the dialog box, make sure the Create PDF Bookmarks option is checked.**

9. **Click OK to return to the Table of Contents Styles dialog box, then click OK to return to the document window.**

10. **Add a new blank page at the end of the document.**

    Unfortunately, PDF bookmarks are not created unless the table of contents is actually placed somewhere in the file. To work around this problem, you are going to place the table of contents on a new page but not include that page in the exported PDF file.

11. **With the new blank page active in the document window, choose Layout>Table of Contents.**

    You should choose the Table of Contents menu option — not the Table of Contents Styles option — to compile the table of contents and place it in your layout.

12. **Make sure PDF Contents is selected in the TOC Style menu, then click OK.**

    Because you defined a table of contents style, you can call those same options by calling the defined style in the TOC Style menu.

13. **Click the loaded text cursor in the empty page to compile the table of contents.**

    Don't worry about the appearance of the list; you are not going to include this page in your final output.

    You're adding the TOC on Page 5 of the layout.

14. **Open the Bookmarks panel (Window>Interactive>Bookmarks).**

    This panel lists all bookmarks in the file. You can double-click an existing bookmark to navigate to that location in the layout. You can also click the New Bookmark button to create a new bookmark — independent of the defined table of contents list — from any selected text or object.

    New Bookmark button

15. **Save the file and continue to the next exercise.**

Define Hyperlinks

Hyperlinks are the most basic interactive elements in digital documents. Every hyperlink has two parts: the hyperlink object (or text) and the destination. The destination is the document, a specific place in the file, or other location that is called by clicking the hyperlink. InDesign's Hyperlinks panel makes it very easy to create and apply hyperlinks to elements of a layout.

1. **With `cac-brochure.indd` open, navigate to Page 4 of the layout and zoom into the bottom of the text frame in the right column.**

2. **Open the Hyperlinks panel (Window>Interactive>Hyperlinks).**

3. **Highlight the web address near the end of the text.**

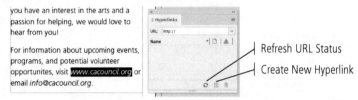

Refresh URL Status

Create New Hyperlink

Note:

If you choose New Hyperlink in the panel Options menu, a new hyperlink is added to the selected text using the default settings.

If you choose New Hyperlink from URL, the new hyperlink of the URL type is automatically created. The type is set to URL, the required http:// protocol is added to the selected URL text, and the default appearance settings are applied.

4. **Click the Create New Hyperlink button at the bottom of the Hyperlinks panel.**

   This automatically opens the New Hyperlink dialog box, where you can define the type and destination of a link, as well as the default appearance of the link in the layout.

5. **In the resulting dialog box, make sure URL is selected in the Link To menu.**

   The Link To menu defaults to the last-used setting; yours might already be set to URL. InDesign supports five different kinds of hyperlinks:

   - **URL** opens a web page at the address you define.

   - **File** opens another file based on the location you define. (This file must be available on a computer or server that users of the file can access. If you define a file on your computer, users working at other computers won't be able to access the file.)

   - **Email** links open a new mail message that is pre-addressed with the address you define.

   - **Page** links navigate to a specific page in the layout.

   - **Text Anchor** opens a page to a specific, defined location.

   - **Shared Destination** allows you to import URL destinations from other InDesign files.

When URL is selected in the Link To menu, text highlighted in the layout (which will be the hyperlink text) automatically appears in the URL field; the required "http://" protocol is automatically added.

InDesign defaults to apply a character style named "Hyperlink" to all hyperlink text. If no such character style exists, a new Hyperlink character style is added to the file; that style changes the type color to blue and

URL is selected in the Link To menu.

The selected text is automatically used as the URL destination.

The required **http://** protocol is automatically added to the beginning of the destination.

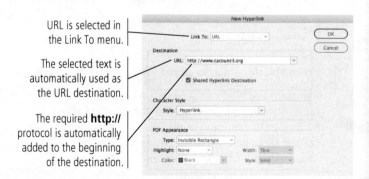

adds the underline type style. In the case of this project, the supplied cac-brochure.indd file includes a predefined Hyperlink style that sets the font style to italic but does not change the font color or underline.

6. **Click OK to close the dialog box.**

   After you define a hyperlink, it is listed in the Hyperlinks panel. You can click the page-number hot link for a hyperlink to select the source of that hyperlink (similar to the hot-text links in the Links panel, which navigate to and select specific images placed in the layout).

   You can also click the Status icon in the right side of the panel to navigate to the hyperlink destination. Clicking this icon opens the required application (a default browser for a URL link, an email client for an email link, etc.) on your desktop and performs the required action (opening the URL, addressing a new email message, etc.).

Status icon

Hyperlink location

7. **Highlight the email address in the last of line of text.**

8. **Click the Create New Hyperlink button at the bottom of the Hyperlink panel.**

9. **In the New Hyperlink dialog box, choose Email in the Link To menu.**

   The selected text automatically appears in the Address field when you choose Email in the Link To menu.

10. **In the Subject Line field, type Re: CAC Spring brochure.**

    When users click an email link, a new mail message opens in their default email client application. The text you enter in the Subject Line field automatically appears in the subject line of the new email message.

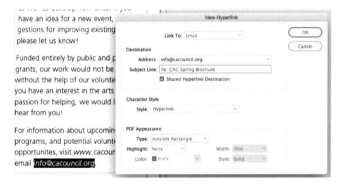

11. **Click OK to create the second hyperlink.**

12. **Save the file and continue to the next exercise.**

Create Text Form Fields

The PDF format allows you to create forms that a user can fill out and submit directly in Acrobat without the need to print and mail the page. Until now, creating these forms has been a time-consuming and tedious process that could only be completed in Adobe Acrobat. If you changed the layout and regenerated the PDF file, you also needed to redo all the form-creation work in Acrobat. Now, however, you can create form objects directly in InDesign.

1. **With Page 4 of `cac-brochure.indd` visible, open the Buttons and Forms panel (Window>Interactive>Buttons and Forms).**

2. **Click to select the empty frame above the "Name" label. In the Buttons and Forms panel, open the Type menu and choose Text Field.**

   As you can see, form objects can easily be created from standard InDesign objects, such as the empty frames in this layout.

3. **At the top of the panel, change the Name field to `Name`. At the bottom of the panel, check the Required option.**

   Form objects, like button objects, can trigger actions. In this simple form, you do not need to assign actions to these basic text fields.

   You do, however, need to make sure people include at least the basic contact information.

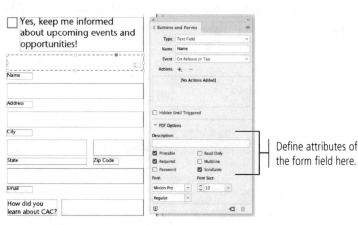

   - The **Printable** box, checked by default, means the form object — in this case, the text frame — will be included in printed output, including when you export a PDF for printing.

   - By checking the **Required** box, users won't be able to submit the form unless they fill out this field.

   - If you check **Password**, content in the field will appear as asterisks.

   - If you check **Read Only**, users will not be able to enter data into the field.

   - If you check the **Multiline** option, the field can contain more than one line of entered text.

   - If the **Scrollable** option is also checked, the field will display scrollbars as soon as more text than will fit into the defined field height is entered.

   You can use the Font and Font Size fields at the bottom of the panel to determine the default font that is used for form field content.

4. **Repeat this same process to convert the Address, City, State, Zip Code, and Email frames to required text fields.**

When frame edges are visible (View>Extras>Show Frame Edges), form fields are identified by a small icon on the right side of the object. When a form field object is selected, it shows a heavy dashed border.

Neither of these indicators is a printable attribute, which means you can create interactive form fields in the same file you use for print output; you don't need to make any special adjustments to preserve the integrity of the printable file.

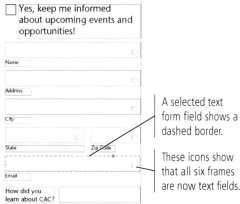

A selected text form field shows a dashed border.

These icons show that all six frames are now text fields.

5. **Save the file and continue to the next exercise.**

 Create a Radio Button Form Field

A radio button is a toggle that allows users to make a yes-or-no choice; the control is either on (selected) or off (not selected). You can also create a radio button group in which users can choose only one of a defined set of options.

1. **With cac-brochure.indd open, zoom in to the frame in front of the word "Yes" at the top of the form area, then click to select it.**

2. **In the Buttons and Forms panel, choose Radio Button in the Type menu.**

3. **Change the Name field to Add to Mailing List.**

When you convert a frame to a radio button, InDesign automatically creates a variety of states in the Appearance section of the Buttons and Forms panel. The selected state is what appears in the layout.

Note:

To create a radio button group, in which a user can select only one of several options, define the same name to each radio button that you want to include in the group.

4. **Click away from the radio button object, then click to select it again.**

If you don't deselect then reselect, the new object name does not register in the Layers panel. This is a small bug in the software but an important one.

5. **In the Layers panel, expand the Add to Mailing List group, then expand the [Normal On] group.**

   The various radio button states are simply groups of InDesign objects — in this case, a circle and a square.

   These objects make up the radio button when the Normal On state is active.

6. **Use the Selected Item icon in the Layers panel to select the circle. Change the Stroke and Fill colors of the circle to Pantone 8863 C.**

   You can edit the elements of a form object just as you would any other object in the layout. You simply need to select the correct object state in the Appearance area of the panel so you can access the pieces you want to change.

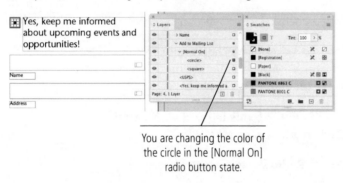

   You are changing the color of the circle in the [Normal On] radio button state.

7. **Click the Normal Off option in the Buttons and Forms panel.**

   When the Normal Off state is selected, it will be the default object state in the resulting PDF file, as well as any printed file you might create.

   As you can see in the panel and in the layout, the Normal Off state does not include the circle object that you saw when the Normal On state was active.

   The active state is the default in the exported form.

   Users must choose the radio button to submit the form.

   The value "yes" is sent for the Add to Mailing List item.

8. **At the bottom of the panel, activate the Required option, and change the Button Value field to Yes.**

   The Button Value is the data that will be sent when a user chooses the radio button and submits the form.

9. **Save the file and continue to the next exercise.**

Create a Combo Box Form Field

A combo box is a type of list in which users click to open the drop down menu of options. An example is the Type menu at the top of the Buttons and Forms panel. You can define a list of options that will appear in the menu; users will be able to make a single choice from the list.

1. **With `cac-brochure.indd` open, select the frame to the right of the question "How did you learn...".**

2. **In the Buttons and Forms panel, choose Combo Box in the Type menu and change the Name field to `Source`.**

   A combo box is a menu in which users can select only one from a defined list of options. You can use the options at the bottom of the Buttons and Forms panel to define the options that appear in the list.

Note:

If you want to allow users to select more than one option in a list, use the List Box field type.

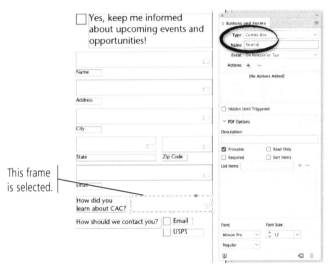

This frame is selected.

3. **Type `Direct mail` in the List Items field and then click the + button.**

Type in this field to add items to the list.

The item appears in the list after clicking the + button.

4. **Using the same method as in Step 3, add four more items to the list:**

City employee	Email
Social Media	Friend/Family

5. **Check the Sort Items option.**

   This option organizes the defined list items alphabetically.

Check Sort Items to alphabetize the list.

6. **Add Select one... as another list item.**

   Because the list is being sorted alphabetically, this new item is added to the bottom of the list (S comes after N). However, the first item in the list appears in the menu in the exported PDF; because you want this item to appear at the top of the list, you need to manually rearrange the list items.

7. **Uncheck the Sort Items option. Click the Select one... item and drag in the list to move it to the top of the panel.**

   A black line identifies where the list item will appear when you release the mouse button.

   Uncheck Sort Items so you can manually reorder the list items.

8. **Save the file and continue to the next exercise.**

 ## Create Check Box Form Fields

A check box is similar to a radio button; users can turn it on or off to select an option or not. If a check box is part of a group, however, users can typically select more than one option — unlike radio button groups, which allow only one choice from the available options.

1. **With cac-brochure.indd open, select the empty frame to the left of the Email label.**

2. **In the Buttons and Forms panel, choose Check Box in the Type menu and change the Name field to Send Email.**

3. **At the bottom of the panel, select the Normal Off state as the default state.**

Note:

This frame has a fill of None, so you have to click the frame edge to select it.

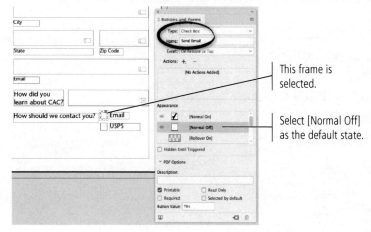

This frame is selected.

Select [Normal Off] as the default state.

4. **Repeat this process to create a second check box named Send Mail for the frame to the left of the "USPS" label.**

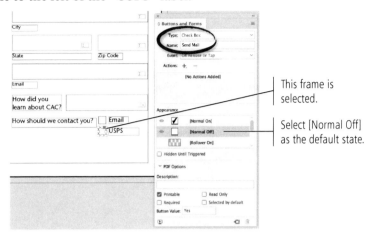

This frame is selected.

Select [Normal Off] as the default state.

5. **Save the file and continue to the next exercise.**

Create Form Control Buttons

The final piece of this form is a set of buttons that allow users to clear and submit the form. You can use built-in tools to create and program buttons to accomplish this task.

1. **With cac-brochure.indd open, open the Buttons and Forms panel Options menu and choose Sample Buttons and Forms.**

   This opens an InDesign Library panel with predefined objects that have already been converted to button objects. You can also create your own buttons by selecting an object on the

   page, then clicking the Convert Object to Button option at the bottom of the Buttons and Forms panel.

2. **Scroll through the resulting library panel until you find the item labeled "124".**

3. **Drag an instance of the button labeled "124" onto the layout and position it as shown in the following image.**

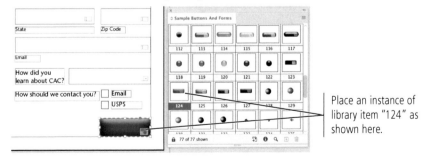

Place an instance of library item "124" as shown here.

4. **In the Buttons and Forms panel, change the selected button object's name to Submit.**

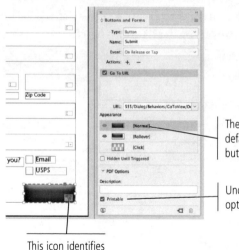

The placed object defaults to become the button's Normal state.

An InDesign button can have three states, which are based on the position of the user's mouse cursor. The default Normal state displays when the cursor is not touching the button; the Rollover and Click states are called by the position and action of the user's mouse.

5. **At the bottom of the panel, uncheck the Printable option.**

Uncheck this option.

When this option is unchecked, the button object will be included in an interactive PDF, but will not appear in printed output or in a PDF for print. Again, because you are using the same file for both output methods, you should make sure any elements affect only the output method you want to affect.

This icon identifies a button object.

6. **With the button object still selected on the page, open the Event menu in the panel and review the options. Make sure On Release or Tap is selected.**

InDesign supports six different types of events:

- **On Release or Tap** triggers when the mouse button is released after clicking or tapped on a touch-screen device.
- **On Click** triggers as soon as the mouse button is clicked.
- **On Roll Over** triggers when the cursor enters the button area.
- **On Roll Off** triggers when the cursor leaves the button area.
- **On Focus (PDF)** triggers when pressing the Tab key highlights the button (called "being in focus").
- **On Blur (PDF)** triggers when the focus moves to another button.

7. **Select the existing action in the list, then click the Delete Selected Action button. Click OK when asked to confirm the deletion.**

The two buttons in your file will both cause something to happen when clicked; the "something" that happens is called an **action**. The default buttons include the Go to URL as a default. Because you want to control states, not web pages, you have to first delete the existing action.

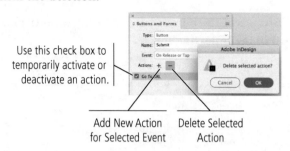

Use this check box to temporarily activate or deactivate an action.

Add New Action for Selected Event

Delete Selected Action

8. **Click the Add New Action button to open the menu of available options.**

The specific action that occurs is defined in this menu:

- **Go To Destination** navigates to a specific bookmark or anchor.
- **Go To [First/Last/Next/Previous] Page** navigates to the specified page in a file.
- **Go To URL** opens a web page in the user's default browser.
- **Show/Hide Buttons and Forms** toggles between showing and hiding specified buttons and form fields in the exported file.
- **Sound** allows you to play, pause, stop, or resume a placed sound file.
- **Video** allows you to play, pause, stop, or resume a placed movie file.
- **Animation** lets you play, pause, stop, or resume a selected animation.
- **Go To Page** navigates to the page that you specify in a defined SWF file.
- **Go To State** navigates to a specific state in a multi-state object.
- **Go To Next/Previous State** navigates to the next or previous state in a multi-state object. These options are especially useful for clicking through a slideshow.
- **Clear Form** resets the defined form fields to their default states.
- **Go To Next View** navigates to a page after going to the previous view (similar to the Forward button in a browser).
- **Go To Previous View** navigates to the most recently viewed page in the PDF file or returns to the last-used zoom size (similar to the Back button in a browser).
- **Open File** opens the specified file in the file's native application (if possible).
- **Print Form** prints the form on the active page.
- **Submit Form** submits the form on the active page.
- **View Zoom** displays the page according to the zoom option you specify.

9. **Choose Submit Form in the menu of actions.**

10. **Click away from the button, then click it again to select it.**

   As with the radio button you created earlier, the Layers panel will not reflect the button object's new assigned name unless you select it and then reselect it.

11. **With the Normal state of the button selected, use the Layers panel to expand the Submit group and the nested Normal group.**

Expand the [Normal] subgroup in the Submit group.

12. **Using the Layers panel, click to select the top rectangle in the Normal group.**

13. **Change the selected object's fill color to 100% of the Pantone 8863 C swatch.**

Change the fill color and tint of the top rectangle object.

14. **Using the Type tool, click inside the selected object to convert it to a type frame.**

When you see this cursor, clicking converts the frame to a type frame.

15. **Type Submit and then apply the Button Text paragraph style that exists in the cac-brochure.indd file.**

16. **Open the Text Frame Options dialog box (Command/Control-B), apply centered vertical alignment, then click OK to close the dialog box.**

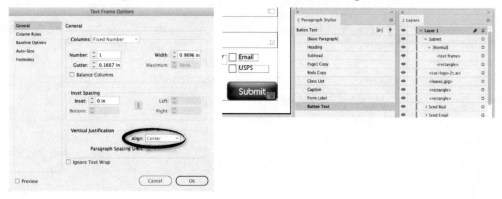

17. **Press Command/Control to temporarily access the Selection tool, and click to select the frame.**

You have to select the actual frame to view or change the button object's properties.

18. **Select the Rollover state in the Buttons and Forms panel.**

The rollover state will display when a user's mouse cursor moves over the button area.

19. **Repeat Steps 11–16 to change the fill color and add the necessary text to the Rollover state object.**

20. **Using the Selection tool, click away from the button object, then click to select the button object group again.**

If you use the Command/Control-click method, you only select the top object in the group that makes up the button state. You have to deselect the active frame, then click to select the entire button object for the next step to work properly.

Note:

The default button object from the library adds a drop shadow to the top rectangle object in the Rollover state.

21. In the Buttons and Forms panel, click the Normal state to make it the active (default) state.

22. Option/Alt-drag the button object to clone it. Place the clone immediately to the left of the existing button.

23. Using what you have already learned about buttons, change the cloned button to clear the form. Use Reset as the button text and Clear Form as the button action.

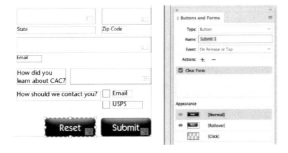

24. Save the file and continue to the next exercise.

 Export an Interactive PDF

Now that you have defined interactive elements, you need to export the PDF file with the appropriate settings. You will use the Export to Interactive PDF options here to create a PDF file that includes your table of contents, hyperlinks, slideshow, and form.

1. With cac-brochure.indd open, choose File>Export.

2. Choose Adobe PDF (Interactive) in the Format/Save as Type menu. Change the file name to cac-brochure-digital.pdf, then click Save.

3. **In the Export to Interactive PDF dialog box, make the following choices in the General pane:**

- **Type 1–4 in the Range field.**

  Remember, you added a fifth page to contain the table of contents that you want to function as bookmarks in the resulting PDF file. By exporting the specific page range, you exclude the unwanted page from the final file.

- **Choose the Export As Pages option.**
- **Choose Fit Page in the View menu.**
- **Uncheck the Open in Full Screen Mode option.**
- **Check the View After Exporting option.**
- **Make sure Include All is selected in the Forms and Media option.**

4. **Make the following choices in the Compression pane:**

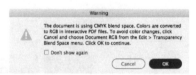

- **Choose Automatic in the Compression menu.**
- **Choose 72 in the Resolution (ppi) menu.**

5. **Click Export. Read the resulting warning, then click OK.**

   Remember, you are exporting from a file that was originally created for commercial print. As the message states, colors (including spot colors) are converted to RGB in interactive PDF files.

   In this case you are safe to simply click OK and let the software make the necessary conversions.

6. **When the new PDF file opens, navigate through the pages and test your bookmarks, hyperlinks, and form elements.**

   Although the form still needs to be officially distributed so that data can be easily gathered, you can still test the functionality of the form fields and buttons.

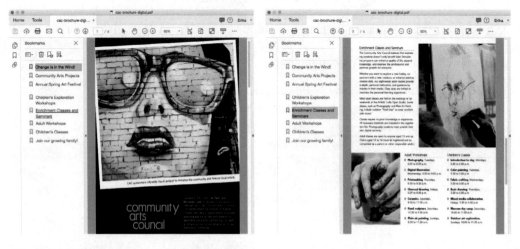

7. **Close the PDF file and return to InDesign.**
8. **Save the InDesign file and continue to the next stage of the project.**

Clients need to be able to distribute their information in as many ways as possible to reach the broadest audience; to meet that need, they utilize a variety of digital media in addition to print communication.

In this stage of this project, you are going to export an HTML file that can be posted for internet distribution. InDesign's built-in tools make it relatively easy to export this format from the same layout that you used to create the static print layout and interactive PDF file.

Note:

The exercises in this project assume no working knowledge of HTML, XML, CSS, or other technologies that drive the HTML and EPUB formats. Our goal is to show you the basics of the process.

We recommend studying applications such as Adobe Dreamweaver if you plan to work as a web design professional.

 ## Anchor Graphics to Text

The images in this layout simply float on the page — an appropriate approach for print design, where the position of objects is fixed wherever you place them. For HTML output, however, objects are exported based on their left-to-right, top-to-bottom order on the page. If you simply export an HTML file from the existing layout, the images will appear in odd places that are inappropriate at best and confusing at worst. To solve this problem, you need to define exactly where the images should go by anchoring them to the related text.

1. **With cac-brochure.indd open, navigate to Page 2.**

2. **Make sure frame edges are visible (View>Extras>Show Frame Edges).**

   Three images appear on the spread; each image is related to the nearby heading. As we already explained, however, you need to physically connect the images to the text so they will be in the correct position when you export the HTML file.

3. **Using the Selection tool, click to select the image on the left side of the page.**

4. **Click the blue square near the top-right corner of the image frame and drag until the insertion point appears at the beginning of the paragraph after the "Community Arts Projects" heading.**

   If you don't see the blue square, choose View>Extras>Show Anchored Object Control.

   When you create the HTML file, anchored images will appear where they are anchored.

   Be careful when you drag to anchor an image; it is very easy to drop the anchor after a character instead of before it, especially if you are using a small view percentage. You can always drag again from the anchor icon to redirect the image to anchor in a different location.

   When you release the mouse button, a dotted line connects the image to the text where it is anchored. If you don't see the dotted line, choose View>Extras>Show Text Threads.

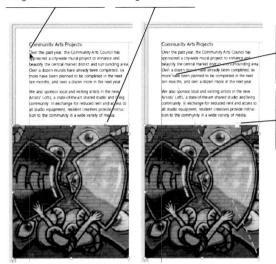

Watch the insertion point to see where the image will be anchored.

Click this icon and drag to anchor the image to the text.

The dotted line shows where the image frame is anchored.

This icon shows that the image frame is anchored to the text.

5. Repeat this process to anchor the other two images on the page as follows:

umbrella image	Beginning of the paragraph after the "Annual Spring Art Festival" heading
chalk image	Beginning of the paragraph after the "Children's Exploration Workshops" heading

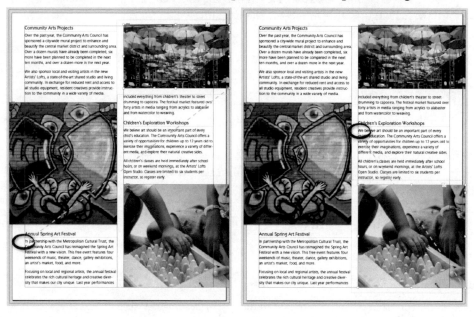

6. Navigate to Page 3 of the layout. Using the same method as for Page 2, anchor the two images on the page as follows:

sketching image	Beginning of the paragraph after the "Enrichment Classes and Seminars" heading
pottery image	Beginning of the "Adult Workshops" heading

Note:

You can unanchor an image by choosing Object>Anchored Object>Release.

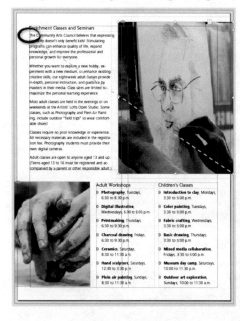
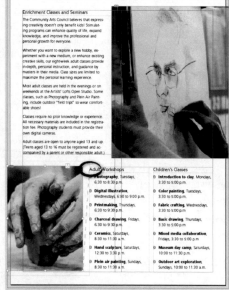

7. Save the file and continue to the next exercise.

Define Articles

You have three options when you export HTML files:

- Export the file based on the existing page layout. This option allows the software to make assumptions based on the top-to-bottom position of objects in the page layout. Every object in the layout is included.

- Export the file based on the content of the Structure pane, which allows you to define the order of tagged content. (You will use the Structure pane in Project 7: Repurposed Content Layouts.)

- Export the file based on a user-defined set of articles. This option allows you to define the content that will be included in the exported file, as well as the order in which it will appear. You will use this approach to complete this exercise.

1. **With `cac-brochure.indd` open, open the Articles panel (Window>Articles).**

2. **Navigate to Page 1 and select the text frame at the bottom of the page.**

This frame is selected.

Create New Article button

3. **Click the Create New Article button at the bottom of the Articles panel.**

4. **In the resulting dialog box, change the article name to `Intro`. With the Include When Exporting option checked, click OK.**

   The articles you define will be used to create the HTML file.

The new article contains the text in the frame.

Note:

You can also click the Add Selection to Articles button at the bottom of the panel to add the selected item to the active article.

5. **Click the panel to deselect the new article.**

   If you don't deselect the existing article, the next one you create will be added as a subarticle inside the previously selected one.

6. **Using the Direct Selection tool or the Content Grabber icon, select the image inside the frame at the top of Page 1.**

   You don't want to include the entire group that includes the image frame and the caption frame, so you are selecting only the image inside the frame before creating a new article.

7. **Click the Create New Article button in the Articles panel. Name the new article Intro Picture and click OK.**

The placed image, but not the containing frame or group, is selected.

8. **In the Articles panel, drag the Intro Picture article above the Intro item.**

The order in which items appear in the Articles panel determines the order in which they will appear in the exported HTML file. New articles are always added at the bottom of the list. You can drag articles to reorder them, drag items within an article, and even drag items from one article to another.

Drag the article in the panel to reorder it.

9. **Collapse the two existing articles, then click the empty area at the bottom of the panel to deselect both existing articles.**

10. **Navigate to Page 2. Select the text frame on the page, then click the Create New Article button. Name the new article Body Copy, then click OK.**

If text threads are visible, you can see that the Page 2 text frame is threaded to the frame on Page 3. When you add a story as an article, the entire story is part of that article; you don't need to add the frames on Page 3 independently.

Also, remember that you anchored the images on Pages 2 and 3. As anchored images, they are technically part of the story; you do not need to add those images to the article.

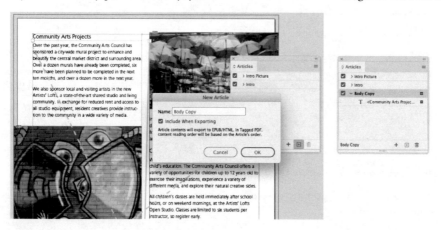

11. **Collapse the Body Copy article in the panel, deselect it, then navigate to Page 4.**

The text frame on this page is not linked to the previous story. If you want to include it, you need to create another article.

12. **Select the text frame on the page, then click the Create New Article button at the bottom of the panel. Name the new article Call To Action, then click OK.**

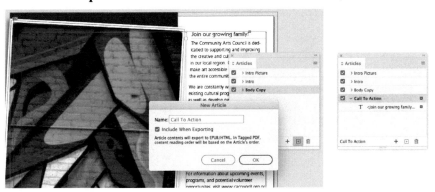

13. **Select the image frame at the top of the page. Drag the selected image into the Articles panel, above the text item in the Call to Action article.**

Although this image is not anchored to the text, you can still add it to the article.

Notice that you did not include the logos or the form objects in the Articles panel. You do not need to include every element in a file when you export to HTML; only items in the Articles panel will be included.

14. **Save the file and continue to the next exercise.**

 # Tag Styles for Exporting

The HTML format supports a specific text structure, which is based on tags that identify different elements of text (headings, paragraphs, and so on). The layout you are working with was designed with several paragraph and character styles that control the appearance of the copy. You can use export tagging to map the existing styles to defined tags that are recognized by the digital formats.

1. **With cac-brochure.indd open, open the Paragraph Styles panel (Window>Styles>Paragraph Styles).**

2. **With nothing selected in the layout, double-click the Heading style in the panel to open the Paragraph Style Options dialog box.**

3. **In the resulting dialog box, display the Export Tagging options.**

These options define how text formatted with the style is mapped to the tags that are supported by EPUB and HTML.

4. **Open the Tag menu in the EPUB and HTML menu and choose h1.**

EPUB and HTML formats include tags for a number of levels of headings; the number in each tag indicates its level of editorial priority. As a general rule, each page should have only one paragraph tagged as h1.

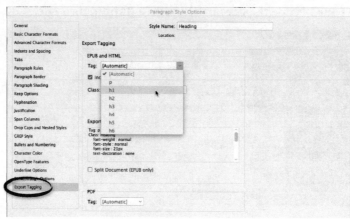

5. **Make sure Include Classes in HTML is checked.**

If this option is not checked, the class information will not be included in the exported HTML, ultimately defeating the purpose of defining the class names.

6. **Type heading in the class field, then press Tab.**

If you don't press Tab (or click to select a different field), the class information does not appear in the Export Details pane.

A class is an option for formatting content in an EPUB or HTML file. If you do not define a class name in the Export Tagging options, the exported file will use the browser's default setting for the applied tags.

As you can see in the Export Details pane, the class information defines the same formatting attributes that are applied in the InDesign paragraph style (or at least, those attributes that are supported in the EPUB and HTML formats).

Classes are important because you can define different formatting options for different styles. For example, say you have a Body Copy style and a Body Copy - No Indent format. Both styles would be tagged as paragraphs (with the p tag), but you can use classes to define different formatting options for each style.

Note:

The class name can be anything; it does not need to be the same as the style name.

7. **Check the Emit CSS and Split Document (EPUB only) options.**

The Emit CSS option causes the class name you define here to take precedence in case there is a conflict with other classes.

The Split Document option forces a new "page" every time the defined style is applied. This option is automatically checked for every heading tag.

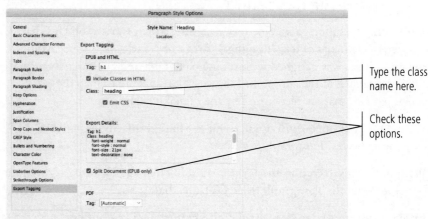

Type the class name here.

Check these options.

8. **Click OK to return to the layout.**

9. **Repeat this process for the Subhead and Body Copy paragraph styles, using the following information:**

Style:	**Subhead**
Tag:	**h2**
Include Classes in HTML:	**checked**
Class:	`subhead`
Emit CSS:	**Checked**
Split Document:	**Unchecked**

Style:	**Page1 Copy**
Tag:	**p**
Include Classes in HTML:	**checked**
Class:	`intro-copy`
Emit CSS:	**Checked**
Split Document:	**Unchecked**

Style:	**Body Copy**
Tag:	**p**
Include Classes in HTML:	**checked**
Class:	`main-text`
Emit CSS:	**Checked**
Split Document:	**Unchecked**

Note:

The p tag identifies a paragraph in HTML code.

10. **In the Character Styles panel, double-click the Class Name style. In the Export Tagging options, define the following options:**

Tag:	**Automatic**
Include Classes in HTML:	**checked**
Class:	`class-name`
Emit CSS:	**checked**

Note:

If you don't define a different class name for a specific style, InDesign automatically defines a class name based on the style name. Spaces are replaced with hyphens because spaces are not allowed in CSS style names.

11. **Click OK to close the Character Style Options dialog box.**

12. **In the Paragraph Styles panel, click the [Basic Paragraph] option.**

13. **In the Character Styles panel, click the [None] option.**

When you double-clicked the style names to open the Style Options dialog boxes, you effectively selected those styles; following the steps in this exercise, the Body Copy paragraph style and Class Name character style were technically selected after Step 10.

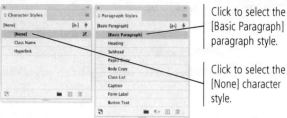

Click to select the [Basic Paragraph] paragraph style.

Click to select the [None] character style.

If a style is selected in either of these panels when nothing is selected in the layout, you are effectively defining the style(s) that apply by default to any new text frame you create. If you do not reset the default styles to [Basic Paragraph] and [None], problems could arise later in your work.

14. **Save the file and continue to the next exercise.**

Export HTML

As you probably know, HTML is the code that defines a web page. Although InDesign is not a professional web design application, you can export HTML code from an existing layout to make repurposing the content far easier than creating the HTML from scratch.

Your client has stated that the HTML file you create is going to be placed into the content area of the primary website; he is mainly concerned with the content — text and images — rather than duplicating the print brochure layout. By completing the previous exercises, you have laid the groundwork for exporting an HTML file that will be an excellent starting point to meet those needs.

1. **With `cac-brochure.indd` open, make sure all items in the Articles panel are checked.**

    The Articles panel determines what will be exported. If you uncheck a specific element in the panel, it will not be included in the exported HTML file.

2. **Choose File>Export. Create a new folder named `Upload` in your WIP>CACouncil folder, and choose that folder as the target location.**

3. **Choose HTML in the Format/Save As Type menu. Uncheck the Use InDesign Document Name as the Output Filename option, and define the file name as `Community-Arts-Council.html`.**

    The file name is essentially the page name, which appears in the browser window's title bar and in the page's document tab, so you are using a slightly more colloquial title than we normally use in InDesign.

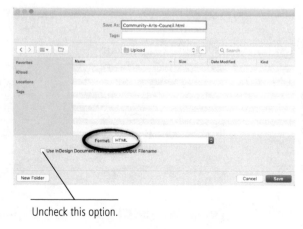

Uncheck this option.

4. **Click Save.**

5. **In the resulting dialog box, review the General options.**

Content Order. This menu defines how content is ordered in the exported file. You can allow InDesign to export the file based on the page layout; order content based on the defined XML structure; or order content based on defined articles (in the Articles panel).

Bullets and Numbers. You can use these menus to map text formatted with these options to the unordered list (ul) and ordered list (ol) tags that are supported by HTML. If you don't want to use those tags, you can choose Convert to Text to treat bullets and numbers as regular text.

View HTML after Exporting. When this option is checked, the resulting file automatically opens in a browser.

6. **Choose the Same as Articles Panel option for Content Order.**

7. **Click Image in the left pane and review the options.**

Copy Images. This option refers to the linking process that is required for HTML to properly display images. Like a print layout, an HTML file links to image files in a defined location. When InDesign exports the HTML file, it creates the optimized images and moves them into the defined target folder. Optimized, the default option in this menu, refers to images that are generated based on the defined Image Conversion settings. You can also choose Original to copy the original images, ignoring the selected optimization options. The Link to Server Path option can be used to define the location of files that exist on a server.

Preserve Appearance from Layout. If this option is checked, InDesign applies image transformations before exporting. For example, consider an image with its opacity reduced to 50%; if this option is not checked, the exported image will have the appearance of regular 100% opacity.

SVG Options. You can use this menu to export the code for SVG images as embedded code or object tags.

Resolution. This menu defines the resolution of exported images. Although monitors only use 72 or 96 ppi, keep in mind that many tablet devices support higher image resolution. Higher resolutions are also important if you want to allow zooming.

Image Size. This menu determines whether images are Fixed (at the size they appear in the layout) or Relative to Page, which refers to the "page" size in the browser.

Image Alignment and Spacing. These options define the position of images, as well as spacing that is added above and below the images in the exported file.

Image Conversion. Use this menu to define the image format(s) that should be used in exported images. Automatic allows InDesign to make the best choice based on image content. You can also specify whether images should export as GIF, JPEG, or PNG files.

GIF Options and **JPEG Options.** For GIF files, you can define a specific color palette to use. For JPEG files, you can determine how much compression should be applied.

Ignore Object Export Settings. You can define object export settings for specific images in the layout by choosing Object>Object Export Settings. The options in that dialog box are the same as the options listed here, except they apply only to the selected object. If this box is checked in the HTML Export Options dialog box, your settings here override any settings that you defined for specific images.

8. **In the Image options, set both Image Spacing fields to 10 pixels.**

9. **Click OK to export the HTML file.**

10. **Review the resulting file in your browser.**

    The resulting file includes as much of your defined formatting as is supported by the HTML/CSS formats. As you can see, this is a very basic HTML file.

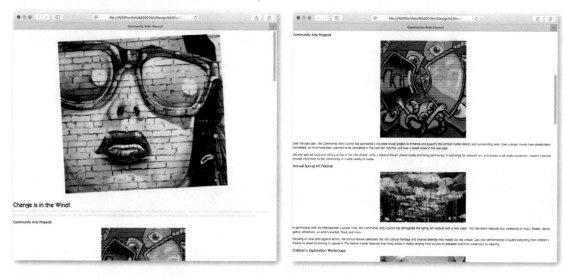

11. **Close the browser window and return to InDesign.**

12. **Choose File>Export again. Without changing any options, click Save. When asked if you want to replace the existing file, click Replace/Yes.**

    As you can see, the export process generates a number of additional files that are required for the HTML file to work properly. When you complete the project, the entire Upload folder needs to be sent to the client.

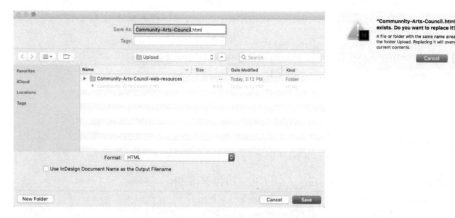

13. **In the Advanced options, uncheck the Generate CSS option.**

    Rather than export CSS from the InDesign file, you are going to attach an external file that was created to format the various elements in the HTML file that will be exported. Unfortunately, InDesign does not include a CSS editor; we used Adobe Dreamweaver to create the external CSS file, although you can accomplish the same task in any text editor if you know how to write CSS code.

14. **Click the Add Style Sheet button. Navigate to `html-styles.css` in your WIP>CACouncil folder, then click Open.**

    A cascading style sheet (CSS) file includes instructions that define the appearance of various tags and classes in an HTML file. You can use these options to not include CSS rules or to embed CSS into the resulting HTML file based on existing document formatting. You can click the Add Style Sheet button to define an existing CSS file that controls the appearance of tags and classes in the resulting EPUB file.

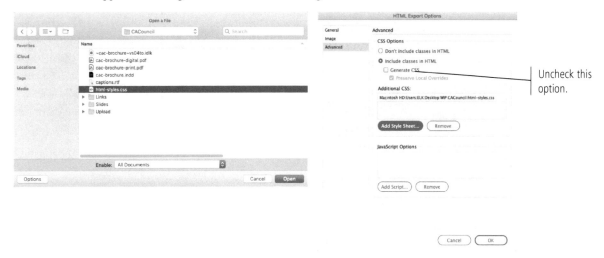

15. **Click OK to export the HTML file again.**

    The CSS file that you attached redefines the appearance of several tags. Most notably, we defined a specific width for the body tag, which contains the entire page. We also assigned fixed sizes and relative positions for the various images.

16. **Close the browser window and return to InDesign.**

17. **Save the InDesign file, then continue to the final stage of the project.**

STAGE 4 / Exporting an EPUB File

The EPUB format is now a de facto standard format for publishing e-content; virtually all devices support the format, except Amazon's Kindle devices. (There are a number of free tools available on the Internet for converting EPUB files to work on Kindle devices.)

EPUB 3 is the current revision of the standard; it includes support for rich media such as video and sound, as well as fixed layouts in which reflowable content is not appropriate — for example, design-rich magazines or promotional brochures such as the one you are working with in this project. In this stage of the project, you are going to create a fixed-layout EPUB with an interactive slideshow that shows multiple images in a single position.

It is important to note that there is much, much more to consider when publishing e-books than the basic concepts we discuss here. Our goal is not to make you an expert on e-book publishing or even the EPUB format; rather, it is simply to show you how to use the tools available in InDesign.

Note:

If you plan to work in the publishing market, we encourage you to learn as much as possible about e-book publishing and, more specifically, the EPUB format.

Create Versions with Layers

Rather than saving and editing multiple versions of the same basic file, you are going to use layers to identify elements that function properly for all output versions and isolating objects that are only appropriate for certain formats.

When you use layers to create multiple versions of a document, the first step is to determine how many layers you need. Elements that will appear in all versions should exist on one layer. Each different version that you create requires its own layer to hold elements that will change from one version to the next.

Note:

Layers are also useful for designing die-cut documents, which are cut in non-rectangular shapes or contain an area cut out within the page. The tab on a manila folder and a folded carton are two examples of die-cut jobs.

1. **With `cac-brochure.indd` open, navigate to Page 1 of the layout.**

2. **In the Layers panel (Window>Layers), double-click the Layer 1 name to open the Layer Options dialog box.**

3. **Change the Name field to `Common Elements`, then click OK to close the Layer Options dialog box.**

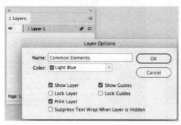

4. **Click the Create New Layer button at the bottom of the Layers panel.**

5. **Double-click Layer 2 in the Layers panel. Change the layer name to Static and click OK.**

6. **Using the Selection tool, click to select the group that includes the image and caption frames at the top of Page 1.**

7. **In the Layers panel, click the arrow to the left of the Common Elements layer to expand it.**

   The Layers panel only shows objects on the active page or spread.

8. **In the Layers panel, click the selected <group> and drag up until a line appears between the Static and Common Elements layers.**

9. **Expand the Static layer in the Layers panel.**

   In the next exercise, you will create an interactive slideshow that will take the place of the main image on Page 1. Because you need to be able to output this file with interactive elements or with static print elements, you need to move the existing image frame to a layer that can be hidden when you export the interactive version.

   Because the Static layer is higher in the stack than the Common Elements layer, the group is now higher in the stack than all other objects on the page. As you can see, the group now obscures the logo in the bottom left corner. To solve this problem, you need to move the logo onto the Static layer, above the group.

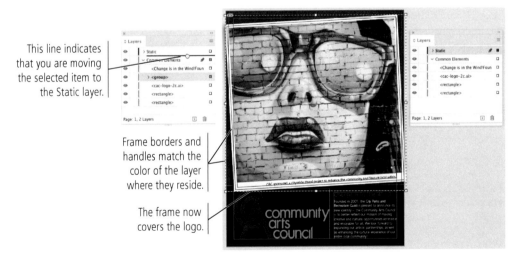

This line indicates that you are moving the selected item to the Static layer.

Frame borders and handles match the color of the layer where they reside.

The frame now covers the logo.

10. **Click the <cac-logo-2c.ai> item in the Layers panel and drag it above the group on the Static layer.**

Drag the logo file above the group.

The logo is again on top of the image frame.

11. **Collapse both layers in the panel.**

12. **Control/right-click the Static layer and choose Duplicate Layer "Static" in the contextual menu.**

13. **Double-click the new Static Copy layer. Rename the layer Animated, choose Green in the Color menu, then click OK.**

   Duplicating a layer applies the same layer color to the duplicate. So you can better see where an object resides, you should change the layer to use a different color.

Note:

Having two layers use the same color defeats the purpose of unique layer identifiers. When you duplicate a layer, it's a good idea to change the layer color for the duplicate.

14. **In the Layers panel, click the visibility icon for the Static layer to hide that layer.**

15. **Save the file and continue to the next exercise.**

Controlling Text Wrap on Different Layers

By default, an object's text wrap attributes affect all text frames that touch that wrap object; the wrap object's position in the stacking order, as well as a layer's position in the layer stack, are both irrelevant.

If you want text wrap to affect only objects on underlying layers, you can activate the Text Wrap Only Affects Text Beneath option in the Composition preferences.

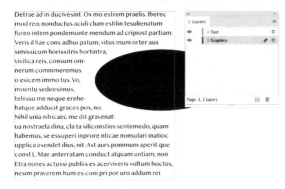

By default, the oval's text wrap affects the text frame regardless of the Graphics layer's position in the stacking order.

When **Text Wrap Only Affects Text Beneath** is active, the oval's text wrap does not affect text on the layer above.

If Suppress Text Wrap When Layer is Hidden is checked in the Layer Options dialog box, text on other layers reflows when the layer is hidden. The text wrap attributes of objects on the layer are applied only when the layer is visible.

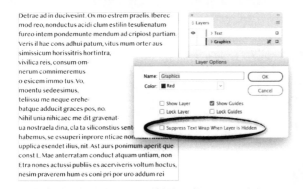

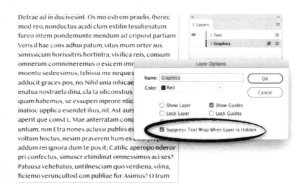

If **Suppress Text Wrap When Layer is Hidden** is not checked, affected text does not reflow when the layer is hidden.

If **Suppress Text Wrap When Layer is Hidden** is checked, affected text reflows when the layer is hidden.

Create a Basic Animation

Fixed-layout EPUB files can include dynamic elements, including objects that move from one place to another. You can use InDesign to add basic animation without the need for a separate application. In this exercise you are going to add motion to the image frame that will contain the different slides in the slideshow.

1. **With Page 1 of `cac-brochure.indd` visible, use the Selection tool to select the group at the top of Page 1.**

2. **Open the Animation panel (Window>Interactive>Animation).**

3. **Open the Preset menu and choose Fly in From Left.**

   InDesign includes a number of animation presets. You can use these as defined or as starting points, modifying the settings to customize the animation.

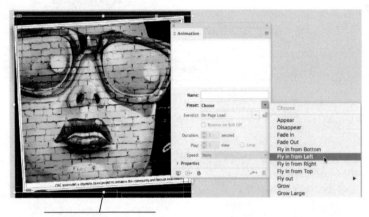

The group on the
Animated layer is selected.

4. **Move your mouse cursor over the preview area in the Animation panel to review the effect of the active settings.**

   The green line is called a **motion path**; it defines the path over which an object will move throughout the animation. Each dot on the path represents a frame in the animation; dot spacing indicates the speed of movement over the duration of the animation.

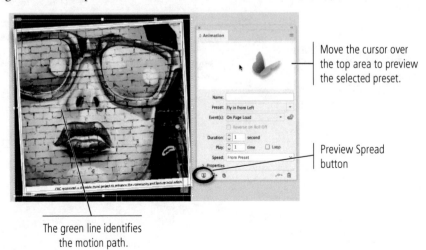

Move the cursor over
the top area to preview
the selected preset.

Preview Spread
button

The green line identifies
the motion path.

5. **Click the Preview Spread button at the bottom of the Animation panel.**

   This opens the EPUB Interactivity Preview panel, which you can use to preview the defined animation using the actual artwork in your file.

6. **Click the bottom-right corner of the panel and drag to enlarge it.**

7. **Click the Play button at the bottom of the panel.**

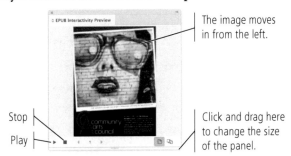

The image moves in from the left.

Stop

Play

Click and drag here to change the size of the panel.

8. **In the Animation panel, change the Duration field to 1.5 seconds.**

   Animations function based on the concept of frames per second, or the number of frames that flash to create the illusion of continuous movement. When you increase the duration of an animation, you add more dots (frames) to the motion path.

9. **Choose None in the Speed menu.**

   Closer spacing between dots represents slower movement; wider spacing represents faster motion. By choosing None in the Speed menu, the dots on the motion path are equally spaced; this animation will have a uniform speed over the entire duration.

Changing the Duration adds dots (frames) to the motion path.

Changing the Speed spreads the dots evenly across the motion path.

Note:

If you click the motion path to select it, you can use the built-in tools (e.g., the Pen tool and its variants) to edit the motion path, effectively editing the direction of an object's movement throughout the animation.

10. **Save the file and continue to the next exercise.**

The Animation Panel in Depth

The Animation panel offers a variety of options for controlling the details of an animation.

Event(s) defines what event triggers the animation:

- **On Page Load**, the default, means the animation plays when the page is opened in the SWF file.
- **On Page Click** triggers when the page is clicked.
- **On Click (Self)** and **On Roll Over (Self)** trigger the animation when the object itself is clicked or moused over, respectively. If you choose On Roll Over (Self), you can also select **Reverse On Roll Off**, which reverses the animation when the mouse moves off the object.

Although you will learn about button events later in this project, you should understand that you can also create a button that triggers the animation. In this case, **On Button Event** is added to the Event(s) menu.

You can click **Create Button Trigger** to use an existing object to trigger the animation. After you click Create Button Trigger, click the object that should act as a trigger; it is converted to a button, and the Buttons and Forms panel opens.

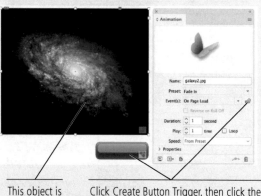

This object is animated.

Click Create Button Trigger, then click the object you want to trigger the animation.

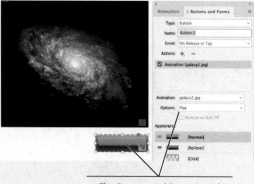

The Buttons and Forms panel controls the new button's behavior.

Duration defines how much time it takes for the animation to play (start to finish).

Play defines the number of times the animation is played. Check the Loop option to play the animation repeatedly.

Speed controls the change in animation speed over time.

- Using None, the animation speed is a steady rate.
- Using Ease In, the animation speeds up over time.
- Using Ease Out, the animation slows down over time.

If you expand the **Properties** section of the Animation panel, you can define additional options.

If you look closely, one end of the motion path includes an arrow, indicating the direction the object will travel. You can change the direction using the **Animate menu**:

- From Current Appearance uses the object's current properties as the animation's starting point.
- To Current Appearance uses the object's properties as the animation's ending point.
- To Current Location uses the current object's properties as the starting point of the animation and the object's position as the ending point.

The effect of the **Rotate**, **Scale**, and **Opacity** properties depends on which option is selected in the Animate menu:

- If From Current Appearance or To Current Location is active, the properties define the ending appearance of the animated object.
- If To Current Appearance is active, the properties define the starting appearance of the animated object.

You can use the **animation proxy** to get a rough idea of how your properties affect the animation.

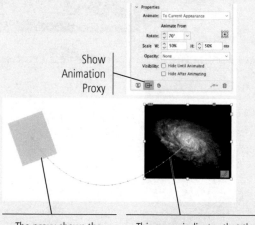

Show Animation Proxy

The proxy shows the starting rotation and scale.

This arrow indicates that the object will move *to* this position.

Define Object States

As you know, you are going to display multiple images in the same space. The Object States panel makes this process not only possible, but also relatively easy.

1. **With Page 1 of `cac-brochure.indd` visible, open the Object States panel (Window>Interactive>Object States).**

2. **Using the Selection tool, double-click the image frame on the Animated layer to enter into the group and select only the image frame.**

   Object states are *object* specific, not *content* specific. You have to select the containing frame — not the frame's content — before converting to a multi-state object.

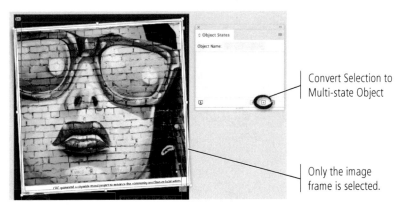

Convert Selection to Multi-state Object

Only the image frame is selected.

3. **Click the Convert Selection to Multi-State Object button at the bottom of the Object States panel.**

   When you convert the image to a multi-state object, a second state is automatically added to the panel. The image that was placed in the frame is the default State 1 image.

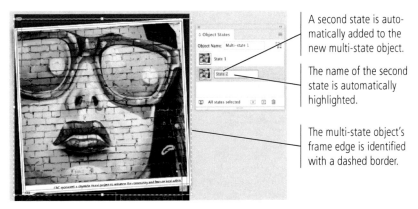

A second state is automatically added to the new multi-state object.

The name of the second state is automatically highlighted.

The multi-state object's frame edge is identified with a dashed border.

4. **Highlight the Object Name field at the top of the panel and type Images.**

5. **Click State 2 in the panel to select it.**

It is important to pay attention to exactly what is selected in a multi-state object. The Object States panel includes different icons to help you identify the active selection.

- When the entire object is selected, you can make transformations (move, resize, etc.) that affect the entire object and all of its states.

- When a specific state is selected, object transformations affect only the active state.

- When the object inside the state is selected, you can change that object — image, text, or other content — in only that state.

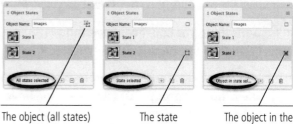

The object (all states) is selected.   The state is selected.   The object in the state is selected.

6. **Using the Content Grabber icon, select the placed image inside the frame.**

In this case, you are replacing the content of the object in each state. You have to select the actual content — not the frame — in order to replace it in each successive state.

7. **Choose File>Place. Select mural2.jpg (in the WIP>CACouncil>Slides folder). Make sure the Replace Selected Item option is checked, then click Open.**

After the new image is placed, the States panel appears empty because nothing is actually selected in the layout.

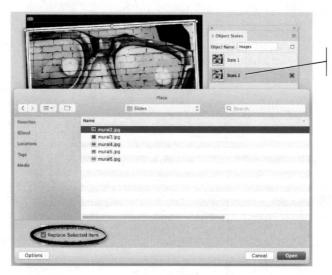

The object in the state is selected.

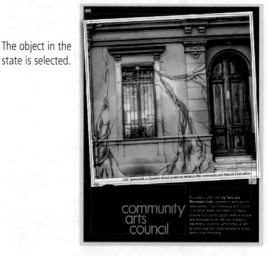

8. **Double-click the image frame to select it.**

   You have to select the object to again show the states in the panel. Because this frame is grouped with the caption frame, you have to double-click the frame to select it.

9. **Click the Create New State button at the bottom of the Object States panel.**

10. **With the new state (State 2 Copy) highlighted, immediately type State 3, then press Return/Enter to finalize the new name.**

    All successive states are named "State X copy"; unfortunately, if you do not immediately rename them, there is no way to do so later.

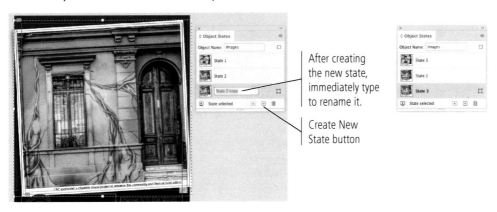

After creating the new state, immediately type to rename it.

Create New State button

11. **With State 3 selected in the Object States panel, select the image inside the frame.**

12. **Choose File>Place. Select mural3.jpg, make sure Replace Selected Item is active, and click Open.**

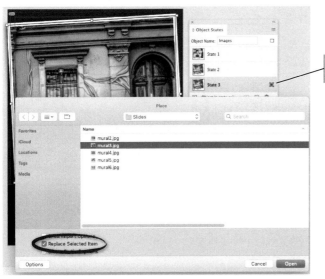

The object in the state is selected.

13. **Repeat the process from Steps 7–11 to add additional states for the remaining images in the Slides folder.**

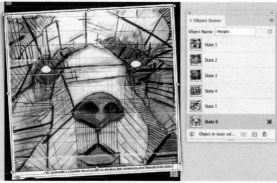

14. **Save the file and continue to the next exercise.**

Create a Multi-State Text Frame

Multi-state objects are not limited to image frames. You can also create a text frame that has different content in different states, which you will do in this exercise to add captions to the various images in the frame above.

1. **Make sure Page 1 of cac-brochure.indd is visible and the Animated layer is active.**

2. **Using the Selection tool, double-click to select the text frame below the image (the frame with the image caption).**

3. **With the text frame selected, click the Convert Selection to Multi-State Object button at the bottom of the Object States panel.**

   As with the image frame, the existing caption automatically becomes the content for State 1 of the new multi-state object.

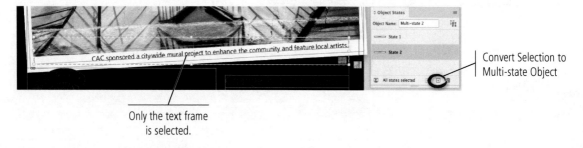

Convert Selection to Multi-state Object

Only the text frame is selected.

4. At the top of the panel, change the Object Name field to Captions.

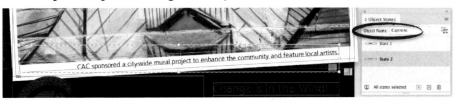

5. Click away from the page to deselect everything.

6. Choose File>Place. Select captions.rtf in the WIP>CACouncil folder, then click Open.

7. Click the loaded Place cursor to place the loaded file on the pasteboard to the right of the page.

   These captions need to be placed into various states of the text frame below the image.

8. Highlight all the placed text and apply the Caption paragraph style that is saved in the cac-brochure.indd file.

   Make sure to clear style overrides if necessary after applying the style.

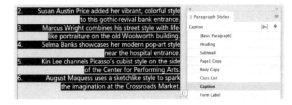

9. Choose the Type tool in the Tools panel.

10. In the text frame on the pasteboard, highlight and cut the text of the caption labeled "2" (excluding the number).

11. Press Command/Control to temporarily access the Selection tool, then click the multi-state text frame to select it.

    Remember, pressing Command/Control temporarily activates the Selection tool so you can select an object. When you release the modifier key, you automatically return to the last-used tool (in this case, the Type tool).

    Note:

    Because the process of creating multiple object states requires a lot of switching from object to content to object again, this shortcut is invaluable to accomplishing your goal in this exercise.

12. Release the Command/Control-key to return to the Type tool.

13. With State 2 highlighted in the Object States panel, highlight the existing caption, then paste the one you cut in Step 10.

    If you exactly followed the instructions in this exercise, the image frame should show the image from State 6 because we did not tell you to select a different state at the end of the last exercise. The caption frame shows the caption in State 2 because that state is active for that object.

14. **Command/Control-click to select the text frame.**

    When the frame is selected, you can again see the various states in the Object States panel.

15. **Click the Create New State button at the bottom of the Object States panel. Rename the new state State 3.**

16. **Using the same basic process outlined above, create new states for each caption in the text file that you placed on the pasteboard.**

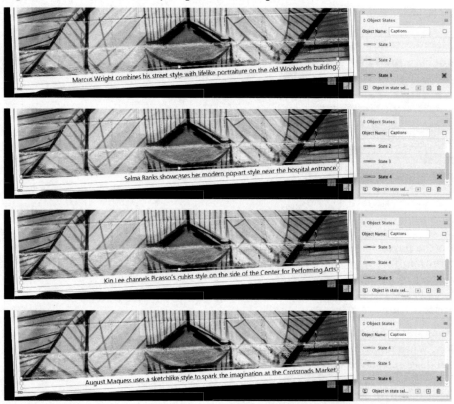

17. **When you're finished creating new states for the captions, delete the text frame from the pasteboard.**

18. **Save the file and continue to the next exercise.**

Create Buttons to Control the Animation

As you already learned, buttons have multiple states based on the position of the user's mouse cursor. In this exercise, you create the final piece of the animated slideshow: buttons that allow the user to navigate through the different pictures and captions.

1. **With Page 1 of `cac-brochure.indd` visible, open the Buttons and Forms panel (Window>Interactive>Buttons and Forms).**

2. **Open the panel Options menu and choose Sample Buttons and Forms.**

3. **From the Sample Buttons and Forms panel, drag an instance of the item labeled "135" onto the page.**

4. **Use the Control panel to resize the placed library item to 125% proportionally, then position it as shown here:**

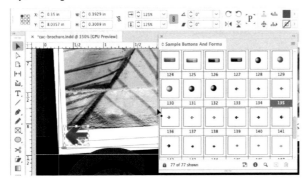

5. **Change the Name field at the top of the Buttons and Forms panel to `Previous Image`.**

   As you saw previously, you can use the built-in buttons as-is or modify them to meet the needs of your project.

6. **With the Normal state selected in the Appearance section of the Buttons and Forms panel, change the object's stroke to 1.5-pt Paper.**

7. **With the button object still selected on the page, make sure On Release or Tap is selected in the Event menu.**

8. **Select the existing action in the list, then click the Delete Selected Action button. Click OK when asked to confirm the deletion.**

   Because you want to control states, not URLs, you have to first delete the existing action.

9. **Open the Add New Action menu and choose Go to Previous State.**

   When you choose this option, an Object menu appears and automatically defaults to the first multi-state object in the file.

   For the Go to Previous State event, the Object menu defaults to the first multi-state object on the page.

10. **Open the Add New Action button again and choose Go to Previous State. In the Object menu, choose Captions.**

   Because you want this button to control two objects, you need to add a second action that controls the state of the Caption multi-state object.

   You are adding a second action to the same button.

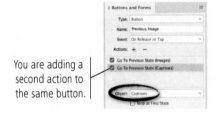

11. **Using the Selection tool, Option/Alt-click and drag to clone the button object. Rotate the clone 180°, then move to the right of the original button.**

12. **In the Buttons and Forms panel, change the button name to Next Image.**

   Because you cloned the existing button, the two Go to Next State actions are already in place. Unfortunately, you can't edit an existing action; you have to delete the ones you don't want and then add what you do want.

13. **Select and delete both existing actions from the button.**

14. **Using the same process from Steps 9–10, add two actions to the button, using the Go to Next State action.**

15. **Click the Preview Spread button at the bottom of the Buttons and Forms panel.**

16. **In the resulting EPUB Interactivity Preview panel, test the buttons' functionality.**

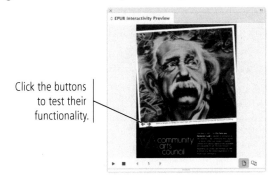

Click the buttons to test their functionality.

17. **Save the file and continue to the next exercise.**

 ## Export a Fixed-Layout EPUB

Now that the animated elements are complete, the final step is to export the EPUB file that you can distribute digitally.

1. **With cac-brochure.indd open, choose File>Export. Navigate to the WIP>CACouncil folder as the target location.**

2. **Choose EPUB (Fixed Layout) in the Format/Save As Type menu.**

3. **Change the file name to Community-Arts-Council.epub, then click Save.**

For an EPUB file, the file name is essentially the book title.

4. **In the General options in the EPUB Export Options dialog box, choose the Range option and type 1-4 in the attached field.**

   Remember, you created an extra page to hold the compiled table-of-contents list that was necessary for the interactive PDF file. You don't want to include that page in the PDF file, so you are exporting only the range that contains the brochure content.

5. **Choose Bookmarks in the Navigation TOC menu.**

   The Navigation TOC menu determines how the table of contents will be generated in the resulting EPUB file.

   - File Name uses the InDesign file name as the EPUB file's table of contents.

   - Multilevel TOC Style uses a defined TOC Style as the EPUB's table of contents.

   - Bookmarks uses bookmarks that are defined in the InDesign file as the EPUB's table of contents.

Note:

The Cover menu defines the image that will appear on the digital book shelf of e-reader apps and devices. You can rasterize the first page of the file or choose another image as the cover.

6. **In the Conversion Settings options, choose PNG in the Format menu. Leave all other options at their default values.**

   The Format menu defines the image format(s) that should be used in the exported images. Automatic allows InDesign to make the best choice based on image content. You can also specify whether all images should export as GIF, JPEG, or PNG files.

   If you choose to export JPEG files, you can determine how much compression should be applied in the JPEG Options area. For GIF files, you can define a specific color palette to use in the GIF Options area.

   You can also use the Resolution menu to define the resolution of exported images. Higher resolutions are important for high-density monitors and devices, as well as if you want to allow zooming.

Note:

The Spread Control menu defines how spreads are exported in the resulting EPUB file.

7. **Click Viewing Apps in the list on the left.**

   If you don't have an e-reader app on your computer, you should download and install one before you export EPUB files from InDesign. Adobe Digital Editions works on both Macintosh and Windows desktops; the current version (4.5 at the time of this writing) supports EPUB 3 and fixed-layout ebooks.

   Many other e-reading apps are available free or for a nominal fee. Once you have installed at least one e-reader app, you can click the Add Application button to alert InDesign which applications are available to open the resulting EPUB file.

Note:

The CSS and JavaScript panes of this dialog box can be used to add external files to the resulting EPUB file.

8. **Check the e-reader app you want to use to preview the EPUB file.**

You can use the check boxes to define which app(s) to launch when the export is complete; as long as one or more boxes are checked, the resulting EPUB file opens automatically.

Note:

We recommend using an actual ebook app, such as Apple Books or Adobe Digital Editions, for testing EPUB export. Interactive functionality is not always supported by more generic applications such as Microsoft Edge.

9. **Click OK to export the EPUB file.**

Because you used the fixed-layout EPUB option, the original page layout is maintained in the resulting EPUB file.

The animated slideshow is controlled by the buttons.

10. **Close the EPUB file and return to InDesign.**

11. **Save the InDesign file and close it.**

Using the Publish Online Service

If you have an individual-user subscription to the Adobe Creative Cloud software, part of your subscription includes the ability to publish an InDesign file to the Adobe CC servers.

You can use this functionality to make a PDF of your file accessible to other users. This will let those users view and comment, or let them download or embed the file into another web page.

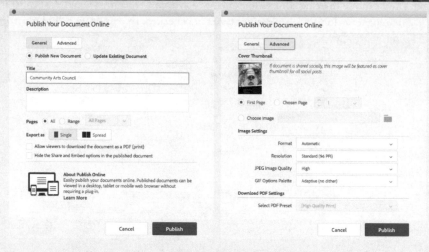

Clicking the Publish Online button in the InDesign application/menu bar presents a dialog box where you can define settings for the file that will be shared. You can publish the existing file as a new document, or choose the Update Existing Document if you have already published the file at an earlier time.

After you click the Publish button, a Preview dialog box shows the upload status.

When the upload is complete, you can click the View Document button to open the published file in your default web browser. You can also use the Social Media buttons to automatically create a post on your Facebook feed, share a link on your Twitter feed, or send an email with a link to the published file.

When you view the published file, moving your mouse cursor over the browser windows reveals a series of buttons at the bottom of the window:

A Toggle Thumbnails

B Zoom In

C Zoom Out

D Full-Screen Mode

E Share (if enabled)

F Report Abuse

PROJECT REVIEW

1. A(n) _____ describes the color reproduction characteristics of a particular input or output device.

2. _____ is the range of possible colors within a specific color model.

3. _____ are the four component colors in process-color output.

4. A _____ hyperlink opens a web page at the address you define.

5. A _____ can be used to display more than one image in the same frame.

6. The _____ format can be used to display dynamic, interactive content.

7. The _____ button action can be used to remove the user's choices from form fields.

8. The _____ format is designed to present content in a web browser.

9. The _____ options in a paragraph style can be used to map styles to HTML and EPUB tags.

10. A _____ can be used to assign different formatting options to various text with the same tag.

1. Briefly explain the difference between additive and subtractive color.

2. Briefly explain the concept of color management as it relates to building a layout in InDesign.

3. Briefly explain at least two considerations when using a single layout to export content to multiple media.

PORTFOLIO BUILDER PROJECT

Use what you learned in this project to complete the following freeform exercise.
Carefully read the art director and client comments, then create your own design to meet the needs of the project.
Use the space below to sketch ideas; when finished, write a brief explanation of your reasoning behind your final design.

art director comments

The Community Arts Council board members were very happy with your work on their rebranding project. Your local city government representatives saw the various pieces at a recent convention, and they would like to create a similar campaign to help promote local tourism.

To complete this project, you should:

❏ Find images (or create your own) that highlight different events and attractions in the local area.

❏ Write compelling copy to promote the area to visitors. Look at the local chamber of commerce and city government websites for ideas or for detailed information about specific events.

❏ Design the print layout first, then repurpose the same content for digital PDF, EPUB, and HTML files.

client comments

We've been trying to reach out to a larger audience to promote the local attractions and events that make our city special.

We'd like to plan and design both a promotional brochure that we can hand out at various events and digital versions that can more easily reach beyond our local community.

We don't have any specific text or images in mind, so we're hoping you can find or create whatever you need to make the project successful.

project justification

This project highlighted a number of methods for repurposing content for multiple output media. Completing this work in a single InDesign file offers a distinct advantage if you need to make editorial changes: you can open the single file, make the necessary changes, then re-export the various formats.

You should realize, however, that this type of repurposing work requires a significant amount of planning and careful consideration. You need to determine what to include in each version, whether for aesthetic purposes or to meet the specific needs and capabilities of a given output medium. You also need to prepare elements to work in various output media and create assets to take best advantage of different delivery methods.

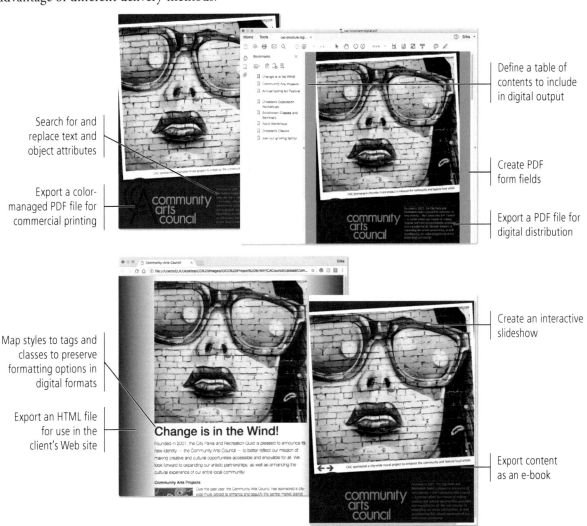

Search for and replace text and object attributes

Export a color-managed PDF file for commercial printing

Define a table of contents to include in digital output

Create PDF form fields

Export a PDF file for digital distribution

Map styles to tags and classes to preserve formatting options in digital formats

Export an HTML file for use in the client's Web site

Create an interactive slideshow

Export content as an e-book

Repurposed Content Layouts

7

Your client is the marketing manager for an extreme sports outfitter company. She wants to create a series of collateral pieces that will be used at tourism centers to lure potential customers. She hired you to produce a one-sheet flyer that will be distributed in print and online, a rack card to be placed in area hotels, a postcard to be given away at various events, and an interactive file that will work on digital tablet devices.

This project incorporates the following skills:

❏ Creating an XML file using tagged frames and content

❏ Building a layout from imported XML content

❏ Controlling the structure of a layout to merge XML content into tagged frames

❏ Placing linked content into alternate layouts

❏ Creating alternate layouts for horizontal and vertical tablet orientations

PROJECT MEETING

We want to create several pieces to introduce our business to new clients. We already have a flyer layout that will be sent as a handout for travel boards and enthusiast clubs, but we want you to create other versions for different purposes:

– The rack card will be placed in hotels near our facilities for potential visitors.

– The postcard will be given away as a souvenir at various events.

– The folio file will be made available on our website for people who want to download it to their digital tablets.

This could be a huge project for our agency if we can showcase our talents to the new client.

InDesign offers several methods for repurposing content into different layouts. I already created basic templates for the rack card and postcard; I want you to use XML to map the flyer content into those template layouts.

For the digital folios, you need to create two versions: horizontal and vertical. They don't need to be exact matches, but they should have all the same content.

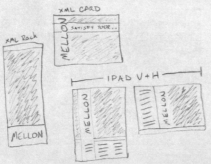

To complete this project, you will:

❑ Tag frames for XML.

❑ Review document structure.

❑ Review XML structure and attributes.

❑ Place unstructured XML content.

❑ Update linked XML data.

❑ Import structured XML.

❑ Create a file for digital publishing.

❑ Use the Content Collector.

❑ Manage linked object options.

❑ Define liquid page rules.

❑ Create an alternate layout.

STAGE 1 / Working with XML

Repurposing content, or placing the same content into different layouts (often for multiple output media), is a common design task. In the first stage of this project, you will use **XML (Extensible Markup Language)** to use the same content in three different print layouts.

For many designers, XML is an intimidating concept. Despite all the complexities that underlie this programming language, InDesign makes it very easy to implement XML in your layout documents.

Tag Frames for XML

As you know, styles define the appearance of content. All paragraphs formatted with the Subhead style display the characteristics defined for that style regardless of the actual content in those headings. XML describes the *actual content* marked with a specific tag; in other words, the heading is the actual text identified by the XML Heading tag regardless of the applied formatting.

The first step in creating an XML file is to identify the elements that make up the document content, each of which will be enclosed within tags as shown below:

<Heading>Much Ado About Nothing</Heading>

The first tag, <Heading>, is the opening tag; it identifies the beginning of the content. The second tag, </Heading>, is the closing tag; it identifies the end of the content.

When InDesign imports an XML file, it finds the content within tags and places that content into the appropriate locations in the layout.

To create the XML file for this project, you first have to define and apply tags for the different elements of the layout.

1. **Download `Sports_ID20_RF.zip` from the Student Files web page. Expand the ZIP archive in your WIP folder (Macintosh), or copy the archive contents into your WIP folder (Windows).**

   This results in a folder named **Sports**, which contains the files you need for this project. You should also use this folder to save the files you create in this project.

2. **Open `sports-flyer.indd` from the WIP>Sports folder.**

   If you get a warning about missing or modified images, update those links in the open file. The two placed image files are in the WIP>Sports>Links folder.

   If you see any Profile or Policy Mismatch warnings, click OK.

3. **Choose Window>Utilities>Tags to open the Tags panel.**

   The Tags panel allows you to create and manage XML tags within an InDesign layout. One tag, "Root," exists by default in every file; it is the basic container tag that encloses all other tags in the document.

   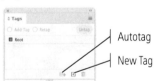

   Autotag

   New Tag

4. **Using the Selection tool, select the large image frame in the layout.**

5. **In the Tags panel, click the Autotag button.**

   The Image tag is automatically created and applied to the selected frame.

6. **If your image is not bordered and overlaid with a purple color, choose View>Structure>Show Tagged Frames.**

   The border and overlay color are for identification purposes. They only appear while you are working in the file; they do not appear when the file is output.

Tagged frames are identified by a heavy border and transparent overlay.

7. **In the Tags panel, double-click the Image tag to open the Tag Options dialog box.**

8. **Change the Name field to Main-Image and click OK.**

   As with all other user-defined elements, it is a good idea to use descriptive names so you (and others) can more easily identify assets at a later date. Tag names cannot include spaces, so you must use a hyphen or underscore character if you want to separate words in the tag name.

   The tag color refers to the color of the nonprinting markers identifying tagged elements in the layout. If Show Tagged Frames is active, the color is used for the frame edge and overlay of tagged frames. If Show Tag Markers is active, this color is used for the brackets surrounding tagged text.

After changing the tag name, it is not highlighted (active) in the panel.

9. **With the large image frame selected in the layout, click Main-Image in the Tags panel to apply it to the selected frame.**

   Although the image frame is selected in the panel, the Main-Image tag does not appear selected in the panel. You need to be sure the correct tag is applied to the frame. (This is a minor bug in the software; it is important to recognize but easy to fix.)

Click the tag to be sure it is applied to the selected frame.

10. **Using the same method, tag the other image frame with a tag named Logo.**

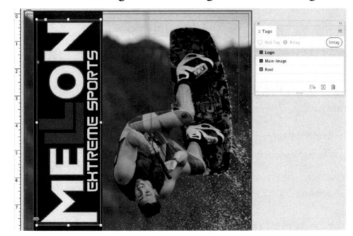

11. **Select the text frame with the web address and click the Autotag button in the Tags panel.**

    Text frames are automatically tagged with the Story tag. You need to identify two different stories in this job, so you should use a unique tag for each.

12. **Double-click the Story tag and change the name to Web-Address. Click OK to close the Tag Options dialog box.**

    This is the same name as the paragraph style applied to the text; using the same name for both elements allows you to easily map the tagged content to styles of the same name, which you will do later.

    Note:

    Make sure you type the tag names exactly as you see them in these steps, including the capitalization.

13. **With the same text frame still selected, click Web-Address in the Tags panel.**

14. **Repeat Steps 11–13 to create a new tag named Main-Text and apply it to the three-column text frame at the bottom of the page.**

    The file now has four tagged frames, each identified by a unique tag.

15. **Choose View>Structure>Hide Tagged Frames to toggle off the tag indicators in the layout.**

16. **Save the file and continue to the next exercise.**

Tag Content for XML

In addition to tagging frames, you can also tag specific content within frames. Doing so enables you to automatically format XML content in other layouts and allows you to access specific content when necessary.

1. **With sports-flyer.indd open, make sure hidden characters are visible (Type>Show Hidden Characters).**

2. **Using the Type tool, highlight the first paragraph in the three-column text frame, excluding the paragraph return character.**

   When you tag different kinds of text, make sure you don't select the final paragraph return character at the end of the selection.

3. **Click the New Tag button at the bottom of the Tags panel.**

   The new Tag1 is automatically added and highlighted.

New Tag

4. **With the tag name highlighted, type Heading and press Return/Enter to finalize the name change.**

   As with tagging frames, the new tag has been renamed, but it has not yet been applied to the selected text.

Note:

If you click the New Tag button to create a tag, that new tag is not automatically applied to the selected object.

5. **With the paragraph still selected in the layout, click the new Heading tag to apply it.**

6. **Click in the paragraph to place the insertion point and remove the text highlighting.**

7. **If you don't see brackets around the paragraph, choose View>Structure> Show Tag Markers.**

   Like the overlay and border on tagged frames, these brackets will not appear in the printed piece.

Brackets indicate that the text is tagged.

The bracket color matches the color swatch for the applied tag.

8. Using the Type tool, select the first paragraph in the second column, excluding the paragraph return character. Create and apply a tag named Body-Copy.

9. Select the subheading paragraph in the second column, excluding the paragraph return character. Create and apply a tag named Subhead.

10. Select the bulleted paragraphs below the subhead, excluding the final paragraph return character. Create and apply a tag named Body-List.

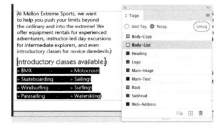

11. Select the first paragraph in the right column, excluding the paragraph return character, and apply the Body-Copy tag.

12. Select the subheading paragraph in the right column, excluding the paragraph return character, and apply the Subhead tag.

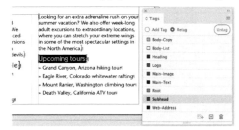

13. Select the bulleted paragraphs below the subhead in the right column, and apply the Body-List tag.

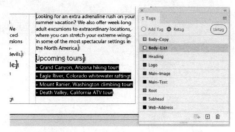

14. Save the file and continue to the next exercise.

 Review XML Structure and Attributes

XML files allow you to share content across multiple files, using either a structured or an unstructured method. Using the unstructured method, which you will utilize to create the postcard in a later exercise, you can simply import the XML into a document, and then drag elements into the layout. Structured repurposing requires more planning but allows you to merge tagged XML content into tagged frames in another layout.

1. With sports-flyer.indd open, choose View>Structure>Show Structure. In the Structure pane, click the arrow to the left of "Root" to expand the file's structure.

The Structure pane appears in the left side of the document window, showing the hierarchical order of tagged elements in the file. Elements appear in the order they were created; any element with an arrow next to its name can be expanded to show nested elements and associated attributes (we explain those attributes shortly).

2. If you don't see the actual web address words to the right of the Web-Address element, open the Structure pane Options menu and choose Show Text Snippets.

When snippets are visible, the first 32 characters of text in that element display in the pane.

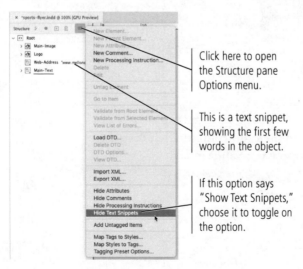

Click here to open the Structure pane Options menu.

This is a text snippet, showing the first few words in the object.

If this option says "Show Text Snippets," choose it to toggle on the option.

Note:

You can drag the bar on the right edge of the Structure pane to make the pane wider or narrower.

3. **Expand all elements by clicking the arrow to the left of each element.**

The Main-Text element contains additional tagged elements.

When expanded, each of the two image elements shows the path to the placed image with the "href" prefix. This path is an attribute of the image element, defining the location of the content placed within the element. This path information tells InDesign which image to use when the file is imported into another layout.

Note:

Attributes, such as the source of a place image, are identified in the Structure pane by a large bullet character.

4. **Choose File>Export and navigate to your WIP>Sports folder as the target destination.**

5. **Choose XML in the Format/Save As Type menu. Change the file name to mellon-sports.xml, then click Save.**

6. **Make sure no boxes are checked in either tab of the Export XML dialog box that appears, and then click Export.**

7. **Continue to the next exercise.**

Export XML Options

When exporting an XML file from an InDesign layout, the following options are available in the General tab:

- **Include DTD Declaration** exports a reference to a defined DTD (Document Type Definition) along with the XML file. This option is only available if a DOCTYPE element is showing in the Structure pane.

- **View XML Using** opens the exported file in the defined browser or editing application.

- **Export From Selected Element** starts exporting from the currently selected element in the Structure pane.

- **Export Untagged Tables As CALS XML** exports untagged tables in CALS XML format (an extension of XML).

- **Remap Break, Whitespace, and Special Characters** converts special characters to their XML code equivalents (if equivalents exist).

- **Apply XSLT** applies a style sheet from the XML file or from an external file. (XSLT stands for Extensible Stylesheet Language Transformation.)

- **Encoding** defines the encoding mechanism for representing international characters in the XML file.

In the Images tab, you can move images identified in the XML code to a folder created during the export process. (This is similar to the Links folder created when you use the Package utility.)

- **Original Images** copies the original image file into an Images subfolder.

- **Optimized Original Images** optimizes and compresses the original image files and places the optimized versions in an Images subfolder.

- **Optimized Formatted Images** permanently applies transformations (rotation, scaling, etc.) in the optimized images that are placed in the Images subfolder.

Using either Optimized option, you can choose the format (GIF or JPEG) to use in the Image Compression menu. You can also define the optimization options for each format. The Optimized options are more useful if you are repurposing the XML content into a web layout; GIF and JPEG are not recommended for print layout design.

Import XML Options

When importing XML data using Merge Content, the XML Import Options dialog box offers the following options:

- **Create Link** links to the XML file, so if the XML file is changed, the XML data in the InDesign document is automatically updated.

- **Apply XSLT** defines a style sheet that transforms XML data from one structure to another.

- **Clone Repeating Text Elements** replicates the formatting applied to tagged placeholder text for repeating content (e.g., formatting applied to different elements of an address placeholder).

- **Only Import Elements That Match Existing Structure** filters imported XML content so only elements from the imported XML file with matching elements in the document are imported. When unchecked, all elements in the XML file are imported into the Structure pane.

- **Import Text Elements Into Tables If Tags Match** imports elements into a table if the tags match the tags applied to the placeholder table and its cells.

- **Do Not Import Contents Of Whitespace-only Elements** leaves existing content in place if the matching XML content contains only whitespace such as a paragraph return character.

- **Delete Elements, Frames, and Content That Do Not Match Imported XML** removes elements from the Structure pane and the document layout if they don't match any elements in the imported XML file.

- **Import CALS Tables As InDesign Tables** imports any CALS tables in the XML file as InDesign tables.

Place Unstructured XML Content

As we mentioned earlier, you can use either an unstructured or a structured method for applying tagged XML content into a new layout. The unstructured method is easier because you can simply drag the content from the Structure pane and place it into your new document.

1. **Open the file card.indt from the WIP>Sports folder to create a new file. Save the new file as card-sports.indd in your WIP>Sports folder.**

   We created this basic postcard template with placeholders for a number of the same elements used in the flyer you just worked with.

2. **Open the Structure pane for the postcard layout. In the Structure pane Options menu, choose Import XML.**

Note:

You can also simply choose File>Import XML.

3. **Navigate to the file mellon-sports.xml in your WIP>Sports folder. Make sure the Show XML Import Options box is checked and click Open.**

Note:

The Merge Content and Append Content radio buttons are available in the Import XML dialog box because you need to make this choice even if you don't review the other import options.

4. **Review the choices in the XML Import Options dialog box.**

   The most important option is the Mode menu.

   - If **Merge Content** is selected, the XML content will be placed into the Root element of the current file. Content in the XML file will be automatically placed into tagged frames in the current layout. If frames in the layout are not tagged, elements from the XML file will be added to the Structure pane.

   - If **Append Content** is selected, the entire XML file will be placed into the Root element of the current document *after* any existing elements.

5. **Make sure Merge Content is selected in the Mode menu and check the Create Link option.**

   The **Create Link** option maintains a dynamic link to the XML file, just as a placed image is linked to the original image file. If content in the XML file changes, you can update the layout to automatically reflect the same changes.

6. **Click OK to import the XML file into the postcard document. In the Structure pane, expand all items.**

7. **With Page 1 of the postcard showing in the document window, drag the Web-Address element from the Structure pane onto the empty frame in the bottom-left corner.**

   Adding content is as easy as dragging it into the layout. If you drag an element into an empty area, a frame is automatically created. When you release the mouse button, the frame is automatically tagged with the Web-Address tag. Content in that tag is automatically placed into the frame. In the Structure pane, a small plus sign in the item icon indicates the item has been placed into the layout.

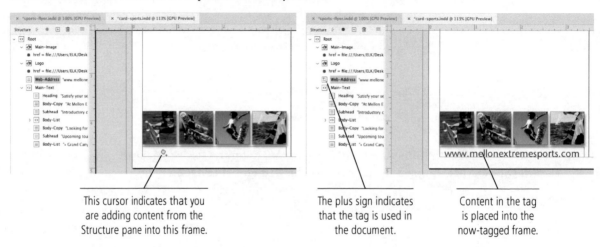

This cursor indicates that you are adding content from the Structure pane into this frame.

The plus sign indicates that the tag is used in the document.

Content in the tag is placed into the now-tagged frame.

8. **Make Page 2 of the postcard layout active in the document window.**

9. **Using the same process as in Step 7, drag the Main-Image element into the large empty frame.**

10. **Drag the Logo element into the smaller frame on the left side of the layout.**

11. **Drag the Heading element from the Main-Text element to the empty, gradient-filled text frame at the top of Page 2.**

When you release the mouse button, the content of the selected Heading element is placed into the frame. As you can see, the formatting defined in the imported content is not appropriate for this layout.

12. **In the Structure pane Options menu, choose Map Tags to Styles.**

Make sure you choose Map Tags to Styles, not Map Styles to Tags.

13. **Click the Map by Name button at the bottom of the dialog box.**

This resulting dialog box allows you to assign specific styles to specific elements.

Using the same names for tags and styles allows you to easily format different elements with the appropriate style. The Heading tag matches the style of the same name, so it is properly mapped to that style. Eight other tags, including Web-Address, are not mapped to any style.

Note:

Each of the template files for this project defines different formatting options appropriate for each layout for the same-named styles. There is no link between the styles in one file and the styles in another, other than the same style names.

14. **Click the words "[Not Mapped]" to the right of the Web-Address tag and choose Web Address from the menu.**

This menu lists all styles defined in the layout. Paragraph, character, table, cell, and object styles are all listed because any of these five might apply to a specific type of tag.

15. **Click OK to apply the defined formatting to the XML tags.**

The text element is automatically formatted because you already mapped that tag (Heading) to the existing document style (Heading).

XML communicates the content, but not the appearance, of the different elements. After mapping the tags to the postcard styles, which we defined in the provided template, the Heading text is formatted with attributes better suited to the postcard layout.

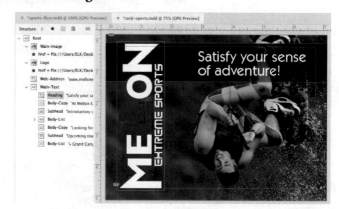

16. **Save the file, then continue to the next exercise.**

Update Linked XML Data

When you placed the XML file into the postcard layout, you checked the Create Link option. This means changes to the XML file can easily be updated in the postcard layout, just as you would update a placed image.

1. **Make sure sports-flyer.indd is open and active.**

2. **Using the Type tool, change the existing web address in the flyer to www. mellonextreme.com, then click away from the type object to deselect it.**

After deselecting the text frame, the text snippet in the Structure pane changes to show the new text in that object.

Change the web address here.

3. **Save the file.**

4. **Choose File>Export and navigate to the WIP>Sports folder as the target. Make sure XML is selected in the Format/Save As Type menu and the file name is mellon-sports.xml, then click Save.**

5. **When asked if you want to overwrite the existing file, click Replace/Yes.**

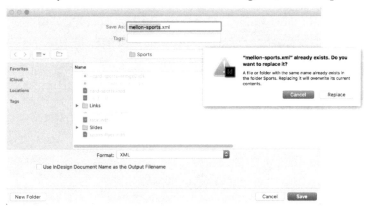

6. **Click Export in the resulting dialog box to rewrite the XML file.**

7. **Make card-sports.indd the active file, and then display the Links panel.**

   The XML file is linked to the document, so it appears (appropriately) in the Links panel. The Warning icon indicates the file was changed since being imported.

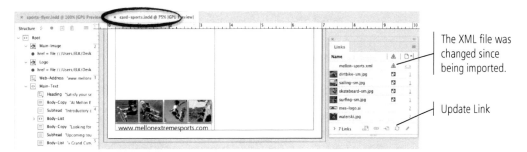

The XML file was changed since being imported.

Update Link

8. **Select mellon-sports.xml in the Links panel and click the Update Link button.**

   When the linked XML file is updated, the change automatically reflects in the postcard.

9. **Save the postcard file and close it.**

10. **Continue to the next exercise.**

Import Structured XML

With some advance planning, you can build a layout with tagged frames to automatically contain elements when the XML file is imported. For this process to work correctly, keep the following points in mind:

- Tag names must be exactly the same in the document file as in the XML data. You can load tags from one InDesign file to another to be sure they match.

- You can automatically format imported XML content by mapping tag names to styles. Style names need to exactly match the tag names.

- The tagged layout should have the same structure as data in the XML file. Remember, the structure in the XML file is based on the order of elements in the Structure pane.

Keep in mind, XML can be far more complex than what you applied in these short documents; entire books have been written on the subject. The point of this project is to introduce you to the concepts of XML and to show you how InDesign's XML capabilities make it relatively easy to work with XML data.

Note:

To learn more about the capabilities of XML, we encourage you to explore www.xml.org. This site offers a wealth of information about XML from experts and standards organizations in multiple industries.

1. **Create a new file by opening the rack.indt template in the WIP>Sports folder. Save the new file as rack-sports.indd in your WIP>Sports folder.**

   This layout includes two pages with placeholder frames for all the same elements used in the flyer. To prepare these frames for XML import, you have to tag those frames with the same tag names used in the XML file you want to import.

2. **In the Tags panel Options menu, choose Load Tags.**

3. **Navigate to sports-flyer.indd in your WIP>Sports folder and click Open.**

   You used this file to generate the XML file, so its tags match those in the XML file. This method of loading tags ensures the tags you add in the rack card file exactly match the tags in the flyer and, thus, in the XML file.

4. **Open the Structure pane for the rack card file (View>Structure> Show Structure).**

   Adding tags to the file does not automatically add elements to the structure. Elements aren't added to the structure until you attach the loaded tags to frames in the layout.

5. **Place the Tags panel next to the Paragraph Styles panel and compare the two lists.**

Remember, for tags to correctly map to styles, the names of the styles must exactly match the names of the tags.

The Body Copy and Body List style names do not match the tag name because the hyphen is missing from paragraph style names.

Note:

Tag names can't have spaces, but style names can, so this type of mismatch is not uncommon.

6. **In the Paragraph Styles panel, click the Body Copy style to select it. Pause a second, then click the style name again to highlight it.**

Double-clicking the style name opens the Paragraph Style Options dialog box, where you can edit the style settings. If you click to select the style, pause, then single-click the name of the active style, you can change its name directly in the panel without opening a dialog box.

7. **Change the style name to Body-Copy, then press Return/Enter to finalize the new style name.**

The style name now matches the tag name.

Single-click a selected style name to highlight it.

Type a new style name, then press Return/Enter to finalize it.

8. **Repeat Steps 6–7 to change the Body List style name to Body-List, adding a hyphen.**

9. **Use the Selection tool to select the empty text frame on Page 1 in the layout, then click the Main-Text tag in the Tags panel.**

After the frame is tagged, the element is added to the Structure pane.

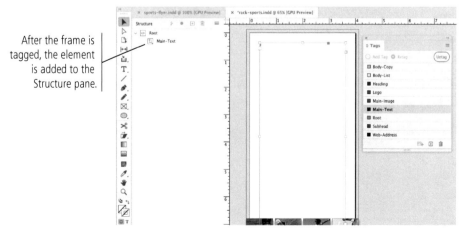

10. **Navigate to Page 2 of the layout. Using the same method as in Step 9, assign the following tags to the frames on Page 2.**

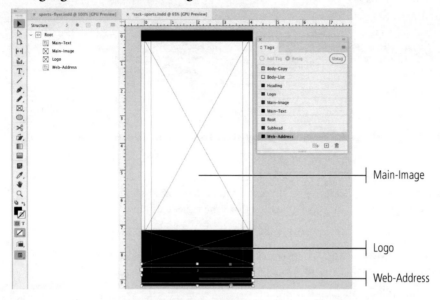

11. **Make sure `sports-flyer.indd` is open, then choose Window>Arrange> 2-up Vertical.**

To be sure the XML will import properly, the tagged document structure should exactly match the structure in the XML file. The two Structure panes show the Main-Text element is not in the same order; you need to fix this before importing the XML file.

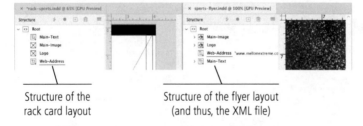

Structure of the rack card layout

Structure of the flyer layout (and thus, the XML file)

12. **In the rack card Structure pane, drag the Main-Text element to appear below the Web-Address element.**

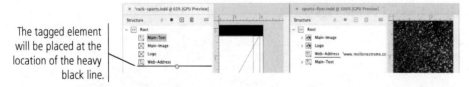

The tagged element will be placed at the location of the heavy black line.

When you drag the tag into a new position, drag away from the existing tag names to avoid creating a nested tag.

13. **Return to the single-document arrangement (Window>Arrange> Consolidate All Windows)and make the rack card file active.**

    Use the Consolidate All document arrangement option.

14. **With the rack card document active, choose File>Import XML.**

    This is the same as choosing the Import XML option in the Structure pane Options menu.

15. **Navigate to the file mellon-sports.xml in your WIP>Sports folder. Uncheck Show XML Import Options and Import Into Selected Element. Choose the Merge Content radio button.**

16. **Click Open to import the XML file into the rack card layout and merge the data into the tagged frames.**

    The tagged elements are all placed into the matching tagged frames, but they do not yet show the appropriate style settings.

17. **In the Structure pane Options menu, choose Map Tags to Styles. In the resulting dialog box, click Map by Name, and then click OK.**

    Again, make sure you choose Map Tags to Styles, not Map Styles to Tags.

    Because you took the time to define style names that exactly matched the tag names, the mapping process requires no additional intervention.

18. **Choose View>Structure>Hide Tagged Frames and View>Structure>Hide Tag Markers to turn off the nonprinting visual indicators.**

19. **Save the file and close it, then continue to the next stage of the project.**

STAGE 2 / Creating Alternate Layouts

As you have already seen throughout this book, there is almost always more than one way to accomplish a specific goal in InDesign. In the first stage of this project, you used XML to feed content into several existing templates. In this second stage, you will use another method to create versions appropriate for digital tablet display.

When designing for mobile devices, one of the problems we face is the range of different hardware — most of which have different physical sizes, even if that difference is slight. There is no single consistent size or resolution from one device to another. It's also important to realize that new devices are being introduced all the time, and each new phase of mobile-communication evolution will almost certainly introduce more variables into the picture.

Ideally, when you design for mobile devices, you would create separate files for each device to take best advantage of the available screen capabilities. However, this would mean dozens of iterations for individual devices, which is not always possible given the deadline-driven nature of some publishing projects. In this stage of the project, you will create layouts at the appropriate sizes for a basic iPad.

Create a File for Digital Publishing

You can now use built-in options to easily create a new file for a number of standard digital media sizes — specifically, common tablets such as iPads and Android devices.

1. **With sports-flyer.indd open, choose File>New>Document.**

2. **Choose the Mobile option at the top of the dialog box.**

3. **Click the View All Presets option in the middle of the dialog box, then choose the iPad preset.**

4. **Make the following changes to the preset details:**

Name:	**ipad-sports**
Orientation:	**Portrait**
Primary Text Frame:	**Unchecked**

   The Mobile intents default to landscape (horizontal) orientation. Although you eventually have to create both orientations for tablet devices, it is often easier to start with the version closer to the file you already have, which is the portrait-orientation flyer).

   You do not need a primary text frame in this file because you will be copying the entire text frame from the flyer layout to the iPad layout.

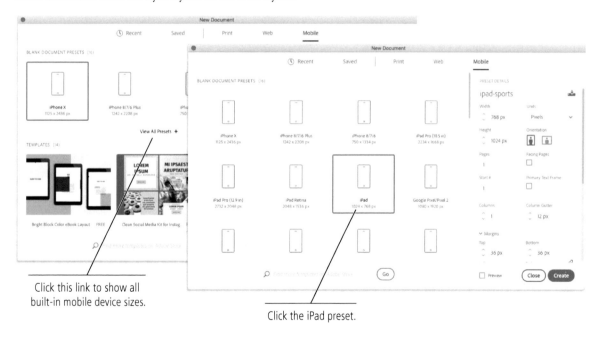

Click this link to show all built-in mobile device sizes.

Click the iPad preset.

5. **Click Create to create the new file.**

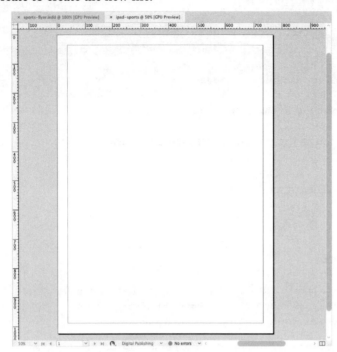

Note:

The mobile presets use pixels as the units of measurement and RGB as the default color mode.

Note:

In this project you will use a number of InDesign features to create a file using the iPad dimensions; in a professional environment, you would likely have to also create files for other mobile devices.

6. **Save the file as ipad-sports.indd in your WIP>Sports folder, then continue to the next exercise.**

Use the Content Collector

The Content Collector/Content Placer toolset is a powerful option for sharing and linking content throughout a layout and across multiple layouts. In this exercise, you are going to use these tools to repurpose the flyer content to a size suitable for an iPad.

1. **Make sports-flyer.indd the active file.**

2. **Choose the Content Collector tool.**

Make sure you choose the *Collector* tool and not the *Placer* tool. The arrow in the Collector tool icon points down. When you choose the Content Collector or Content Placer tool, the Content Conveyor automatically appears.

Note:

When the Tools panel is in two-column mode, the Content Placer tool appears to the right of the Content Collector tool instead of nested under it.

Content Collector tool

Content Conveyor

3. **Click the text frame with the web address on the page to select it.**

   When you select an object with the Content Collector, it is added to the Content Conveyor. The cursor icon shows how many objects are currently stored in the conveyor.

Clicking an item with the Content Collector tool loads that item into the conveyor.

The cursor icon (enlarged here) shows how many items are loaded in the conveyor.

4. **Click the three-column text frame to select it.**

   A second item is added to the Content Conveyor; the cursor icon now shows two items are available.

Note:

If you click the Load Conveyor button on the right side of the panel, you can load the conveyor with all objects in the active selection, on a specific page, or on all pages. You can load these objects as individual items or as a single set.

5. **Draw a selection marquee touching all three frames in the top half of the page: the large image frame, the red-filled frame, and the logo frame.**

   When you select more than one object at a time, those objects are added to the conveyor as a **set**. The cursor icon shows three objects (the large image frame, the red-filled frame, and the logo frame) are now stored in the conveyor. In the conveyor, the set thumbnail shows the set contains three items.

Note:

Press ESC to remove the active item from the Content Conveyor.

The thumbnail shows the number of items in the set.

6. **Make the `ipad-sports` file active, then press B to switch to the Content Placer tool.**

When the Content Placer tool is active, the cursor shows the number of items loaded in the conveyor, a thumbnail of the active item, and an icon indicating the type of active item (text frame, image, set, etc.).

Note:

You can also use the buttons at the bottom of the conveyor to switch tools.

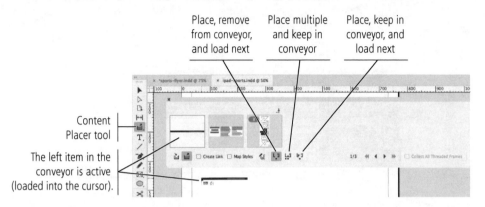

Place, remove from conveyor, and load next

Place multiple and keep in conveyor

Place, keep in conveyor, and load next

Content Placer tool

The left item in the conveyor is active (loaded into the cursor).

7. **Check the Create Link and Map Styles options at the bottom of the Content Conveyor.**

These options are explained in the next exercise. For now, simply make sure they are checked.

8. **Make sure the first placement option is selected at the bottom of the Content Conveyor.**

The buttons in the conveyor determine what will happen when you drop an item.

- **Place, remove from conveyor, and load next (▯).** Clicking places the active item; that item is removed from the conveyor, and the next is automatically loaded into the cursor.

- **Place multiple and keep in conveyor (▯).** The active item in the conveyor remains active until you intentionally change to another item; this allows you to place multiple copies of the same item.

- **Place, keep in conveyor, and load next (▯).** After placing the active item, the next item becomes active; all items remain in the conveyor.

Note:

You can hide the content conveyor by choosing View>Extras>Hide Conveyor. If you hide it, it remains hidden even after you select the Content Collector or Placer tool.

If you choose the Content Collector or Content Placer tool and do not see the Content Conveyor, choose View>Extras>Show Conveyor.

9. **Press the Right Arrow key two times to navigate to the third item in the Content Conveyor.**

The left item in the conveyor is the active one, which will be placed when you click. You can use the navigation buttons at the bottom of the conveyor to change the active item, or use the Left and Right Arrow keys to move from one item to the next.

Note:

If the active item is a text object, you can click inside an existing text frame to place the loaded story into that frame.

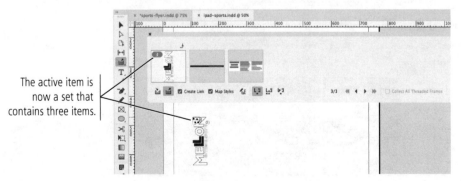

The active item is now a set that contains three items.

10. **With the Content Placer tool still active, press the Down Arrow key to display the set items in the Content Conveyor.**

When the active item is a set and the Content Placer tool (*not* the Content Collector) is active, you can press the Down Arrow key to show the individual items in the set.

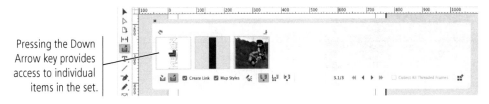

Pressing the Down Arrow key provides access to individual items in the set.

11. **Press the Up Arrow key to make the entire set active again.**

12. **Click the top-left corner of the page and drag until the preview shows the new object filling the entire page width.**

When a set is active in the Conveyor, you place the entire set at one time.

You can simply click to place the item, or click and drag to place the item at a different size than the original; when you drag, the frame preview shows the object's original aspect is maintained in the new frame.

If you want to place a copy without maintaining the original aspect ratio, press Shift while you drag the new object's shape. (This is the only time the Shift key does not constrain a transformation.)

Clicking and dragging maintains the same aspect ratio as the original.

When you release the mouse button, the three frames are placed in the layout.

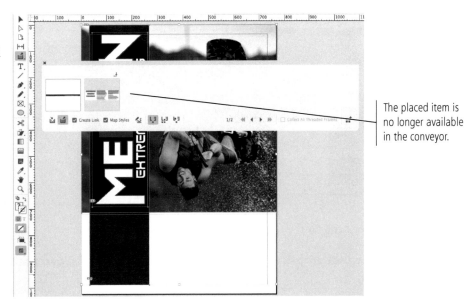

The placed item is no longer available in the conveyor.

13. **With the web-address item active in the Conveyor, click and drag from the left page edge to the right page edge, immediately below the large image frame.**

Use the following image as a guide.

When you release the mouse button, the web-address text frame is placed in the appropriate location.

14. **With the Content Placer tool still active, click to place the active item (the three-column text frame) in the empty space at the bottom of the layout.**

If you click inside the area of the red frame, text from the shared item will be placed into the red frame. You have to click in a blank area to place the actual three-column text frame. You will adjust it shortly to fit the iPad layout.

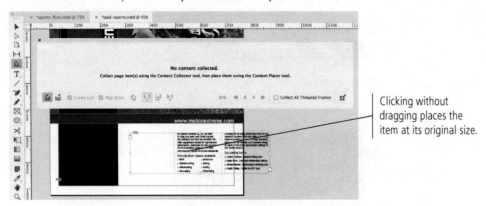

Clicking without dragging places the item at its original size.

15. **Deselect everything in the ipad-sports layout, then save the file.**

16. **Save and close the sports-flyer.indd file, then continue to the next exercise.**

Manage Linked Object Options

When you use the Content Placer with the Create Links option checked, the content you place is linked to the original file instead of simply being a copy. If you need to make changes, you can edit the flyer content, and the changes can be automatically updated in the iPad file's linked objects.

Because InDesign keeps track of link update status — just as it does for regular placed images — you don't need to worry about forgetting to make changes in any specific file. However, if you make a change to a linked object and then later update the links, you are warned that your edits in the linked copies will be lost.

Compare this to the XML workflow in the first stage of this project. Using that process, you have to re-export the XML file if you make changes in the original flyer file, and then update the linked XML file in any secondary layouts. Using the Content Collector/Placer, you don't need to take that extra step.

In this project, you are going to modify the linked objects and define settings that will protect your changes.

Note:

Choosing the Edit>Place and Link command has the same general effect as selecting an item with the Content Collector tool.

Note:

*There is no dynamic link **from** the linked copies back to the original or to other copies of the same object. If you want changes to reflect in all linked copies, you have to edit the original object. This is easily accomplished by Control/right-clicking any of the copies — in the layout or in the Links panel — and choosing **Go to Source** in the contextual menu.*

1. **With ipad-sports.indd open, open the Links panel and review the list.**

2. **Expand the Links panel as necessary so you can see most of the items' names and the Format column.**

   The Links panel lists each item you placed in the previous exercise as a separate item. The software also creates separate links for objects/frames and those objects' content. Stories — the actual text in the shared fames — are identified by an icon that looks like a small text document; the actual frames do not display icons.

Linked items list the source document.

Icons identify the type of linked content.

Click this line and drag to make the item name list wider.

Click here and drag to make the panel wider.

Because frames and contents are linked separately, you can update the linked content without affecting the object attributes and vice versa:

- Update individual items or contents by selecting a specific listing in the Links panel and clicking the Update Links button. This method allows you to update the item without affecting the content and vice versa.

- Update individual copies by clicking the Modified icon on individual items in the layout using the Selection tool. If you use this method, both the item and the item content will be updated.

3. **Using the Selection tool, select the three-column text frame. Define its position as X: 36 px, Y: 770 px based on the top-left reference point.**

   When you placed the text frame, you simply clicked to place it. You did not click and drag to define the placed text frame's size. You are making this change to better fit the available space in the iPad layout.

4. **Click the bottom-right corner of the text frame and drag to the bottom-right margin.**

These two items refer separately to the selected frame and the content inside the frame.

5. **Click away from the text frame to deselect it.**

6. **In the Links panel, click to select only the three-column text frame object.**

The frame does *not* have an identifying icon.

The actual story does have an identifying icon.

The snippet in the item name shows the first few words in the frame.

7. **Control/right-click the text frame item for the flyer copy. Choose Link Options in the contextual menu.**

8. **In the Preserve Local Edits area, check the Size and Shape option. Click OK.**

Because the object is linked to the object in the print flyer, any changes to the frame size or shape in the print layout would cause this item to show a Modified link. If you update the link, the frame in the iPad file would revert to the same size as the frame in the print layout.

Note:

It is important to realize that the Preserve Local Edits options relate to all objects in the file. You cannot define different settings for individual objects.

You can use the **Preserve Local Edits** section to define which options you want to keep in the linked copies when you update the links. By checking the Size and Shape option, you are telling InDesign to keep the frame's size and shape you defined in the iPad layout; you have essentially unlinked specific properties, while other attributes of the frame (appearance, etc.) are still linked to the print flyer frame.

9. **Open the Paragraph Styles panel.**

When you resized the frame, you should have noticed the text reflowed. The text formatting applied in the print layout left a lot of empty space at the bottom of the page. You should adjust the text size to best take advantage of the available space.

Note:

When you use the Content Placer tool to make copies, any assets (styles, color swatches, etc.) required by the linked object are added to the file where you place the copy.

10. **Make the following changes to the paragraph styles:**

Heading   **Change the type size to 42 pt**

Subhead   **Change the type size to 16 pt**

Body-Copy   **Change the type size to 11 pt**

                      Change the leading size to 14 pt

There is no link between the styles in the original file (the flyer) and the styles in the file where copies are placed (the iPad layout). You can use styles to change the appearance of the type in either location without affecting the other.

The Body-List style is based on the Body-Copy style; both are changed when you edit the Body-Copy style.

11. **Using the Selection tool, select the image frame in the layout.**

When you select an object in the layout, the object and the object contents are both selected in the Links panel.

If you select the frame in the layout, both the object and the object contents are highlighted in the Links panel.

12. **Deselect everything in the layout.**

13. **In the Links panel, click to select only the image frame. Control/right-click the frame listing and choose Unlink in the contextual menu.**

You are going to use this frame to create an interactive slideshow that displays when someone opens the file on a tablet device. To avoid problems if you make changes to the image frame in the flyer file, you are breaking the link for only this frame.

Unlink the frame, not the frame's content.

The image frame remains in the layout, and it still shows the link icon because this is still a linked image — linked to the actual image source file. There is no longer any link to the original object in the flyer file.

The frame is no longer linked; it has been removed from the Links panel.

14. **Save the file and continue to the next exercise.**

Defining Style Mapping Rules

In the previous exercise, you saw that styles applied in the placed content are automatically copied into the file where you place that content. If the target file has existing styles with the same name as the styles in the source file, the target-file style definition is automatically applied in the placed content. In other words, the target file style overrides the same-named style in the source file.

If you are placing content into a file that has existing styles, but those styles don't have the same names as the styles in the source file, you can define style mapping rules to determine which styles in the target file will be used instead of styles in the source file.

When the Content Placer tool is active, you can click the Edit Custom Style Mapping button in the Content Conveyor to determine what styles you want to apply in the file where you place the content.

Edit Custom Style Mapping

In the Custom Style Mapping dialog box, first choose the **Source Document** that contains the styles you want to replace. You can use the **Style Type** menu to create style mapping rules for paragraph, character, table, and cell styles.

Clicking the **New Style Mapping** button adds an item to the list. In the left side of the dialog box, choose the style you want to replace from the source file; in the right side of the dialog box, choose the style you want to apply (the mapped style, from the destination file).

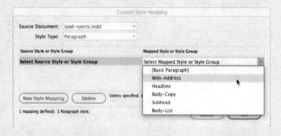

Once you define style mapping rules, those choices will be applied as long as the Map Styles option is checked in the Content Conveyor.

Create an Interactive Overlay

You might have noticed that you did not include the second image from the print layout in the iPad layout. As you know, print is static; objects stay where you put them, and they do not change. If you want to show two pictures, you place two pictures into the layout.

If you completed Project 6: Digital Layout Variations, you have already seen that digital publishing is not subject to this restriction. You can use a single frame to show multiple images or even play a video. In this exercise, you will use an interactive overlay to display multiple images in the same frame in the final app.

Understanding Interactive Overlay Options

When you create a file to be viewed on a digital tablet, the visible content — including text — is often rasterized into a single image. Interactivity is technically added on top of the image as a separate "layer" on top of the existing content (hence the term "overlay").

The interactive layer is not a true InDesign layer that you can turn on and off; you can't directly access the layer containing the interactivity. Instead, you use the Overlays panel (Window>Overlays) to define interactive settings, which will be used to generate the necessary code in the final file.

The **Hyperlink** overlay can be applied to any object that has been defined as a hyperlink (using the Hyperlinks panel) or to a button object that uses the Go to URL action.

The **Web Content** overlay can be used to feed HTML content into a frame in the layout.

The **Slideshow** overlay can be applied to a multi-state object. It provides controls similar to those you created using buttons in Project 6: Digital Layout Variations.

The **Pan & Zoom** overlay can be applied to any image frame in which the image has been cropped by the frame edges; the frame defines the scrollable area that is visible in the folio file. If you choose Pan & Zoom, users can use pinch gestures to zoom in to a specific image area.

The **Image Sequence** overlay creates a slideshow from a folder of images. You can apply this overlay to any rectangle frame, whether or not it already contains an image.

The **Scrollable Frame** option creates a frame in which the user can scroll to see more content.

To create a scrollable frame, you have to first create the frame that will define the scrollable area and the content objects that you want to be included in the frame. Next, you have to select the content object(s) with the Selection tool, choose Edit>Cut, select the frame object, and choose Edit>Paste Into.

The **Audio** and **Video** overlays add controls to audio and video files that are placed in the layout.

Finally, apply the Scrollable Frame overlay to the frame object, and define the properties in the Overlays panel.

1. **With ipad-sports.indd open, open the Overlays panel (Window>Overlays).**

   This panel includes a number of common interactive elements that can be added to a digital publication using only tools in the InDesign interface. You don't need an external application to create these elements.

2. **Using the Selection tool, select the image frame in the layout, then click Image Sequence in the Overlays panel.**

   After applying an overlay to a frame, the bottom half of the panel shows options related to the specific type of overlay.

Note:

Unfortunately, you will not be able to preview the effect of an overlay on your desktop. These interactive elements work only in the special file format used for an Adobe Experience Manager Mobile Article; they do not function in interactive PDF or EPUB files.

3. **Click the Folder icon to the right of the Load Images field.**

4. **Navigate to the Slides folder in the WIP>Sports folder, then click Choose/Select Folder.**

   This folder contains a number of images that will be used in the interactive slideshow.

   At this point, there is no visible indication that the frame in the layout has changed. By default, the image currently placed in the frame will appear when the file opens.

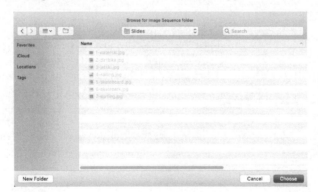

5. **In the Overlays panel, check the option to Show First Image Initially.**

   When you activate the Show First Image Initially option for the Image Sequence overlay, the frame automatically resizes to fit the image at 100%.

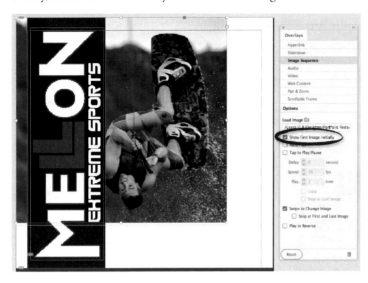

6. **Using the Selection tool, resize the frame to occupy the same space it did before Step 5.**

Resize the frame to occupy the same space as it did before Step 5.

7. **In the Properties panel, locate the Frame Fitting options. Click the Options button to open the Frame Fitting Options dialog box.**

Click the Options button to open the Frame Fittting Options dialog box.

8. **Define the following settings in the Frame Fitting Options dialog box:**

- **Check the Auto-Fit option**
- **Choose Fill Frame Proportionally in the Fitting menu**
- **Choose the Center point in the Align From proxy**
- **Type 0 in all four Clip Amount fields**

These options mean the images in the Slides folder will automatically scale to fill the frame when each image loads.

9. **Click OK to apply the new frame fitting options.**

10. **With the image frame still selected, make the following choices in the Options section of the Overlays panel:**

- **Check the Auto Play option**
- **Check the Tap to Play/Pause option**
- **Change the Delay to 2 secs**
- **Change the Speed to 1 fps**
- **Check the Loop option**
- **Uncheck the Swipe to Change Image option**

These options should be self-explanatory, which is a testament to the ease with which you can create interactive elements directly in InDesign.

In our testing, the Delay field accurately controlled the image sequence timing on Android devices but not on the iPad. Changing the frames per second (fps) to 1 second also accurately controlled the image timing on the iPad.

11. **Save the file, then continue to the next exercise.**

Define Liquid Page Rules

If you have a tablet device, you already know it can display content both horizontally and vertically depending on the device's physical position. When you publish files for digital tablets, you can create different layout versions to take best advantage of each orientation.

1. With **ipad-sports.indd** open, select the text frame at the bottom of the page.

2. Press **Command/Control-B to open the Text Frame Options dialog box.**

3. With the **General options visible, choose Flexible Width in the Columns menu and change the Maximum field to 250 px.**

   When you assign a frame to have flexible column widths, you can define the maximum width allowed when you resize the page or the frame. (This will make more sense shortly when you resize the page.)

4. Click **OK to return to the layout.**

5. Choose the **Page tool in the Tools panel and open the Liquid Layout panel (Window>Interactive>Liquid Layout).**

6. In the **Control panel or Liquid Layout panel, choose Object-Based in the Liquid Page Rule menu.**

   When the Page tool is active, the Liquid Page Rule menu defines how existing objects react when you change the page size or create an alternate layout.

7. Click **the three-column text frame with the Page tool to make sure that object is selected.**

   When the Object-Based rule is applied and you select an object with the Page tool, you can use on-screen controls to define how the image will behave when you resize the page. Circles outside the frame edges refer to the frame's position relative to the page edges; circles on the frame edges refer to the frame's height and width.

Note:

The options in the Liquid Layout panel correlate to the on-screen controls for the selected object.

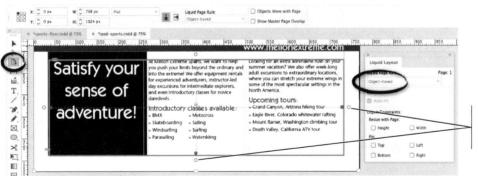

Circles control the object's liquid layout properties.

Understanding Column Options

Fixed Number means the frame has a defined number of columns. When you resize the frame, the columns resize to equally divide the frame width.

The number of columns is constant, regardless of the frame width.

Fixed Width means columns in the frame always have the exact width defined in this box. If you resize the frame, columns are added or removed based on the available space. Using this option, the frame will always be exactly wide enough to contain the defined number of columns, including gutters.

Say you define Fixed Width columns of 2" with a gutter of 0.25". With two columns, the frame will be 4.25" wide. If you widen the frame, it automatically snaps to the next size that accommodates the defined column width (6.5", 8.75", etc.).

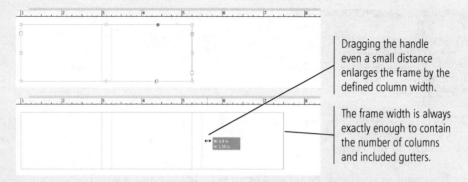

Dragging the handle even a small distance enlarges the frame by the defined column width.

The frame width is always exactly enough to contain the number of columns and included gutters.

Flexible Width means the number of columns in a frame adjusts dynamically when the frame is resized. When you change a frame's overall width, columns resize until the maximum width triggers the addition or removal of a column.

Say you define flexible-width columns with a maximum width of 2" and a gutter of 0.25". When the overall frame width is more than 4.25" (2" column + 0.25" gutter + 2" column), another column is added. The column width varies based on the overall frame width.

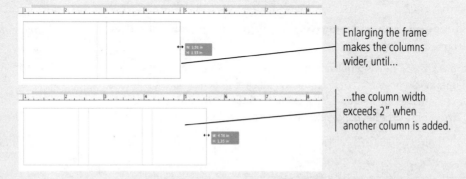

Enlarging the frame makes the columns wider, until...

...the column width exceeds 2" when another column is added.

8. **Click the bottom-right corner of the page and drag to approximate the size of a horizontal iPad.**

Using the Page tool, you can drag a page handle to preview the effect of resizing the page. Remember, both frame dimensions are pinned, but the frame is not pinned to any page edge. As you can see, the text frame retains the same size, centered horizontally in the resized page area.

Note:

You can press Option/ Alt to retain the new page size when you release the mouse button.

Using the Page tool, drag one of the handles to preview the page contents at a different page size.

9. **Release the mouse button.**

When you release the mouse button, the page — and objects on the page — return to their original state.

10. **Click the bottom, left, and right hollow circles outside the frame edges.**

In the on-screen controls, hollow circles outside the frame edges mean the object is not locked (pinned) to the page edges; solid circles on the frame edges and the lock icons inside the frame mean the object's dimensions are pinned.

Because you pinned the object to the left and right sides of the page, the frame's width is automatically unlocked — a frame can't be pinned on both sides and locked in the same orientation.

Note:

Zooming in can be helpful to see the on-screen controls.

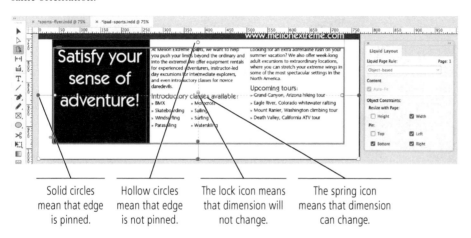

Solid circles mean that edge is pinned.

Hollow circles mean that edge is not pinned.

The lock icon means that dimension will not change.

The spring icon means that dimension can change.

11. **Click the bottom-right page handle, and drag again to approximate the size of a horizontal iPad.**

Remember, your object-based rules allow the text frame to widen. You also allowed the frame to have a flexible column width, up to 250 px. When the frame becomes wider than three 250-px columns, plus the defined gutter width, the frame automatically changes to have four columns.

Note:

When you move the mouse over the on-screen controls, tool tips tell you the function of each icon.

A fourth column is added when the frame width requires it.

The text frame is pinned to the bottom, left, and right edges.

12. **Release the mouse button to restore the original page size.**

13. **With the Page tool still active, click the image frame at the top of the layout. In the Liquid Layout panel, check the Top and Right pin options.**

This means the image frame will remain attached to the top and right edges; the frame will not resize when the page is resized.

These options correlate to the on-screen controls.

14. Using either method (the on-screen controls or the Liquid Layout panel), pin the top and right edges of the logo frame. Do not allow the object to resize.

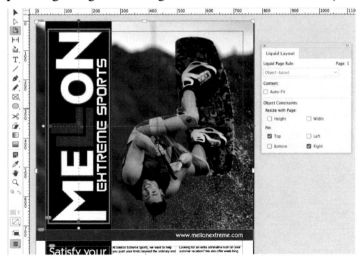

15. Pin the top and right edges of the red frame behind the logo. In the Liquid Layout panel, check the option to allow the object's height to resize.

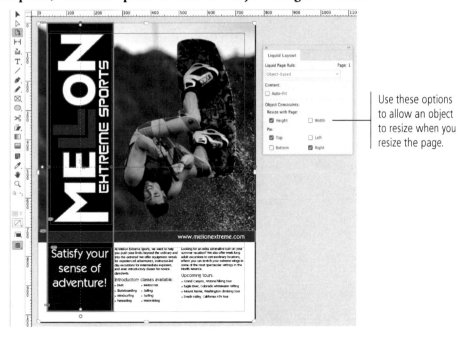

Use these options to allow an object to resize when you resize the page.

Understanding Liquid Page Rules

If the **Show Master Page Overlay** option is checked in the Control panel, the active master page appears in the bottom-left corner of the active page.

Using the **Off** liquid page rule, resizing the page has no effect on placed objects.

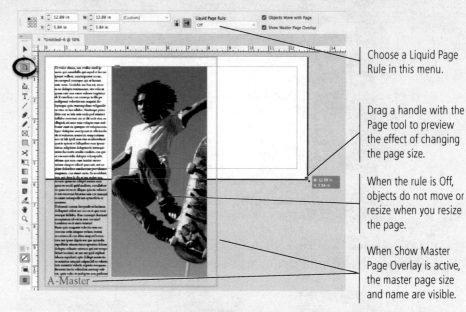

Choose a Liquid Page Rule in this menu.

Drag a handle with the Page tool to preview the effect of changing the page size.

When the rule is Off, objects do not move or resize when you resize the page.

When Show Master Page Overlay is active, the master page size and name are visible.

Using the **Scale** liquid page rule, content is scaled proportionally, adding or removing space around the page if the content can't be scaled in a specific direction.

When the Scale rule is active, objects scale to fit inside the adjusted page size.

Using the **Re-center** liquid page rule, content is centered in the new page area; its size is not affected.

When the Re-center rule is active, objects remain centered to the new page size; they are not scaled.

Using the **Guide-Based** liquid page rule, you can use the Page tool to drag "liquid" guides; any object touched by a liquid guide will resize when you change the layout size. Horizontal liquid guides allow objects to resize vertically, and vertical liquid guides allow an object to resize horizontally. You can select a guide with the Selection tool, then click the icon on the end of the guide to convert it from a page guide to a liquid guide or from a liquid guide to a page guide.

When the Guide-Based rule is active, objects are resized if they intersect liquid guides.

Using the **Object-Based** liquid page rule, you can use on-screen and panel-based controls to resize and reposition individual objects. This rule gives you the most control over the layout. (You will use this option in this project.)

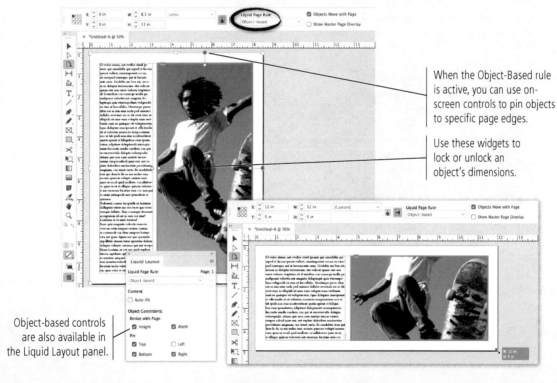

When the Object-Based rule is active, you can use on-screen controls to pin objects to specific page edges.

Use these widgets to lock or unlock an object's dimensions.

Object-based controls are also available in the Liquid Layout panel.

If the **Controlled by Master** option is selected, the rules that are applied to the active master page will be applied if you resize the layout page. If you resize a layout page and the Controlled by Master rule is selected, the applied master page resizes as well.

16. Pin the top and right edges of the frame with the web address. In the Liquid Layout panel, check the option to allow the object's width to resize.

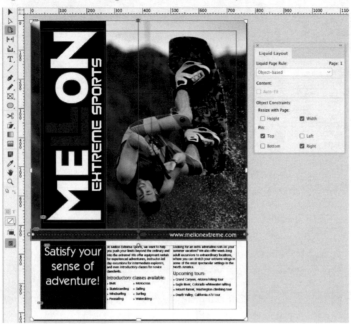

17. Click the bottom-right page handle, and drag again to approximate the size of a horizontal iPad.

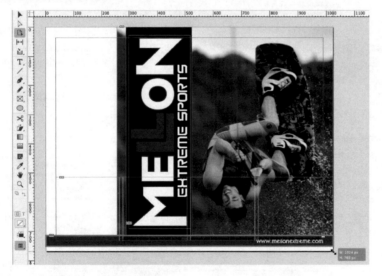

18. Release the mouse button to restore the original page size.

19. Save the file and continue to the next exercise.

Create an Alternate Layout

Rather than creating multiple files for each possible variation, InDesign makes it very easy to create an alternate layout for the existing pages all in the same file. Keep in mind, of course, that repurposing content for multiple layouts is almost never a one-click process. Even though InDesign makes the process much easier than ever before, some elements will still require choices and manual intervention to best take advantage of the available space.

1. **With ipad-sports.indd open, open the Pages panel.**

   When you use the built-in presets, InDesign recognizes the layout name and orientation you are creating. The Pages panel reflects both above the existing page icons.

2. **Open the Pages panel Options menu and choose Create Alternate Layout.**

3. **Review the options in the resulting dialog box.**

   Because you already have the iPad V (vertical) layout created, the dialog box defaults to create the opposite orientation of the same layout — in this case, the iPad H (horizontal) layout.

   You can choose a different page size in the menu, or choose Custom to define a new preset with dimensions other than those already defined in a preset.

   The Liquid Page Rule defaults to Preserve Existing, which applies the settings you manually defined while the Page tool was active. You can also use the menu to override the existing settings by calling one of the built-in rules (off, scale, re-center, guide-based, or object-based).

4. **Make sure the Link Stories option is checked.**

   When this option is checked, the objects in the alternate layout are linked to the same objects in the original layout, which, if you remember, are linked to the objects in the print flyer layout.

5. **Make sure the Copy Text Styles to New Style Group option is checked.**

   When this option is checked, the styles in your layout will be moved into a style group named according to the original layout (in this case "iPad V"). Another copy of those styles is placed in a second group (named "iPad H"), so you can change the style definition in one layout without affecting the same-named styles in the alternate layout.

6. Uncheck the Smart Text Reflow option.

If this option is checked, changing the size of the primary text frame will automatically result in extra pages being added to the layout. This layout does not use a primary text frame, so the option is irrelevant in this case.

(If you do use the primary text frame and want exactly the same number of pages in the alternate layout, make sure you turn off this option.)

7. Click OK to generate the alternate layout.

The Pages panel now shows both layouts. You can navigate to either layout just as you navigate pages: double-click a page icon to show that page in the document window regardless of which layout it belongs to.

8. Double-click the iPad H Page 1 icon.

As you can see, your defined liquid page rules defined the position and size of each object:

- The black text frame did not resize; it is still attached to the top and left page edges.
- The image frame did not resize; it is still attached to the top and right page edges.
- The text frame resized horizontally, and a fourth column was added. It is still attached to the left, bottom, and right page edges; the same margin is maintained between the frame and page edges.

You can also tell some work still needs to be done. The two orientations do not need to have the same approximate layouts; in fact, they don't even need to have the same content (although they probably should, in most cases).

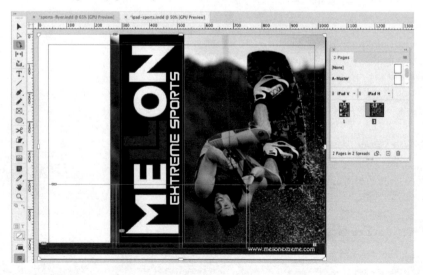

9. **Select the four-column text frame with the Selection tool. Change its parameters to:**

> X: 36 px   W: 210 px
>
> Y: 36 px   H: 660 px

Because you allowed a column width up to 250 px, the new frame width shows only a single column. Nothing appears to be in the text frame because the Heading style uses the Paper color and the Body-Copy style is defined to start in the next column.

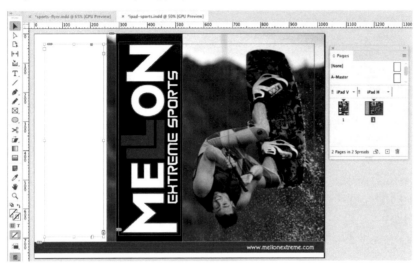

10. **Click away from the text frame to deselect it.**

11. **Open the Paragraph Styles panel and expand both style groups.**

12. **Double-click the Heading style in the iPad H group to edit that style.**

Make sure you edit the style in the iPad H group.

13. **Make sure the Preview option is checked. In the Character Color options, change the character fill color to C=0 M=100 Y=100 K=20.**

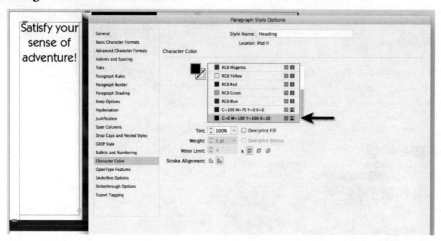

14. **Click OK to return to the layout.**

15. **In the Paragraph Styles panel, double-click the Body-Copy style in the iPad H group to edit that style. In the Keep options, choose Anywhere in the Start Paragraph menu.**

    Changing the Keep options allows all three sections to fit in the same column.

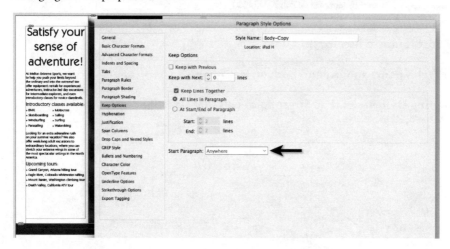

16. **Click OK to return to the layout.**

    Because you created the style groups for each alternate layout, you can edit the styles in one layout without affecting the styles in the other.

17. **Using the Selection tool, drag the bottom-center handle of the web-address text frame until it snaps to the bottom page edge.**

18. **Click the Split Window button in the bottom-right corner of the document window.**

19. **With the left pane active, choose View>Fit Page in Window.**

20. **Click in the right pane to make it active. Double-click the iPad V layout in the Pages panel, then choose View>Fit Page in Window.**

    The split window option allows you to view both alternate layouts at once. Each pane can have a separate view percentage.

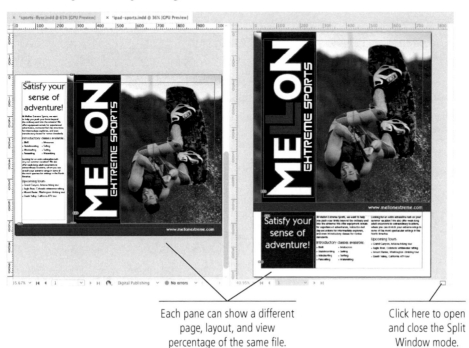

Each pane can show a different page, layout, and view percentage of the same file.

Click here to open and close the Split Window mode.

21. **Click the Split Window button again to close the split pane.**

22. **Save and close any open files.**

PROJECT REVIEW

fill in the blank

1. You can use the _____ to review the content and hierarchy of tagged frames.

2. The _____ tool is used to select objects you want to share multiple times across one or more layouts.

3. When placing shared content, the _____ displays items and sets that are ready for sharing.

4. Press _____ while dragging to place shared content at an aspect ratio other than the original.

5. True or false: The Links panel includes content placed using the Content Placer tool. _____

6. _____ is the proper name of a style that should map to a tag named Body-Copy.

7. When working with shared content, you can use the _____ options to define which options you want to keep in the linked copies when you update the links.

8. Using the _____ option, the number of columns in a text frame adjusts dynamically when the frame is resized; columns are limited to a maximum user-defined width.

9. Press _____ while dragging a page handle with the Page tool to permanently change the page size.

10. Using the _____ liquid page rule, you can pin the edges and/or dimensions of a frame, preventing that object from moving when you create an alternate layout.

short answer

1. Briefly explain the concept of using XML for repurposing content.

2. Briefly explain the differences between using XML and using the Content Collector/Placer to repurpose content.

3. Briefly explain how to prevent updated linked content from overriding changes to frame size.

PORTFOLIO BUILDER PROJECT

Use what you learned in this project to complete the following freeform exercise.
Carefully read the art director and client comments, then create your own design to meet the needs of the project.
Use the space below to sketch ideas; when finished, write a brief explanation of your reasoning behind your final design.

In order to increase marketing opportunities, your agency would like to create several more examples to showcase the ability to repurpose content for multiple media. Every designer in your agency has been asked to create a "How-To" piece in both print and digital formats.

❏ Think of something you know how to do.

❏ Write clear instructions detailing how to create or accomplish the topic you are explaining.

❏ Find or create graphics or images to illustrate your topic.

❏ Design an 8.5" × 11" print document to present the content of your tutorial.

❏ Create digital versions of your tutorial, including HTML and EPUB, as well as different variations for an iPad.

Cross-media publishing is not only the future — it's the present. The National Parks campaign is an excellent portfolio piece to showcase our capabilities, but I would like our salespeople to be able to show off more than one example when they meet with current and potential clients.

To increase our agency's portfolio, I've asked every staff designer to create a new example of cross-media publishing. I want this to be fun for you, and I want a range of different types of projects.

So, rather than give you a specific topic to work with, I want you to create a one-sheet tutorial on anything that interests you — how to rebuild a transmission, how to knit a sweater, how to sky dive, how to train a pet turtle. Your tutorial should focus on something you are good at or feel passionate about.

After you create the print version, repurpose it to prepare it for digital media.

PROJECT SUMMARY

Repurposing the same content in multiple different layouts is becoming increasingly common in the design world. This project explored two different methods for repurposing content, both for multiple print formats and for digital media.

You used unstructured XML to drag specific types of content into a layout, and you used a more structured approach to automatically place content into tagged frames of a different layout. By maintaining a link to the XML file, you were able to automatically update the placed content to reflect changes in the text.

You also used the content sharing and alternate layout capabilities built into InDesign to create different layouts from existing content. You also added interactive overlays to take better advantage of the capabilities of digital media.

Use structured XML to create a layout from all content

Use unstructured XML to create a layout from selected content

Use content sharing tools to create layouts for digital media

Create alternate layouts for different device orientations

Multi-Chapter Booklet

8

Your client, Against The Clock (ATC), publishes books related to the computer graphics industry. In addition to application-specific books, it is also creating a series of "companion" titles that discuss the concepts underlying the use of digital software: basic design principles, type, color, and so on. You were hired to build an "excerpt" booklet of the companion titles, which ATC will use for marketing purposes.

This project incorporates the following skills:

❏ Combining multiple InDesign files into a single book

❏ Synchronizing the assets in multiple files to ensure consistency from one piece to the next

❏ Building a unified table of contents for the entire book

❏ Building an index that covers all chapters of the book

❏ Using variable data to build a personalized letter

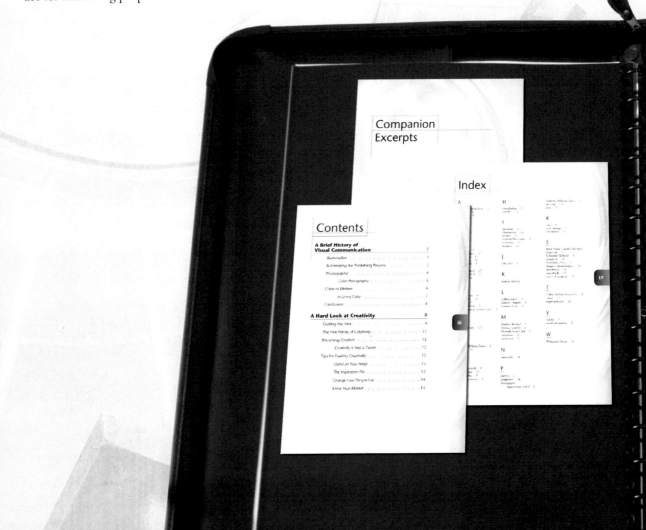

PROJECT MEETING

client comments

We are launching a new series of books that will complement our application-specific books. We want to use the existing InDesign files to create a sample excerpt booklet that we can use in digital and print advertising.

We sent you the files for the first chapters from two of the books. Unfortunately, we can't find the final file that was tagged for the *Color Companion* index. We want the booklet to include a representative index, though, so we'd like you to tag a few entries in the *Color Companion* chapter and build a mini-index for the sample. The booklet should also have its own title page and table of contents.

These booklets will be printed and mailed to clients that we selected from our database. We're asking these clients to review the sample chapters and provide quotes that we can use in marketing materials. We provided you with a comma-delimited data file that was exported from our database. We also sent you the text for a thank-you letter we want to include with the booklet.

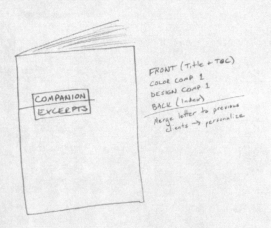

art director comments

Long documents such as books (especially non-fiction) require special elements, including a table of contents and an index. Publishers spend countless hours manually composing these elements; they literally flip through pages and handwrite every entry in a spreadsheet. Fortunately, InDesign has built-in tools that make this process far easier.

If you use styles consistently, you can build a table of contents based on those styles. An index is a bit more complicated. Although the tools for tagging and compiling ease the process, identifying index content remains a largely manual process.

The advantage of using these tools is that you need to complete the process only once. Making changes late in the process — which happens almost every time — used to mean manually recompiling the table of contents and index. Using InDesign's built-in tools, you can easily recompile both elements as often as necessary, and you can format them automatically using other styles.

project objectives

To complete this project, you will:

- ❑ Create an InDesign book file.
- ❑ Manage different files as chapters of a single book.
- ❑ Control section and page numbering across multiple chapter files.
- ❑ Synchronize assets in all files of the book.
- ❑ Build a table of contents based on styles.
- ❑ Tag index entries in each file of the book.
- ❑ Compile the index for all book chapters at once.
- ❑ Create a variable-data letter addressed to previous ATC clients.

STAGE 1 / Combining Documents into Books

Publication design is a unique subset of graphic design. Attention to detail is critical. You must ensure subhead formatting in early chapters matches subhead formatting in later chapters, captions are all set in the same font, body copy is the same size throughout the document, and so on. Regardless of whether one or several designers work on the project, consistency is essential from the first page of the book to the last. To make long-document design easier, InDesign allows you to create a special type of book file for combining and managing multiple chapters as a single unit.

Long documents are frequently split into multiple files, then combined at the end of the process to create the final job. This workflow offers several advantages:

- Layouts with numerous images can become very large; dividing these layouts into pieces helps keep the file size smaller.

- If a long document is divided into multiple stand-alone files, several designers can work on different files of the same book without the risk of accidentally overwriting another designer's work.

- If a long document is split into several files, you won't lose the entire job if a single file becomes corrupt.

InDesign's book-building tools make long-document design much easier by automating many of the tasks that used to be done manually. Of course, even though the InDesign book utilities automate much of the process, you must still — and always — pay close attention to the details of your work.

Build an InDesign Book

An InDesign book is simply a container file into which multiple InDesign files are placed for easier organization and management. The InDesign book utility offers several benefits, including:

- Synchronizing styles, colors, and other assets to the book's master file

- Monitoring page and section numbering of each individual file in the book, and the book as a whole

- Building a table of contents and index from all book files at once

- Printing or exporting the entire book, or outputting only selected chapters

1. **Download Excerpts_ID20_RF.zip from the Student Files web page.**

2. **Expand the ZIP archive in your WIP folder (Macintosh), or copy the archive contents into your WIP folder (Windows).**

   This results in a folder named **Excerpts**, which contains the files you need for this project. You should also use this folder to save the files you create in this project.

3. **With nothing open in InDesign, choose File>New>Book. Navigate to your WIP>Excerpts folder as the target location.**

   Unlike creating a new file, creating a new book requires you to immediately name and save the book file.

Note:

When a single design project is made up of several files, it is even more important to maintain consistency from one file to the next. If the font is slightly different from one issue of a newsletter to the next, few people are likely to spot the difference. That difference is far more noticeable, however, when two or more files are bound together in the same publication.

Note:

When you work with book files, you frequently open, save, and close the chapters of the book files; in fact, some operations happen without your direct intervention. Book chapter files need to be stored on a writable disk as long as you are still working on the book.

4. **Change the book name to Excerpts.indb and click Save.**

   The correct extension is automatically added for you, but if you accidentally remove it, add it to the file name.

   Clicking Save opens the Book panel; the file name you defined ("Excerpts") appears in the panel tab. By default, the Book panel floats in the workspace; you can drag it anywhere you prefer (including into a specific panel group, whether docked or not).

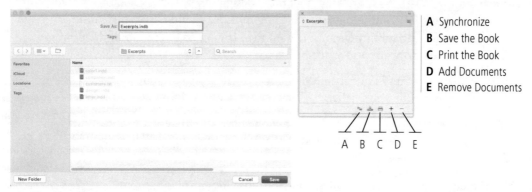

   A Synchronize
   B Save the Book
   C Print the Book
   D Add Documents
   E Remove Documents

5. **Continue to the next exercise.**

Add Book Chapters

Once the book file has been defined, adding chapters is easy. The first chapter you add becomes the style source chapter, and other chapters can be synchronized to it. You can change the book's style source by clicking the empty space to the left of a chapter.

Note:

You can save a book with a different name by choosing Save Book As from the panel Options menu.

1. **With the Excerpts book file open, click the Add Documents button at the bottom of the Book panel.**

2. **Navigate to color1.indd in your WIP>Excerpts folder and click Open.**

   Depending on the size of the chapter, it might take a few seconds to process the file. When the process is complete, the file name appears in the Book panel.

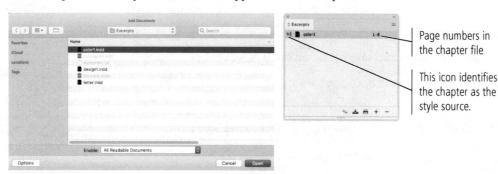

   Page numbers in the chapter file

   This icon identifies the chapter as the style source.

3. **Click the Add Documents button again. Navigate to design1.indd in your WIP>Excerpts folder and click Open.**

   New files are automatically added below the previously selected chapter. If no chapter is selected in the panel, new files are added to the end of the book.

   If you haven't changed the section or page numbering options for the files you add, new book chapters are automatically numbered sequentially from one file to the next.

4. **Create a new file by opening `companion.indt` from your WIP> Excerpts folder.**

   If you get a Profile or Policy Mismatch warning at any point in this project, select the option to leave the document as is, and click OK.

   This is the template from which the companion chapters were created. Although the two excerpt chapters are already laid out, you need to create a front matter document to hold a title page and the table of contents for the combined excerpts.

5. **In the Pages panel, drag the F-Title Page master page icon onto the Page 1 icon.**

   The front matter document will include the title page and table of contents, both conventional parts of book design, which have been planned for in the existing master page layouts. By dragging the F-Title Page master onto Page 1, you're applying the existing master page to the first page of the front matter file.

   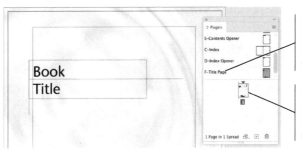

   Scroll through the master page area to find the F-Title Page master at the bottom of the list.

   Drag the F-Title Page master onto the Page 1 icon in the lower section of the Pages panel.

6. **Press Command/Control-Shift and click the Book Title text frame to detach only that object from the master page.**

   The text frame for the book title is placed on the master page; to change the text and enter the actual book title, you either have to make the change on the master page or detach the master items on the regular layout page.

7. **Using the Type tool, highlight the text "Book Title" in the text frame and type `Companion Excerpts`.**

8. **Drag the right-center handle of the text frame until the word "Excerpts" moves entirely to the second line and the right edge of the frame is approximately 1/8″ from the edge of the text.**

   Only this text frame has been detached from the master page layout.

9. **Save the file as `front-matter.indd` in your WIP>Excerpts folder, and then close the file.**

   Front matter typically refers to the information preceding the main content of a book, including a title page, table of contents, copyright information and acknowledgements, and other important elements.

10. **In the Excerpts Book panel, click the Add Documents button.**

Note:

You can open a book file the same way you open a regular document file (File>Open).

Note:

You can remove a file from a book by clicking the Remove Documents button at the bottom of the Book panel. Once you remove a chapter from a book, you can't undo the deletion. The file still exists in its original location, how-ever, so you can simply add the file back into the book, if necessary.

11. **Navigate to the `front-matter.indd` file you just created and add it to the book file.**

12. **Click the front-matter file in the panel and drag up until a heavy line appears above color1 in the panel.**

When you release the mouse button, front-matter becomes the first chapter in the book. However, color1 is still the style source; the style source does not need to be the first chapter in the book.

This line indicates the new position of the chapter.

color1 is still the style source for the book file.

Note:

When you drag a file within a book, align the thumb on the cursor icon with the location where you want to place the file.

13. **Click the Save the Book button at the bottom of the panel.**

14. **Continue to the next exercise.**

Managing Book Chapters FOUNDATIONS

When you place a file into a book, the book file acts as a container. An InDesign layout stores the path to a placed image as a reference. Books use the same methodology, storing references to the files contained within the book; the book file does not contain the actual chapter files, only links to those chapters.

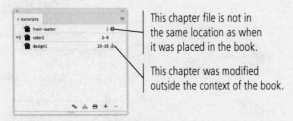

This chapter file is not in the same location as when it was placed in the book.

This chapter was modified outside the context of the book.

If the chapter files have been moved since being added to the book, the Book panel shows a missing-link warning icon. When you double-click a missing book chapter, InDesign asks if you want to replace the missing file; clicking Yes opens a

navigation dialog box so you can locate the missing file or identify a replacement file. You can also select a missing file in the panel and choose Replace Document from the Book panel Options menu.

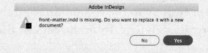

If you open a chapter using the Book panel, changes automatically reflect in the containing book. When you open a book chapter outside the context of the book, the Book panel displays a modified-link icon for that file.

You can update a modified book chapter by simply double-clicking the file in the panel to open it. When you save the chapter and close it, InDesign updates the book chapter link to reflect the most current version of the file. Once a chapter has been added to a book file, it is best to make changes only within the context of the book.

Control Section and Page Numbering

After moving the front matter chapter in front of the color chapter, the page numbers for each chapter automatically change to reflect their new positions in the book. The problem, however, is that the second file (color1) begins on Page 2 and the third file (design1) begins on Page 10. Even-numbered pages are left-facing, but book design conventions dictate that book chapters begin on right-facing (odd-numbered) pages.

1. **With the Excerpts book file open, choose Book Page Numbering Options from the Book panel Options menu.**

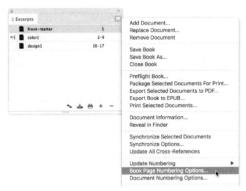

2. **In the Book Page Numbering Options dialog box, choose the Continue on Next Odd Page option.**

   You can use this dialog box to control exactly where new chapter files begin:

   - **Continue from Previous Document**, the default option, allows new chapters to pick up numbering from the end of the previous file. This option allows new chapters to begin on odd- or even-numbered pages.

   - **Continue on Next Odd Page** forces new chapter files to begin on odd-numbered pages. If your layouts use facing pages, this means new chapters will always begin on right-facing pages.

   - **Continue on Next Even Page** forces new chapter files to begin on even-numbered pages. If your layouts use facing pages, this means new chapters will always begin on left-facing pages.

Note:

Although some book designs intentionally break from convention and begin chapters on left-facing pages, this is not the norm. Right-facing chapter-starts are so common, in fact, that InDesign's long-document tools include the ability to force chapters to begin on the right side of the spread.

3. **Check the Insert Blank Page option and leave the Automatically Update option checked.**

   The Insert Blank Page option adds a blank page into any file where the defined page order leaves a blank space in the page numbering. When the Automatically Update option is checked, as it is by default, files in the book automatically adjust to reflect additional choices in this dialog box.

4. **Click OK to apply your changes.**

   The second and third files in the book now begin on odd-numbered (right-facing) pages. Blank pages have been added as necessary to fill empty spaces caused by moving the chapters to the appropriate side of the spread.

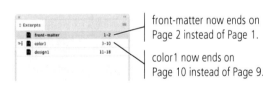

front-matter now ends on Page 2 instead of Page 1.

color1 now ends on Page 10 instead of Page 9.

Understanding Book Page Numbering

If you had not checked Insert Blank Pages in the Book Page Numbering Options dialog box, each chapter in your book would begin on a right-facing (odd-numbered) page. However, the last page in each file would remain unchanged. The image here shows the original pagination in comparison to the renumbered pages; the first page of each file is highlighted in pink. In the middle version, which shows the result of the steps you just took, blank pages are highlighted in yellow.

The third version shows what would have happened if you had not selected the Insert Blank Pages option. Although the second and third files would have begun on odd-numbered (right-facing) pages, the blank pages would not have been added to fill the space. This could cause significant problems when the book is imposed into printer's spreads for commercial printing. (Refer to Project 4: Museum Exhibits Booklet for an explanation of printer's spreads.)

Original pagination		Modified pagination inserting blank pages		Pagination without inserting blank pages	
	1		1		1
2	3	2	3		3
4	5	4	5	4	5
6	7	6	7	6	7
8	9	8	9	8	9
10	11	10	11	10	11
12	13	12	13		13
14	15	14	15	14	15
16		16	17	16	17
		18		18	

5. **In the Book panel, click the front-matter file to select it.**

6. **Open the Book panel Options menu, then choose Document Numbering Options.**

In addition to controlling the page numbering from one file to another, you can also control the page numbering for a specific file. This option is useful if, for example, you want the front matter of a book to be numbered separately from the main body of the document.

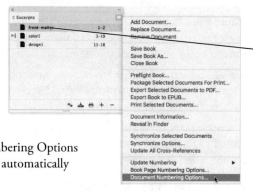

The front-matter file is selected in the Book panel.

To change document-specific settings, such as page numbering and sections, the document must be open. When you choose Document Numbering Options in the Book panel Options menu, the selected file automatically opens so you can make changes.

7. **Choose lowercase Roman numerals in the Page Numbering Style menu.**

This is another convention in book design and layout: the front matter is numbered separately from the main part of the book, commonly in lowercase Roman numerals.

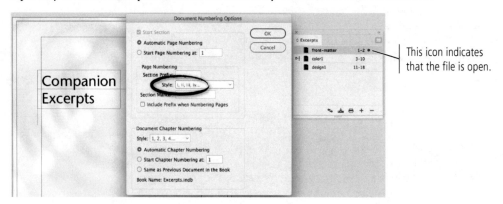

This icon indicates that the file is open.

8. **Click OK to apply the change, save the open layout, and then close the file.**

   In the Book panel, the front-matter file reflects the new numbering style. The problem, however, is that the first *content* chapter begins on Page 3; publishing convention typically specifies that the main content of a book begins on Page 1. To accomplish this goal, you can start a new section with the color1 chapter.

9. **Double-click color1 in the Book panel.**

   Double-clicking a file in the Book panel automatically opens that file.

10. **Control/right-click the Page 3 icon in the Pages panel and choose Numbering & Section Options.**

    This command opens a dialog box similar to the Document Numbering Options dialog box. The primary difference is that this dialog box provides options for controlling a specific page (in this case, Page 3, which you Control/right-clicked to access the dialog box).

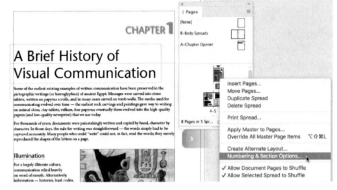

11. **In the Numbering & Section Options dialog box, choose the Start Page Numbering At option and change the number in the field to 1.**

    InDesign's default behavior — the Automatic Page Numbering option — causes pages to number sequentially from one file to the next in the book. By choosing the Start Page Numbering At option, you can override the default page numbering and determine the exact page number of any file in the book.

Note:

The page numbering of a book relies on the Current Page Number marker (Type>Insert Special Character>Markers> Current Page Number).

12. **Click OK to apply the new page number to the first page of the color1 file.**

    Because you haven't changed the numbering options for the design1 file or any specific page in that file, it is still automatically numbered in sequence with the color1 file.

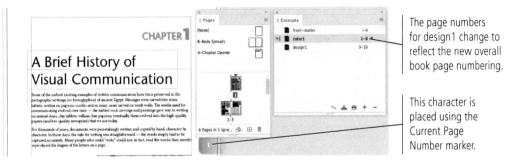

The page numbers for design1 change to reflect the new overall book page numbering.

This character is placed using the Current Page Number marker.

13. **Save the open document (color1) and close it.**

14. **In the Book panel, click the Save the Book button, and then continue to the next exercise.**

Section and Page Numbering in a Single File

Sections allow you to create different page numbering sequences within a single file. For any section start page, you can restart page numbering at a specific page number, change the style of page numbers in the section, define a section marker for the section, and/or include the section prefix in the page number.

When you choose Numbering & Section Options in the contextual menu of a page that isn't already a section start, the New Section dialog box opens with the Start Section option automatically checked. If you choose Numbering & Section Options for an existing section start page, the choices in the resulting dialog box are exactly the same as those in the New Section dialog box; the only differences are the title bar and the choices already selected when you open the dialog box.

When you click OK in the New Section dialog box, the selected page is designated as a section start.

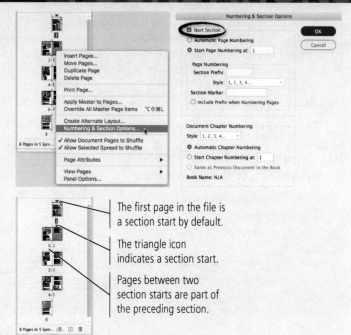

The first page in the file is a section start by default.

The triangle icon indicates a section start.

Pages between two section starts are part of the preceding section.

Adding Section Prefixes

If you use Page Number markers (Type>Insert Special Character>Markers>Current/Next/Previous Page Number), you can add a prefix to page numbers by checking the Include Prefix when Numbering Pages option. Whatever you type in the Section Prefix field is added in front of the page number.

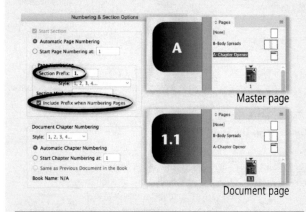

Master page

Document page

Chapter Numbering

When you work with book files, you can also define Document Chapter Numbering options, which is basically file numbering.

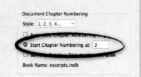

If you define a specific chapter number in the Numbering & Section Options dialog box, you can place the built-in Chapter Number variable (Type>Text Variables>Insert Variable>Chapter Number) to reflect the current chapter number.

Adding Section Markers

Section markers are a type of variable. You can define the Section Marker text for a specific section, and then place the marker into the layout (Type>Insert Special Character>Markers>Section Marker).

The Section Marker special character displays the text in the Section Marker field of the Numbering & Section Options dialog box. If a section has no defined Section Marker text, the special character displays nothing.

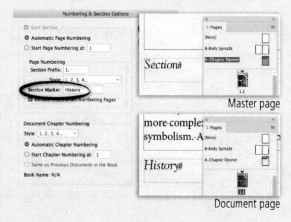

Master page

Document page

Synchronize Book Files

A primary advantage of using the InDesign book-building functionality is the ability to easily synchronize various assets — swatches, styles, etc. — across multiple chapter files to ensure consistency throughout a publication.

When a book is synchronized, assets in the style source file are applied to all other files in the book. (The synchronization process does not affect elements that are not in the style source file.)

- If an asset in the Style Source file does not exist in other book files, it is simply added to the other files.

- If an asset already exists in the other book files, the element definition from the Style Source file is applied to the same-named element in the other files.

In this exercise, you synchronize the assets in the Companion Excerpts files to ensure both the highlight color has the same definition in all files and the appearance of text styles is consistent throughout the document.

1. **With the Excerpts book file open, double-click the front-matter file to open that document.**

2. **Open the Swatches panel, and then open the Swatch Options dialog box for the Companion Color swatch.**

3. **Change the swatch definition to C=70 M=100 Y=0 K=0 and make sure the Name with Color Value option is not checked.**

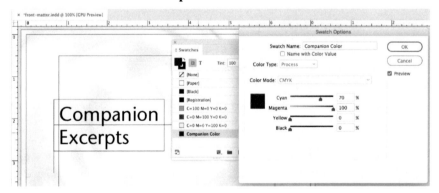

Note:

The synchronization process does not create any type of report showing what has been done in which files. Some experts prefer to back up their book files before synchronization in case they need to go back to the pre-synchronized files for any reason.

Each book in the Companion series was printed with a different highlight color. When combining chapters from different books in the series, the highlight color needs to be unified for consistency throughout the "combo" document. In this excerpt booklet, the client decided to use a purple shade as the highlight color.

This is an instance where there is good reason to break from the color-naming convention based on color definition. The swatch is different in all companion books, but the swatch is named the same in all files of all books. By synchronizing the color in all book files to this new definition, you can change the Companion Color swatch in multiple files at one time.

4. **Click OK to close the Swatch Options dialog box, save the document and close it, but leave the book file open.**

5. **In the Book panel, click the empty space to the left of the front-matter file to redefine the style source.**

Since the front-matter.indd file now has the Companion Color swatch definition you want to use for the entire document, you need to synchronize other files in the book to the excerpt front file.

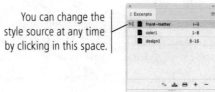

You can change the style source at any time by clicking in this space.

6. **Click in the empty area at the bottom of the Book panel to deselect all files.**

If nothing is selected in the Book panel, all chapter files will be synchronized to the style source file. You can also synchronize specific files by selecting them in the Book panel before clicking the Synchronize button. Of course, synchronizing only certain files defeats the purpose of synchronizing, but the option is available nonetheless.

7. **In the Book panel Options menu, choose Synchronize Options.**

Click in this space to deselect all chapters in the book.

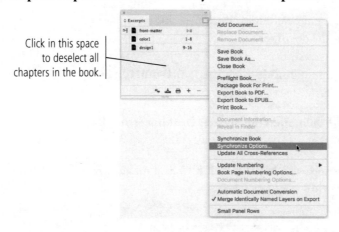

8. **In the Synchronize Options dialog box, uncheck all options except Character Styles, Paragraph Styles, and Swatches. At the bottom of the dialog box, leave the Smart Match Style Groups checked.**

In this simple project, your primary concern is consistency of appearance between existing files from the same series of books. The three selected options are sufficient for this project. In other cases where you combine radically different files from multiple designers, it might be useful — or even vital — to synchronize the other types of assets as well.

9. **Click OK to close the dialog box.**

10. **In the Book panel, click the Synchronize button.**

11. **Click OK in the resulting warning.**

As we mentioned, synchronizing book files can cause problems. InDesign is smart enough to recognize and warn you about one of the most common and serious problems: overset text.

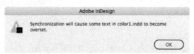

12. When the process is complete, click OK to dismiss the resulting message.

This message warns you of a potential problem caused by synchronization: documents might have changed. When you synchronize book files, you should carefully review the pages to be sure content is still where it belongs.

13. Double-click color1 in the Book panel to open that file, and navigate to Page 8.

When you synchronize files, you often have no idea what caused the problem: but you still need to fix it. You have several options:

- Edit the text to fit the overset line in the available space. (This assumes you have permission to edit text, which you usually do not.)

- Add text frames to the chain. This typically assumes you can add pages to a file, which you often can't.

- Change style definitions to fit text into the available space. If you synchronize again later, your changes will again be overwritten.

- Adjust local formatting of specific text to make the layout work properly.

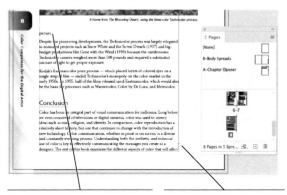

The last line of the last paragraph on Page 7 now appears on Page 8.

The reflowed text causes the overset text icon to appear.

14. On Page 7 of the file, click four times to select the entire last paragraph. Using the Character panel, change the tracking of the selected paragraph to -10.

After changing the tracking for the selected paragraph, the last line again fits on Page 7.

Note:

Layout designers frequently manipulate and tweak to force-fit text into available space, to make a runaround work correctly, or to achieve a specific effect. When the files are combined into a book, these adjustments can cause problems.

15. Navigate to Page 8 and review the text.

The end-of-story character now shows, and the overset text icon no longer appears.

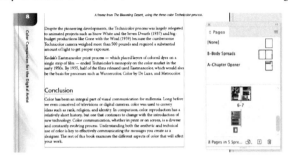

Note:

Instead of placing only one line of text on Page 9 and inserting a blank Page 10, the Tracking setting for the body text style was reduced in the original color1 file to fit the text in eight pages.

16. Save the document and close it.

17. Save the book file and continue to the next stage of the project.

Smart Matching Style Groups

The Smart Match Style Groups option is useful if you use groups (folders) to organize styles in your layout files. The following images show the results of synchronizing styles that are stored in style groups.

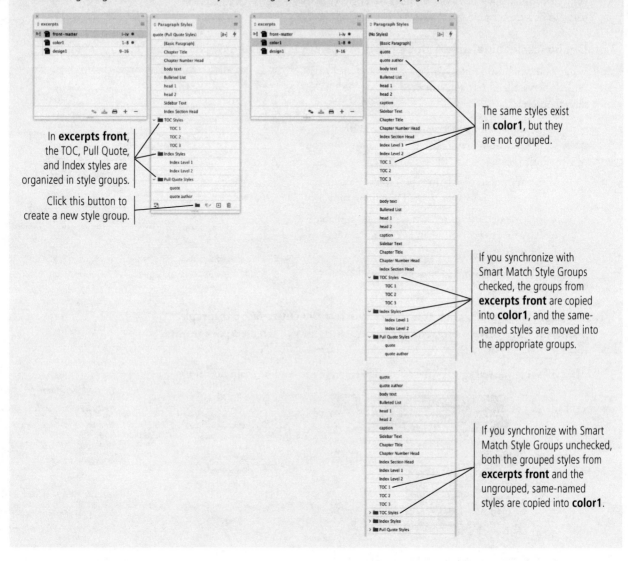

In **excerpts front**, the TOC, Pull Quote, and Index styles are organized in style groups.

Click this button to create a new style group.

The same styles exist in **color1**, but they are not grouped.

If you synchronize with Smart Match Style Groups checked, the groups from **excerpts front** are copied into **color1**, and the same-named styles are moved into the appropriate groups.

If you synchronize with Smart Match Style Groups unchecked, both the grouped styles from **excerpts front** and the ungrouped, same-named styles are copied into **color1**.

STAGE 2 / Building a Table of Contents

Before desktop-publishing software automated the document-design process, tables of contents and other lists (figures, tables, etc.) were created manually from page proofs — by turning each page and writing down the appropriate text and page number and then sorting and typesetting those hard-copy lists into the final document. The process was extremely time-consuming and required precise attention to detail. If the document changed after the lists were completed, the entire piece had to be rechecked, one page at a time.

Fortunately, InDesign includes a Table of Contents feature to automate this process, greatly decreasing production time and making it easier to maintain accuracy. InDesign tables of contents are based on the paragraph styles used in a layout. If you are conscientious about applying styles when you build a layout, you can easily create a thorough, accurate table of contents based on those styles.

You can define the styles included in the compiled table of contents. For example, a table of contents might include Heading 1, Heading 2, and Heading 3 paragraph styles; any text set in those styles will appear in the list.

You can also determine the styles used to format different elements in the compiled table of contents. Using the same example, TOC1 can be assigned to Heading 1 list items, TOC2 to Heading 2 items, and so on. When you compile the table of contents into the file, it is formatted automatically.

Define a Table of Contents Style

A table of contents (TOC) can be defined and applied in a single process. You can also create and save table of contents styles, which you can apply as needed in the active file, as well as import into and apply in other files. Because of the versatility allowed by styles of all types (paragraph, table, object, etc.), we recommend creating table of contents styles rather than defining a single-case table of contents.

1. **With the Excerpts book file open, double-click the front-matter file in the panel to open that file.**

2. **Drag the E-Contents Opener master page to the right of the Page ii icon.**

   When the new page is added, another blank page is also added because of your choices (Insert Blank Page) in the Book Page Numbering Options dialog box.

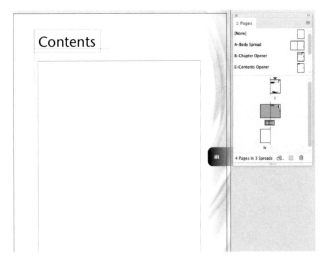

3. **Choose Layout>Table of Contents Styles.**

   You can create new styles, edit or delete existing styles, or load styles from other files.

4. **Click New. In the resulting New Table of Contents Style dialog box, type** Companion Contents **in the TOC Style field.**

   The TOC Style field defines the style name. It is basically the same as a paragraph style name (an identifier).

5. **Delete the text from the Title field.**

   The Title field, on the other hand, is actual text that is included at the top of the compiled table of contents. Because the "Contents" title for this layout is built into the master page, you should not include a title in the compiled table of contents.

6. **If necessary, click the More Options button on the right side of the dialog box.**

   When More Options are showing, you can control the appearance of page numbers in the table of contents.

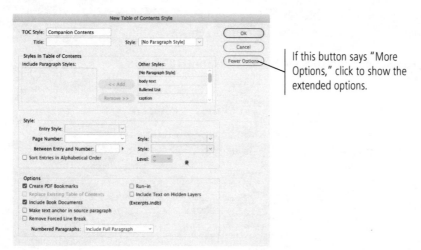

If this button says "More Options," click to show the extended options.

7. **Scroll though the Other Styles list, select Chapter Title, and click the Add button.**

8. **In the middle section of the dialog box, choose TOC 1 in the Entry Style menu.**

9. Choose After Entry in the Page Number field, and choose TOC Page Number in the associated Style menu. Leave all other options at their default settings.

You can define a number of options for each style included in a table of contents:

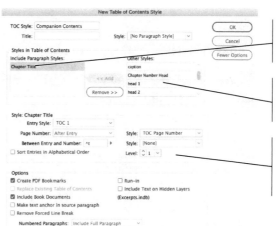

This list shows styles included in the table of contents.

This is the list of paragraph styles available in the file.

These options define the appearance and content of listings in the table of contents.

- **Entry Style** defines the paragraph style applied to those entries in the compiled list.

- **Page Number** determines where the page number will be included for each entry (After Entry or Before Entry). You can also choose No Page Number to add the list entry without the associated page number.

- **Between Entry and Number** defines the character(s) placed between the list entry and the associated page number. The default option (^t) is the code for a Tab character. The attached menu includes a number of common special characters, or you can type the code for a specific special character.

- You can use the **Style** menus in the right column to define separate character styles for the page number and the character between the entry and page number. If you don't choose a character style in one or both of these menus, those element will be formatted with the paragraph style settings defined for the list entry.

- If the **Sort Entries in Alphabetical Order** option is checked, the compiled list entries will appear in alphabetical order rather than page-number order.

- By default, each new style in the Include pane is added one level lower than the previous style. You can use the **Level** menu to change the hierarchy of styles in the list.

10. In the Other Styles list, highlight head 1 and click Add. In the Style section of the dialog box, define the following options:

- **Entry Style:** TOC 2
- **Page Number:** After Entry
- **[Page Number] Style:** TOC Page Number

This label shows the active style, for which you are defining formatting options.

11. **In the Other Styles list, highlight head 2 and click Add. Define the following Style options:**

- **Entry Style:** TOC 3
- **Page Number:** After Entry
- **[Page Number] Style:** TOC Page Number

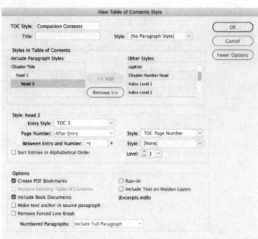

12. **In the Options area, check the Create PDF Bookmarks and Include Book Documents options.**

- **Create PDF Bookmarks** tags the table of contents entries to appear in the Bookmarks panel of Adobe Acrobat or Adobe Reader when the document is exported to PDF.

- **Replace Existing Table of Contents** is only available if a table of contents has already been built in the open file. This option is more relevant when you build the table of contents than when you define a table of contents style.

- **Include Book Documents** allows you to build a single table of contents for all files in an InDesign book file. This option is only available if the open file is part of an InDesign book.

- **Run-in** builds a list in which all entries run into a single paragraph; individual entries are separated by a semicolon.

- **Include Text on Hidden Layers** adds list entries even if the text is on a hidden layer. This option is unchecked by default, and it should almost always remain that way — unless you have a very specific reason for listing elements that do not actually appear in the document.

- The **Numbered Paragraphs** menu determines whether the list entry includes the full numbered paragraph (number and text), only the numbers, or only the text.

13. **Click OK to return to the Table of Contents Styles dialog box.**

14. **Click OK to close the Table of Contents Styles dialog box and return to the document window.**

15. **Save the file and continue to the next exercise.**

Note:

Different types of projects call for different types of lists. Although called the Table of Contents utility, you can use it to build a list of any editorial element formatted with a paragraph style. For example, some publications call for a separate table of contents for illustrations. If you define and apply a Figure Heading paragraph style, you can create a list of all entries formatted with that style.

Build and Update a Table of Contents

Once a list is defined, you can build it into the layout very easily. In fact, when you build a table of contents, the compiled list loads into the cursor; you can click to place the loaded list just as you would place any other text element.

1. **With front-matter.indd open from the Excerpts Book panel, choose Layout>Table of Contents.**

   This dialog box has the same options as those available when you defined a TOC style. The only difference is that here you define a one-time table of contents list, although you can click the Save Style button to create a style based on your choices.

2. **Make sure Companion Contents is selected in the TOC Style menu.**

   Because it is the only style in the open file, it should be selected by default. The options in this dialog box should already reflect the choices you defined in the Table of Contents style in the previous exercise.

3. **Click OK.**

   When the list is ready, it loads into the cursor. This process might take a while to complete depending on the size of your book, so don't panic or try to force-quit the application. If you're working on a very large book (such as this 500-plus-page Portfolio Series book), now is probably a good time for a coffee break.

4. **Click the loaded cursor in the middle of Page iii to place the TOC into the text frame on the page.**

   That's all there is to building a table of contents, whether for a single file or multiple documents in an InDesign book file. After a TOC is built into a document, it is a static block of text. The applied styles can be changed like any other styles, and you can change the text frame in which a list is placed. You can change or delete items from the list without affecting the main layout.

   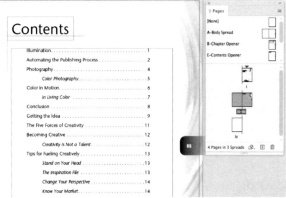

5. **Double-click color1 in the Book panel to open the file, and navigate to Page 1. Command/Control-Shift-click the frame containing the document title to detach that frame from the master page.**

The table of contents built for this file reveals one problem: text that exists on the master page only is not included in the compiled lists. The text frames for each chapter title have not been detached from the master pages, which means that text only exists on the

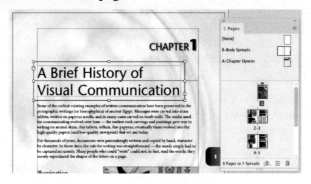

master pages, so the chapter titles do not appear in the compiled list.

Note:

Be careful when building a table of contents for an InDesign book. For a book TOC to function properly, the styles must be consistent in every chapter file. In other words, you shouldn't format second-level headings with "Head 2" in one chapter, "H2" in another chapter, and "Heading 2" in other chapters. If you do, the TOC has to include all three of those styles as separate list items.

Capitalization counts, too; when building a table of contents, "Head 2" is not the same as "head 2."

6. **Save the file and close it.**

7. **Repeat Steps 5–6 on the first page of the design1 file (Page 9 in the book) to detach the title text frame from the master page.**

8. **With Page iii of the front-matter file showing, place the insertion point anywhere within the current table of contents and then choose Layout>Update Table of Contents. Click OK in the resulting message.**

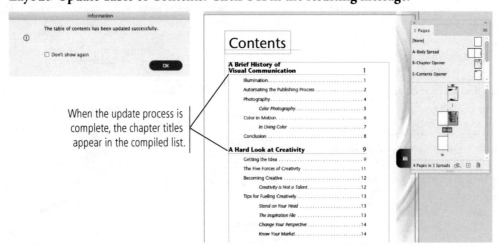

When the update process is complete, the chapter titles appear in the compiled list.

9. **Save your changes and close the document.**

10. **Save the book file and continue to the next stage of the project.**

STAGE 3 / Building an Index

As with tables of contents, creating an index used to be an extremely time-consuming and labor-intensive process. However, InDesign includes an Index tool to manage and automate part of the indexing process, improving the production workflow and saving considerable time when changes are inevitably made. Nonetheless, the process of identifying relevant terms and tagging them for inclusion in the index must still be done manually. Despite the manual nature of the process, some advance planning can make your indexing life easier. While you can always change the style definitions later in the process, indexing involves a number of styles you *should* plan in advance:

- Paragraph styles for index headings (if you decide to use them).

- Paragraph styles for up to four levels of index entries. If you don't define these styles in advance, they will be automatically created for you when you generate the index.

- Character styles for the page numbers of each index entry (if you want them to be formatted differently than the paragraph style used for the index entry).

- Character styles for cross-references (if you want them to be formatted differently than the index entry).

Tag Basic and Reversed Index Topics

1. **Double-click color1 in the Excerpts Book panel to open that document.**

2. **Choose Window>Type & Tables>Index to open the Index panel.**

3. **On Page 1 of the open document, highlight the word "hieroglyphics" in the middle of the second line of text.**

   A Go to Selected Marker
   B Update Preview
   C Generate Index
   D Create New Index Entry
   E Delete Selected Entry

A B C D E

Note:

Reference mode (the default) is used to add index entries in a layout. Topic mode is used to define a list of topics and review the hierarchy of included topics before compiling the index.

4. **Click the Create New Index Entry button at the bottom of the Index panel.**

   The New Page Reference dialog box shows the highlighted text in the first Topic Levels field.

5. **Make sure the Type menu is set to Current Page and click OK.**

   You can define a number of different types of index entries; the Current Page option adds a reference to the page number where the text is currently highlighted.

   When you close the New Page Reference dialog box, you see the highlighted text is preceded by a large carat character. This nonprinting character is an **index marker**. It indicates the location of a tagged reference, but it will not appear in the output job.

6. **If hidden characters are not showing, choose Type>Show Hidden Characters.**

7. **In the Index panel, click the arrow to the left of the "H", and then click the arrow to the left of the word "hieroglyphics".**

   You can see the topic was added using the text in the Topic Levels field, and the reference was added with the Current Page number of the highlighted text.

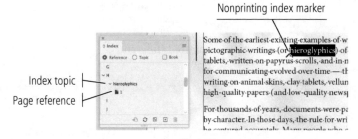

Nonprinting index marker

Index topic

Page reference

8. **Click the arrow to collapse the "H" section of the Index panel.**

9. **Highlight the word "papyrus" in the next line.**

10. **Macintosh: Press Command-Option-Shift-Left Bracket ([).**
    Windows: Press Control-Alt-Shift-Left Bracket ([).

    This key command adds a new Current Page reference without opening the New Page Reference dialog box.

11. **In the Index panel, expand the "P" list and the "papyrus" topic.**

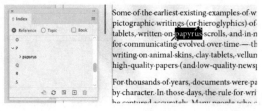

12. **Create new Current Page references to "rock carvings", "clay tablets", and "vellum" in the same paragraph.**

13. **On Page 2 of the document, highlight the words "Johannes Gutenberg" in the second line of the first paragraph after the "Automating…" heading.**

14. **Macintosh: Press Command-Option-Shift-Right Bracket (])**
    Windows: Press Control-Alt-Shift-Right Bracket (])

    This key command adds a reversed topic reference to this name.

15. In the Index panel, expand the "G" list and the nested index topic.

The highlighted text was added in reverse order (last word, first word). The reference for index markers is always the current page unless you intentionally change the reference type in the New Page Reference dialog box.

16. On Page 4 of the layout, highlight the words "William Henry Fox Talbot" in the first line of the second paragraph.

17. Press Command-Option-Shift-] (Macintosh) or Control-Alt-Shift-] (Windows) to add a reversed topic reference to this name. Review the entry in the Index panel.

Only the last word of the highlighted text is placed before the comma in the index topic.

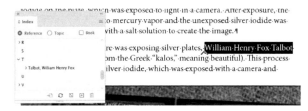

This index topic is technically correct because some people might look for the last name "Talbot" to find information about this person. Others, however, might look for his full last name ("Fox Talbot"), so you should add another index entry for the same text.

18. In the text, highlight the space character between the words "Fox" and "Talbot". Choose Type>Insert White Space>Nonbreaking Space.

Note:

The key command for a nonbreaking space is Command-Option-X/Control-Alt-X.

19. Highlight the entire name again and press Command-Option-Shift-] or Control-Alt-Shift-] to add a reversed topic reference to this name. Review the entry in the Index panel.

"^S" is the code for a non-breaking space.

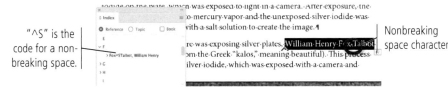

Nonbreaking space character

20. Scan the text of the document and add Current Page index entries to all people mentioned in the chapter. Add all names in reverse order, using nonbreaking spaces as necessary to keep compound last names together.

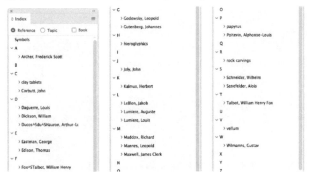

21. Save the document and continue to the next exercise.

Add Multiple Page References

In some cases, you need to add multiple references to a specific index topic. Rather than searching through the text to find every instance of the topic, you can use the Add All button in the New Page Reference dialog box.

1. **With the color1.indd file open from the Excerpts Book panel, navigate to Page 3 of the layout.**

2. **Highlight the word "Printing" at the beginning of the first full paragraph, then click the Create New Index Entry button at the bottom of the Index panel.**

3. **In the New Page Reference dialog box, click the Add All button.**

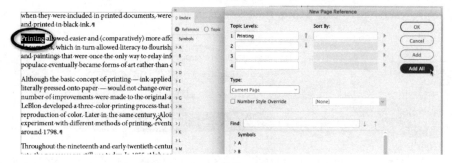

4. **Click Done to close the New Page Reference dialog box.**

5. **In the Index panel, expand the "Printing" topic in the "P" list.**

   When creating an index, topics are case-sensitive. "Printing" is not the same as "printing." The word "Printing" is capitalized only once in the layout, so the Add All function added only one reference to the topic "Printing".

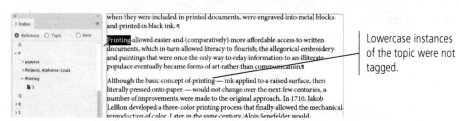

Lowercase instances of the topic were not tagged.

6. **Highlight the word "printing" in the first line of the second full paragraph and click the Create New Index Entry button.**

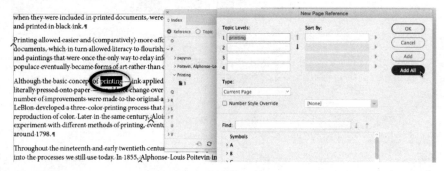

7. **In the New Page Reference dialog box, click the Add All button and then click Done.**

Note:

After you click Add or Add All in the New Page Reference dialog box, the OK button changes to Done.

8. **Review the new topic and references in the Index panel.**

Your index now includes two references to the same term, one capitalized and one lowercase. This is not good practice, so you need to combine the two terms.

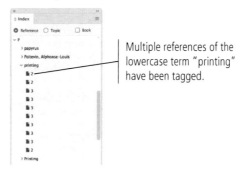

Multiple references of the lowercase term "printing" have been tagged.

9. **In the Index panel, double-click the capitalized "Printing" topic.**

Double-clicking a term in the panel opens the Topic Options dialog box.

10. **In the pane at the bottom of the Topic Options dialog box, expand the "P" list.**

This pane shows all topics currently used in the document or book. In this case, you are working with an InDesign book; topics defined in the other book files, such as "Perspective," are also included in the topic list.

11. **Double-click "printing" in the topic list.**

Double-clicking an existing topic changes the text in the Topic Levels field.

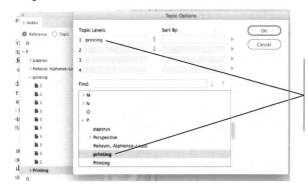

Double-clicking the lowercase "printing" topic in the list changes the text of the topic ("Printing") you are editing.

This method of choosing an existing topic also works in the New Page Reference dialog box. When you double-click a topic in the list at the bottom of the dialog box, text in the Topic Levels field changes to reflect the topic you double-click. The index marker will be placed at the location of the highlighted text, but the reference will be added for whatever was shown in the Topic Levels field.

12. **Click OK to close the dialog box, and then review the "P" list in the Index panel.**

Your index now includes a single reference to the term "printing." The page reference for the previously capitalized term has been merged into the references for the lowercase term.

13. **Save the file and continue to the next exercise.**

Add Page-Range References

Index references are not limited to single page numbers. You can use the Type menu in the New Page Reference dialog box to define several other reference types:

- **Current Page** includes a single-page reference for the index entry.

- **To Next Style Change** references a page range that starts at the insertion point and ends at the first point where a different paragraph style has been applied.

- **To Next Use of Style** references a page range that starts at the insertion point and ends at the first instance in the story where a specific paragraph style has been applied. You select the style that ends the range.

- **To End of Story** references a page range that starts at the insertion point and ends at the last page of the current story.

- **To End of Document** references a page range that starts at the insertion point and ends at the last page of the current document.

- **To End of Section** references a page range that starts at the insertion point and ends at the last page of the current section.

- **For Next # of Paragraphs** references a page range that starts at the insertion point and ends after the defined number of paragraphs.

- **For Next # of Pages** references a page range that starts at the insertion point and ends after the defined number of pages.

- **Suppress Page Range** references a topic with no associated page number.

1. With the **color1.indd** file open from the **Excerpts** Book panel, navigate to Page 1 of the layout.

2. Highlight the word "History" in the chapter title and click the Create New Index Entry button in the Index panel.

3. In the New Page Reference dialog box, change the capital "H" in the first Topic Levels field to a lowercase "h".

4. Choose To End of Document in the Type menu and click the Add button.

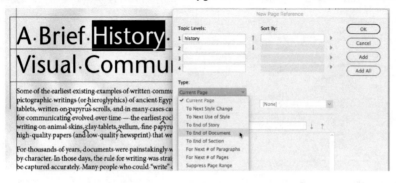

5. Click Done to close the dialog box and then review the new topic and reference in the Index panel.

The page-range reference has been added; the document ends on Page 8, so the reference extends from Pages 1–8.

6. Highlight the word "Illumination" in the heading on Page 1 and click the Create New Index Entry button.

7. In the Type menu, choose To Next Use of Style. In the related Style menu, choose head 1.

This heading is formatted with the head 1 style. You are adding a reference that spans all text between this heading and the next instance of the head 1 style.

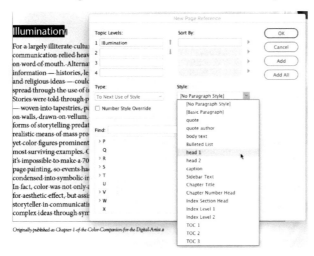

8. Click Add, and then click Done to close the dialog box.

9. Review the new topic and reference in the Index panel.

The new reference points to the current page only and not to the actual next instance of the head 1 style.

This problem highlights an apparent bug in the software or at least something that does not work intuitively. When you highlight text formatted with the same style defined in the To Next Use of Style menu, InDesign identifies the highlighted text as the next use of the style, and the reference points to the location of the highlighted text only. Solving this problem requires a work-around.

10. In the Index panel, click the "1" reference to the "Illumination" topic and click the panel's Delete button.

11. In the resulting message, click Yes to confirm the deletion.

Note:

If you delete a term from the index, all references to that term are also deleted.

12. In the document, highlight the word "For" at the beginning of the paragraph after the Illumination heading.

13. Click the Create New Index Entry button in the Index panel.

14. Change the text in the first Topic Level field to illumination.

15. In the Type menu, choose To Next Use of Style. In the related Style menu, choose head 1.

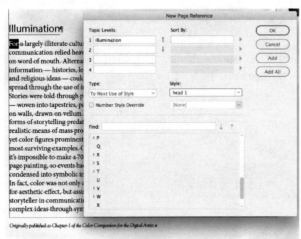

16. Click Add, and then click Done to close the dialog box.

17. Review the new topic and reference in the Index panel.

The new reference shows the correct range between the selected text and the next instance of the head 1 paragraph style (on Page 2 of the document).

18. Save the file and continue to the next exercise.

Add Multiple-Level References

You might have noticed the New Page Reference dialog box includes four fields in the Topic Levels area. These fields allow you to created multilevel or nested index entries. You can create up to four levels of nested index entries, depending on the complexity a particular project requires.

1. **With the `color1.indd` file open through the `Excerpts` Book panel, navigate to Page 4 of the layout.**

2. **Highlight the words "daguerreotype method" in the second line of the first paragraph. Click the Create New Index Entry button in the Index panel.**

3. **In the New Page Reference dialog box, click the down-arrow button in the Topic Levels area.**

   This button moves the selected term down one level to become a second-level index term. Of course, when you add a second-level term, you also need to define the parent term for that nested entry.

4. **Click the first Topic Levels field and type `photography`.**

   You can select an existing topic as the first level or type a new term in the field.

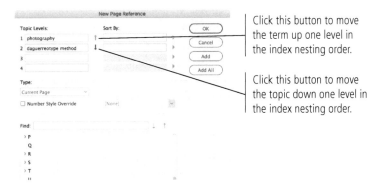

Click this button to move the term up one level in the index nesting order.

Click this button to move the topic down one level in the index nesting order.

5. **Click OK to add the term and reference to the index.**

6. **In the Index panel, expand the "photography" entry in the "P" list.**

This second-level term is listed under the new first-level "photography" term.

7. **Save the color1 file and close it, then continue to the next exercise.**

Changing Topic Sort Order

The Sort By field allows you to change the alphabetical order of an index topic in the built index. When the index is built, the entries will appear in the list based on the Sort By text, but the entry text will still be the text defined in the Topic Levels field.

This option is particularly useful for indexing abbreviations and proper names. In the examples shown here, the abbreviated text "Mt." will be alphabetized according to the full word "Mount". The name "Benjamin Franklin" will appear in the index under F instead of B, alphabetized by last name but appearing in the text in standard first name/last name order.

Defining Cross-References

A cross-referenced item refers the reader to another index entry. For example, the index entry for "CIELAB" might say, "See LAB color." If you choose to create an entry as a cross-reference, you also need to define the type of notation. The Referenced field defines the topic to which a cross-reference will point; you can type in the field or drag a topic into the field from the list at the bottom of the dialog box.

- **See [also]** allows InDesign to choose the appropriate cross-reference method: "See" if the topic has no page references of its own or "See also" if the topic includes page numbers.

- **See** refers the reader to another topic or topics; the entry has no page number, only text listing the cross-referenced topic. For example, if the index entry is "Dogs", the cross-reference might be "See Canine".

- **See also** directs attention to the current topic, as well as other information elsewhere in the index. For example, an index item called "Dogs" may have its own list of page numbers and then a cross-reference to "See also Pets".

- **See herein** and **See also herein** refer the reader to entries within the current index entry. For example, if the main (Level 1) index entry is "Dogs", you might want to direct the index to a subentry (Level 2 or Level 3 item) that might not be expected under this heading, such as "See herein Wolf".

- **[Custom Cross-Reference]** allows you to define the text that will be used as the cross-reference, such as "Go to" or some similar text.

Build the Book's Index

Building an index into a document is very similar to building a table of contents. Once the index has been generated, it is loaded into the cursor so you can place it in the layout. When you are working with a book file, you can build the index into an existing chapter file, or you can add a separate back matter file to hold the index.

1. Open the **companion.indt** template from the WIP>Excerpts folder to create a new file.

2. Drag the D-Index Opener master page onto the Page 1 icon.

3. Save the file as **back-matter.indd** in your WIP>Excerpts folder, then close it.

   Back matter is anything after the primary chapters of a document, such as appendices and an index.

4. In the **Excerpts** Book panel, make sure nothing is selected in the panel and click the Add Documents button.

5. Navigate to the file **back-matter.indd** in your WIP>Excerpts folder and click Open.

6. Open the Synchronize Options dialog box from the Book panel Options menu.

7. Deselect all options but the Swatches check box. At the bottom of the dialog box, leave the Smart Match Style Groups checked. Click OK.

8. **Make sure no files are selected in the Book panel and click the Synchronize button at the bottom of the panel. Click OK to acknowledge the synchronization is complete.**

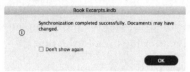

Note:

You can preview all index entries in a book file by opening the individual chapter files and checking the Book option at the top of the Index panel. (The panel only shows entries for files that are currently open.)

9. **Double-click the `back-matter` file in the Book panel to open the file.**

   This file has no defined index markers, so nothing appears in the panel.

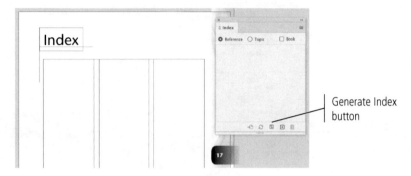

Generate Index button

10. **At the bottom of the Index panel, click the Generate Index button.**

11. **In the Generate Index dialog box, delete the word "Index" from the Title field.**

   The Title and Title Style options are the same as the related options for building a table of contents. Because the master page you're using already includes the title "Index", you should not include a title in the built index.

12. **Select the Include Book Documents option.**

   Even though there are no index references in this back-matter file, it is part of the book with files that have index markers.

13. **If the third button on the right reads "More Options," click the button to expand the dialog box.**

14. Click the Following Topic menu and choose Em Space as the character that will appear between the entry text and the associated references.

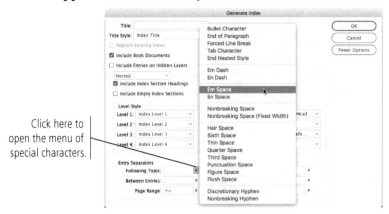

Click here to open the menu of special characters.

Options for Generating an Index

When you generate an index, you have a number of options for automatically formatting the compiled list. In many cases, the default settings will work perfectly well, but you can change any or all of the following options as necessary:

- The **Nested** or **Run-in** menu determines how individual entries in the index are placed. Nested creates each entry on its own line. Run-In forces all index entries to run together in the same paragraph.

- If **Include Index Section Headings** is checked, alphabetical headings (A, B, C, etc.) are added to the index.

- If **Include Empty Index Sections** is checked, all letter headings are added to the built index, even if that letter has no associated terms.

- The **Level Style** menu defines paragraph styles used to format different levels of index entries. If you don't choose different styles in these menus, the default options (Index Level 1, etc.) are created and applied to the headings. If you define your own style named "Index Level 1," your settings are applied in the built index.

- The **Section Heading** menu defines paragraph styles used to format the section headings in the index. If you don't choose a different style, the default Index Section Head is created and applied to the headings. If you define your own style named "Index Section Head," your settings are applied in the built index.

- The **Page Number** menu defines the character style applied to page numbers in the generated index.

- The **Cross-Reference** menu defines the character style applied to the cross-references in the index (for example, the "See also" part of "See also LAB color").

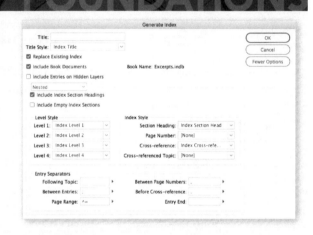

- The **Cross-Referenced Topic** menu defines the character style applied to the text of a cross-reference (for example, the "LAB color" part of "See also LAB color").

- The **Entry Separators** area defines the characters used in specific parts of the index:

  - **Following Topic** is used between the entry text and the entry page references.

  - **Between Page Numbers** is used between individual page references.

  - **Between Entries** is used between entries in a run-in index.

  - **Before Cross-reference** is used before the text of a cross-reference.

  - **Page Range** separates numbers in a page range.

  - **Entry End** is added at the end of individual entries.

15. **Click OK to generate the index. Click the loaded cursor in the three-column text frame to place the index.**

Some of these entries are from the second chapter (the file from the *Design Companion*); these tags were already created in the file provided by the publisher.

Your index might be slightly different than our example depending on which names you added in the previous exercise.

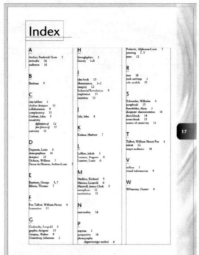

16. **Save the file and close it.**

17. **Save the book file and continue to the next stage of the project.**

STAGE 4 / Exporting Book Files

Another advantage of combining multiple files is the ability to output those files all at once, choosing print or export settings once instead of opening each file and changing the print or export settings individually. Using the Book panel, you can output all chapter files simultaneously, or you can output specific selected chapters.

Export PDF Files for Print and Digital Distribution

Your client asked for two separate files: one that can be printed at high quality and one that can be posted on the company's website and sent via email. Because you're working with a single file for the entire book, you can easily create these two output files in a few steps.

1. **With the Excerpts Book panel open, click the empty area at the bottom of the panel to deselect all files in the book.**

2. **Choose Export Book to PDF in the panel Options menu.**

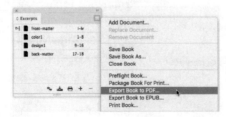

Note:

If any files are selected, the menu option changes to Export Selected Documents to PDF.

3. Navigate to your WIP>Excerpts folder as the target and change the file name to **Excerpts-print.pdf**. Choose Adobe PDF (Print) in the Format/ Save As Type menu, and then click Save.

4. In the Export Adobe PDF dialog box, choose [High Quality Print] in the Adobe PDF Preset menu.

5. In the Marks and Bleeds options, check the Crop Marks option. Change the Offset field to **0.125 in**, and change all four Bleed fields to **0.125 in**.

If your fields show some other unit of measurement, you can type the value you need, including the ″ character, and the software will make the appropriate conversion for you.

6. Click Export.

Exporting a book does not occur in the background. You have to wait for the export process to finish.

7. When the export process is complete, close the PDF file if necessary and return to InDesign.

8. Choose Export Book to PDF in the Book panel Options menu.

9. Choose **Adobe PDF (Interactive)** in the Format/Save As Type menu. Name the second file **Excerpts-digital.pdf** and click Save.

10. In the General options, make the following choices:

    • Choose the **[Export As] Pages** radio button.

    • Choose **Fit Page** in the View menu.

    • Choose **Single Page** in the Layout menu.

    • Check the **View After Exporting** option.

11. Click Export. When the PDF file opens, navigate to Page iii of the file. Move your cursor over any of the listings, then click to navigate to that section of the document.

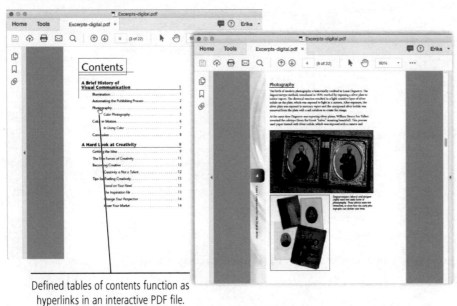

Defined tables of contents function as hyperlinks in an interactive PDF file.

12. **Close the PDF file and return in InDesign.**

13. **Open the book panel Options menu and choose Close Book. When asked if you want to save the book file, click Save/Yes.**

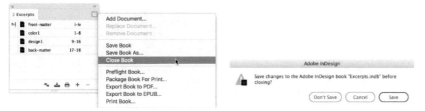

14. **Continue to the next stage of the project.**

STAGE 5 / Merging Data into a Page Layout

Personalized printing uses data to produce layouts targeting a specific region, a demographic group, or even an individual person. A national company might create a single weekly sale ad with one page that varies according to the local distribution; why, for example, would a company want to advertise snow shovels in southern California?

Data merge is a fairly sophisticated utility in most word-processing applications; it allows you to combine text with information stored in a database or spreadsheet (such as a Microsoft Excel file). Through a data merge, you can write one letter, click a few buttons, and print or export multiple copies of the letter, each with a different mailing address, for example. InDesign's Data Merge capabilities can be used for this type of personal letter generation, and — with a bit of advance planning — it can also be used for more sophisticated database-driven layouts such as catalogs with graphics.

InDesign's Data Merge feature makes it fairly simple to create a layout incorporating variable data. Once the data source file has been established, you can create any layout you want, add the data, and create multiple versions of a finished layout in one action. For the final stage of this project, you need to create a thank-you note from the publisher to previous clients. This note will be included with the printed copies of the Excerpts booklet when the sample is mailed to the clients. The publisher provided a comma-delimited file with the client mailing addresses; this file also identifies which book each client purchased.

 Create the Merged Document and Load the Source Data

The target document for a data merge needs to include placeholders or locations where the data will appear after the data merge is complete. Once you have established the data source for the InDesign file, you can easily create these placeholders anywhere in the document.

1. **Open the file letter.indd from your WIP>Excerpts folder.**

   Your client wrote this letter using her InDesign letterhead template. She used all capital letters to indicate where she wants database information to be added in the letter text.

A database is made up of **fields** that contain information. Each field has a **field name**, which is usually descriptive text that defines the contents of the field. Each listing in a database is called a **record**; each record contains every field in the database, even if a particular field contains no information for a given record.

In the following example, Name and Address are both fields. The first line of the file contains the field names "Name" and "Address." Each record appears on a separate line.

Name	Address
James Smith	123 This St., Someplace, MI 99999
Susan Jones	3208 Street Ct., Small Town, ID 55555

InDesign's Data Merge feature does not interact directly with a database application. Data must first be exported from a database into a tab- or comma-delimited ASCII text file.

In the text file, the information in each field (called a **text string**) is separated by the delimiter (comma or tab), which tells the software that the next text string belongs in the next field. Records are separated by a paragraph return, so each record begins on a new line.

If a particular text string requires one of the delimiter characters (for example, a comma within an address), that string is surrounded by double quotation marks in the text file.

A comma within quotation marks is treated as a text character, not as a delimiter.

The first line of the text file should list the field names. If your database application does not export field names as the first line of the text-only file, you need to open the file in a text editor, and add the field name line at the beginning.

Cleaning up Data

Placeholders in InDesign are made up of the field name enclosed within double brackets, such as <<Name>>, inserted anywhere in the target document.

<<Name>>
<<Address>>

Dear <<Name>>,

Congratulations! Your house at <<Address>> has been selected for a free facelift!

Once data from the source file has been merged into the document, it looks like this:

James Smith
123 This St., Someplace, MI 99999

Dear James Smith,

Congratulations! Your house at 123 Anywhere St., Someplace, MI 99999 has been selected for a free facelift!

The same document is reproduced for every record in the data file, personalizing each letter for the intended recipient.

Notice that the address is entirely on one line of text, and that the "Dear" line includes the person's whole name. This type of personalization is certainly better than addressing the recipient as "Dear Occupant," but it is still not as conversational as a letter using only the addressee's first name.

The previous example would benefit greatly from a different arrangement:

First_Name,Last_Name,Street_Address,City,State,Zip

James,Smith,"123 This St.",Someplace,MI,99999

The target file, using more specific placeholders, can then appear much more personal:

<<First_Name>> <<Last_Name>>
<<Street Address>>
<<City>, <<State>> <<Zip>>

Dear <<First_Name>>,

Congratulations! Your house at <<Street_Address>> has been selected for a free facelift!

Once data from the source file has been merged into this version, it looks like this:

James Smith
123 This St.
Someplace, MI 99999

Dear James,

Congratulations! Your house at 123 This St. has been selected for a free facelift!

2. **Choose Window>Utilities>Data Merge to open the Data Merge panel.**

Before you define a source file, the Data Merge panel provides instructions for use.

3. **Open the Data Merge panel Options menu and choose Select Data Source.**

4. **Navigate to the file customers.txt in your WIP>Excerpts folder and click Open.**

When the file is processed, the available fields (defined by the first line in the data file) are listed in the Data Merge panel.

The T icons indicate that these fields are text strings.

5. **In the document, turn on hidden characters (Type>Show Hidden Characters).**

6. **Highlight the first line in the letter (excluding the paragraph return character), and then click the First Name item in the Data Merge panel.**

Highlight this line of placeholder text (excluding the paragraph return character).

Clicking an item in the Data Merge panel replaces the highlighted text with a placeholder for that data field.

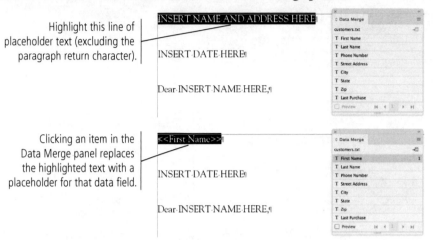

Note:

Like a text variable, a placeholder is treated as a single character in the layout.

Highlighting a few letters in any field name in the document automatically highlights the entire field name, including the brackets.

7. **Click to place the insertion point after the placeholder. Press the Spacebar, and then click the Last Name item in the Data Merge panel.**

8. **Press Return/Enter to start a new paragraph in the document and then click the Street Address item in the Data Merge panel.**

9. **Press Return/Enter again. Add the City, State, and Zip fields on the third line, separated by the appropriate punctuation and spaces.**

10. **Highlight the All Caps text in the salutation line, and then replace it with the First Name data field placeholder.**

11. **In the third paragraph of the letter, replace the All Caps text with the Last Purchase data field placeholder.**

12. **With the Last Purchase placeholder selected, change the font to ATC Pyrite Italic.**

    After placeholders have been entered in the document, you can apply text and paragraph formatting as you would for any other text element.

Note:

If you were going to reuse this letter, you might consider using a type variable for the date instead of typing an actual date.

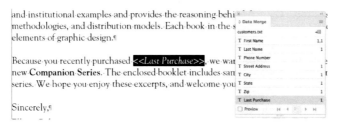

13. **Highlight the text "INSERT DATE HERE" and type today's date.**

14. **Save the file and continue to the next exercise.**

Complete the Merged Document

Once you have created your target document and formatted all the elements, you can preview the data and create the merged document. InDesign uses the data source file and the target layout to create a third document — the merged file. This third file is not linked to the data source; any changes you make to the data are not applied to the merged document. If you change the data file, you have to repeat the merge of the original layout file with the changed data.

1. **With letter.indd open from your WIP>Excerpts folder, activate the Preview check box at the bottom of the Data Merge panel.**

    You can preview your document at any time by activating the Preview check box in the Data Merge panel. When turned on, the actual data from the source file replaces the placeholder markers. The arrows to the left and right of the record number in the panel allow you to preview each record in the merged document.

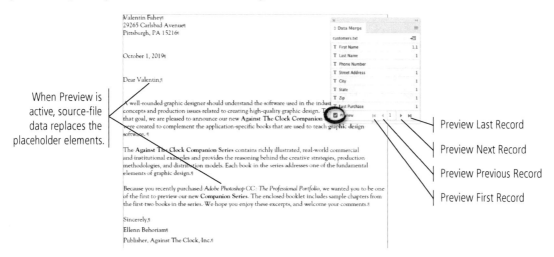

When Preview is active, source-file data replaces the placeholder elements.

Preview Last Record

Preview Next Record

Preview Previous Record

Preview First Record

2. **Choose Export to PDF in the Data Merge panel Options menu.**

In the Create Merged Document dialog box, you can define specific options for your merged document. The Records tab determines which records (all, one single record, or a specified range) will be included in the merged document.

The two check boxes at the bottom of the dialog box provide feedback after you create the data merge. Checked by default, these important options allow you to make sure all your data is available and fits into the spaces you defined.

Note:

If you choose Create Merged Document, the merge process results in an InDesign file with the necessary number of copies. The Export to PDF option skips this intermediary step.

3. **Click OK in the Create Merged Document dialog box.**

4. **Choose the [High Quality Print] preset in the Export Adobe PDF dialog box. Check the View PDF after Exporting option, then click Export.**

Note:

The Records per Document Page option allows you to place multiple records on a single page in the merged document. This option can be useful for creating catalog listings, multiple labels, or other projects with more than one database record on a single page.

5. **In the resulting dialog box, navigate to your WIP>Excerpts folder as the target location, and then click Save.**

6. **When you see the message that the data merge resulted in no overset text, click OK.**

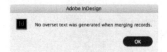

7. Review the resulting PDF file.

Because there were 44 records in the data source file, the new document has 44 pages (one page for each record/letter).

8. Close the PDF file, return to InDesign, and then save and close the letter.indd file.

Working with Long Text Fields

A text placeholder can be inserted anywhere in a document. Keep in mind, however, that the text frame must be large enough to hold the longest piece of data that exists for that field. Frames will not automatically enlarge or shrink to match the content.

When you preview the records, you can see how the formatting will apply once the data merge is complete. Even if the text for one record fits into a defined frame, that doesn't mean that all records will necessarily fit. Make sure a text frame is large enough to fit the longest possible record field.

Previewing allows you to verify that the text for each record fits into the space you defined.

Incorporating Images in a Data Merge

You can also incorporate images in the data source file to create variable images in a layout. To do so, your data source file must include a field that contains the full path to the image, beginning with the drive name where the image resides, called an **absolute path**. In the field names, the name of the image field should start with the "@" symbol (for example, "@image").

The absolute path for an image tells the Data Merge processor where to find the necessary file. On a Macintosh, the components in the path name are separated by colons:

Macintosh HD:Catalog Files:Pictures:image.tif

On Windows, the path name begins with the drive letter:

C:\My Documents\Pictures\image.tif

The only spaces in the path name are those that exist in the name of a file or folder; no spaces should separate any of the colon or backslash characters.

When a data source includes an image field, the Data Merge panel shows a small picture icon for that field. You can attach an image placeholder to any graphics frame by selecting the

frame in the layout and double-clicking the image item in the Data Merge panel.

When you use images from a data source file, you can choose Content Placement Options in the Data Merge panel Options menu to predetermine the appearance of the image in relation to the placeholder frame.

- The **Fitting** menu includes the same options that are available for fitting placed images in a graphics frame.

- If **Center in Frame** is checked, the image is centered within the placeholder frame after the Fitting option has been applied.

- The **Link Images** check box, active by default, links the data source images to the layout that is created when you generate the merged document. If this option is not checked, images are embedded in the resulting file. (Embedding images drastically increases file size; as a general rule, you should leave Link Images checked.)

You can preview variable images just as you preview text. If an image path is incorrect, you will see a warning when you try to preview that record.

The image placeholder will hold images defined in the @images field.

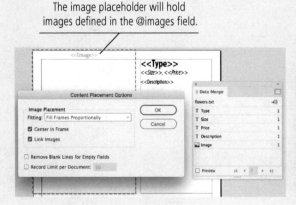

Merging Multiple Records on a Single Page

You can merge more than one record onto a single page by selecting Multiple Records in the Records per Document Page menu. When this option is selected, the Multiple Record Layout tab determines how records are placed and separated in the merged document.

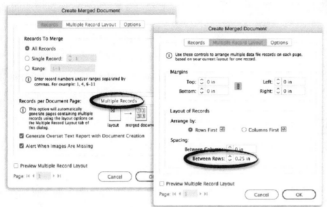

Two records fit on each page in the merged document; 0.25" is added between each row.

Managing Empty Data Fields

When you merge data, you should be aware that one or more fields for a specific record might be empty. For example, a specific record might not include a company name. If your target document includes a company name placeholder, the merged document might end up with an empty line where that placeholder appears.

In the Options tab of the Create Merged Document dialog box, the Remove Blank Lines for Empty Fields option solves this potential problem. When this option is checked, placeholders are ignored for fields that have no content. (The same option is available in the Content Placement Options dialog box, accessed in the Data Merge panel Options menu.)

Placeholders in original document

Merged document with blank lines

Merged document without blank lines

PROJECT REVIEW

fill in the blank

1. The _____ is used to organize and manage multiple chapter files in a book.

2. If a chapter file shows a _____ icon, it has been edited outside the context of the InDesign book.

3. Book chapters typically begin on _____-numbered, _____-facing pages.

4. _____, typically including a title page and table of contents, is the content preceding the main body of a book.

5. _____, typically containing indexes and appendices, appears after the primary content of a book.

6. The _____ option can be used to renumber any specific page in a document.

7. You can change the _____ of an index entry to rearrange its alphabetical position in the compiled index.

8. Clicking the _____ button in the New Page Reference dialog box is case-sensitive. "Printing" will not be tagged if the topic is "printing".

9. A(n) _____ is useful for tagging references to people based on their last names without changing the text in the document.

10. You can delete a(n) _____ without deleting its parent topic from the Index panel. The reverse is not true; deleting a parent topic deletes all _____ for that topic.

short answer

1. Describe three conventions that relate to and govern long-document design.

2. Briefly explain the concept of synchronization, including potential problems that might arise from it.

3. Briefly explain two advantages and two disadvantages of the InDesign indexing functionality.

PORTFOLIO BUILDER PROJECT

Use what you learned in this project to complete the following freeform exercise.
Carefully read the art director and client comments, then create your own design to meet the needs of the project.
Use the space below to sketch ideas; when finished, write a brief explanation of your reasoning behind your final design.

art director comments

All professional designers need a portfolio of their work. If you've completed the projects in this book, you should now have a number of different examples to show off your skills using InDesign CC.

The eight projects in this book were specifically designed to include a broad range of *types* of projects; your portfolio should use the same principle.

client comments

Gather your best work, and create printed and digital versions of your portfolio:

❏ Include as many different types of work as possible: one-page layouts, folding brochures, multi-page booklets, etc.

❏ Print clean copies of each finished piece you want to include.

❏ For each example in your portfolio, write a one or two paragraph synopsis of the project. Explain the purpose of the piece, as well as your role in the creative and production processes.

❏ Design a personal promotion brochure. Create a layout that both highlights your technical skills and reflects your personal style.

❏ Create a digital version of your portfolio so you can send your portfolio via email, post it on job sites, and keep it with you on a flash drive.

project justification

_____
_____
_____
_____
_____
_____
_____
_____
_____
_____
_____
_____
_____
_____

PROJECT SUMMARY

As you completed the exercises in this project, you learned to use InDesign tools to define special formatting, combine multiple files, build tables of contents and indexes, and merge variable data into a page layout.

Consistency is the key to effective long-document design. InDesign's book utility allows you to combine multiple chapter files into a single book and synchronize those files so related elements remain consistent from page to page and chapter to chapter. This book-building functionality works equally well for combining single-page documents or lengthy chapters with many pages.

By automating as much of the process as possible to build tables of contents and indexes — which used to require days of manual checking and rechecking if even a single page in the layout changed — InDesign greatly improves the efficiency of your workflow. Effectively implementing styles throughout a long document makes it relatively easy to compile a thorough table of contents that includes every heading from Page 1 to the final page.

Although no software is "smart" enough to identify which terms are important enough to appear in a document's index, the ability to store index markers in a document means compiling and recompiling the final index is far simpler than building and compiling the list by hand.

These skills are relatively rare in the graphics marketplace. Your ability to master them makes you much more marketable as a professional graphic designer.

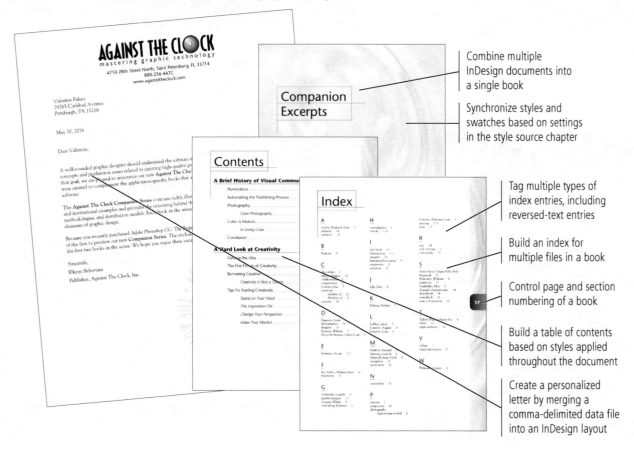

Combine multiple InDesign documents into a single book

Synchronize styles and swatches based on settings in the style source chapter

Tag multiple types of index entries, including reversed-text entries

Build an index for multiple files in a book

Control page and section numbering of a book

Build a table of contents based on styles applied throughout the document

Create a personalized letter by merging a comma-delimited data file into an InDesign layout

INDEX

INDEX

INDEX

INDEX

INDEX

INDEX